A MILITARY HISTORY OF ITALY

A MILITARY HISTORY OF ITALY

Ciro Paoletti

PRAEGER SECURITY INTERNATIONAL
Westport, Connecticut · London

Library of Congress Cataloging-in-Publication Data

Paoletti, Ciro, 1962–
   A military history of Italy / Ciro Paoletti.
      p. cm.
   Includes bibliographical references and index.
   ISBN: 978-0-275-98505-9 (alk. paper)
      1. Italy—History, Military.   I. Title.
   DG482.P36 2008
   355.00945—dc22   2007036162

British Library Cataloguing in Publication Data is available.

Library of Congress Catalog Card Number: 2007036162
ISBN: 978-0-275-98505-9

First published in 2008

Praeger Security International, 88 Post Road West, Westport, CT 06881
An imprint of Greenwood Publishing Group, Inc.
www.praeger.com

Printed in the United States of America

The paper used in this book complies with the
Permanent Paper Standard issued by the National
Information Standards Organization (Z39.48–1984).

10 9 8 7 6 5 4 3 2 1

Contents

A photo essay follows page 128.

Acknowledgments

My first deepest and foremost thanks go to Frederick C. Schneid, whose help was incomparably important. Without his support, work, experience, revisions, and suggestions this work probably would never have been published.

My second deepest and foremost thanks go to Heather Staines: It was only thanks to her patience and activity that the whole work, in spite of some strange adventures, was achieved and published.

Introduction

The Historical Service of the Italian Army originally commissioned this work in 1995. The idea was to create a general survey of Italian military history from the beginning of the Modern Age to the present. This meant a book beginning with the discovery of America by Columbus—or, as Italian books often say, from the death of Lorenzo the Magnificent to the end of the Cold War. Nothing comparable existed and, after twenty years of studying military history, I needed only two years (and something more than three thousand titles) to write the book. Published by the Italian Army Historical Service in 2002 under the title *Gli Italiani in armi—cinque secoli di storia militare nazionale, 1495–2000* (*The Italians at Arms: Five Centuries of National Military History, 1495–2000*), it was successfully reviewed in the *International Bibliography of Military History* and in the United States in the *Journal of Military History*. Then it was chosen as an "officially suggested text" by the ISSMI, the Italian Joint Staff Interforce Institute, but never republished.

Of course, when Praeger asked me to write a military history of Italy, this book found new life, but this is not a pure translation of the old work. This is something quite different. The Italian book was 650 pages in length and had 3,300 titles in its bibliography; this book has 8,500. The original book for the army focused on armies and land warfare, only leaving room for basic information about the Italian navy and air force. While this book is well balanced, it provides a general account of the development of military technology in Italy and how it was implemented by its armed forces. Finally, the original was intended to be read largely by Italian officers and scholars; it did not contain information understood in the context of Italian historical memory or general knowledge, yet this book was written with an understanding that this information is new to a non-Italian audience. I have been careful to include contextual explanations when needed.

At the time when I prepared the original work, I realized that the lack of general information concerning Italian military history was commonplace. Entire periods, such as the seventeenth century, had been completely forgotten, because they were no longer studied. The social history, focusing on specific facts, or classes, or people, abandoned an overview any good historian must have to understand events. Moreover, this "new history" led to the rejection of fields related to military history.

There is, of course, a good reason to explain such a lack of knowledge. The

French Revolution caused a deep change in Italian ruling classes. It allowed the bourgeoisie to overthrow the aristocracy and force monarchies to grant constitutions. Half a century after the end of Napoleonic rule, the bourgeoisie and a large reform-minded portion of the aristocracy pursued national unification under the banner of a constitutional Kingdom of Italy founded by the House of Savoy. As a result, after 1861 the histories of preunification Italy were no longer studied. The new histories, beginning in the late nineteenth century, focused on the history of the House of Savoy, and of course on its own state, the Duchy of Savoy, later the Kingdom of Piedmont-Sardinia. This would have been enough to create problems for any historian.

The ruling groups in the new kingdom were direct descendants of those who cooperated with Napoleon; this meant the government held an official position on the Napoleonic era. In 1845, Charles Albert of Sardinia—that is to say the House of Savoy—accepted the mantle of revolution, whose heritage was traced to the French Revolution. Between 1848–60, in order to justify their current situation, the French and their collaborators in Italy (1797–1814) were considered heroes and their enemies villains. Moreover, this game was easier when discrediting other Italian states. The Risorgimento had been against Austria—a Napoleonic foe, the papacy—subordinated to Napoleon, and the king of Naples, whose dynasty, according to the Risorgimento propaganda, opposed the Italian unification as far back as 1799.

When in 1876, fifteen years after unification, the political coalition known as the Historical Left gained power, the process accelerated. The Historical Left was composed of nationalists belonging to former revolutionary groups, who needed to demonstrate that they were on the right side of revolution. They focused their energy on magnifying the recent Risorgimento and used the Napoleonic period as the source for everything good and a demonstration of their own correctness. There was a problem, however, when applying this methodology to the armed forces. How does one establish a historical heritage for the newly created Italian army?

The seventeenth and eighteenth centuries, with all their victories against the French, Austrians, Turks, and Spanish, were forgotten, especially because the new ruling class had taken no part in them. As well, these centuries lacked political relevance. In fact, it was considered unpatriotic to study the old states, which later opposed national unification, and it could be a symptom of a weak patriotic spirit to study those states—like Venice—which disappeared before the Risorgimento. Ignoring these states and their history meant forgetting their military history, and the abandonment of military history made it impossible to speak of the Italians as a military people. The new nationalist spirit, however, wanted to demonstrate that the Third Rome, the Rome of united Italy, the capital of the new kingdom, commanded a European power.

Attention turned to Napoleon's Italian Army, and it became difficult to find any history addressing military campaigns prior to 1796. Indeed, polemics and propaganda distorted the histories written thereafter. For instance, the two 1866 battles of Custoza and Lissa were used to attack the contemporary government.

The same happened after the colonial defeat of Adowa in 1896, when the press transformed it into a strategic disaster and a national shame, forcing Prime Minister Crispi to disappear.

This process continued in the following years and distorted political interpretations, affected the histories of the Great War, Fascism and its wars, and, of course, the Second World War. All of this complicated the panorama of Italian military history. As a result, after the end of World War II, military history was out of favor. The Partisans who fought against Fascism in 1943–45 were, in a certain sense, the same ruling class the Fascists had defeated when taking power in 1922. In fact, many members of the Resistance had been members of Parliament or of the government until 1925, when Mussolini's dictatorship began.

The year 1946 inaugurated a new era in writing military history. The Italian left, notably the Communists, struggled to gain political power, and they heavily influenced intellectuals. Their perception of military history meant to speak a priori of Fascism as the evil and of the Resistance as the good. And when, after consultation with archival sources, someone—as did Renzo De Felice—wrote that Fascism was not the absolute evil and Mussolini had not been the worst man in the whole of history, he was attacked and accused of being a Fascist, that is to say a sort of intellectual leper.

The political climate and context of postwar Italy and the prevailing negative view of military history led to a tragic lack of research. For these reasons Italy saw few military historians. Piero Pieri, generally regarded as the best Italian military historian of the twentieth century, left a large number of general studies, but only one pupil: Giorgio Rochat, who, belonging to the left, spent his life studying the Italian military history of 1870–1945, as did Lucio Ceva. Raimondo Luraghi, who studied under Italy's expert on the seventeenth century—Guido Quazza—soon abandoned his old and much-loved studies and found new interest in the Confederate navy in the American Civil War. Ennio Concina moved away from studying the Venetian armed forces to medieval and early Renaissance maritime affairs.

There were truly few good historians who dealt with the nineteenth and twentieth centuries. Ferdinando Pedriali wrote many books on the Italian Air Force, as Riccardo Nassigh wrote on naval power in the Adriatic. Rear Admiral Pier Paolo Ramoino educated an entire generation of naval officers by looking at the lessons of the past, often a very far past, to divine the future. Mariano Gabriele, Alberto Santoni, and Giuliano Colliva wrote some good works about the Italian Royal Navy produced after many years of research. Ugo Barlozzetti and Nicola Pignato definitively studied Italian military motorization. Virgilio Ilari prepared the only existing work about the military service in Italy, *Storia del servizio militare in Italia*, 5 volumes (Roma: Ce.Mi.S.S.—Rivista Militare, 1991), but began writing books about Italian military history prior to the twentieth century after he collaborated with me. All the other military historians dealt only with the Second World War and the Resistance.

The same can be said for the generation of historians born in the sixties: Enrico Cernigoi wrote many very good books about the Great War, Italian submarines, and about World War II and national identity; Filippo Cappellano is the best expert on firearms; and Flavio Carbone produced new studies about the police services and Carabineers from their origins, giving a new and clearer perspective of their role. No general overview of Italian military history, however, existed before my book (and until now no other came after it). No one seemed attracted to the idea. Furthermore, when someone studied the pre-Napoleonic past, it was very narrow and disassociated from its relationship to the economic, political, and social situation of Italy at that time.

The best authors focused only on the last century, and that is why it is so difficult to find recent works (within the last seventy years) about Italian wars prior to the twentieth century. The few Italian authors who studied the old states were mostly in their thirties and, being as they were preparing their works at the same time I was preparing my book, they were completely unknown to the public. This is why I discovered so late, after having published my first book in 1995, Niccolò Capponi's studies on seventeenth-century Tuscany, Paolo Giacomone-Piana's work about Genoa's military resources, Andrea De Consoli's book on Savoy's seventeenth-century military administration, Bruno Mugnai's works on seventeenth-century Turkish and Imperial armies; and, of course, none of them were accepted into the Academy, despite the high quality of their work. This is why, when preparing this original manuscript for the Italian Army, I was forced to consult the original sources. It was great luck. I could research the entire period without prejudice or influence from this or that historiographical school or scholar. Conversely, this was both quite difficult and quite good, and generated a good result.

Italian military history has been misunderstood. For instance, few associated Italian conflicts with the Thirty Years' War; not from books, but from the situation depicted by contemporary documents. I remember the harsh and nasty attack made by a Finnish historian against me in Prague, in summer 1997, when for the first time I presented a paper about Italy and the Thirty Years' War. It was based upon facts and figures, but he told me it was "useless" as it spoke of unknown Italian places and little towns. I simply answered that I was very sorry: Figures and facts came out of archives. I did not pretend to give them more importance than that they had; I only presented them. And, for what concerned the "unknown little cities," well, I was sorry again, but I assumed that Venice, Milan, Naples, Florence, and Rome to be generally well known and not so little to be ignored by the public.

Another new issue was Italy's strategic relevance during the War of Spanish Succession. Italian historians were unaware of the critical role of Italy as a theater of war because nobody studied it anymore. Then the Napoleonic era changed my perspective on the Risorgimento and, when dealing with the twentieth century, I had some surprises concerning the Great War and topics that followed.

This was enough about Italian historiography and Italian scholars, but the situation was obviously worse when looking at Italian affairs in foreign literature. Italian is the language of the cultured, the deeply cultured, but the deeply cultured people are few. It was therefore very hard to find a non-Italian historian who had the time and the knowledge (and often the funding) to study Italian documents in order to prepare a book. But, also if a non-Italian historian would have time and means, the other problem was a dearth of books on Italian military history before 1900, other than ones on general colonial issues. It must be regarded as a miracle if some scholars in France, Great Britain, and the United States spent time studying Italian issues, but they are so few that it is quite hard to find their works and, of course, the most important topics are—for them, too—those related to the twentieth century.

Here, however, emerged another problem; the current and most common opinion about Italy and Italian military history is negative. I discuss the origins of this in the book, but this current opinion heavily affected many people who wrote about Italian topics. Even histories that were supposed to be objective were in one way or in another affected by this notion.

How did it happen and why? Readers who look at Anglo-Saxon and French literature before the Second World War can easily discern contemporary opinions about Italy. For instance, British historians admired the Risorgimento and spoke and wrote well of Italy. They read reports about the Piedmontese army in the Crimea in 1855–56 and, in 1915, British propaganda had to support the idea of a heroic and good Italian army joining the Allied cause. Of course, national pride rendered implicitly clear that the Italians were not—and could not be—as good as the British, but, in a sense, the Italians were not so bad. The same occurred with the French; and no American really took care to discuss Italy at that time. Then, all changed during and after the Second World War.

Why? I got the answer from one of the world authorities in military history, when I met him for the only time in my life, in High Point, North Carolina, in February 2004, a few months before his death. Professor Gunther Rothenberg was very kind and talked a lot with me. When he told me he had been in the British Eighth Army during World War II and, after the Italian armistice in 1943, had been a British liaison officer to our troops fighting on the Allied side in 1943–45, I asked him for his sincere opinion about them. He was ever a sincere man. He was very kind, but this simply meant that he could say the more severe things in the kindest, gentlest, clearest, and best way. It was quite a surprise for me to listen to his answer that, for what he had personally seen in Africa and in Italy, the Italian troops had been "as good as any other, on both sides." This was astonishing for me, because in my experience it was the first time a non-Italian did not pronounce a negative opinion about Italian troops and, of course, because of the authority who pronounced it. "So," I asked, "why this largely expressed crude opinion about them?" "Oh," he said, "just propaganda." As he told me, the British had needed, as all nations need in such a case, to ridicule the enemy, to denigrate him for propaganda purposes. This was the main reason for the very poor opinion expressed by many Britons. Moreover, as it is well known, with little exception, historians copy each from the other. When someone writes, all others report his errors in their work, and when the error is also supported by prejudice, as in this case, the game is over.

Apart what Professor Rothenberg told me, there is also another reason heavily affecting and complicating the work of a foreign historian dealing with Italian affairs; the existing Italian literature. Having described the current situation, it should be clear why and how it is possible for a foreign scholar to have problems understanding what happened in Italy. If we take into consideration the problem of the missing recent printed sources about the pre-twentieth century; the reduced comprehension of the Italian language, especially among Anglo-Saxon scholars; the politically affected—and misleading—Italian literature and the existing—often old and affected by prejudice—literature in English, we must conclude that only a miracle or a very strong will can produce a non-Italian historian dealing with Italian military affairs who produces good and reliable work.

It is also the case that the less the Italian language is known, the more non-Italian scholars are discouraged to study Italian military history. The more they are discouraged, the less they publish about it in their own languages. The less they publish in their own languages, especially in English, the more the readers look for information from non-Italian sources. The final result is poor information—that is to say, no information at all.

All of this explains why there are so few real experts on Italian military history, and that's why they can be considered a phenomena. Historians such as Jeremy Black, John Gooch, Sir John Hale, Gregory Hanlon, MacGregor Knox, James J. Sadcovich, Frederick C. Schneid, Christopher Storrs, Brian R. Sullivan, Geoffrey Symcox, and Bruce C. Vandervort spent a long time studying Italian documents and searching Italian archives with very good results. The best Mussolini biography out of Italy and, I suspect, also in Italy (also officially a biography of Mussolini's mistress Margherita Sarfatti) is by Brian Sullivan. John Gooch's book about the Italian armed forces from unification until the end of the Great War has been adopted as official text in at least two Italian universities. Bruce Vandervort's remarks about the Italian colonial army in 1880–1912 are the best I've ever seen, Italian literature included. Frederick Schneid's books on Napoleon's Italian army may be considered of fundamental importance and Sir John Hale's work on the Venetian army in the Renaissance is a masterpiece. Jeremy Black reached interesting conclusions about the strategic role of Italy in the Early Modern Era and especially in the early eighteenth century, as well as Christopher Storrs and Geoffrey Symcox, who recently wrote about the Duchy of Savoy's development in the last days of the seventeenth and the early eighteenth century. James Sadcovich's book about the Italian Navy is quite good. Finally, Gregory Hanlon provides a good general account concerning Italian military history from the Renaissance until the Napoleonic age, even if the title, *Twilight of a Military Tradition*, could generate some discussion about the "twilight" itself. It is now up to the reader of this book to decide if, and how much, Italy was in the twilight of its military traditions.

PART I

THE SIXTEENTH CENTURY

CHAPTER 1

Before the Deluge

Italy from the Fall of the Roman Empire to the Renaissance

The political structure of Italy in 1492 was peculiar. The region possessed a homogeneous cultural entity dating from the end of the collapse of the Roman Empire. Roman Catholicism was dominant. Religion and laws were derived from the Roman system, and a common art and culture unified the peninsula. The Italian language, a derivation of Latin, has been spoken since the seventh century. As early as the twelfth century, poets of the Sicilian school wrote in an Italian that is still possible to fully understand. Despite these commonalities, Italy was anything but politically homogeneous. After the fall of the Western Roman Empire, German tribes overran northern Italy, establishing independent kingdoms. They fought the Byzantines, who claimed to be the true heirs of the Western Empire. Small territories escaped the invasions. Some were protected by mountains and by the sea, such as Genoa or Amalfi, while some simply declared themselves dependencies of the Byzantine Empire. This was the case for Venice. People from the Venetian *terraferma* escaped the barbarian invasions to the small islands in the lagoon and built a city, which in the year 697 became a dependency of Byzantium.

In the absence of a central and established political power, the Roman Catholic Church was the only surviving institution of the Western Empire and gradually took responsibility for the administration of government. In the sixth century the Lombards established a kingdom in northern Italy. By the end of the seventh century Italy was divided into three parts: the Lombard kingdom in the north, the Roman Church in the center and the south, and the islands of Corsica, Sicily, and Sardinia under the Byzantines.

The conflict between the Church and the Lombards ended with a Frankish invasion in 774 led by Charlemagne. He established Italy as a kingdom separate from the Holy Roman Empire. After Charlemagne's death in 814, however, northern and central Italy became part of the Holy Roman Empire, except for Venice and Genoa.

In the eleventh century the Normans conquered southern Italy and Sicily from the Muslims. The pope recognized their new kingdom of Naples and it became a feudal dependency of the Church. In subsequent centuries Italy's geographic position in the Mediterranean made it an increasingly important marketplace. The kingdoms and territories grew in wealth; a banking system emerged, eventually expanding throughout Continental Europe as Italian merchants became the middlemen for goods traded between the Middle East, North Africa, and Europe.

The wealthier Italy became, the weaker was the authority of the Holy Roman Emperor. Wealth increased the power and independence of Italian towns and cities. When the German emperor, Frederick I "Barbarossa," tried to reassert his authority in Italy, the cities—the Commons, as they called themselves—formed an alliance, the Lombard League, and defeated him at Legnano in May 1176. This was a turning point in Italian political history. The Peace of Constance signed in 1183 confirmed the autonomy of Italian Commons. The papacy supported the Commons, as did the king of Naples.

At the conclusion of the fifteenth century, Italy remained divided. There were four kingdoms: Sardinia, Sicily, Corsica, and Naples; many republics such as Venice, Genoa, Florence, Lucca, Siena, San Marino, Ragusa (in Dalmatia); small principalities, Piombino, Monaco; and the duchies of Savoy, Modena, Mantua, Milan, Ferrara, Massa, Carrara, and Urbino. Parts of Italy were under foreign rule. The Habsburgs controlled the Trentino, Upper Adige, Gorizia, and Trieste. Sardinia belonged to the kingdom of Aragon. Many Italian states, however, held territories outside of the peninsula. The duke of Savoy possessed the Italian region of Piedmont and the French-speaking Duchy of Savoy along with the counties of Geneva and Nice. Venice owned Crete, Cyprus, Dalmatia, and many Greek islands. The Banco di San Giorgio, the privately owned bank of the republic of Genoa, possessed the kingdom of Corsica. Italian princes also held titles and fiefdoms in neighboring states. Indeed, the duke of Savoy could also claim that he was heir and a descendant of the crusader kings of Cyprus and Jerusalem. All of this confusion often remained a source of contention in Italian politics.

The Muslims became the greatest threat to security when the Arabs occupied Sicily in the ninth century. Later Muslim attempts to conquer central Italy failed as a result of papal resistance. Although the Norman conquest of southern Italy and Sicily removed the immediate threat. Muslim ships raided the Italian coast until the 1820s.

This conflict with Islam resulted in substantial Italian participation in the Crusades. The Crusader military orders such as the Templars and the Order of Saint John were populated by a great number of Italian knights. Italian merchants, too, established their own warehouses and agencies in the eastern Mediterranean and Black Sea. Thanks to the Crusades, Venice and Genoa increased their influence as well. They expanded their colonies, their revenues, and their importance to the Crusader kingdoms. Their wealth exceeded that of many European kingdoms.

The fall of the Crusader kingdoms, the Turkish conquests, and the fall of Constantinople by 1453 led to two significant consequences: the increasing influence of Byzantine and Greek culture in Italian society, and the growing Turkish threat to Italian territorial possessions in the Mediterranean. The conflict between Italians and Muslims was complex. For centuries Italians and Muslims were trading partners. So the wars between the Turks and Venetians therefore consisted of a combination of bloody campaigns, privateering, commerce, and maritime war lasting more than 350 years.

Despite a common enemy, common commercial and financial interests, a common language, and a common culture, Italian politics remained disparate and divisive. For much of the fifteenth century the states spent their time fighting each other over disputed territorial rights. Although they referred to themselves as Florentines, Lombards, Venetians, Genoese, or Neapolitans, when relating themselves to outsiders, such as Muslims, French, Germans, and other Europeans, they self-identified as "Italians."

The Organization of Renaissance Armies

The lack of significant external threats led to the reduction in size of Italian armies. The cost of maintaining standing armies or employing their citizenry in permanent militias was too expensive and reduced the productivity of the population. Italian city-states, duchies, and principalities preferred to employ professional armies when needed, as they were extremely costly to hire. Larger states, such as the Republic of Venice, the Kingdom of Naples and the Papal States possessed a limited permanent force, but the remainder of the Italian states had little more than city guards, or small garrisons. Nevertheless, Italian Renaissance armies, when organized, were divided into infantry and cavalry. Artillery was in its infancy and remained a severely limited in application. Cavalry was composed of heavy or armored cavalry, *genti d'arme* (men at arms), and light cavalry. Since the Middle Ages, *genti d'arme* were divided into "lances" composed of a "lance chief"—or corporal—a rider, and a boy. They were mounted on a warhorse, a charger, and a jade respectively. The single knight with his squire was known as *lancia spezzata*—literally "brokenspear," or *anspessade*.

Infantry was divided into banners. Every banner was composed of a captain, two corporals, two boys, ten crossbowmen, nine *palvesai*, soldiers carrying the great medieval Italian shields called *palvesi*, and a servant for the captain. Generally the ratio of cavalry to infantry was one to ten. There was no organized artillery by the end of the fifteenth century, as it was relatively new to European armies.

Piracy, Galleys, and Sailing Ships

The greatest threat to Italy was piracy. Mediterranean pirates and privateers were both Christian and Muslim, and there was little difference between them in violence and cruelty; but Italians generally considered the Muslim pirates their major enemy. Barbarian regencies of Tripoli—in Libya—Tunis, and Algiers in North Africa were centers of piracy. In theory, they were dependencies of the

Ottoman Empire, but the Sultan's authority was weak and Istanbul far away. The Uscocks, Croatian pirates, preyed upon Adriatic shipping, as their ports lay on the Dalmatian coast under Habsburg protection. Venetian and Turkish vessels were their primary targets.

There was a difference between pirates and privateers. Privateers were formally permitted by a sovereign to fight against that sovereign's enemies. They could only attack vessels under an enemy flag. Pirates attacked everything, independently of flag. When captured, privateers were considered as prisoners of war; pirates could be killed or hanged. Death, however, was not enough to stop them. Northern African regencies needed piracy because it was their primary source of revenue. Their domestic economy was largely agricultural and few goods produced were exported.

In fact, pillaging a vessel or a coastal town gave them money and goods to be sold for money, and, above all, slaves. Before steam power, the easiest and cheapest available manpower was the slave. Captured seamen and passengers, or peasants, fishermen, and citizens were carried to northern African and Ottoman ports to be sold. Wealthier captives were often ransomed. Many of the strongest slaves were not sold but used on galleys as oarsmen. Slavery substantially disappeared in Italy in the Middle Ages, but Muslim prisoners were used largely as oarsmen, or galley slaves. As the need for oarsmen became greater, Italian coastal states condemned their criminals to serve on the galleys as oarsmen, hence the word "galley" became synonymous with "prison" as well the term "bath"—the place where the slaves normally stayed—for "penal bath."

Pirates had vessels set for their tasks. Their targets had to be taken by surprise. A coastal town had to be reached in spite of low waters, and the vessel had to be able to move as quickly as possible to escape as well as to reach an enemy. This meant small and light ships were generally employed for purposes of raiding. More-over, light ships could move by oars no matter the weather, and the Mediterranean had less wind than the Atlantic. Sometimes the ships had an opposite wind or no wind at all. That's why the ancient galleys, for two thousand years, were propelled by sails and oars. A galley could be as fast as a sailing ship—as the Venetians tested—and it moved also without wind. Of course, it needed a lot of men—slaves, voluntary oarsmen, seamen, marine infantrymen, gunners—and this meant a high consumption of food and water, so that the ship had only a four-to-seven-day sea range. The Mediterranean, however, is relatively compact; its shores can be quickly reached to find water and fresh foods, thus galleys were the best choice. And galleys were integral parts of Italian navies until the French Revolution and Napoleonic era. They disappeared only after 1814, when the Royal Sardinian Navy abandoned them. As piracy was a persistent menace and the galley the only good weapon to fight it, all the Italian navies were primarily composed of galleys. Of course, many possessed sailing ships, too, but they were not as relevant as galleys in quantity and importance. Naval officers serving on galleys held a higher rank than those serving on vessels.

Since the seventeenth century, Italian fleets were divided into *Squadra delle*

Galere—literally being the Italian the word *squadrone* used only for cavalry, the "squad of galleys"—and the *Squadra dei Vascelli*—the "squad of vessels"—or, as the Venetians referred to them: the Light Squadron and the Heavy, or the Big, Squadron, also called "the Big Army," and the "the Light Army." The Heavy Squadron included all the square-sailed vessels; the Light one included rowing ships—galleys, galleasses, half galleys, and galliots—as well as the lateen-sailed vessels like schooners, tartans, and ketches. In all the Italian states, except Venice, the Light Squadron comprised the entire fleet and usually had no more than six galleys.

If we consider Italy's long coasts, it was impossible to patrol blue waters to protect merchant traffic and the coast with so few ships. The Adriatic was generally safe. The Republic of Venice protected the northern Adriatic, her fleet was strong and, moreover, the Most Serene Republic had an agreement with Istanbul: No man-of-war under sultan's formal authority—which included Barbary pirates—was allowed to sail in the Adriatic. This agreement remained in effect until the fall of the republic in 1797. Venice maintained permanent naval squadrons protecting her commercial routes. The "*Guardia* in Candia," based in the capital of Crete, controlled eastern Mediterranean waters. The "*Guardia* in Golfo"—guard in the Gulf—at Corfù, protected the entrance to the Adriatic Sea, at that time proudly called "the Gulf of Venice."

Beyond the protection of Venice, the southern—Ionian and western Tyrrhenian—seas were open to piracy. Maltese, Neapolitan, Sicilian, Sardinian, Tuscan, Genoese, and papal fleets hardly totaled more than forty-five galleys. They had no centralized command, no coordination, and they had to protect 2,600 miles of coastline. This meant that in the best possible situation, using all the galleys at the same time, there could be no more than one galley every fifty-seven miles. In fact, when considering that normally a six-galley fleet had two galleys on patrol, two galleys just back or coming back to the port, and two galleys preparing to go out, every galley had to patrol 173 miles coastline, and none in blue waters. It was clearly impossible to stop pirates. The only way to reduce the threat consisted of land-based standing forces. That's why the Italian coast, from Nice in the northern Tyrrhenian Sea to the Gargano promontory in the southern Adriatic Sea—just out of Venetian waters—was filled with watchtowers. Every tower had cannons to fire against pirates and wood for a signal fire, to warn the towns and the villages of the approaching menace and to call infantry and cavalry from the castles in the interior. All of this, however, remained insufficient to stem the threat, and Italian coastal populations concentrated in the well-fortified port cities or escaped to the interior. Towns were built on the top of hills or mountains. Coastal routes were abandoned as well as the country near the sea. Marshes became larger and larger, especially from south of Pisa down to north of Naples, because no one drained the country as the Etruscans and Romans had. Mosquitoes increased and carried malaria—literally "naughty air" or "evil air"—and this disease, which was supposed to come from the country air, forced the people to concentrate in the cities, were malaria was not so terrible or did not exist at all.

CHAPTER 2

The Italian Wars in the Early Sixteenth Century

Charles VIII of France and the Italian States

In the second half of fifteenth century, Italian states began a process of expansion. They all possessed relative military parity, they were all very rich, and the geopolitical situation was balanced. The Kingdom of Naples, the Republic of Venice, the papacy, the Republic of Florence, and the Duchy of Milan competed with each other for the dominant position in Italy. The balance of power was disturbed, and external forces returned to the peninsula when the duke of Milan, Ludovico il Moro, opened a Pandora's box and asked the king of France, Charles VIII, for assistance. Ludovico feared that the king of Naples, Alfonso of Aragon, brother of the Spanish king Ferdinand of Aragon, was fomenting an Italian alliance against him. Charles VIII responded promptly, arriving in Italy in the early days of September 1494 with an army of 30,000 men with 150 cannons.

The French invasion of Italy ended the stalemate and altered the course of Italian history. France was allied with the Republic of Genoa, and Charles was able to pass with his army unmolested along the coast and the south, passing through Florence. He found no opposition. His rapid advance into central Italy allowed him to engage and defeat Neapolitan troops at San Germano sul Garigliano, and then he entered Naples at the end of the winter in 1495 and proclaimed himself king. Venice, Ludovico il Moro's old enemy, feared the considerable success of the Milanese-French alliance and on March 31, 1495, organized the Italic League, an alliance against them. The Pope Alexander VI, Alfonso of Aragon and Naples, and eventually Ludovico il Moro—now fearing the French, joined the League. The extent of the French conquest brought Charles VIII's rivals to the peninsula. Ferdinand of Aragon and Maximilian von Habsburg worried for their dynastic possessions because of the French invasion. They responded by actively supporting the Italic League and dispatching funds and forces to Italy. Ferdinand sent a Spanish army commanded by Great Captain Consalvo de Cordova, which landed in Naples in the spring of 1495.

The Spaniards defeated the French in Naples and forced them north. The army of the Italic League with 40,000 men intercepted and attacked Charles VIII at Fornovo on July 8, 1495. Charles's army escaped complete destruction, but he lost money and materials in excess of 300,000 ducats and more than 1,000 men. His great invasion ended with a rapid retreat to France. Both sides claimed Fornovo as a victory, but it was a hollow one for the French. Their route was blocked by the League army, however, in the end they were able to force their way through. Indeed, Fornovo is significant in Italian history because it was the first time an Italian army fought for "Italy's honor," or "Italy's liberty" as said in that time. The national idea was essentially a cultural one, but at Fornovo cultural unity appeared in political and military form.

As often happens in alliances, after the conclusion of the war, the allies' divergent interests manifested themselves and the members of the League returned to their petty rivalries. Italy now became a battlefield for dynastic competition for the next three hundred years. After the first French attempt in 1494, it was evident that the Republic of Venice was the only real contender for dominance in the peninsula. Venice's strong position, however, was complicated by papal resistance to accept such an alteration to Italian geopolitics.

The Problem of the Papacy

The papacy found this new conflict and the changing nature of Italian politics a serious threat to its religious and political influence on the peninsula, with implications extending across Catholic Europe. The pope, as vicar of Christ and the depository and defender of the integrity of the Christian doctrine, may be the worst possible person as it was at this time—the Spanish Alexander VI Borgia—yet his responsibility is to maintain the integrity of Church doctrine. The pope can not alter doctrine, as it has its source in Jesus Christ, and therefore coming directly from God it is impossible to change it. This meant that the Church could not and still can not allow interference by a state or a king. The most important interference had determined the schism between the Roman and the Orthodox churches. Both were Catholic, but the Orthodox hierarchy submitted to the Byzantine emperor, while the Roman rejected any authority above it, a part God himself. The Church successfully preserved its religious autonomy, which was followed by political independence. Political policy was a consequence of religion and a tool to preserve the integrity of the doctrine.

At the end of the fifteenth century the papacy was weak and worried by the consequences of the Italian war. Alexander VI decided to strengthen its position in Italy and within its own borders. Roman barons were too independent and too strong, and Venice could not be accepted by the pope as the leading power in Italy because the Venetians lost no time in affirming their supremacy over the Church on political and, occasionally, on religious issues.

Papal response to these threats came in two forms: Internally the barons were reduced through four military campaigns by the "Very Holy Army" between 1496 and 1503; externally the Venetian problem was resolved in the worst possible way when foreign powers were invited into Italy. This dynamic, beginning with the Milanese alliance with France in 1494, was repeated throughout the sixteenth century. Every time a foreign power became too strong in Italy, the papacy, fearing for its political autonomy and for related religious autonomy, backed another foreign power, often its dynastic rival. Within a few years both the French and Spanish received papal pleas, sometimes in alliance with Italian states, sometimes against them. The result of this seesaw strategy during the first thirty years of the sixteenth century left all the Italian States, but Venice, weakened so much that they lost their independence.

The Venetian Problem

The only Italian power wealthy enough to resist French and Spanish power was Venice. Unfortunately, "the Venetian Lords" had two enemies apart from the other Italian states. In addition to Spain and France, the Holy Roman Emperor was the third external enemy. He was the master of Trentino, Upper Adige, Friuli, Slovenia, and Croatia, whose coastline was Venetian Dalmatia, and he wanted it. The fourth enemy was the Great Lord of the Sublime Gate of Happiness, the sultan of the Ottoman Turks, master of the East, whose armies were slowly moving north in the Balkans and west into the Mediterranean, menacing Venetian dominions on land and sea.

How could the Most Serene Republic survive? It was impossible to fight against all four enemies at once. The Venetian Senate prioritized its foreign policy with its potential threats. The life of the republic depended upon commerce; therefore the primary effort had to be focused against the Turks. The second priority was to deploy military forces to protect the Venetian domains in Italy against the Habsburgs—the Holy Roman Emperors and rulers of Austria. Finally, Venetian diplomacy was designed to balance France and Spain, because it was impossible to fight these two great powers without the help of the other Italian states.

The Habsburg threat to Venice took precedent when Charles of Habsburg ascended to both the Spanish and Austrian thrones. His mother was the daughter of king Ferdinand of Aragon and queen Isabella of Castille, and his father was the son of the holy roman emperor Maximilian. Charles inherited all the territories of his grandparents; Spain in 1516 and the Empire in 1519. This meant that Charles V, as he was called in Germany—Charles I in Spain—was the master of Germany, Spain, the Low Countries, Naples, Sicily, and Sardinia. This meant that Venice's enemy to the north as well as in southern Italy and the southern Adriatic was the same. It was therefore necessary to reduce Habsburg pressure on Venetian territories with all possible allies, in all possible ways. France was the logical choice. Encircled by Habsburgs, as was Venice, King Francis I of France found an ally there. Furthermore, he pursued another powerful potential ally, the Turks. For the

French this strategic perspective provided a great opportunity because as the sultan, Suleiman the Magnificent, moved west or north, Habsburg pressure on France was reduced. This worked quite well for France, but became a complete disaster for Venice, because the republic found itself wedged between an Austrian-Spanish dynasty and a Franco-Turkish alliance. Venice's previous four enemies now became only two, but they were linked in such a way that it seemed impossible for Venice to survive. Only the desperate energy and ability of its Senate allowed Venice to resist for the next two and a half centuries.

Establishing Spanish Rule

In a few years all the Italian states were forced to play a balancing act between Charles V and the king of France, Francis I. The union of Austrian and Spanish resources as well as the supremacy of the Spanish military system gradually reduced French power in Italy. Unfortunately, the Spaniards understood the art of ruling very well and they were more able than the French in exploiting opportunities offered by the political situation in Italy. Within a few years France was finally excluded from Italy, and Spanish rule was established.

After Fornovo, the French came back in 1500. They took Milan, looking for a new conquest of southern Italy. In July 1501 they entered Naples, but soon a Spanish army came and, supported by Italian allies, defeated the French and conquered Naples in June 1503. The decisive battle was fought in December on the Garigliano River, where, thanks to a maneuver planned by the Italian captain Bartolomeo d'Alviano, the Spanish army destroyed the French reinforcement. "Bartolomeo was the one who deprived us of the Kingdom," commented French cardinal D'Amboise.[1] The end came in 1526 when the Holy See organized the so-called League of Cognac. In the French city of Cognac, Venice, Rome, Florence, France, and Milan signed a military alliance against Spain, later joined by England.

When the emperor came to Italy, only Venice seemed to stand against Spain and the Empire. Pope Clement VII made the worst possible mistake. His policy was not directed against the French or Spanish, because they were considered as "birds flying over Italy, unable to stay there indefinitely."[2] The Holy See perceived Venice as its greatest threat as they "are in Italy and understand very well the art of ruling."[3] Fearing Venetian supremacy, the pope did not act strongly against the Spaniards. The League of Cognac was ineffective and as a result the Imperials reached and pillaged Rome in 1527 and forced Clement to accept an armistice. In 1529 then, only Florence and Venice remained in the field. They faced the resources of Spain, Germany, Flanders, Austria, and southern Italy, paid with new silver from the Americas. Instead of continuing the conflict, Florence and Venice were surprised when Charles V invited them to a great peace conference at Bologna. It was an imperial peace, but generous enough, and better than a destructive war.

Florence was required to abandon its republican government in favor of a ducal rule under the Medici family. When the Florentines refused, it led to war and the city appealed to all its best men. Michelangelo was responsible for the city fortress. Niccolò Machiavelli's ideas about drilling and organizing an army were considered as the best, but they proved inadequate against overwhelming imperial force. In 1530 the republic was defeated and the Medici family obtained Florence and its dependencies. Florence was now considered a fief of the Empire, or, according to others, dependent upon Spain.

Five years later the last duke of Milan died. He had no heirs, and the duchy fell into the hands of the emperor. In 1536 the king of France claimed his rights to Milan and sent an army to Italy. The war ended in 1538. The agreement was founded on the *uti possidetis*, that is to say on the principle of every conqueror keeps his own conquests. France did not possess Milan—held strongly by Spain—but maintained control of the Piedmont, which gave it free passage through the Alps.

An Evolution in Military Affairs, or the So-Called "Military Revolution"

Artillery was in its infancy during the fifteenth century, but in the early days of the sixteenth century, a quick and impressive development began. The Battle of Ravenna in 1512 marked the first decisive employment of cannons as field artillery. Soon infantry and cavalry realized the power of artillery and proceeded to alter their tactics to avoid or at least to reduce the damage. Moreover, the increasing power of artillery demonstrated the weakness of medieval castles and led to a transformation of military architecture. The traditional castle wall was vertical and tall and could be smashed by cannon-fired balls. In response, the new Italian-styled fortress appeared. Its walls were lower and oblique instead of perpendicular to the ground. The walls resisted cannonballs better, as their energy could also be diverted by the obliquity of the wall itself. Then, the pentagonal design was determined as best for a fortress, and each angle of the pentagon was reinforced by another smaller pentagon, called a bastion. It appeared as the main defensive work and was protected by many external defensive works, intended to break and scatter the enemy's attack. The fifteenth-century Florentine walls in Volterra have many bastion elements, but the first Italian-styled fortress was at Civitavecchia, the harbor for the papal fleet, forty miles north of Rome. It was erected by Giuliano da Sangallo in 1519, but recent studies suggest that Sangallo exploited an older draft by Michelangelo.[4]

The classical scheme of the Italian-styled fortress often referred to as the *trace italienne* was established in the second half of the sixteenth century. Its elegant efficiency was recognized by all powers. European sovereigns called upon Italian military architects to build these new fortresses in their countries. Antwerp, Parma, Vienna, Györ, Karlovac, Ersekujvar, Breda, Ostend, S'Hertogenbosch, Lyon, Charleville, La Valletta, and Amiens all exhibited the style and ability of Giuliano da Sangallo, Francesco Paciotti, Pompeo Targone, Gerolamo Martini, and many other military architects, who disseminated a style and a culture to the entire Continent.

The pentagonal style was further developed by Vauban and soon reached America, too, where many fortresses and military buildings were built on a pentagonal scheme.

This evolution in military architecture—generally known as "the Military Revolution"—meant order and uniformity. A revolution also occurred in uniforms and weapons. Venetian infantrymen shipping on galleys for the 1571 naval campaign were all dressed in the same way;[5] and papal troops shown in two 1583 frescoes are dressed in yellow and red, or in white and red, depending on the company to which they belonged.[6] Likewise, papal admiral Marcantonio Colonna, in 1571, ordered his captains to provide all their soldiers with "merion in the modern style, great velveted flasks for the powder, as fine as possible, and all with well ammunitioned match arquebuses . . . "[7] Of course, uniformity remained a dream, especially when compared with eighteenth- or nineteenth-century styles, but it was a first step.

Although a revolution in artillery and fortifications remained a significant aspect of the military revolution, captains faced the problem of increasing firepower. The Swiss went to battle in squared formations, but it proved to be unsatisfactory against artillery. Similarly, portable weapons could not fire and be reloaded fast enough, and it soon became apparent that armies needed a mixture of pike and firearms. The increasing range and effectiveness of firearms made speed on the field more important. It was clear that the more a captain could have a fast fire–armed maneuvering mass, the better the result in battle. Machiavelli examined this issue; he was as bad a military theorist as he was a formidable political theorist. He suggested the use of two men on horseback: a rider and a *scoppiettiere*—a "handgunner"—on the same horse. It was the first kind of mounted infantry in the modern era. Giovanni de'Medici, the brave Florentine captain known as Giovanni of the Black Band, adopted this system. Another contemporary Florentine captain, Pietro Strozzi, who reduced the men on horseback to only one, developed the same system. He fought against Florence and Spain, then he passed to the French flag at the end of the Italian Wars. When in France, he organized a unit based upon his previous experience. It was composed of firearmed riders, considered mounted infantrymen, referred to as dragoons.

Thirty More Years of Wars in Italy, and the Beginning of a Unifying Policy of the House of Savoy: 1530–1560

After 1530, Italy was practically under Spanish rule. Spanish viceroys were in Naples, Palermo, and Cagliari, and a Spanish governor was resident in Milan. The Republic of Genoa and Duchy of Florence were allied to Spain. The duchies of Parma, Modena, and Mantua completely submitted. The Duchy of Savoy practically disappeared after a war between France and Spain from 1541 to 1544, and a further one from 1552 to 1559. Spain won, but the French were allowed to occupy the whole Piedmont. The duke tried as he could to stop the French, but no Spanish help came, and his son, the young heir Emmanuel Philibert of Savoy, soon had to go abroad to fight as a general in his uncle's army; and his uncle was emperor Charles V.

Cosimo de'Medici, duke of Florence, took advantage of the Spanish supremacy. He established a strong alliance with Spain and, after a long war from 1553 to 1559, conquered the Republic of Siena, giving him all of southern Tuscany except for a little group of coastal towns known as the *Presidii*—the Garrisons. They were an important intermediate port on the route from Naples to Genoa.

The papacy found itself surrounded by Spain or its allies. On a map his state looked like a sock. Spain was under the foot, on his southern border in Naples. Spain was on half of his northern border in Milan. The little duchies of Parma and Modena covered the northwestern border. The western border looked to Tuscany—allied to Spain—and the eastern border was on the Adriatic, a closed sea. The pope could act within his borders—as he did in 1539, crushing an insurrection in the city of Perugia—and could also act against some of his feudatories, as Pope Paul III did with a campaign against the Colonna family in 1540, but no more. In fact, strategic encirclement and its effects appeared clearly when the pope tried to destroy his most powerful feudal subject, the said Colonna family.

In 1556, Pope Paul IV, who was strongly against Spain, ordered the Colonnas to leave the fief of Paliano. The chief of the family refused and, being also constable of the Kingdom of Naples, he asked that king—that is to say Philip II, new king of Spain—for military support. The war lasted until 1557 and saw Spanish troops arriving literally at the gates of Rome before the pope accepted to a peace, leaving Paliano to the Colonna family. In these conditions it appeared that papal policy was strongly conditioned by Spain and the House of Habsburg, leaving the only possible alliance with France.

Unfortunately, France was weak. Its army had been involved in many wars with the Imperial army and was destroyed in August 1557 in the French village of Saint Quentin. The Imperials, led by Emmanuel Philibert, duke of Savoy, won a decisive victory. France agreed to sign the Peace of Cateau-Cambresis, giving backq Emmanuel Philibert all his possessions in Italy and Savoy. This allowed him to reorganize his states and establish a strong military state on both sides of the Alps.

Emmanuel Philibert decided that it was impossible to expand his possessions on the western side of the Alps. France was too strong and impossible to be defeated without a Spanish aid. The only possible solution was to expand east of the Alps, into Italy.

The Italian states were divided and weak. They were roughly the same size as the Duchy of Savoy. Emmanuel Philibert, however, had no army. On December 28, 1560, in the city of Vercelli, he issued an edict creating a standing army. As a former Spanish general, he applied the Spanish scheme to the newly established Savoyard army. All males between eighteen and fifty were liable for the levy. The best were ordered to "arm and equip themselves, according to instructions delivered from their superiors to them."[8]

At the same time, the duke organized a small navy, composed of a galley squadron, and began construction of a defensive ring of fortified cities, having at its center the fortified capital, the city of Turin. Emmanuel Philibert's program was successfully pursued by his heirs. Gradually, because the opposition of Spain and France, the House of Savoy increased its territory, obtained the royal crown in the eighteenth century, and in the nineteenth century achieved the goal of unifying Italy.

CHAPTER **3**

Between France and the Muslims: 1565–1601

The Siege of Malta

In the latter half of the sixteenth century, the *Sublime Porte* continued to export its power into the Balkans and Mediterranean. Strategically, the Mediterranean world was divided into two spheres of influence, with Italy as its geographic boundary. The Muslim sphere under Turkish rule, included the eastern Mediterranean, North Africa, the Middle East, and the Balkans. The Christian sphere under essentially Spanish control included the western Mediterranean from Gibraltar to Italy. The sultan, Suleiman the Magnificent, pursued a horizontal expansion, from east to west with Italy at the epicenter. Muslim efforts to conquer Italy had failed in the fifteenth and early sixteenth centuries. Neapolitan troops repeatedly repelled Turkish landing forces in Apulia, at the heel of the Italian boot. The last time, in 1537, an enormous Turkish fleet approached Apulia along the Adriatic coast, confident of Venetian neutrality. The entire operation failed because of the sudden appearance of a Venetian squadron. Venice later explained to the *Porte* that the squadron commander had misunderstood his orders, but Istanbul suspected Venetian duplicity and decided not to attempt a second invasion.

Suleiman considered an alternative strategy, not wanting to add Venice to his list of enemies. If he could not conquer Italy, or at the very least Naples, Suleiman decided to bypass the peninsula, sending his fleet into the western Mediterranean through the Channel of Sicily, between Tunisia and Sicily. This operation, however, would only succeed if the Turks could seize the strategically critical island of Malta. The Knights Hospitalars of Saint John, better known as the Knights of Malta, defended the island. Malta possessed a valuable harbor and would be a critical base for the conquest of the western Mediterranean.

In the spring of 1565, 188 Turkish vessels sailed to Malta along with 48 additional war galleys from Tripoli, Tunis, and Algiers. They escorted an enormous invasion fleet, which carried 38,000 soldiers, 25,000 pioneers, and powerful siege artillery. News of the Turkish assault spread rapidly throughout Europe. Venice reinforced its Mediterranean garrisons, and the duke of Tuscany, the Republic of

Genoa, and the papacy sent reinforcements to the island. The duke of Savoy provided supplies and dispatched his galleys. King Philip II of Spain ordered the Neapolitan, Sicilian, Sardinian, and Spanish galley squadrons to assemble at the Sicilian city of Messina to aid Malta. The king of France, Francis II, did nothing, as he maintained a secret agreement with the Turks.

On May 20, 1565, the Turkish fleet under Pialì Pasha reached Malta. Grand Master Jean de La Valette had only 541 knights—169 of them Italians—6,000 Maltese, and 2,600 Spanish soldiers garrisoning the three forts, Saint Elmo, San Michele, and Saint Angelo. The Turks failed to take Sant'Elmo by storm for a price of 3,000 dead compared to only 120 knights. In the following days the Turks isolated and repeatedly attacked the fort, finally prevailing on June 17. No quarter was given, and the few prisoners were flayed alive. They were then fixed on planks, and the planks were launched into the sea under the horrified eyes of the knights in the two other forts. The Turks subsequently attacked San Michele. Their first assault cost 2,000 dead and failed. Pialì Pasha then employed alternate bombardment and infantry attacks. The fort held and, on September 7, a Christian fleet reached Malta. Composed of sixty galleys from Tuscany, Naples, Sicily, Savoy, Genoa, Sardinia, and Rome, they landed an expeditionary force of infantry and cavalry. Divided into three columns, 8,000 Italian and Spanish soldiers attacked the Turks. Their attempt to deploy their army for battle failed due to a charge by Tuscan cavalry, which threw the Turks into disarray, cutting them in pieces. Pialì Pasha's army was destroyed, only 3,000 remained on the field. The routed army fled to the ships and abandoned the invasion. After a 110-day siege, Turkish casualties amounted to 20,000 men. The Christians lost 214 knights and some 5,000 soldiers. Malta was saved, and Suleiman's plans for the invasion of the western Mediterranean failed.

The War for Cyprus and the Victory of Lepanto

Sultan Suleiman the Magnificent died in 1566. His son and heir Selim II altered Turkish strategy once more. The failure to take Malta meant it was impossible to successfully control the western Mediterranean. Selim decided to secure internal lines in the eastern Mediterranean before attempting a second strike in the west. Although the eastern Mediterranean was a Muslim-controlled lake, it had two major Venetian bases, Cyprus and Crete, in its enter. They threatened Turkish sea routes from the Balkans to Egypt and to the Middle East. It was therefore necessary to seize them despite previous understandings between the republic and the Ottoman Empire. The sultan decided to proceed methodically, eyeing Cyprus first.

The Ottomans and Venetians had last fought a war from 1537 to 1539. Venice lost its possessions in Greece, particularly the cities of Naples in Romania and Naples in Malvasia (whose name is now Nauplion). This was largely due to the lack of support by other Christian powers and French duplicity in favor of the Turks. Confident in victory, Selim pursued war, but desired Venice to break their previous agreements. Venice, however, was cautious and avoided every possible pretext for war. In the course of this diplomatic game, Selim prepared a galley fleet of 150 ships and concentrated thousands of soldiers in Alexandria, Rhodes, and in the Layazzo Gulf. The Venetian Senate worried about the impending conflict as they lacked sufficient strength to face the full power of the Turkish empire. Moreover, it was impossible to find allies, because France was a friend of the Turks and Spain was an enemy of Venice. Indeed, the Venetians had not contributed ships or men to the relief of Malta only five years earlier that's why the Italian princes had little sympathy for Venice.

In the spring of 1570 the Turkish ambassador presented an ultimatum to the republic. It was rejected and, after the ambassador's departure, 40 Venetian galleys left for Corfu. Despite their purposeful failure to participate in the defense of Malta, the Venetians sought assistance from the papacy, Philip II, and assorted Italian princes. They found the responses far more favorable than anticipated. The pope, the dukes of Tuscany, of Urbino, and of Savoy, the king of Spain, and the Knights of Malta sent 189 ships, but they were too late. A Turkish invasion force of 150 galleys and 106 transports fleet had landed 50,000 men in Cyprus. The garrison of Nicosia was overwhelmed after a forty-five-day siege. The entire garrison of 4,000 men was killed. Turkish troops entered the city, massacring the population. They killed 25,000 civilians and all the Venetian officials, who were tortured to death. They beheaded the city's commander, Nicolò Dandolo. Then the Turkish commander took the head to Famagosta—the other Venetian garrison—and showed it to the local Venetian commander. General Marc Antonio Bragadin was not impressed and refused to surrender. The siege commenced and resistance was fierce. Bragadin had 8,400 men and his garrison was outnumbered 25 to 1. He resisted until August 1571. On August 1 the Venetian garrison was reduced to 1,800 men and retired in the citadel; but Turkish casualties were extremely heavy. Mustafà Pasha, the Turkish commander, offered very good terms to Bragadin. If the garrison surrendered, the Venetians would be allowed to go to Crete with their weapons and five cannons. Bragadin agreed, but it was a mistake. Upon surrendering on August 4, he was kept by the Turks, who cut off his nose and ears. He was then flayed alive. His skin was filled with straw and suspended from the mast of a ship, which was sent to all ports of the eastern Mediterranean to show what the enemies of the sultan could expect.

The united Christian fleet, forged by a papal-negotiated alliance referred to as the Holy League, remained inactive because the Spanish commander, Don Juan of Austria, had been ordered by Madrid not to assist the Venetians. Spain wanted Venice to be weakened as much as possible, but after a whole year of inaction, Pope Pius V was so angry that it was impossible for the fleet to remain at port. Don Juan's fleet was composed of 208 galleys, six galleasses, and 30 smaller ships. Of these ships, 109 galleys and all the galleasses were from Venice, 12 came from Tuscany, three were sent by the duke of Savoy, three were from Malta, 14 from Spain, 13 from Genoa, and the remainder from Naples, Sicily, and Sardinia. It was an Italian fleet with a substantial number of Spanish soldiers on board.

On the morning of October 7, 1571, in the Greek gulf of Lepanto, the Christian fleet engaged the Turkish fleet of 282 ships. By five o'clock in the evening Don Juan's victory was complete. Only 43 Turkish ships fled, while 80 Ottoman galleys were sunk and 160 captured. The Turks lost 30,000 men and 5,000 prisoners, and the Holy League lost 15 galleys and 8,500 men. More than 15,000 Christian slaves were freed from Turkish ships. The Battle of Lepanto was the greatest triumph of the Italian navies. According to tradition, on the same day in the Vatican, Pope Pius V was conducting business, then suddenly stood up and went to the window. He looked eastward for a long time, then turned and said to the cardinals: "Let attend to this business no more. Let us go to thank the Lord: the Christian fleet just gained the victory."[1] The cardinals were surprised and took note of the time and the day: It was five o'clock in the evening. They were astonished when, after many days, messengers came from Venice announcing the victory and confirming the day and the time.

Unfortunately, the Spaniards did not want to exploit the victory. They had no strategic interest in the eastern Mediterranean and their major task was to avoid a Venetian success. The Venetian Senate quickly realized they could not expect further help from Spain and its Italian dependencies or Italian states allied to Spain. The Venetian fleet was strong, but not strong enough to sustain a war against the Ottomans. This dilemma was resolved when the Venetian Senate made peace with the Turks, at the expense of the Spanish and despite papal protestations.

Italy between Spain and France: 1580–1601

The political situation in Italy did not change in the last quarter of the sixteenth century. Spanish supremacy remained firm; its power was based in Italy and centered on the Kingdom of Naples. Naples consistently provided Philip II with great quantities of money and men. When needed, more troops could be concentrated in Naples from Sicily and occasionally Sardinia. They could then march northward along the Adriatic coast, but they normally took ship in the Tyrrhenian Sea via galleys. After an intermediate stop in the *Presidii* on the Tuscan coast, they landed near Genoa and marched along the Ticino river to the Alps. Passing through Grisons-Swiss–owned Val Tellina, they reached the Rhine-Danube watershed. If they had to go to the Low Countries, they marched along the Rhine Valley. If they had to reach Austria or central or eastern Germany, they marched along Danube Valley. This was the so-called *Cammino di Fiandra*—literally "the path of Flander"—better known in English as "the Spanish Road." It was the vital strategic artery of the whole Spanish military and political system.

Italian troops under Spanish colors served throughout Europe. They fought in Germany, in France, in Italy, the Low Countries, in Northern Africa, on the fleet—on the Invincible Armada (1588), too—and in Central and South America, with very good results. In the seventeenth century Italian troops had the honor of receiving the second rank in the Spanish army, immediately after the Spanish and before all others. Italian generals in Spanish service were considered quite formidable. They had successful careers, obtaining commands in Europe and in America. Two of the most famous generals in Spanish service were Italians. Duke Alessandro Farnese, known more commonly as "Parma" because he was the duke of Parma, commanded Spanish troops in Flanders in the late sixteenth century, and Ambrogio Spinola, a nobleman from Genoa, succeeded him later, achieving major victories against the Dutch—such as Breda—and ending his career in northern Italy around 1630.

The cost of maintaining the Spanish empire was enormous. In spite of gold and silver from the Americas, in 1504 Spain demanded a "gift" from Naples. The first was 311,000 ducats. This was more than all the money spent by the people of the kingdom each year for clothes. The following years the gift increased. From 1532 to 1553, Naples gave Spain 6,500,000 ducats. In 1560 the gift became annual, instead of biennial as it had been before, and Madrid fixed it to 1,200,000 ducats per year. The financial burden was too great for the kingdom and Naples suffered severe economic decline. The kings of Spain, Charles I (Charles V as the emperor) and later his son Philip II—also kings of Naples—continued to draw revenue to support Spanish policy in Europe and around the world.

During the sixteenth century, following the Peace of Cateau-Cambresis, the House of Savoy tried to enlarge its Italian possessions "by hook or crook." It fought a war supporting Catholics against Huguenots in southern France from 1589 to 1601, with no results, and conquered the Marquisade of Saluzzo, owned by France in the Piedmont. Madrid did not support their wily Italian client because although France was an enemy, the Spanish did not want to enable Italian princes, even allies, to increase their power.

The pope had to balance Spain and France, two Catholic powers, but it was extremely difficult, as religious uniformity did not translate into dynastic alliances. In fact, France was weakened by civil and religious war between Catholics and Protestants during the latter half of the sixteenth century. The pope supported the French Catholic monarchy, but Spain was important as the arm of the Counter-Reformation in Europe. This meant that the papacy was closely linked to the Habsburgs, but Rome did not like Madrid very much. This is the underlying reason for prompt papal recognition of the conversion of Henry de Bourbon, the former Huguenot leader, who became Henry IV, king of France. He ended the civil war between Catholics and Huguenots and pursued a decidedly anti-Spanish, anti-Habsburg foreign policy that provided the papacy with options for the first time in more than a century. Henry renewed French interest in Italy as part of his anti-Spanish policies; and Italian interests in France increased as it provided an alternative Catholic polity.

PART II

THE SEVENTEENTH CENTURY

The Thirty Years' War in Italy

Before the Thirty Years' War: The Triple War of 1613-1617: Gradisca, the Uscocks, and the First War of the Mantuan Succession

At the dawn of the seventeenth century, Spain's position in Italy appeared impregnable, but appearances can be deceiving. The Italian princes used their small armies for short campaigns, such as Pope Clement VIII—who sent an expeditionary force against the Muslims in Hungary in 1595 and in 1601–2—or the Duchy of Modena, which waged war against the smaller Republic of Lucca in 1613.

Venice was the only independently powerful state in Italy. The intrinsic desire to remain independent of all influences often placed it at odds with Spain and the papacy. Venice's senate compelled the papacy to seek senatorial approval for papal edicts issued in the republic. If the Senate disagreed with papal policy, it rejected decrees. This religious autonomy further exacerbated the rift between Rome and the republic.

In 1605 the disagreements between Venice and Rome finally reached a critical stage. Spain pledged Rome all possible military support, but failed to back its pledge with tangible forces. They feared possible French intervention, and thus a stalemate ensued. The diplomatic situation in Italy was complex, and thus in 1613 a confused and peculiar war was fought. Venice had difficulties with Dalmatian pirates, protected by the Austrian Habsburgs. A Venetian fleet attacked the pirates in their ports, and soon a maritime war expanded to the Italian mainland where Venetian troops attacked an Austrian army in Friuli. They fought on the same battlefields were, exactly three centuries later, Italians and Austrians would clash during World War I, on Carso and around the city of Gorizia. The Habsburg garrison was commanded by count Albrecht von Wallenstein, future general of Habsburg forces in Germany during the Thirty Years' War.

The war at sea was known as the Uscock War, after the name of the Dalmatian pirates. The war against Austria was called the War of Gradisca, after the city attacked by Venetian forces. In the course of these wars Spain mobilized its forces in Milan to assist their Austrian Habsburg cousins. At the moment an expanded Habsburg-Venetian war appeared imminent, Duke Charles Emmanuel I of Savoy demanded the Duchy of Mantua for his house or, at least, the Marquisat of Monferrat. Spanish opposition to Savoyard expansion in April 1613 generated a war between the Italian duchy and Spain. Although the weight of forces favored Spain, the Spanish army from Milan was defeated and the duke resisted further Spanish threats. Surviving for the moment, Charles Emmanuel actively pursued a Venetian alliance. He sent an ambassador to Venice. Although the Senate welcomed the opportunity, it decided that this Spanish distraction served them better than an active war between Venice and Spain. They decided not to declare war against Spain but covertly cooperate with Savoy without an official alliance. Venice subsidized the Savoyard army; Charles Emmanuel sent troops to the Venetian army and with his war occupied Spanish resources in Italy.

The Neapolitan—that is to say Spanish—fleet appeared in the southern Adriatic, but the Venetian fleet was more than adequate to meet the challenge. The war stalemated, and soon the French became active in the Alps. The threat of French intervention compelled Philip III, king of Spain, to end the war before his territories in Italy were fully threatened by a French-Savoyard-Venetian alliance. In 1617, Madrid, Vienna, Turin, and Venice came to terms. Despite the conclusion of this Italian war, it was soon eclipsed by the greater European conflict looming on the horizon, the Thirty Years' War.

Causes

The European conflict known as the Thirty Years' War originated in 1618 as a result of an internal conflict between the king of Bohemia, Ferdinand II—Holy Roman Emperor and head of the Austrian Habsburgs—and the Protestant lords in Bohemia. They threw Ferdinand's envoy and his assistants out of the castle window in Prague—the Defenestration of Prague—and then requested military support from the Evangelical Union in the Holy Roman Empire. Bohemia, a kingdom of the Austrian Habsburg realm, was one of the seven electoral territories in the Holy Roman Empire. The defiant Bohemian lords looked to the German Protestant princes in their rebellion against Ferdinand II, and offered Frederick, elector of the Palatinate, the crown of Bohemia.

The Holy Roman Emperor of the German Nation was elected by prince electors. If the House of Habsburg lost the crown of Bohemia, it lost the electoral capability as well as the possibility of maintaining the imperial crown in its hands. At the onset of this struggle for Bohemia, the House of Habsburg moved quickly to deal with this crisis, although it found itself overwhelmed with additional rebellions in Austria, too. All of this provided an opportunity for Frederick, as the Protestant Evangelical Union had no standing army and no diplomatic support abroad. Venice gave diplomatic support, because an enemy of Austria was a friend of the republic. Sweden and Denmark did the same, but Venice was richer and closer to Austria and Bohemia than Denmark and Sweden, therefore its support was of major importance to Frederick.

The problem remained building an army. It is here that Charles Emmanuel of Savoy became a central player. In 1617 he raised in Germany and paid in advance for an army of five thousand professional soldiers under General Ernst von Mansfeld. Initially, he wanted to employ it against Spain in northern Italy. With the war in Italy interrupted and the Evangelical Union needing an army, he left his forces in Germany. The Union's ambassadors agreed that in exchange for his army, they support his interest in the imperial crown. As a prince of the empire they could vote for him. Charles Emmanuel accepted the proposition and his army went to Prague. Frederick had now diplomatic support and an army. He refused any possible accommodation with the Habsburgs, and the Thirty Years' War began. The Evangelical Union did not keep its word; nonetheless, both Savoy and Venice had successfully diverted the Habsburg menace from Italy.

The emperor, Ferdinand II, was strongly funded by the Catholic world. His Spanish cousin, Philip III, gave him 1 million florins *una tantum*, but this was a trifle compared to the funds raised in Italy. Pope Paul V pledged 20,000 florins per month for the duration of the conflict. Then he permitted the emperor to levy a war tax in Italy, which brought in 250,000 scudi per year. The twelve congregations of the Catholic Church sent a 100,000-scudi gift, and this meant that, after 1623, the pope gave the emperor more money than Spain did. Moreover, the duke of Tuscany gave financial support and maintained a cavalry regiment in Germany throughout the war.

Thousands of Italians took part in the war, many of whom served as high-ranking officers in the imperial army. Famed soldiers such as Collalto, Galasso, Piccolomini, and Raimondo Montecuccoli fought under imperial and Spanish colors. Italian troops formed a significant part of the army that defeated Frederick and the Evangelical army at White Mountain in 1618; 14,000 were later led by the duke of Feria from Italy to Bavaria, as well as 16,000 led by the Habsburg Archduke Ferdinand (later Ferdinand III), who fought and won at Nördlingen in 1634.[1] The greater part of Habsburg forces and finances were drawn from Italy.

The Spanish Road and the Struggle for Its Control: 1619–1640

Soon after the war began, Spain moved its troops north along the Spanish Road. It was impossible to prevent their movement in Italy, but it was possible to cut the Spanish Road in Switzerland, in the Valtelline. The Grisons were the masters of that Catholic and Italian-speaking valley, and they were Protestant. The advent of the Thirty Years' War in Bohemia therefore affected Switzerland, too. A long and complicated war, the First Valtelline War began in 1620, when the local Catholics massacred all the Protestants living in the valley and, supported by the Spaniards, destroyed Protestant Swiss reinforcements coming from the north. The French, directed by Cardinal Richelieu, tried to cut the Spanish Road but repeatedly failed. Richelieu's objective was to weaken the Habsburgs in Italy and Germany by supporting the local autonomies against Spain and Austria. He anticipated that this would compel Madrid and Vienna to use their military resources and their capital in Switzerland and Italy, to keep the Spanish Road opened, reducing their forces in Germany.

This policy of distracting the Habsburgs from their dynastic ambitions was drafted by King Henry IV and, after his assassination, it was continued and successfully exploited by his son's minister Cardinal de Richelieu. From the early days of seventeenth century, the primary objective of French foreign policy was to supplant Habsburg power in Italy and Germany; failing that, to keep the Habsburgs weak in both regions. When in 1623 the major French effort to cut the Spanish Road in the Valtelline failed, France approached Savoy for an alliance. Richelieu's intention was to conquer Genoa in order to cut the Spanish Road at its landing point in Liguria. In 1625, Charles Emmanuel of Savoy led a victorious campaign against Genoa, but as he anticipated consolidating his hold on the republic, French disorganization and Spanish intervention stopped him. Piedmontese troops were forced to leave Liguria and Spanish troops invaded Piedmont, thereby securing the the Spanish Road. In 1626 the Spanish army surrounded the key Piedmontese city of Verrua. The siege was long, terribly hard, and expensive. The Spaniards failed to take the city and decided to negotiate an end to the war. In any case, France failed again to cut the Spanish Road, and soon Spanish troops continued their march to Germany to support Catholic and Habsburg causes. The Protestants were defeated in Bohemia and in western and central Germany. Imperial troops defeated a Danish army under Christian IV and reached the borders of Jutland when the death of the duke of Mantua altered the course of the conflict.

Mantua was small, rich, and possessed major strategic importance in northern Italy. If the Spanish Road was cut, imperial troops could move from Germany to Italy only along a second, less protected, and less comfortable route. Venice owned the land in northern Italy from Switzerland to Adriatic coast, between Austrian and Spanish territories. Imperial troops could pass through the mountains separating the Trentino from Lombardy, then reach Lake Garda and sail down the Mincio river. Although the route passed through Venetian territory, the Venetians would allow them to sail down the river under condition of not landing on Venetian territory. Mantua was the terminal at the end of the journey. The master of the city controlled the only other imperial route through Italy.

In 1628, when duke Vincenzo Gonzaga died, his closest heir was the duke of Gonzaga-Nevers, descended from a branch of the family established in France. When the Spaniards realized that a French noble was the legal heir of Mantua and master of their second most important strategic city, they immediately threw their support behind the second Gonzaga branch, that of the former dukes of Ferrara. Venice and Paris declared their armies prepared to back Charles of Gonzaga-Nevers. Ferdinand II then ordered his troops to Italy. The return of the imperial armies from Germany to Italy was a long-standing nightmare of the Church. Pope Urban VIII concentrated an army on his northern border, the bank of the Po river in front of Mantua, to prevent the introduction of imperial troops any farther south.

Cardinal de Richelieu saw Mantua as a new opportunity. A French-born duke in Mantua could cut the Habsburg's strategic nerve. Mantua was far from the French frontier, and Richelieu's army needed a secure passage through the Alps and a supply base in northern Italy. Lombardy was Spanish, but Mantua owned Monferrat, which was in Piedmont. If France could obtain free passage across the Alps with permission of Savoy, it could establish a horizontal strategic line running from the Alps through Casale—the capital of Monferrat—to Mantua, cutting both the Spanish Road, very close to Casale, and the Mantua route. The objective was so vital to French grand strategy that Richelieu personally led the French army into the Piedmont.

Charles Emmanuel I of Savoy was allied to Spain at this time, having been betrayed by the Evangelical Union and courted by Madrid. Richelieu tried to bargain, but the duke was clever. He negotiated with the cardinal while assembling his army. At the same time the new duke of Mantua raised an army; and both Venetian and imperial troops marched to Mantua. Gradually, more than 100,000 men from Savoy, Venice, Spain, the Papal States, Mantua, France, Naples, and the empire concentrated on the Padana Plain. It was the biggest concentration of troops ever seen during the Thirty Years' War; and it occurred in Italy instead of in Germany.

In 1629, after the Danish phase of the Thirty Years' War and prior to Swedish intervention, the turning point was reached in Italy. As C. V. Wedgwood remarked: "Insignificant in itself, the Mantuan crisis was the turning point of the Thirty Years' War, for it precipitated the final division of the Catholic Church against itself, alienated the pope from the Habsburg dynasty, and made morally possible the calling of Protestant allies by Catholic powers to redress the balance."[2] Habsburg generals Ambrogio Spinola and Rambaldo di Collalto—both Italians— coordinated their efforts and, on July 18, 1630, Mantua fell and was pillaged by the imperials. Richelieu had captured Pinerolo, at the foot of the Piedmontese Alps, by this time, and the French and Mantuan garrison of Casale successfully kept the Spanish at bay. When this short and bloody war ended in 1630, the Treaty of Regensburg recognized the French presence in Italy and their possession of a passage across the Alps. The Spanish Road could now be cut from Casale; and the city-fortress could be supported by the French garrison at Pinerolo; and Pinerolo could be supplied from France thanks to the passage across the Alps. Richelieu had achieved a remarkable strategic success.

All was quiet on the Italian front for the following five years. Germany became the major operational theater once more; and Spain focused its attention and troops there. Long columns of soldiers under Spanish colors marched along the Spanish Road from Italy to Germany to fight and die on Dutch and German battlefields. The Spanish raised an enormous amount of money in Italy.

Their troops sailed from Italy to South America after 1624, when the Dutch attacked Brazil. Spain absorbed Portugal and its colonies until the 1640s, and found them susceptible to Dutch raids after 1621, when the twelve-year truce ended. The first Italian troops reached Saõ Joaõ da Bahia in 1625 and fought successfully against the Dutch. In 1635 the Neapolitan nobleman Giovan Vincenzo Sanfelice was appointed supreme commander of the Spanish troops in Brazil, and in 1638 he defeated Dutch troops attacking Bahia under John Maurice of Nassau.

The entire conflict in Europe changed in 1635 when France entered the war, backing the Protestants. Richelieu opened the Italian front with an alliance between France, Savoy, Mantua and Parma against Spain. Then a French army reentered the Valtelline to cut the Spanish Road. Spanish troops from Milan ejected the French; and Richelieu moved his army to Piedmont, while the duke of Modena joined Spain. After two years, a new peace was signed over the Valtelline, but the war continued in Piedmont until 1640. Piedmont, however, was racked by civil war between the duchess—sister of Louis XIII of France and mother of the young Duke Charles Emmanuel II—and princes Maurice and Thomas of Savoy who, as the brothers of the late Duke Victor Amadeus I, wanted the regency until their nephew could receive the crown.

France supported Duchess Christine and Spain backed the princes. After a three-year war, France and the duchess prevailed. The French retained their positions in Piedmont and menaced the Spanish Road once again. Richelieu followed up this change of fortune with another indirect attempt to weaken Spanish control of Italy. A local war exploded in central Italy in 1640. The so called Castro War, after the name of a little fief some sixty miles north of Rome, involved a coalition composed of Venice, Parma, Modena and Tuscany in a conflict against the pope. The clash had no impact on the war in Germany, but it diverted men and resources and forced Spain to retain troops in Italy. All the Italian states involved recalled their best men serving abroad. Among them was Raimondo Montecuccoli, appointed commander of the Modenese troops who conducted an impressive campaign against papal troops around Bologna.

This bloody war, with casualties on both sides exceeding 14,000 men in twenty-three months, ended in 1644, with no significant changes to the political situation in Italy.

Cardinal Mazarin, successor to Richelieu, decided to act directly against Spain. In 1646 a 10,000-man French expeditionary force landed in the *Presidii* to cut the maritime portion of the Spanish Road. Operations went on slowly, but in 1647, Naples, the financial and military center of Spanish power in Italy revolted against the Spanish viceroy. The root cause of the revolt was the excessive taxation by the Spanish to sustain their war in the Netherlands and Germany. When in July 1647 a new tax was levied on fruits and vegetables, the people revolted. No less than 115,000 people took arms against the viceroy, who escaped to Naples' main castle. The Spanish garrison was unable to stop the riots, and in October the revolution expanded throughout southern Italy. Madrid dispatched all available galleys and troops to Naples. No less than 40 galleys and vessels and more than 3,000 cannons, including those in the fortresses, were employed. The expedition failed; and Naples fell to the rebellion. The Royal Neapolitan Republic—as the revolutionary govern-ment named itself—requested assistance from France. A French fleet arrived before the city on December 24, 1647, and fought a naval battle against the Spanish while the French duke of Guiche was proclaimed chief of the Royal Neapolitan Republic.

Spain increased troops and ships in the area. At the same time the Spanish promised money and honors to all who would help them, as well as a general pardon to the city and its inhabitants. In spring 1648 the money succeeded where the weapons had failed; and the duke of Guiche was captured by Spanish forces.

The Peace of Westphalia ended the war in Europe, but the Thirty Years' War left unresolved problems and new animosities. France attained its strategic goals. Germany and Italy remained divided into small weak states. According to the treaty, France could intervene in German affairs to defend Protestant rights. Ger-man princes could seek French protection when in conflict with the emperor. France used this power for diplomatic and military purposes into the eighteenth century.

The situation in Italy differed because the Treaties of Westphalia did not address the situation in the peninsula. France, however, retained control of the Alpine passes and the fortress of Pinerolo. This gave them a direct control over the Pied-mont and the effective means to cut the Spanish Road and the Spanish logistical system.

Fifteen More Years of Strife: 1649–1663

Spain certainly did not benefit from the strategic results of the Thirty Years' War. As soon as possible, the Spanish tried to reaffirm their rule in Italy. The result was a lengthy war in Italy. Furthemore, the Peace of Westphalia did not end the Franco-Spanish war, which continued until 1659. The strategic objective was control of the Piedmontese fortresses. Spain wanted to eliminate France from the eastern side of the Alps. Conversely, France was looking for a complete and secure strategic line from the Alps to Mantua and to the Venetian border. France also found allies in Modena, whose duke—not by chance—married one of the nieces of Cardinal Mazzarin, the Italian-born prime minister of France and successor to Richelieu.

The conflict saw another French expedition to Naples in 1650, to restore the duke of Guiche. It failed, but in northern Italy the French achieved a strategic victory. Piedmont became a satellite of France, and in 1659 all the consequences of the Thirty Years' War in Italy ended with a peace treaty between Modena and Spain, signed at Guastalla, and with Spain and France in the Peace of the Pyrenees.

The Second Half of the Century

The Candia War: 1645–1669

In the last years of the Thirty Years' War, the Ottoman sultan Ibrahim resumed Ottoman imperial expansion. The only non–Ottoman enclave still remaining in the eastern Mediterranean was the Venetian-owned island of Crete. Its geographic position on the route from Egypt to Greece and the Dardanelles was quite strategic. On June 23, 1645, a powerful Turkish fleet of 348 ships landed a 51,000-man expeditionary force in Crete. The invasion was coordinated with an offensive in the Balkans, threatening Austrian Habsburg possessions and Venetian-held Dalmatia. Pope Innocent X proclaimed a Crusade; and thousands of volunteers answered the call serving under the imperial banner and Venetian Saint Mark's colors. All the Italian states sent their galleys to Corfu, where the Venetian fleet gathered.

The preparation for the relief of Crete came too late for many of the small Venetian-held towns on the island. The surviving Venetian troops concentrated in the capital city of Candia in the autumn of 1645. The strategic difficulty of waging war in Crete was complicated for both armies. The Turks failed to take the island by surprise and found themselves fighting a war of attrition at a distance. The Turks required an immense amount of resources in order to maintain the pressure on Candia. Their supplies were concentrated in ports throughout the eastern Mediterranean, with the central magazines at Istanbul. Turkish convoys sailed from the Dardanelles to Crete, but they needed protection; and this meant the full commitment of the Turkish fleet.

Venice had a similar problem. It had to sustain its garrison in Candia. Their fleet needed to interdict the enemy's maritime supply lines, too. The Venetian fleet therefore had to operate against the Turkish convoys as well as protect its own. Moreover, the Ottoman offensive in the Balkans threatened the Dalmatian coast and could potentially cut Venetian routes in Adriatic. To secure Adriatic coast and routes, the Senate organized a second front in Dalmatia under General Leonardo Foscolo. The Venetians won three campaigns, in 1646, 1647, and 1648, yet the Turks held the cities in the interior and continued to menace the Venetian-held coast. The Senate concentrated all its resources on the maritime war while reinforcing the coastal towns. Venice was hard-pressed. A city, albeit a rich one, with little territory, was standing against the Ottoman Empire. Less than 1 million Italians were resisting some 50 million Muslims under Ottoman rule. It was probably the first attrition war ever fought in the Western world. Venice could not win, but she continued to resist.

Historians agree that more than 2,700 clashes occurred around the city of Candia during the twenty-three-year-long siege from 1646 to 1669; averaging one every three days.[1] Nevertheless, the major engagements occurred at sea. The Venetian fleet was smaller, but Venetian sailors were more experienced and veteran. Normally, Venetian galleys of the Light Squadron held post around Candia, while the Heavy Squadron was stationed at the egress of the Dardanelles. Unfortunately, they were not strong enough to intercept all outbound Turkish convoys from Istanbul. They disrupted one or two regularly, but the numbers of enemy vessels were too great to institute an effective blockade. The Venetian fleet was able to close the Dardanelles on occasion, but when the fleet was called to support operations in Candia, as happened in 1648, the Turkish straits were abandoned and the enemy sailed into the Aegean without disruption.

In 1649 an Ottoman fleet of 93 galleys and vessels left the Dardanelles en route to Candia. Venetian admiral Da Riva, commanding the Heavy Squadron, could not intercept due to contrary winds. Once the winds changed, he pursued the Turks to the Bay of Focea. Da Riva attacked and destroyed the Ottoman fleet, although outnumbered five to one. Despite the Venetian victory, the Turks sent another fleet of 83 galleys, 63 vessels, and many smaller ships to Candia the following month. They landed 7,000 men and detached 40 galleys for operations against the small Venetian-held Cretan town of Suda. General Pietro Diedo repelled the attack and the Turkish admiral was killed, but this did not alter the situation. The convoy reached Crete and supplies were landed.

The next year, Venetian admiral Mocenigo, whose fleet was outnumbered two to one, attacked an Ottoman fleet of 114 ships. He destroyed 17 Turkish vessels without loss. The Turks retreated to Rhodes and then, as soon as possible, sent another convoy of 46 galleys to Crete with money to pay the besieging army. In 1654, Venetian ships twice intercepted the 164-ship Turkish convoy. They won both the times, but, being outnumbered four to one, they could not stop the entire fleet; and the Turkish army in Crete received its supplies. The next year Venice put to sea 55 ships and galleys. It was considered a great achievement because its fleet was only outnumbered 2.8 to 1. The result was the same: a great clash, a partial Venetian victory; and a 12-galley Turkish convoy reaching Crete with supplies. In 1656 the Venetian "Sea Captain General"—the supreme commander of the fleet—Lorenzo Marcello, attacked the Dardanelles with 63 ships. On June 26, 1656, at noon, Turkish admiral Sinan Pasha with 96 vessels and galleys engaged Marcello. It was the worst Turkish defeat since Lepanto. At the end of the afternoon, only 14 Ottoman galleys escaped to Constantinople. Marcello lost only three vessels and 300 men. He killed 10,000 Turks and liberated 500 Christian slaves.

All of these victories against the Turks did little to save Crete and Candia. The immense resources of the Ottoman Empire were immediately used to build 100 galleys, 100 vessels, and 200 transports by the following spring. The year 1657 witnessed another Venetian tactical victory and another Turkish strategic success in supplying Crete. The republic could only look for help from Italy and Europe, but the more the time passed, the more unlikely it was to find allies.

Having seen that it was impossible to completely stop enemy convoys at their point of departure, Venice concentrated its fleet around Crete to intercept them at arrival. The new Sea Captain General, Andrea Cornaro, scattered the fleet in small squadrons patrolling blue and coastal waters, but this proved worthless. Francesco Morosini replaced Cornaro in 1658. He is considered the best admiral employed by Venice because he destroyed more Turkish vessels than any other and became the soul of the resistance. Although he succeeded in destroying the first convoy, the enemy had so many ships that it could easily reach the island, landing supplies and men and escaping before the small Venetian fleet could arrive.

Fighting for every inch, the walls of Candia gradually crumbled under cannon-balls. Terrible general assaults carried on by tens of thousands of Turks involved hand-to-hand fighting on the walls, bloody sorties and counterattacks, and horrible close-quarter combat in deep and obscure galleries invaded by poisonous smoke. The defense of Candia became the nightmare of every combatant. Perhaps only World War I saw similar desperate sacrifice and cruel violence on its battlefields and in its trenches.

Spain did not send aid and France contributed very little. His Most Catholic Majesty Louis XIV, king of France, proclaimed the cause of Christendom but, being allied to the sultan, he had no reason to help Venice. A victory could weaken the Ottoman Empire, and a weak Ottoman Empire was a gift to the Holy Roman Empire and to the House of Habsburg, his traditional enemy. Italian states regularly gave their support, but they were drained, too. The dukes of Savoy and Tuscany each maintained an infantry regiment in Candia for the entire war. Popes Innocent X, Alexander VII, and Clement IX sent funds and a galley squadron every year between 1645 and 1669. The Knights of Malta did the same. The Republic of Lucca and the Duchies of Modena and Parma generally contributed gunpowder and money. Many German princes dispatched troops, money, and powder to Crete or to the imperial army, but it was insufficient. Venice desperately needed money to continue the war. The Turks experienced similar economic crises between 1651 and 1656.

The Senate exhibited its desperation when they opened "the Golden Book," listing all the families of the Venetian patritiate. Those willing to pay huge sums were admitted to the patritiate—the ruling class—and the funds were used to finance the war effort. The response was enthusiastic, but it was not enough. Thus, in September 1669, Venetian troops in Candia capitulated. They had twelve good-weather days to leave the city. They could take with them all they could carry. All those who wanted to leave were permitted. The republic, under the principle of *Uti possidetis* (what you have), maintained three small islands around Crete and all the Dalmatian cities and towns captured during the war. On September 26, 1669, the last Venetian ships left Candia. All the clergy and all of the holy relics and the contents of the churches, monasteries, and private houses were taken to Venice. On October 4 the grand vizier entered Candia. Despite his promise in the capitulation, all the churches were destroyed, excluding four, which were transformed into mosques. So began 230 years of Ottoman rule in Crete.

The war for Crete (Candia) had been a terrible and costly conflict. No precise figure is available for casualties. It is particularly difficult to calculate because of the great variations in size and scope of the operations each year. If 1667 is taken as an example, there were 20,000 Turkish dead compared to 400 officers and 2,600 Venetian soldiers. Yet, in the first half of 1668, the Venetian garrison lost 600 officers and 6,500 men. The period 1667–69 was the hardest, with 29,088 Christians and an estimated 70,000 Turks dying, and no fewer than 38,000 slaves and Cretan peasants forced by the Turks to dig trenches. According to Venetian reports, losses from the war only in Candia totaled 30,985 Venetian soldiers and 118,754 Turkish soldiers. This figure excludes casualties on the Dalmatian front, at sea, and during the first operations in Crete. It is possible that if these figures are included, casualties for both sides should be doubled.

The financial costs had been terrible. Venice spent 126 million ducats, more than 5 million per year. One million was used annually for military expenditure; the remainder covered all other war-related expenses. At war's end the republic had a deficit of 64 million ducats. To compare, the contemporary purchasing value of one Venetian ducat is approximately $2,000, that is to say more than $250 billion was spent on the war. The immediate cost was nothing compared to the commercial devastation suffered by the Venetian republic. Venice lost its last and biggest commercial center in the eastern Mediterranean.

During the course of the war Venetian commercial traffic from the Mediterranean to northern Europe decreased. This reduction in the availability of Mediterranean goods led to increased prices in Britain and the Low Countries. After a few years, English and Dutch merchants saw opportunity. As England and the Netherlands were neutral powers, their ships could trade in the Mediterranean with little concern. The price of their Mediterranean goods was less than the Venetians or other Italian states. Their business increased, especially because they traded with the Turks, too. When the war ended, Venice had lost a lot of men, a lot of money, a vital colony, and, above all, its monopoly on East-West trade in Mediterranean. The Candia War was a complete disaster.

The Wars in Italy: 1670–1682

The following two decades passed with two remarkable conflicts in Italy, products of the wars of Louis XIV. In 1672, Piedmont tried to seize Genoa. The republic was no more a maritime power. At the end of the Italian Wars in the first half of sixteenth century, due to a personal alliance between Genoese admiral Andrea Doria and the Habsburg emperor Charles V, Genoa was a client state of the Spanish imperium. At the end of the century, her ruling class found it beneficial to act as the bank for the Spanish empire as opposed to struggle to maintain existing markets or look for new ones. This relationship with Spain led Duke Charles Emmanuel II of Savoy to attack Genoa in 1672. He believed that as Spain was occupied with France during the Dutch War, there would be little help for the republic. His military operations fell flat against Genoese resistance and Spanish aid, and after a year French diplomatic intervention ended the war in January 1673. Louis XIV did not want a second front opened in Italy if Charles Emmanuel was defeated. He therefore encouraged a peaceful settlement, for his own ends.

As one threat to the Spanish empire in Italy abated, another emerged. In 1674 the city of Messina in Sicily revolted against Spanish rule. As in Naples in 1647, the people did not appreciate their local officers imposed by Madrid. Riots exploded on July 7, and in a few days Spanish troops arrived from Palermo to crush the revolt. The city council sent emissaries to Rome to make contact with the French ambassador at the Vatican. Louis XIV had great interest in intervening, as Messina possessed a good strategic position. The city controlled the channel dividing Italy from Sicily, but a fleet based in Messina could also command the sea between Sicily and Tunisia, that is to say the passage from western to eastern Mediterranean. Although already at war with Spain, Louis made legal claim to Sicily as the French House of Anjou had ruled it in the Middle Ages. Messina, therefore, could be the first step to seizing the entire Kingdom of Sicily.

Charles II, king of Spain, reacted desperately in the early days of 1675 when a French expeditionary force reached the city. Spanish troops from Naples, Sicily, and Sardinia had already placed Messina under siege, but all attempts to take the port failed. Neapolitan, Sicilian, and Sardinian galley squadrons blockaded the city, but the French squadron was composed of sailing ships and the Italo-Spanish galleys were no match. A galley carried only three large cannon and numerous smaller ones. A sailing vessel could have 60 to 80 cannons. Two French fleets united under Admiral Duquesne, comprising 39 sails, easily dispersed the blockading ships.

The Dutch War in 1672–78 made for strange alliances. Louis XIV's invasion of the Netherlands, in 1672, was preceded by the violation of French armies marching through the Spanish Netherlands (Belgium). Traditional enemies made common cause. Spain requested naval assistance from the Netherlands. In response, the States-General, the Dutch parliament, sent a fleet of seventeen ships under Admiral de Ruyter to the Mediterranean. The Spanish concentrated all their supplies in Calabria, the southern part of the kingdom of Naples and then shipped them to Sicily. The French fleet tried to cut this logistical nerve, but the Dutch-Spanish fleet engaged them in battle for the first time in January 1676, without result. On April 22, Spanish troops attacked the city of Augusta, previously seized by Messinian and French troops. The allied fleet was supporting the operation from the sea when Duquesne attacked it. After three hours of fighting, de Ruyter was mortally wounded and his squadron withdrew. Following up this victory, the French attempted to take Palermo but had no success.

Louis XIV reviewed the situation in Sicily as operations in the Low Countries and western Germany were concluding. The French controlled only Messina and Augusta after two years of fighting. The remainder of Sicily was firmly in Spanish hands. The French expedition did not realize its strategic objective; and Louis withdrew his troops. Messina was abandoned. Fearing the return and retribution of the Spanish, 7,000 people fled with the French. When the Spanish finally recaptured the city, it was deprived of all its benefits and privileges; and those involved in the revolt were arrested and hanged.

Italian Armies in the Late Seventeenth Century

In the second half of the seventeenth century, armies, weapons, and military organizations evolved throughout Europe. Italian states transformed their provisional forces into standing armies. Normally major states, such as Venice, the papacy, and Piedmont, maintained a peacetime army of 9,000 to 10,000 men, which no more than doubled in wartime. Middle-sized or small states as well as Spanish dependencies had half that complement, roughly 4,000 to 5,000 men. All Italian states established permanent regiments. The most important Italian army to emerge was that of the House of Savoy. Two centuries later, it would form the core of the modern Italian army, in the way that the Prussians became the German army.

Duke Charles Emmanuel II reorganized his army between 1660 and 1664. He declared six infantry regiments as "standing." They were created out of units established and maintained during the first half of the century. The Savoy Infantry Regiment—later 1st and 2nd Savoia Infantry Regiments, and then "Re"—the "King"—Infantry Regiment—was originally raised in 1639. The Piedmont Infantry Regiment—later the 3rd and 4th Piemonte Infantry Regiments—formed in 1636 as the Catalano Alfieri Regiment. Prior to 1660 several other regiments were organized: The Guards, later the 1st Grenadiers of Sardinia Regiment; Aosta (later 5th and 6th Aosta Infantry Regiments), Nice and Monferrato Infantry Regiments, His Highness's Dragoon Regiment, and the Royal Madame's Regiment of Dragoons. Italian princes kept foreign professional regiments in their pay, too; so, Swiss and German infantry units served under practically every color in Italy from the sixteenth through the eighteenth centuries.

Grenadier units were established after the French example. Just as shields disappeared before the first half of the sixteenth century, pikes disappeared by the end of seventeenth century. Savoy's army was the first to provide its soldiers exclusively with firearms. The increasing use of firearms included an equal need for gunpowder and balls. Artillery and its ammunitions needed carriages and horses. Year after year logistics became a growing concern; and supply, march, and communication routes became more important.

As in the rest of Europe, operations in Italy began in early spring. Major operations were routinely conducted during the summer and first months of autumn— generally through the end of October. Armies entered winter quarters in November as bad weather and mud caused by rain and snow made routes impracticable and often impassible, especially to heavy carts. The consequence could be a reduction, if not an interruption, in supply; and each army halted operations until the following spring. Only limited operations, made mostly by cavalry or, rarely, by some infantry companies, were carried out for purposes of foraging or reconnaissance.

Cavalry was divided between light and heavy regiments; and dragoons were increasingly employed as cavalry instead of infantry. Artillery was considered a civilian-composed unit under the control of military officers. The same applied for the engineering corps. No real "marine corps" existed, but Savoy and Naples had regiments specifically established to serve on ships; the La Marina Regiment for Savoy and the Tercio Viejo de la Mar de Napoles for Naples. The latter was composed of Spaniards who served on Neapolitan galleys, while Tercio de la Mar Océano was composed of Neapolitans who served in the Spanish Atlantic fleet. Venice used its infantry both on land and at sea, as did Genoa, Tuscany, and the Papal States.

All the Italian states maintained local militias, which were employed as a complementary military organization to be called in case of war.[2] Militiamen generally had to drill once per season and were organized into infantry and cavalry regiments. This system proved quite useful in Savoy and, in the seventeenth century, in Tuscany, too, but it did not work very well in other Italian states.

Officer corps were composed of professionals, drawn domestically or from abroad. Italian and non-Italian officers spent their lives serving in Italian armies. Venice and Genoa were the exception. Both republics used the ancient Roman system of mixing civil and military careers. It was not uncommon for a Venetian Sea Captain General to have substantial experience as a local administrator, civil governor, army officer, central administrator, and diplomat. On occasion, if he was quite successful—as was Francesco Morosini—he could be elected Doge: the chief of the republic.

Venice, the Holy League, and the First Morea War: 1684-1699

It was the summer of 1683 when the Turks besieged Vienna. Previously in 1664, they were stopped "thanks to God and to Count Montecuccoli," as the Emperor Leopold I had said. Less than twenty years later the Turks returned.

Pope Innocent XI proclaimed a Crusade; and again princes raised thousands of volunteers across Europe to fight against the Ottomans. He also negotiated a military agreement between the emperor and King Jan Sobieski of Poland. Venice closed the Saint Mark's evangel on her flags, because in wartime no banner could have *Pax tibi Marce*—Peace to thou, Mark—written on it.

A coalition of imperial forces and the Polish army under Sobieski destroyed the Turks outside the gates of Vienna and, on January 19, 1684, another "Holy League" was forged. Venice, the pope, the king of Poland, the emperor, and—thirteen years later, in 1696—Czar Peter I "the Great" of Russia, marched against the Ottomans in Hungary and the Balkans. Malta and Tuscany joined the League, too, and the duke of Parma sent an infantry regiment. The Most Serene Republic of Venice was given charge of the maritime campaign and of operations in Dalmatia and Bosnia.

Francesco Morosini was elected Sea Captain General. The Senate accorded him liberty of action and provided him with a fleet of 48 ships. The pope, the Knights of Malta, and the grand duke of Tuscany provided him with an additional 17 ships. Morosini left Venice on June 10. Three months later he swept the Turks from the Greek coast, conquering Vonitsa, Xeronero, Missolonghi, and Prevesa. The following year the Turkish fleet practically disappeared while Venetian troops conquered the entire Peloponnesian peninsula, or, as it was called at that time, the Morea. In 1687, while campaigning in Dalmatia, General Cornaro extended Venetian possessions. The Venetian troops under Morosini besieged Athens. They shelled the Turkish powder magazine. It was in the Parthenon and, when a well-directed Venetian shell exploded there, the Parthenon exploded, too, and remained as it is now. Without ammunition and powder the Turks surrendered within six days.

The Venetian Senate—according to ancient Roman tradition—gave Morosini the title of "Peloponnesiacus" and, an honor not previously accorded in Venice, ordered that a statue of him be put in the Ducal Palace, although he was still alive. On March 27, 1688, Doge Giustiniani died; and the Senate elected Francesco Morosini to succeed him. The Senate accompanied his elevation by naming him supreme commander of military forces.

Sultan Suleiman III ascended the throne in the midst of a devastating war. His position improved marginally when, in 1688, France suddenly attacked the Holy Roman Empire and Austrian and imperial troops were deployed to the Rhine. Venetian operations, however, continued. A Turkish army of 100,000 men, dedicated to reconquering the Peloponnesus, was destroyed; and the Turkish fleet survived by avoiding battle. Although Morosini died in January 1694, Venice continued its string of successes. After five more years of fighting, and the end of the War of the League of Augsburg, or Nine Years' War, 1689–98 in western Europe, imperial troops returned to the Balkans. Their commander, Prince Eugene of Savoy, completely destroyed the Ottoman army at Zenta in 1697, and the next year he captured Belgrade.

Defeated by the imperials in the Balkans and by the Venetians in Greece, the Turks accepted the peace in 1699. The Treaty of Carlowitz ended the war and gave the Most Serene Republic possession of Greece.

CHAPTER 6

The League of Augsburg: 1690-1696

The War of Devolution in 1667–68 and the Dutch War of 1672–78 made Louis XIV the most powerful king in Europe. He sought the imperial crown of Germany, and his aggressive policies became bolder each year. Subsequently, in 1686 the German princes, encouraged by Emperor Leopold I, formed a defensive alliance to protect the empire, named after the city of Augsburg where they signed the pact.

The Turkish defeat at the gates of Vienna in 1683 and Venetian victories in the Morea War weakened a significant French ally. In 1688 the House of Habsburg expanded its territory with the conquest of Hungary. The emperor was widening his borders in the Balkans. Moreover, Venice enlarged its possessions in the eastern Mediterranean. A weak Ottoman Empire was not a threat to the Holy Roman Emperor; but a more powerful emperor was a problem for France. In 1688, French troops passed the Rhine, invading the empire and pillaging the Palatinate. The League of Augsburg organized the defense of the empire in the midst of this unprovoked French invasion.

Indeed, in that same year the Glorious Revolution in Britain removed James II from the throne. Britain had been a close ally of France. Charles II—a cousin of Louis XIV—had been strictly linked to France, and British troops had fought in the Low Countries with the French. All of this changed because the new king of England—the Dutch William III of Orange—was an enemy of Louis XIV.

Britain joined the League of Augsburg, now called "the Great Alliance." It was composed of the German princes, the Austrian and Spanish Habsburgs, and the kings of Denmark and Sweden. The French were forced from the right bank of the Rhine, but the Allies were unable to invade France. The war widened overseas and reached America, too, where it was remembered as the King William's War, but with little result. This equilibrium forced France and the Great Alliance to look for new allies, particularly the House of Savoy.

The young Duke Victor Amadeus II reigned in Turin. He pursued the traditional Savoyard policy of enlarging the state, making it the premier power in Italy. The greatest obstacle was the French garrison in Pinerolo, there since the time of

Richelieu. Moreover, the duke of Mantua rented the fortress of Casale to Louis XIV in 1683, and Savoy was still a French satellite. The League offered Victor Amadeus Pinerolo and freedom from French influence. He joined the League in the spring of 1690 and prepared to attack the French.

He had merely 10,000 men when he went to war. Spain and the empire sent him an additional 20,000, while Britain and Netherland gave him 30,000 scudi per month: two-thirds from London and one-third from Amsterdam.[1] Victor Amadeus was appointed supreme commander of allied troops in Italy. His cousin, Prince Eugene of Savoy, commanded the imperial troops. In 1683, Prince Eugene had offered his services as a young man to Louis XIV, who curtly refused. The prince then turned to Leopold in Vienna, who gladly accepted his fealty.

The war in Italy was rather peculiar. Savoy's army resisted very well and maintained control of the country, but the French consistently defeated the Allies in battle, at Staffarda in 1690 and Marsaglia in 1693. Fortunately, logistical difficulties prevented the French from capitalizing on their victories, but soon Victor Amadeus realized that Austria and Spain had only limited commitments in Italy. Both Madrid and Vienna feared a strong Piedmont as much as a French presence in Italy. However, William III did not see the situation similarly as his allies did. He perceived the Italian front to be the most critical. He wanted allied troops to enter southern France, carrying the war to the enemy's territory as never happened under Louis XIV. William's letters, especially in 1691 and 1692, are very clear about it.[2]

Despite defeats in field, Victor Amadeus conducted a successful expedition with Prince Eugene in southern France in 1692. In 1695, rumors about secret negotiations between the Maritime Powers—as Britain and the Netherlands were called at that time—and France reached him. Not trusting his allies, and fearing Austria and Spain would make an agreement without him, Victor Amadeus concluded a separate peace with Louis XIV in 1696. France gave him Pinerolo. The fortifications at Casale were dismantled; and the city was returned to the duke of Mantua instead of to Spain or the empire. Furthermore, France gave Savoy all the territories it possessed in Piedmont and accepted an alliance to secure Italy's neutrality. The Maritime Powers and the emperor were furious and considered Victor Amadeus a traitor.

The Franco-Piedmontese peace allowed the French to send their troops from Italy to Flanders; and this forced the Allies to accept a general peace in 1698.

Savoy's position was secure. The duchy had no foreign garrisons within its borders, and it was lodged between Spain—master of Milan—and France. In case of war, one or the other could support it. It was the first time that an Italian state, other than Venice, had conducted an independent policy since the death of Lorenzo the Magnificent in 1492. The situation was stable and the duke was pleased, but soon catastrophe struck when Charles II, king of Spain, died.

PART **III**

THE EIGHTEENTH CENTURY

CHAPTER 7

The Spanish Succession: 1700-1713

Charles II, the Spanish Habsburg king of Spain, of Naples, of Sicily, of Sardinia, and duke of Milan, died on November 1, 1700. He had no direct heirs; and the monarchs of Europe had spent many years discussing what to do after his death. Nevertheless, all existing treaties were voided when the late king's will clearly proclaimed the duke of Anjou, grandson of Louis XIV, heir to his realms. The Holy Roman Emperor, and Austrian Habsburg, Leopold, contested the will, claiming all the crowns of Spain for his second son, Charles, and organized an army to support him. In the spring 1701 an imperial army commanded by Prince Eugene of Savoy moved into northern Italy, while a second army formed in Germany.

The historical presence of the Spanish in Italy, and the relationship of that dynasty to the Austrians, counterbalanced by French power created a complicated dilemma for Italian princes. The Spanish viceroys in Cagliari, Palermo, and Naples, and the governor in Milan, formally accepted Philip V Bourbon as the king of Spain. Their attitude determined Savoy's posture. Victor Amadeus benefited from having opposing powers as neighbors, but as Spain was now allied to France, he was trapped by this alliance and could only hope for rapid and decisive Austrian intervention. The emperor, however, lacked money and men; and a calculating Victor Amadeus subsequently joined the Spanish-French Bourbon alliance. He had few options. Any attempt to avoid a French alliance meant the destruction of his states by both French and Spanish armies. He dedicated 10,000 men—half of his army—to the Bourbons. At the same time, he maintained secret contacts with the emperor. Victor Amadeus desperately needed an enemy of France in Milan, and looked for every opportunity to change allegiances. William III of England and Emperor Leopold I understood his position perfectly.

Louis XIV suspected the accession of his grandson to the Spanish throne would lead to hostilities, but believed the emperor too weak to challenge the Bourbon succession. Leopold possessed merely 42,000 men, while Louis had 200,000 and could deploy no less than 75,000 men in northern Italy, including Spanish and Piedmontese forces. The imperial army in Italy led by Prince Eugene faced another problem. Venice owned all the territory between the Duchy of Milan and Austria. It was impossible to use the Spanish Road, because Milan was in Bourbon hands. The second route down the Mincio river to Mantua was cut, because that city was quickly seized by the Bourbons. The Austrians then requested from Venice permission for transit. Leopold hoped Venice would join the anti-Bourbon coalition as the Holy League technically linked Venice and Vienna, yet that alliance was dedicated solely against the Turks.

The Venetian government had a difficult task, determining their position in this conflict. France and the Ottoman Empire were clandestine allies, thus allying with Austria against France could lead to a renewed war with the Ottomans. The results of the previous war demonstrated that Austria could provide military support in the Balkans, but no help at sea. What if the French Mediterranean fleet moved into the Adriatic, joined the Turks, and attacked Venetian possessions in Dalmatia and Greece? Likewise, the Austrians may have intended to use *Venetian Terraferma* as a bastion against France. Venice could suffer to Austria's advantage.

A Franco-Venetian alliance was not advantageous either. Venice and Austria shared a lengthy common border in Italy and an even longer one in Dalmatia. Venice would withstand the worst of an Austro-imperial offensive into Italy before the emperor's army reached Milan. Indeed, the Turks could profit significantly in Dalmatia and Greece if a break occurred in Austro-Venetian relations. History illustrated that in this case, Venice could not count on French aid. The Senate chose a third way: neutrality; because Venice could afford one powerful enemy with allies, but they were not so foolish to believe they could fight two powerful enemies without allies.

The other Italian states preferred neutrality as well, but it was quite difficult. Mantua, Parma, and Modena were officially members of the Holy Roman Empire as Imperial Italy, but the French occupied the strategic city of Mantua at the onset of war. Parma guaranteed its neutrality under the protection of the Roman Catholic Church. The duke put the papal flag on his capital and sent ambassadors to the French army. Neutrality was observed, but the duchy suffered severely as foreign armies used his state for transit, and the occasional battle. The duke of Modena faced similar troubles, but he was lucky enough to preserve his neutrality. The pope and the grand-duke of Tuscany remained neutral as well.

In early 1701, Prince Eugene crossed into Italy, taking the Franco-Spanish army by surprise on the Padana Plain at Carpi di Villa Bartolomea. Soon the former members of the Great Alliance realized that a French-Spanish union was a mortal political and economic threat to Europe. The Netherlands and Britain joined the emperor; and the war widened. Fighting expanded throughout Europe, in Asia, along the African coasts and, a bit later, in America, where it was remembered as Queen Anne's War.[1]

Louis XIV supposed that the emperor and the Maritime Powers would accept the arrangement when he accepted the Spanish crowns for his grandson. Once war became reality, he pursued an aggressive strategy later employed in all the Succession Wars as well as in the Revolutionary and Napoleonic period. One French army passed the Rhine, moving through the Bavarian Plateau to Austria. The second crossed the Alps, marching through Padana Plain—the large northern Italy plain extending from Turin to Venice—to the Trentino and across the Brenner Pass, where it would join the other French army in Austria. Thereafter the two armies would advance upon Vienna.

The campaign in Germany presented practically no problems and, in the summer 1703, French troops, along with their Bavarian allies, were poised along the Austro-Bavarian border. Eugene's army in Italy offered significant resistance in 1701 and 1702, but in 1703 the prince was recalled to Vienna. His success in Italy led to his appointment to reorganize the entire Habsburg military system, which had proved so weak in the previous two years of war. Deprived of its genial commander, the imperial army in Italy found itself pressed by the Franco-Spanish army. In September 1703 the French approached Trente close to the Brenner Pass. The threat to Austria abated only when Victor Amadeus changed sides. This cut French supply and communications to France; and the army was immediately withdrawn to Piedmont.

Victor Amadeus threw in his lot with the Allies because he believed a Bourbon victory would ruin the independence of his kingdom. Initially he wanted to wait until his triennial alliance with France and Spain ended in 1703. Then, he intended to reorganize his army during the winter, and sign an official pact with the Great Alliance.

Louis XIV, however, had many spies, who informed him of the Savoyard plans. In September 1703 the Sun King ordered his generals in Italy to seize the Piedmontese expeditionary Corps and destroy the Duchy of Savoy. On September 28 they succeeded in arresting Piedmontese troops—whose forces the duke previously reduced to three thousand men—but that was only a portion of Savoy's army. In fact, Victor Amadeus rapidly fielded a new one by calling the militia to arms.

As we know, in the late sixteenth century, Duke Emmanuel Philibert of Savoy constructed a fortified defense system. It was an oval ring with its center at the citadel of Turin. Victor Amadeus simply concentrated his troops in those fortresses and resisted. The French took all of 1704 and 1705 to reduce the fortresses before reaching Turin. Although the French threatened the Piedmontese capital, it required an enormous expenditure of men and material to occupy the duchy and its fortifications. The Austrian army, however, did not remain inactive throughout, and the French and Spanish had to dedicate substantial forces to wage war in Lombardy, too.

The general strategic situation for the Bourbons deteriorated. During the summer of 1704, Eugene of Savoy and the duke of Marlborough, the Anglo-Dutch commander, decisively defeated the Franco-Bavarian army between Hochstädt and Blenheim. In a terrible battle, they eliminated the threat through Germany to Austria. In the following months, French troops retreated to the Rhine while British forces captured Gibraltar and, together with Portuguese and Austrian troops, invaded Spain, too. In 1705 a first imperial attempt to relieve Victor Amadeus failed. In 1706 the decisive campaign began.

Victor Amadeus held his capital—Turin—and controlled some peripheral valleys. In the early days of summer 1706 he left the city to join the advancing imperial army, led by his cousin Eugene. Piedmontese forces engaged the French in guerrilla warfare in the valleys. At the same time, the garrison of Turin repelled all French attempts to take the city. The siege was terrible and bloody; and Piedmontese artillery proved itself. The Piedmontese Grand Master of Artillery, General Giuseppe Maria Solaro Count della Margarita, ordered all his gunners to concentrate their fire on specific targets instead of maintaining the general fire normally used at that time in Europe. The principle of concentration of fire appeared with great success.

On September 7, 1706, Eugene and Victor Amadeus's combined armies attacked the French and Spanish besieging Turin. By the afternoon the Allies had routed the Bourbons, relieving the city and gaining a strategic victory. The southern axis of French operations was eliminated, and the remaining French army in Italy was cut off from France and soon forced to abandon Italy. The following year saw the imperial and Piedmontese invasion of southern France. The objective was Toulon, the base of the French Mediterranean fleet. Eugene and Victor Amadeus reached the city and placed it under siege. Britain wanted to occupy Toulon, but Eugene did not want to tie down his army. He demonstrated he was right; and the Allied Army, ineffectively supported by the British and Dutch fleet, returned to Italy. Allied shelling, however, completely destroyed the French Mediterranean fleet. At the same time, the offensive forced the French to withdraw troops from Flanders and Spain. This prevented the French from destroying allied forces in Spain and kept the Flemish situation balanced, as Marlborough was outnumbered by French troops.

If 1706 marked a turning point—if not "the" turning point—of the war, then 1707 practically ended operations in Italy. Prince Eugene's victories in Piedmont and Toulon ended the crisis on the Italian front; and he was transferred to Flanders to assist Marlborough.

Victor Amadeus continued limited operations from the Alps into southern France; and the Austrians conquered the Kingdom of Naples. Then the Bourbons established a league of Italian princes against the emperor, but only Pope Clement XI tried to fight. Each time an Italian League fought the imperials, the French deprived them of support. After a short conflict, the pope, menaced by Austria, concluded a peace in the last days of 1708. Although the war continued through 1712, it was fought mainly in Flanders and Spain and, when the Maritime Powers negotiated a settlement with France, Victor Amadeus immediately accepted the peace.

On April 11, 1713, the Treaty of Utrecht ended the War of the Spanish Succession. Britain was the real winner. Europe was now divided into two spheres; the Bourbon kingdoms of France and Spain, and the Habsburg realms the other. The Bourbons held Spain, but the emperor obtained Milan, Naples, and Sardinia. France was expelled from Italy, and Victor Amadeus found his kingdom between France and Habsburg-owned Lombardy. He had achieved his prewar objectives.

Victor Amadeus also managed to expand his possessions, as all French enclaves on the Alpine frontier were returned to Piedmont.[2] He further obtained the royal crown of Sicily with British backing.

London wanted to secure the central Mediterranean. Sicily's geographic position made it a perfect checkpoint and a crucial commercial crossroads. It would have been far too expensive for Britain to occupy the island, and they could not accept having it go to a great power such as Spain, France, or Austria. It was better to give it to a weak state. Victor Amadeus was a friend of Britain, his army was good, but not too powerful, and he had no fleet, so Savoy could not compete as a maritime power. Furthermore, his wife was a cousin of Queen Anne, being the daughter of a sister of Charles II of England. Thanks to London, the House of Savoy became the Royal House of Savoy and, in 1713, Victor Amadeus was crowned king of Sicily. He was now one of only ten kings in Europe and the only one in Italy. His prestige was great, and his House was considered the most important referee in Italian affairs. After Emmanuel Philibert's restoration in 1560, this was the first step on the road to Italian unity under the House of Savoy.

CHAPTER **8**

The Second Morea War, the Quadruple Alliance, and the Corsican Troubles: 1715–1733

After the First Morea War, or the War of the Holy League, in 1699, the Ottomans decided to deal with their enemies piecemeal. The Russians were defeated on the river Pruth and forced to accept a peace. The Sultan, Mustafa II, then moved against Venice. The Senate received worried reports by the "Bailiff to the Ottoman Porte," as its ambassador in Istanbul was called, but did not act. Venice expected assistance, in case of war, from the Emperor Charles VI. They naively believed an imperial diplomatic threat would be sufficient to dissuade Turkish action. Charles, however, was perfectly aware of the situation, but did nothing. The Habsburgs wanted a weak Venice. When in the summer 1715 the Ottomans finally declared war on Venice, Austria did not move. The Senate reminded the emperor of their association in the Holy League, but Charles VI found all possible pretexts not to intervene.

In this tragic situation, Venice did what it could. Venice disposed a paltry 7,000 men garrisoned in six fortresses in Greece. What could they do when 100,000 Turks attacked? During the summer 1715, all Greek and Cretan fortresses fell into Ottoman hands. The Senate raised 18,000 men, but they were too late to save the situation in Greece. Instead these troops were deployed to the Ionian Islands, to hold Corfu, gateway of the Adriatic. Likewise, the Venetians protected the islands by sea. The Ottomans dispatched 58 sails, 30 galleys, 60 galliots, 5 fire ships, and an enormous number of transports to the Ionian Islands.

In autumn, Andrea Pisani, the Venetian sea captain general, with reinforcements from Tuscany, Malta, and the papacy, had a mere 26 sails, 2 fire ships, 18 galleys, 12 galliots, and 2 galeasses at his disposal. He was outnumbered 2.55 to 1 and decided not to chance a naval engagement, but instead save the fleet for the defense of Corfu.

The Ottomans landed an army of 30,000 men in Corfu supported by two naval squadrons. The garrison of Corfu repelled Turkish assaults and the Venetian fleet conducted operations around the island. On August 24, 1716, the Ottomans lifted the siege and withdrew their fleet, having lost 15,000 men. Venetian casualties were comparatively light, 3,000 men: "God remembered on which side his men were," recalled one chronicler.

The years following the Peace of Utrecht saw extensive Austrian intervention in the Balkans. No plans against the Turks had been prepared in 1714 and, when they attacked Greece, it troubled Vienna. When the Venetians asked for help, Prince Eugene wrote to the emperor that they could not expect too much from Austria, as Austria needed a lot of time to gather the army still in the west. A year and a half passed from the Turkish declaration of war, whose news arrived in Vienna on December 14, 1714, against Venice to the Austrian offensive in late June 1716. Although Austria had no money and no troops at that moment, the following year, in late June 1716, the imperial army had 65,980 infantrymen in 31 regiments and 32,944 cavalrymen (34 regiments), with 90 field artillery cannons and some 100 siege guns. Garrisons included 53,380 more men and some 15,000 borderers.

With this army, Prince Eugene of Savoy routed the Turks at Peterwaradin in 1716 and captured Belgrade in 1717, while the Venetian fleet attacked the Ottomans in the Mediterranean. Despite these victories, when the Peace of Passarowitz was signed in 1718, Venice did not regain Greece. Vienna negotiated in its own interest and left the Venetians to their own devices. Venice could not combat the Turkish empire without imperial help and was forced to accept a bad peace that was clearly not to their advantage. This Second Morea War was the last conflict fought by "the Most Serene Republic."

Concomitant with this war in the Balkans, Spain moved against its rivals in Italy. Philip V's counselor, Abbot Giulio Alberoni and Philip's wife Elizabeth Farnese, came both from the Duchy of Parma.

In 1702, Alberoni served as ducal ambassador to the duke de Vendôme, the French supreme commander in Italy during the War of Spanish Succession. Vendôme valued Alberoni's counsel and subsequently took him to Flanders and then to Spain. When Vendôme died, Alberoni remained at the Spanish court, becoming one of its most important figures. When the first queen of Spain died, Alberoni suggested that Philip V marry Elizabeth Farnese, niece of the duke of Parma. The king agreed: Elizabeth became the new queen and Alberoni the most important minister.

Alberoni proceeded to reorganize the Spanish royal administration, but, before he finished his work, the Austrian military buildup in the Padana Plain endangered the autonomy of the duke of Parma, Alberoni's former master, who requested Spanish intervention. Alberoni, now a cardinal, had little desire to pursue war with Austria. Spain was recovering from the Succession War and did not need another draining conflict. Although Alberoni's position allowed him to put off the duke of Parma, his new queen, Elizabeth Farnese, ordered him to act.[1] In July 1717 a

Spanish fleet landed an expeditionary force of 33,000 men in Sardinia. The imperial garrison was quickly overwhelmed; and the Spanish moved against Sicily. In July 1718 the Flemish Marquis van Leden, with 20,000 Spaniards, landed near Palermo. The Savoyard garrison of Sicily included 10,000 men and lacked field artillery. The viceroy, Count Maffei, left enough troops to defend the fortresses and concentrated the majority in Syracuse. Then he waited for imperial aid while the Spanish promptly placed the city under siege.

Spanish intervention caused a diplomatic tempest. France, Netherlands, Britain, and the empire signed a Quadruple Alliance. The British fleet entered the Mediterranean, reached Sicily, and—without a declaration of war—destroyed the Spanish fleet at Capo Passero, not far from Syracuse, while the timely arrival of imperial troops forced the Spanish to raise the siege.

Although the Quadruple Alliance prevented a decisive Spanish victory, it was not a godsend for Savoy. In return for military assistance, Victor Amadeus was forced to give the emperor Sicily in exchange for Sardinia. He remained a king, but Sardinia was incomparably poorer than Sicily. Moreover, Savoy's administration had begun to reorganize Sicily. The previous Spanish administration was chaotic, but, above all, lacked justice; and the aristocracy did what it pleased. To protect themselves against the aristocratic oppression, Sicilians formed secret societies. These societies fought the barons and their men, and generally they were not only secret, but violent. It was the beginning of Mafia. In less than five years, Savoy's administration reduced the power and destroyed the abuses of the local aristocracy, and secret associations no longer had a reason to exist.

Unfortunately, when the Austrians gained Sicily, their administration was so poor that the aristocracy regained its powers. When the Spanish occupied the island again in 1734 and a branch of the Spanish dynasty ascended to the thrones of Naples and Sicily, the situation remained the same. So, the Mafia remained and increased under the Neapolitan Bourbons and thereafter.

Fifteen years passed calmly until 1730, when the kingdom of Corsica, still owned by Genoa, revolted against that Most Serene Republic. Corsica was taxed without representation; and, when its demand for representation was refused, the Corsicans revolted. Genoa failed to put down the revolt because the majority of its troops were composed of Corsicans. So, it asked the empire provide troops and, in 1739, promised to reduce taxation and allow limited representation: The revolt ended without further crisis.

CHAPTER 9

The Polish Succession: 1733-1739

In February 1733, Augustus of Saxony, king of Poland, died. Poland was an elective monarchy and both Louis XV of France and Charles VI, Holy Roman Emperor, proposed their own candidates. Vienna supported Augustus III, the elector of Saxony; Versailles wanted a former king of Poland, Stanislas Leszczynski, father-in-law to Louis XV. Neither could compromise on a candidate and war erupted. France prepared two armies and a separate expeditionary corps dispatched by sea to Poland, while the armies marched against Austria using the same routes as previous wars: the Bavarian Plateau and northern Italy.

Spain allied itself to France through a Bourbon family compact. The Spanish crown wanted to reclaim southern Italy and, if possible, Milan. Both had been part of the Spanish empire prior to 1715, but the Peace of Utrecht removed them from the Spanish Bourbon realm.

Queen Elizabeth Farnese had two sons by Philip V. As the king had two sons through his first marriage, she wanted to secure their future by giving each a crown. The eldest, Charles, received the Duchy of Parma, after last duke's death in 1730, but with the new war her plans changed. Philip, at the queen's behest, appointed Charles commander of the Spanish army in Italy. His objective was the reconquest of the Kingdom of Naples.

France, however, needed the support of the Piedmontese to cross the Alps and invade Milan.

Charles Emmanuel III of Savoy, who ascended to the Piedmontese throne after his father Victor Amadeus left him the crown in 1730, waited for an opportunity to resume his family's traditional policy of expansion in northern Italy. France promised him the Duchy of Milan in return for his aid. He accepted the French proposal and in a few days Piedmontese troops occupied western Lombardy, entered Milan, and besieged its citadel. Concomitant with Franco-Piedmontese operations, the Spanish army passed through the Papal States and entered Naples.

Having assessed the situation and observed no significant alterations to global European policy, Venice chose neutrality rather than take sides. The republic recalled many regiments from its Dalmatian garrisons and prohibited the movement of foreign armies through its territory. The emperor, however, needed right of passage for his forces. He had quickly prepared three weak armies. The first in Germany, superbly commanded by Prince Eugene, maneuvered so well that the French could not leave the right bank of the Rhine; and the Bavarians did not have the courage to declare war without the support of a French army.

The second Imperial army—roughly ten thousand men—was in Naples and clearly unable to adequately defend the kingdom. The third, under the count of Mercy, came from Austria to northern Italy in the spring of 1734. Its strategic task was to reach Naples, to support local troops, and destroy the Spanish army. The Franco-Piedmontese army led by Charles Emmanuel III made it impossible. Allied troops defeated the Austrians twice: in Parma in May and, later, on September 19, 1734, near Guastalla. These victories allowed the Spaniards to defeat Austrian troops at Bitonto. The Kingdom of Naples was conquered and Philip V presented it to his son Charles, who became Charles VII of Naples and who—later, after his father's and his two older half brother's deaths—became King Charles III of Spain.

In January 1735, Charles VII landed in Sicily with his army. The island was conquered as quickly as the Kingdom of Naples had been. Subsequently, the Spanish army marched north to reinforce the French in the Milanese, but the fighting ended prior to their arrival. Austria approached France looking to negotiate; and the French accepted. An armistice was signed and, after a couple of years of discussions, peace came.

The elector of Saxony, Augustus III, received the Polish crown. His competitor, Stanislas Leszczynski, received the Duchy of Lorraine, which belonged to the Holy Roman Empire. At his death, Lorraine passed to his daughter, the queen of France. Duke Francis of Lorraine received compensation through his marriage to the daughter and heir of the Emperor Charles VI, Maria Theresa. He also received Tuscany, whose ruling family, the Medici, had nearly died out, as the last grand duke had no heirs.

Spain maintained its conquests as long as they remained under Charles VII and independent of Spain. Thus, Spain returned to Italy.

Austria and Britain found this settlement quite problematic. Tuscany was insufficient to balance the geopolitical shift in Italy. In order to maintain the equilibrium in Italy, the general agreement returned Lombardy to the House of Habsburg instead of to Charles Emmanuel of Savoy. Obviously, the king of Sardinia had insufficient resources to forcefully object, particularly after the French approved the terms. His delusions of grandeur failed to become manifest, but a new opportunity was on the horizon.

10

The War of Austrian Succession: 1740-1748

In October 1740, Emperor Charles VI died. In his youth he had held title as the Archduke Charles, claimant to the Spanish crown and for whom the Habsburgs waged the War for the Spanish Succession. He left a single heir, his daughter the Archduchess Maria Theresa.

The Holy Roman Empire was an elective monarchy. Charles VI, however, negotiated with the ruling houses of Europe and the magnates of his monarchy to accept Maria Theresa as his legitimate and rightful heir and the next empress. Having secured domestic recognition of his daughter's right to succeed him, he also acquired international recognition embodied in the document, the Pragmatic Sanction. It did not work. As soon as he died, the Bavarian and Saxon electors competed for the crown; and King Frederick II of Prussia, newly ascended to the throne, rejected Maria Theresa's legitimacy and invaded Silesia, wealthiest of the Habsburg territories. France did not enter the war, but a French auxiliary corps was dispatched to central Germany in accordance with the Treaty of Westphalia, "to defend German liberties."

The Spanish royal family decided the war offered an opportunity to reclaim Milan. Prince Philip of Bourbon, the youngest son of Philip V and Elizabeth Farnese, needed a crown; and Milan, along with Parma, suited him. A Spanish army landed in Tuscany—a neutral—and marched north to the Padana Plain. Then, Philip V asked his son Charles VII of Naples to return the army he lent him in 1733 to the Neapolitan and Sicilian thrones. Neapolitan troops marched north to join the Spanish army.

France too required allies. They requested Piedmontese permission to cross the Alps and march on Milan, but Charles Emmanuel III did not want to involve his state in this conflict. He realized that, in case of a French and Spanish victory, Piedmont would be caught between the Bourbons. It meant the end of any autonomous policy and of any possible dream of expanding his power in Italy. Moreover, he threatened the approaching Spanish army that if it entered the Padana Plain, his army would its his route to Milan.

At the same time, Britain perceived the precarious situation as a threat to the Balance of Power. Piedmont and Austria were alone against much of Europe, save Russia. London therefore committed its resources to the Habsburg cause. Charles Emmanuel received a £250,000 annual subsidy to keep his army on a war footing. Then, a British squadron entered the Mediterranean under Admiral Matthews, ordered to act in support of Charles Emmanuel. The British ships entered Naples harbor with some five thousand marines. Charles VII knew it. He had no fleet and very few men to defend the city because his army had marched north. So, when Matthews presented an ultimatum: recall all his regiments with the Spanish army, or the city would be shelled and the marines landed, Charles VII had little recourse but to accept the terms.

The defection of Naples eased Charles Emmanuel's army action against the Spanish in the Padana Plain. Not wanting to face isolation, the Spanish withdrew through the Papal States along the Adriatic coast. Soon after, Charles Emmanuel countermarched rapidly to meet a second Spanish army entering Savoy via France. He won the campaign, but it was clear that the war was becoming harder to manage.

In 1743 the Spanish threatened Piedmont with two armies. Charles Emmanuel possessed no more than 42,000 men and could use only half against each Spanish army. Nonetheless, he crushed Prince Philip's army, marching from France, at Casteldelfino. Simultaneously, the Piedmontese with their Habsburg allies fought and defeated the second army under de Gages at Camposanto, on the other side of Italy and pressed it to the Neapolitan-Papal States border on the Adriatic coast, where it sought refuge from the Neapolitan king.

In the autumn of 1743, Britain joined Piedmont and Austria in a formal league. The treaty signed in Wörms widened the scope of the conflict from Europe to Asia, Africa, and America, where it was known as King George's War.

The 1744 campaign was hard fought. Unfortunately, Maria Theresa wanted Naples because, according to the Peace of Utrecht, it should have remained in Habsburg hands, yet the War of Polish Succession had reversed that agreement.

Charles Emmanuel warned the Austrian ruler that this would only increase the strategic dilemma. Why expand the conflict when victory was not in sight? Regardless of the free advice, she ordered her army to destroy de Gages's Spanish army still waiting on the Neapolitan frontier. Charles VII of Naples, aware of the Austrian menace, declared war and once again united his troops with his father's army.

An Austrian army marched south, passing through the Papal States from the Adriatic to the Tyrrhenian coast. Charles VII gathered the Spanish and Neapolitan army and encamped near Velletri, south of Rome. The Austrians attacked in August and were repulsed with great loss.

The defeat forced the Habsburgs to abandon central Italy in November. The Neapolitan-Spanish army followed on their heels, arriving in northern Italy. What a present for Charles Emmanuel, who had his own troubles.

In fact, France officially entered the war in that same year. A French army united with Prince Philip's army passed the Alps, defeated the local Piedmontese resistance, and besieged Cuneo. Charles Emmanuel tried to relieve the city, but failed. He then directed the militia against the enemy's ordnance and supply lines and, thanks to these guerrilla tactics and to Cuneo's resistance, the Bourbon armies raised the siege and withdrew to France to take winter quarters.

In the early days of 1745, Genoa entered the conflict. The Most Serene Republic sought neutrality, just as Venice had done for the third time in forty-five years. Unfortunately, while Venice could defend its neutrality with 40,000 men, Genoa could not; and, moreover, Britain and Austria promised to give Charles Emmanuel the Marquisate of Finale, a little imperial fief in Liguria owned by the republic as a feudatory of the empire. Charles Emmanuel desired it as a port, an additional window to the Mediterranean.

In order to protect its territory, Genoa signed a treaty in Aranjuez and joined the Bourbon alliance. It was a disaster for Charles Emmanuel. The Genoese accession to the League provided the Spanish-French army with an opened route from France through Genoese territory, and now they could mass the army from France with the army from Naples via Velletri, adding to it 10,000 Genoese troops. This was the real disaster as it increased the powerful Bourbon army to 90,000 men.

As the war in Flanders continued, Charles Emmanuel received no support from Austria.

He had a mere 43,000 men. Maneuvering them well to avoid battle, he lost many fortresses but preserved his army. Despite this, he was compelled to accept an armistice in December 1745. Fortunately, Prussia accepted peace terms offered by Austria, allowing Vienna to send 12,000 men to Italy. It was not an impressive army, but enough to permit Charles Emmanuel to take the field upon the expiration of the armistice. In the spring 1746 he attacked and the Bourbons were defeated. Milan was reconquered, Piedmont liberated, and Genoa overrun by the Austrians. The Piedmontese army occupied western Liguria and the French and Spanish fled, abandoning the republic.

While Charles Emmanuel prepared an invasion of southern France, he sent a regiment to support the Corsican revolution against Genoese rule.

Genoa found itself under occupation and threatened with destruction if it did not pay 3 million scudi to Austria. Subsequently the city revolted, and the Austrian garrison was ejected. Charles Emmanuel halted his operations against France and marched to support Austrian operations against the city. The Genoese fleet, supported by coastal defenses, prevented the British fleet from shelling Genoa, but the Austrian and Piedmontese armies cut the city off from the outside world by land, while the French supplied its ally with men and material by sea.

In the spring of 1747, a new French army marched along the Mediterranean coast. Charles Emmanuel ordered his troops to hold Nice, but soon he knew that another French expeditionary force was approaching the Alps from the west. If they crossed the Alps, they could effectively threaten Turin.

Charles Emmanuel had no troops to stem the invasion. He scraped together what troops he could find. On July 19, 1747, at Assietta Hill, 30,000 French with artillery attacked 5,400 Piedmontese and 2,000 Austrians. At sunset, the French had lost 5,800 men and left more than 600 wounded[1] to the victorious defenders. General Count Bricherasio lost only 192 Piedmontese and 27 Austrians; it was clearly a triumph.

Assietta Hill was the last battle of the war on the Italian front. A peace was signed on October 30, 1748, at Aix-la-Chapelle.[2] Everything remained as it was before the war, except that Prince Philip of Spain obtained the duchy of Parma and Charles Emmanuel received from Maria Theresa two West Lombardy provinces, Vigevano, and Anghiera County, and a part of the territory of Pavia, setting the Milanese-Piedmontese border along the Ticino river.

CHAPTER 11

Italy from the Corsican Rebellion to the French Revolution through the First Cold War: 1748–1792

The Italian Situation

In 1740 the Corsican rebellion against Genoa had begun; and France looked at the island as an opportunity to gain a foothold in the Mediterranean: a potential strategic naval base to protect her southern coast and further menace Italy. The French Foreign Ministry adopted the Chauvelin Plan, after its originator. France would aid Genoa by dispatching troops to the island and in turn they would establish a French presence in Corsica. As time passed, French influence would grow and eventually surpass the Genoese.

The Republic of Genoa managed the whole affair poorly. It denied the Corsicans any representation and regularly broke their agreements after earlier revolts. Despite military successes in 1755 and 1756, the republic's troops controlled only the coast and major coastal cities. After the War of Austrian Succession, the Genoese had little trust in the Habsburgs, they feared Spain and Naples, and saw Piedmont as their primary enemy. For these reasons they turned to France for support in Corsica, and an alliance against its enemies. Genoa allowed the French to retain garrisons on the island after 1764; and in 1768 officially transferred Corsica to France.

The Chauvelin Plan succeeded, primarily because of the republic's arrogance and inability to govern the island. Genoa preferred to give Corsica—an Italian-speaking country—to France instead of to the papacy or to another Italian prince; thus world history changed. The year after France received Corsica, Napoleon Buonaparte was born a subject of France, in Ajaccio, the Corsican capital. If Genoa had maintained a good administration, or at least accepted political autonomy for Corsica, Napoleon would probably have been an unknown lawyer, or an abbot; and Europe would have been spared war and tragedy.

In the midst of the Corsican question in 1755, Austria offered France an alliance. The treaty ended the long dynastic struggle between the House of Habsburg and the French royal house. This diplomatic *volte-face* had its origins in an anti-Prussia, anti-British coalition. It was the precursor to the Seven Years' War.

The Seven Years' War was a conflict not directly involving the Italian states or Italy as a battlefield. Venice and the pope were neutral, and, except for the Bourbon-ruled states of Naples and Parma, and the Habsburg-owned territories such as Lombardy and Tuscany, the only possible actor could be Piedmont. But Piedmont remained neutral, too.

The Piedmontese army—or the Royal Sardinian Troops as it was called at that time—proved to be one of the best armies of that period. It was—in modern terms—a good example of a middle-power army, for hire and highly flexible. It possessed solid sustainability and a capability to project itself beyond its frontiers. This was due entirely to the kingdom's administration—enviously commented upon by Austrian generals[1]—and its diplomats were considered some of the best in Europe.[2]

Unfortunately, Piedmont was a minor actor on the grand European stage. The frequent comparison to Prussia is often overdone. Frederick the Great held Charles Emmanuel and his army in high esteem, but Prussia was larger, richer, and more populated than the Savoyard states. Moreover, Piedmont directly bordered dynastic Austria in Milan and France, having neutral Switzerland to the north and Bourbon-friendly Genoa to the south. Prussia had no common border with France, a limited one with Austria, and many small and weak German territories and Poland on its borders. For these reasons Charles Emmanuel did not participate in the Seven Years' War. Thanks to the dramatic realignment of European alliances, he found his kingdom trapped between Bourbons and Habsburgs. Britain's distance and the lack of direct Prussian assistance would leave Piedmont open to an invasion from Lombardy and France.

Prussia fought that war because Frederick had no choice but to preempt the coalition. Charles Emmanuel, however, was not allied to Prussia and therefore had little interest or motivation in participating in the war, considering his strategic dilemma.

Tuscany—still owned by the House of Lorraine—sent an infantry regiment to the Austrian army in Germany. Indeed, the Austrian army included regiments from Lombardy—such as Marquis Clerici's infantry regiment—and many seamen were allowed by their Italian rulers to enroll in the French and Spanish navies.

Spain was not directly involved in the Seven Years' War until 1762, but in 1761 the Bourbon houses renewed their Family Compact. France, Spain, Naples, and Parma moved to marginalize, if not eliminate, British influence in Italy. Gradually, British officers, and advisers left the peninsula to be replaced by local personnel or the French. The Italian states remained wealthy and the peninsula would always be considered a strategically vital point for travel to the Middle and Far East. So, Britain tried to improve its weakened position in Italy and its diplomats continued to send detailed reports to London regarding the Italian states' respective economies, trade, navies, and armies.[3]

When the American Revolution began, Britain turned its attention from Mediterranean to the Atlantic. Italian intellectuals and aristocrats found the American Revolution facinating, but no Italian states supported it or dispatched troops to America. It was far away and did not concern Italian affairs. Although the French supplanted the British in the peninsula, there was no reason to act with hostility toward an important commercial partner; and the Italian sovereigns kept to the European Continent, and their perennial problems.

Italian navies continued to fight piracy as they had in the previous centuries. The situation had changed very little. Fleets were still mainly composed of galleys, and only Venice and Naples had effective sailing ships, not considering the two frigates composing the entire Piedmontese bluewater fleet.

The Venetian fleet had previously experienced problems during the first Morea War. Sea Captain General Alessandro Molin found the operational cooperation between galleys and sailing ships problematic due to their difference in speed and maneuverability. In his final report, he recommended that the Most Serene Republic abandon galleys and reorganize its fleet, employing only sailing vessels. Although galleasses were struck from the fleet in 1746, galleys remained on duty in the Venetian fleet until the end of the republic in 1797, while the Piedmontese fleet used them after the 1814 Restoration, too.

Venetian and Neapolitan fleets acted promptly against the Barbary pirates. The Neapolitan fleet conducted numerous raids and participated in the joint Spanish-Portuguese-Neapolitan-Maltese expedition against Algiers in the summer of 1784. Venice directed several expeditions against pirates from Tripoli and Tunis. Raids against Tunis in 1784, 1785, and 1786 were brilliantly commanded by Extraordinary Admiral Angelo Emo. He employed floating mortar batteries, then normally used by Italian navies.

Piedmont, under new king Victor Amadeus III, focused its resources on its army. The first son of Charles Emmanuel III, he ascended the throne after his father's death in 1773. He reformed the army, abandoning the old eighteenth-century organic order and using a new one. Previously his army had had no unit organizations larger than regiments. Brigades existed, but were ad hoc formations established only in time of war. In 1786, Victor Amadeus divided his regiments into two lines, or "wings." Each line was divided in two departments. Each department was composed of two divisions, and a division consisted of two brigades, comprising two regiments respectively. Two battalions formed a regiment, and a battalion had two centuries. The century consisted of two companies of two platoons each. Platoons were divided into two dormitories, which were divided in two maniples. A company had 60 men in wartime and 40 in peace. This resulted in weak regiments and proved unsatisfactory in war, but the idea was good, if it came twenty-five years too soon.

Artillery too, was rather advanced for such a minor power. Savoy's troops had used breech-loading cannons since at least 1703, and, shortly before the War for the Austrian Succession, they possessed mountain cannons that could be disassembled into three pieces. The Piedmontese also had leather cannons that could be used only once.

In terms of civil government, Italian sovereigns were not so bad by eighteenth-century standards. Some histories portray Italy during the absolutist era as being rather tyrannical, but this is not completely true. Several princes, in fact, granted their subjects religious toleration. The Kingdom of Piedmont-Sardinia gave refuge to the Waldensians. It was also possible for a Protestant to be found among the highest ranks of the Italian armies, particularly in Venice and Piedmont. The same could not be said of Roman Catholics in the British army until the end of the Napoleonic Wars. This religious toleration was not limited to Christians. A Dominican monk wrote in 1714 that Muslim Turkish slaves served on the galleys of the papal fleet, "for what concerns religion are absolutely not vexed."[4] Seventy years later the French traveler Du Paty wrote the same about Turkish galley slaves in Genoa. He added that the republic had allowed them to build a mosque, while in France in that same period the Protestants could not have a single church.[5] The Jews in Leghorn, in the Grand Duchy of Tuscany, were completely free, and their condition was in all aspects comparable to that of Christians. The same could be said of Venice.

Victor Amadeus II of Savoy had remarkable success in reducing the role of the Church in his kingdom immediately after the Treaty of Utrecht in 1714. His son Charles Emmanuel III did the same from 1730 to 1773. Their example was followed in the duchies of Parma and Modena, and in the Kingdom of Naples. This occurred more than twenty years before the arrival of the French.

Women, too, found conditions in Italy generally more favorable than elsewhere in Europe. A woman held a university chair and obtained tenure in Bologna, Papal State, in 1737. Previously, other women taught at the same university as assistant professors in the medical faculty in the seventeenth century.

And what about the judiciary system? Two Italians were the first to write against the use of torture.[6] After their works, it was subsequently reduced in all Italian states, except Naples; and the Grand Duchy of Tuscany completely abolished the death penalty.

Of course, public security was as poor as in the rest of Europe. Beggars and thieves populated cities, but the cliché of the Italian brigand did not exist at that time. It came later, during the Romantic age. Brigands were a real problem, but less diffused than in contemporary England. So Italian states used special military units in police service, especially in the countryside. Police within urban walls were called *sbirri*, a sort of armed civilian group under the authority of the *bargello*. In Sardinia the Dragoons of Sardinia Regiment was employed as constabulary. Genoa used dragoons and light cavalry units in Corsica. The Papal States had the Corsican Regiment. It consisted of two battalions, later reduced to two companies. They were scattered throughout the Papal States in small garrisons, from 5 to 15 men outside the cities and from 50 to 100 men in the cities. Another papal police military unit was the Compagnia de'Carabini rinforzati, o de' cacciabanditi a cavallo—a Company of Reinforced Carabineers, or of Mounted Bandit-Chasers—which remained active until the Napoleonic era. It patrolled the route from Bologna, across the Apennines, to Florence.

The general situation in Italy was not so bad according to eighteenth-century European standards—and that's why the French encyclopaedists considered contemporary Italian culture remarkable for the Enlightenment. It is clear that prior to the French Revolution, Italy presented a panorama in light and shade, depending upon the particular Italian state. In general, however, Italy presented more light and Enlightment than many European states, if not the Continent.

The First Cold War: 1748–1792

While the French-Habsburg condominium established a general peace in Italy after 1748, France and Britain waged a cold war.

The struggle for supremacy began in 1689 with the League of Augsburg. France wanted to establish its dominance in Europe by subjugating the Netherlands and marginalizing England, and supplanting Habsburg with Bourbon influence in the Holy Roman Empire. France was Britain's most perilous enemy; and Austria its natural Continental ally. France attempted to reduce Austria to a secondary power in the War of Polish Succession. At that time England remained outside the conflict due to Walpole's administration.

The War for the Austrian Succession had been another failed French attempt at European and colonial supremacy. When Austria proposed an alliance against Prussia, France accepted and then signed it on May 1, 1756. The union of France and Austria would cut England off from the Continent.

In 1756 the British colonial empire expanded in India, where they conducted a war against the French India Company. British interest in reaching India by a safe and protected route was paramount to their foreign policy. It was impossible to use the Mediterranean because the Austrian-French alliance had surrounded and neutralized the only ally England had in Italy, Piedmont-Sardinia. This meant all of Italy was neutralized, that is to say it was submitted to joint Bourbon and Habsburg control. This also meant that the Mediterranean route to the East was cut.

Britain found its colonial empire surrounded by France, Spain, and their colonies. The Spanish empire in Central and South America was too strong to attack head-on, but a determined effort in North America, using Canada as a base of operations, could yield significant results. Moreover, maritime routes from Spain and France to Central and South America were hard to cut because they were too far from Britain, but English maritime routes to North America were the same as those from France. Quebec and French territory along the Mississippi encircled the only British colonies in America; and this became the most significant reason to attack the French in North America.[7] The French and Indian War began in 1754, and British and American colonial troops seized French Canada. By 1763 then, the British had opened the new continent for expansion. The French lost their position in India, too. It became clear that they needed to alter their strategic policies toward Great Britain.

For the first time in the modern era, two world powers waged a cold war.[8] At first, British influence—or what remained of British influence—was eroded in Continental Europe. Then the French and Spanish fleets pursued a naval building program until the sum of their vessels surpassed that of the Royal Navy. The opportunity to restore French colonies in America at Britain's expense came thirteen years after the end of the Seven Years' War, when in July 1776 the British colonies in America declared their independence. From the perspective of Versailles, the American Revolution provided a ready ally against England.

French aid proved decisive. The French fleet in the Chesapeake played a major role in isolating the British army at Yorktown. A French expeditionary force under the Comte de Rochambeau became critical to American operations, particularly at Yorktown. Victory in the American Revolution did not translate into substantial gains for France. England had been able to resist to the French-Spanish-American-Dutch coalition and, just prior to the end of the war, had conquered the major Dutch colonies in Asia. In economic terms the war was an abject disaster for France. From 1688 to 1783, France fought a war against the Grand Alliance, the long, terrible War of Spanish Succession, the War of the Quadruple Alliance, the War of Polish Succession, the War for the Austrian Succession, the Seven Years' War, and the Revolutionary War in America. Each war cost millions, and the sum total was in billions. France paid her war expenses with loans; and the loans were paid with further loans because the French administrative system was unable to raise sufficient tax revenue. French commerce could not compensate, thus foreign loans seemed the answer. In the eighteenth century, however, there were only five large financial markets in Europe—Frankfurt, Genoa, Venice, Amsterdam, and London—and only two were sufficiently rich to raise the money needed: Amsterdam and London. As London was the enemy, it was impossible for France to ask for a loan there, but, as the Netherlands had lost its most important colonies, the Dutch could not afford to underwrite a loan. When in 1788, French state finances reached the breaking point, France had to find a domestic solution; and the result was a revolution, and then a twenty-three-year-long war.

12

The Revolutionary
Hurricane: 1792-1799

1792-1795

The French Revolution affected Italy profoundly. In August 1789, Louis XVI's brothers, the Comte de Provence and the Comte d'Artois, escaped to Turin, seeking refuge with their father-in-law, Victor Amadeus III of Piedmont-Sardinia.[1] After Louis XVI's arrest, his sisters fled to Rome, while the queen of Naples and the grand duke of Tuscany worried about the fate of their sister, Marie Antoinette, queen of France. After the battle of Valmy in September 1792, a French army invaded Germany. The previous summer, France asked Piedmont for permission of transit through Piedmont to Austrian Lombardy. Victor Amadeus refused and, on September 22, 1792, French troops occupied Savoy and the county of Nice. The French National Convention declared the Alps and the Rhine to be natural frontiers of France and invaded the Austrian Low Countries (Belgium) for a second time.

The traditional line of British foreign policy began in the eighteenth century was to prevent any European power from ruling the entire Channel coast from France to Holland. It is for this reason that, after the War for Spanish Succession, Britain favored a Habsburg imperial domain in Flanders as opposed to Dutch or French rule. And that's why, when French rule on the whole coast seemed possible, London in early 1793 organized the first of seven coalitions, which fought against France from 1792 through 1815. The First Coalition comprised Great Britain, Empire, Prussia, Russia, Spain, Naples, Piedmont-Sardinia, the Papal States, and Tuscany.

The overthrow of the French monarchy in August 1792 infuriated the emperor, the grand duke, and the queen of Naples. In response, Ferdinand IV of Naples on August 24, 1792, refused to receive the new French ambassador. A French fleet appeared off the Neapolitan coast and threatened the kingdom. Ferdinand forcibly accepted the ambassador, but as soon as the Coalition was established, he joined it. Unfortunately, many officers of the French fleet had spread their political propaganda in Naples; and this caused terrible problems within six years.

In 1793 the French launched an offensive into Italy. The Piedmontese army—32,000 men divided into four separate corps—fought all along the Alps. They defeated the French at Authion Hill on June 12, 1793, but their plans for recapturing Savoy and Nice failed because the Piedmontese army, commanded by the duke of Aosta, was unable to execute the long and complex operation foreseen by the plan. The Coalition took advantage of the uprisings in France and sent an expeditionary force to the rebellious city of Toulon. Britain organized a multinational force to attack and destroy the French Mediterranean fleet at port. British, Neapolitan, Spanish, and Piedmontese troops entered the city to support the French rebels. In December 1793, however, a young artillery captain, Napoleon Buonaparte, directed the French siege and succeeded in retaking the city.

Throughout 1794 the Piedmontese repelled all French attempts to force the Alpine passes into northern Italy. General Andre Massena, the Italian-speaking and Nice-born French commander, had tactical successes but no strategic result. This was particularly so at Testa della Nava on April 25 and at Saccarello on April 27: Massena eventually succeeded and forced the Piedmontese to retreat to Briga. Then, after ten more days of clashes and skirmishes, on May 10 they were forced to withdraw to Borgo San Dalmazzo but he could not really defeat them. Military results created diplomatic benefit, as the emperor Leopold II—former grand duke of Tuscany[2]—agreed to formal military support. According to the treaty signed at Valenciennes, however, Piedmont was responsible for active defense, while Austrian forces would be deployed as a strategic reserve in the Padana Plain. At the same time, Austria assumed the supreme coalition command in Italy. The agreement did not provide financial subsidies for Piedmont, making the burden of Italian defense very expensive. It was clear that the Austrians did not want to fight in Italy. They only looked for good results with the lowest possible effort. Germany and the Austrian Low Countries remained their primary focus. Piedmont thus had to fight; and Austria expected the benefits. Victor Amadeus III did not like this situation, but had little choice.

The 1795 Alpine campaign was simple. The Piedmontese thwarted two French offensives in June. On the heels of these victories the Austrian general De Vins was asked by the Piedmontese commander, General Colli, to commit his forces to a counteroffensive. He did not oblige his allies; and the respite permitted the French to reorganize their army. In November, Massena defeated the Austrians in Loano and opened the route to Lombardy by occupying Liguria (Genoa), which was compelled to accept the French presence to avoid further domestic intereference. On November 26 the Piedmontese attacked Massena at Spinarda Hill and achieved a significant strategic result. Massena withdrew his army to winter quarters to recuperate.

At the conclusion of 1795 then, the Italian front remained beyond the grasp of French armies, although they had achieved substantial results in Spain and Germany. This was largely due to the nature of the terrain. The Alps hampered operations. Contemporary accounts depict a situation closer to World War I instead of traditional eighteenth- or nineteenth-century battlefields. Troops on both sides spent long periods guarding trenches and field fortifications. They lived in small and smokey bunkers, which they could enter only on their knees. Cold, rain, snow, and mud were considered normal weather. Patrols as well as artillery duels were commonplace. On occasion, raids were conducted. The mountain battlefield prevented the French from fully utilizing their new tactics. The French minister of war, Lazare Carnot, had organized a new army. He decreed that it had to *agir toujours en masse*[3]—to act ever in mass—because winning needed only "fire, steel and patriotism."[4]

Inspired by this new doctrine, supported by new, light, and easy-to-repair Gribeauval cannons and by general conscription established on August 23, 1793, the army of 750,000 overwhelmed the allied armies. Outnumbered by the French, disoriented by their speed and by their scattered battle order, Coalition troops were defeated everywhere; everywhere except in the Alps. But all of this changed in 1796 when a relatively unknown artillery general was appointed commander in chief of the French Army of Italy.

1796

Napoleon Buonaparte—who changed his family name to Bonaparte to ease the French pronunciation—was a former Jacobin. After Robespierre's death, he was briefly jailed, but then went to Paris.

One of the most important and influential members of the French Directory—the new government after 1794—was Paul Barras. A corrupt man, ever looking for pretty women and bags of money, Barras faced the critical situation that France was exhausted from war and revolution. Barras had been appointed commander of the Interior Army with the task of maintaining public order. He needed a good professional soldier as an assistant, and he chose that young and hungry Corsican general who often, if not every evening, was around him at Madame Tallien's soirées. He had seen Napoleon in action at Toulon. Barras was a *representative en mission* at the city along with Augustin Robespierre—brother of the revolutionary leader—and Christophe Saliceti, the Corsican revolutionary. That's why Barras appointed Napoleon vice commander of the Interior Army. Shortly thereafter, a Royalist coup provided Napoleon with the opportunity to show his mettle. He acted promptly, and firmly, crushing the revolt with a "whiff of grapeshot." Seeing how reliable he was, Barras gave him as a wife one of his former lovers, Josephine de Beauharnais, and then command of the Army of Italy.

The Directors sought to settle affairs abroad in order to calm the domestic front. They successfully pursued negotiations with Prussia and Spain. The former kingdom was far more concerned about Russian designs on the rump of Poland and wanted the freedom to focus their efforts in the east. Spain had suffered terribly from French invasion and wanted to withdraw from the Coalition before the French marched on Madrid. All of this was settled at the Peace of Basel in 1795, concluding war with Prussia, and later Spain. Austria and Britain remained France's sole enemies. As war with Britain meant war at sea, the Continental effort was now concentrated fully against Austria in Germany—that is to say the Holy Empire—and Italy.

Lazare Carnot remained in charge of military affairs and presented a clear plan for French operations in 1796. It was simple and resembled French strategy during the War of Spanish Succession. Two armies advanced through southern Germany and northern Italy to meet in Tyrol and then attack Vienna. Accordingly, Victor Amadeus III had to be forced from the Coalition. This would facilitate the movement of a French army through northern Italy without worrying about their lines of communications across the Alps.

Coincidentally, at this time Piedmont was experiencing significant financial and strategic difficulties. War expenses increased substantially and Austrian support was poor. Alliance conditions were hard to maintain in the face of increasing French pressure, and it was clear that no more help could be expected from the other members of the Coalition. Piedmont wanted to reach a separate and not dishonorable peace. How? The situation was rather complex and would require an entire volume to address adequately.[5]

Contacts existed between Barras and the French royal family in exile. The Bourbons persuaded Victor Amadeus III, their father-in-law, to reach an agreement with France. We can deduce this by what happened later. Piedmont would accept peace in exchange for Lombardy. France would have thus secured its army's communications and improved its position in its war against Austria. Piedmont would have lost Savoy and Nice, but Lombardy was sufficient compensation. French troops would have reached Trent and, through the Brenner Pass, Innsbruck and later Vienna. Austria would have been defeated and victory achieved. All of this is speculation, but what we know for sure is that the Bourbon ambassador in Turin acted according to these plans.[6]

The British ambassador in Turin, Mr. Trevor, divined the imminent armistice between France and Piedmont. He wrote to his colleague in Vienna, warning him that France had offered Lombardy to Piedmont in December 1795.[7] The Austrian ambassador in Turin, Marquis Gherardini, warned his government, too. In January 1796 he wrote about French offers to Piedmont and, on February 13, that the king of France—that is to say the exiled Louis XVIII—proposed that his father-in-law accept the peace and an alliance with France.[8] On February 6, 1796, Trevor warned London and Vienna that if no Austrian help came, Piedmont would accept a separate peace and plans for the neutralization of Italy.

What did this mean in regard to Napoleon? It meant that when Napoleon was appointed commander of the Army of Italy, the game was over. Everything had been decided. Piedmont needed only a comedy instead of a war. Turin lost Savoy and Nice to gain Lombardy, two poor territories in exchange for the richest part of Italy. Napoleon was only a puppet who had to play the role Barras and the others wrote for him. Nobody could then divine what sort of military genius he was. He himself did not know. He simply knew that all was ready to finish the war. In fact, some twenty years later, when on Saint Helena, he pronounced these revealing words: "Vendemiaire and Montenotte too did not lead me to believe that I was a superior man. Only after Lodi I realized I could, in conclusion, be an important feature on the political scene. Then the first spark set off my great ambition."[9]

Now, Montenotte was a fine battle and the only possible explanation for such words is that he knew he won because the battle had been prearranged, its result beeing previously negotiated between Paris and Turin. Only after he won a real engagement, such as Lodi, did he realize what a genius general he was.

On March 6, 1796, Napoleon received very detailed operational instructions prepared by Carnot. He had to pass rapidly through Piedmont, not caring to take Turin or destroy Piedmont. He had to seize Mantua and Trente and invade Austria as soon as possible. The 1796 campaign is so well known that is definitely irrelevant to describe it here in detail. Piedmontese troops fought well, but they could not change something previously decided at the top levels; and within a few weeks the campaign was over. On April 26, 1796, Victor Amadeus III signed an armistice. Now Napoleon could concentrate on the Austrian army, supported by a Neapolitan cavalry brigade.

The Italian Situation in 1796-1797

In order to understand what happened in Italy in 1796–97, and why the disaster was so wide, we must try to think as the Italians did at that time. It was the fifth time in one hundred years and the fourth in the eighteenth century that a French army had fought against Habsburg armies in Italy: the War of the Grand Alliance (1689–98), and the three wars for Spanish, Polish, and Austrian Succession. Old people could easily remember the last of those conflicts, fifty years before; and every family had at least listened to grandparents speaking of the previous wars between the French and the Holy Roman Emperor.

Piedmont pursued a separate peace in 1696. France occupied Piedmont twice: in 1703–6 and in 1745. The French entered Lombardy in 1701, 1733, and in 1745. France imposed war contributions on Parma and Modena in the previous three wars. So, what was new?

In 1796 the French were approaching the *Terraferma* of the Most Serene Republic of Venice; and the Austrians were preparing to defend it.

Venice again faced war in Italy and Turks in the Balkans. The Ottomans were still a problem, or, at least, they could still be a problem. The French still maintained relations with the Turks; and the Austrians did not change their Balkan policy. The obvious conclusion was that this war was similar to all the others. It was not in Venice's interest to become involved in this conflict, and for this reason Venice chose neutrality, for the last fatal time.

Unfortunately for Venice, the French Revolutionary Wars were the first total war. According to previous experience, promises had to be kept, neutrality had to be respected, and states were not supposed to be destroyed after a war. Previous experience, however, did not apply to this war, nor did those rules of engagement. Victor Amadeus did not receive Lombardy, and Venetian neutrality was not respected. In the end at Campo Formio, France sold Venice to Vienna in exchange for Lombardy and Belgium.

During late summer 1796, after the Austrian defeat in Lombardy, Napoleon signed a peace with Naples. It deprived the Austrians of a very good cavalry brigade, which had repeatedly defeated French troops, at Fombio and Guardamiglio. While Neapolitan dragoons left Lombardy, Napoleon established a puppet government in Milan and invaded the Venetian *Terraferma*. He secretly supported local insurgencies in name of "Liberty, Equality and Fraternity." This caused a further problem. The middle class realized it could gain political power.

In all the old states, a bourgeois could not reach a high political office. The only way to gain power or to have political power was to be admitted in the aristocracy, but this was quite difficult. The middle class, mostly composed of lawyers, physicians, and merchants, were cut off from the opportunity to gain power. The same occurred for some noble families, as it happened to the nobles of the Venetian *Terraferma* or to cadets: other than the eldest sons of noblemen. The coming of the French provided an opportunity to achieve power. In fact, the French needed men to administer their puppet states. For instance, in Lombardy, soon after their arrival, many small republics appeared like mushrooms after the rain. They were ruled by Italians but controlled by the French. So a large part of the Italian middle class supported the French and their advance in Italy in order to obtain ranks and honors. Obviously the ranks and the honors were subordinate to the French rulers.

The lower classes opposed the French and the middle class, preferring to support the traditional sovereigns. Moreover, the French attitude was definitely antireligious, and this caused a lot of tension and violence. This was a problem; however, in summer 1796 the greatest issue facing Napoleon was the presence of an Austrian army in Mantua and another army in the Trentino. Napoleon found his army between two enemy armies.

Venice had some twenty thousand men as well and could prove difficult. Napoleon therefore supported insurgencies in *Terraferma* to weaken Venetian control. Throughout northeastern Italy the situation was similar; local nobles and the middle class organized insurrections. They asked the local Venetian officers to leave the city and, soon after, they asked the French army in Milan or the closest units to provide support.

The Venetian government was fully confused. It was unclear how much the French were involved in those riots. At the same time, negotiations with Napoleon proceeded; and any hostile actions would be counterproductive. Thanks to negotiations, Napoleon avoided a Venetian decision in favor of Austria. At the same time, he besieged Mantua and maneuvered to prevent any possible Austrian attempt to relieve the city. He succeeded. Supposing the political and military situation was similar to past wars, the Venetian Senate did not take the initiative. When Mantua surrendered, Napoleon became increasingly arrogant toward them. Venetian troops and the population revolted against the French in Padua and other towns. Then Napoleon threatened the Senate and, in the end, after he reached the final agreement with Austria in 1797, he simply declared the republic disbanded. At that moment the French had garrisons in all Venetian towns and cities, except Venice. Venetian rule in Dalmatia and Corfu remained strong, and troops and ships were still there, but unfortunately, some self–professed "patriots" supported a transition of the aristocratic republic into a democratic one, and this divided the Senate, too. Moreover, Venice could not afford a war when all the other states had signed treaties with France. The republic stood alone and, reluctantly, accepted its transformation into the Venetian Republic, as occurred to Genoa when it became the Ligurian Republic.

Insurgencies and Repression: 1796–1800

At the dawn of 1797, northern Italy was composed of puppet states created by France. The House of Savoy, deprived of Nice and Savoy, still ruled Piedmont and Sardinia. The aristocratic Republic of Genoa had been transformed into a so-called democratic Ligurian Republic. The Venetian Republic was soon absorbed into a bigger entity, composed of former Venetian *Terraferma* and Lombardy, including the little republics of Brescia and Bergamo, called the Transpadane Republic, literally "the Republic on the other side of the Po river." The former republics of Bologna, Ferrara, Modena, Massa, and Carrara were grouped into a Cispadane Republic—"the Republic on this side of the Po river." In autumn 1796, the Transpadane Republic established an army, the first unit being the Lombard Legion. On October 11, 1796, Napoleon wrote to the Directory, announcing the creation of the Legion and adding: "The national colors they have adopted are green, white, and red."[10] In fact, the Legion was dressed in green. Discussion is open about the reason why these three colors were chosen, though red and white came from the French flag; but what about green? Some argue it was because green was the Corsican national color; someone suggested a Masonic symbolism; some, more simply, think of a big green tissue ingloriously used for Transpadane uniforms. We do not know. What is sure is that the Cispadane Republic officially adopted the green-white-red tricolor as its national flag. Later, when on July 9, 1797, the Transpadane and Cispadane Republics united as the Cisalpine Republic—"the Republic on this side of the Alps"—the same tricolor became the national flag and, later, of the Napoleonic Kingdom of Italy.

The Cisalpine Army combined the Lombard and Cispadane legions. It was organized on the French model and of division strength. There were seven legions of Italian infantry and an eighth composed of Polish expatriates. The legions were grouped into two infantry brigades and an artillery brigade. General Giuseppe Lechi commanded the First Brigade and General Giuseppe Lahoz commanded the second. Chief of Brigade Lalace commanded the artillery. In theory the Cisalpine Army totaled 32,000 men. No volunteers enlisted, and it only reached 22,500 men. Moreover, the Cisalpine army drained much of the state revenue because France gave the Cisalpine Republic the honor of paying for 25,000 French soldiers, which became part of the Cisalpine Army. It was not particularly a national army.

In 1798 war returned to Europe. In 1796, the French army had fought only against Piedmont, Austria, the pope, and Naples. Tuscany had remained neutral, as had Parma, Genoa, and Modena. In 1798, however, Pope Pius VI caused a problem, which expanded French occupation in Italy. The French did not help matters when they violated their agreements with Piedmont. At the encouragement of their French allies, the Genoese and Cisalpine republics attacked the Savoyard kingdom, whose requests for military assistance from France fell on deaf ears. Despite this surprise, Piedmontese troops defeated the invading armies. Royal Troops condemned Cisalpine prisoners of war to be hanged with their tricolor flags. It was only under these circumstances that the French intervened. The kingdom was occupied, and King Charles Emmanuel IV abdicated the throne. He escaped to Sardinia while France absorbed Piedmont.

Now France secured the strategic passes through the Alps, as it had in the previous two centuries. In fact, Italy's position in the middle of the Mediterranean and as a base for any projection of power from Western Europe to the Middle East made it a vital geographical possession. It was unnecessary to seize the entire peninsula, but the city of Ancona—a good harbor on Adriatic coast, north of the Apennines—was enough. Easily reached from France through the Padana Plain, it was the starting point of the shortest maritime route to the Middle East. Unfortunately, Ancona belonged to the pope, and Pius VI did not like the idea of leaving it to France. In 1796, General Pierre Augereau defeated papal troops in a quick secondary campaign, forcing the pope to sign an armistice on June 23. When discussing the peace in Paris, the Directory forced the papacy to pay incredible amounts of money, hand over artistic masterpieces and rare books and manuscripts, and adopt the civil constitution of the French clergy, too. It meant accepting the submission of the Catholic Church to the state in France, something Pius VI had previously rejected, and placed the French Republic under interdict when instituted in 1791. The pope refused. The French threatened military intervention; but the people supported the pope. Volunteers flowed in from all parts. Unfortunately, the papal army was enthusiastic but inexperienced. The French easily defeated it, and the pope signed a new armistice and then was jailed. Subsequently, the French established a republic in Rome.

The French disease of revolution had approached the Neapolitan border, and the king of Naples found it most disturbing. Furthermore, en route to Egypt, Napoleon occupied Malta. The knights were disbanded, but Malta was a fiefdom of the Kingdom of Sicily and, as Ferdinand IV of Naples was king of Sicily, too, he considered this an act of war. While Napoleon was in Egypt, on May 19, 1798, Naples entered into an alliance with Austria. Austrian and Russian troops prepared their offensive into Italy; and Britain employed its navy to cripple the French in the Mediterranean. Admiral Horatio Nelson destroyed the French fleet in Aboukir and, in November, fifty thousand Neapolitan soldiers marched on Rome commanded by Austrian general Karl Leiberich von Mack, later defeated by Napoleon in 1805.

Neapolitan troops liberated the Holy City and marched northward, but within a few weeks, thanks to Mack's over confidence, they were defeated near Civita Castellana by French, Cisalpine, and Roman troops. Their retreat was a disaster. The French reached the steps of Naples; and the king and his court sailed to Sicily. Ferdinand left a regency, which promptly surrendered to the French general Championnet.

The French established another puppet republic in Naples and compelled them to provide money and men to the cause. They were also expected to bear the burden of French occupation. But the situation in southern Italy was quite different, however, from that in the rest of the peninsula. All the other states had been occupied and their rulers forced into agreements; only later did the French establish puppet states. This did not happen in Naples. The king still ruled a large portion of his territory—Sicily—and it was impossible to reach him. In fact, the remaining Neapolitan fleet and the British navy mastered the sea, while the French had no ships.[11]

Ferdinand IV reorganized an army in Sicily while consenting to a plan presented by Cardinal Fabrizio Ruffo. A former secretary of the papal navy, Ruffo belonged to a noble family from Calabria. When Ferdinand IV fled to Palermo, he followed. He asked the king for permission to organize a counterrevolution. The king accepted; and Ruffo landed in Calabria with few men and a little money. Within a few weeks, however, Ruffo succeeded in raising much of the kingdom in rebellion.

According to the generally accepted history, the French enlightened Italy. Napoleon was a sort of marvelous and incredible hero, and the coming of the French was an absolute benefit for Italy, the dawn of a new era, an era of modernity and the start of the Risorgimento. The French coming meant no more torture, equal civil rights for Jews and Protestants, the end of the supremacy of the Catholic Church on civil affairs, and the birth of democracy. This is a fallacy. As stated in previous chapters, in 1789, Italy was more enlightened than France; and the arrival of the French was anything but fortunate for Italy. In 1796, a country composed of small, pacific states was brutally occupied by an army that was not at war with the Italian states, apart from Piedmont and Naples. This foreign army—the French—destroyed ancient, venerated, and sometimes wise institutions and killed thousands of civilians. Its cruelty was evident. As an example, in 1799 the French killed more than seven thousand civilians in only one day in the southern town of San Severo, which resisted the revolution, and this was not an exception.

No one is able to compute all the casualties, but one may suggest, in a population of perhaps 15 million and a half, a figure of half a million dead from 1798 to 1799, that is to say 3.2 percent of the population of the Italian peninsula. By comparison, the percentage of U.S. soldiers killed in World War II amounted to around 0.27% of the population, distributed over forty-five months. A 3.2 percent figure translates to 6.8 million American dead in only two years, that is to say in 1798–99, Italy had ten times the amount of U.S. dead in World War II and, moreover, concentrated in half the time. In fact, the French army pillaged and stole billions of dollars and masterpieces of art and archives. The same army organized puppet states and filled them with collaborators, and then forced the same puppet states and their people to participate in their glorious and bloody wars. These puppet states—the Roman Republic, the Cisalpine Republic, and, especially the Neapolitan Republic—were filled with foreigners. They were hated by the Church, by the former rulers, and by the general population. They were accessories to the French wars and crimes, and existed only because French bayonets supported them.

Riots and insurrections occurred throughout Italy after 1796. In May 1796 the people of Lodi and Pavia revolted against French pillaging. Then Padua and Verona in the Venetian *Terraferma* revolted, as well as the people in the mountains. The same occurred in Tuscany when the French arrived, as well as in the Papal States. Why? Because of French anticlericalism and deist attitudes, which offended the Italians; because of local political reasons; because of personal interests damaged by the invasion; and because of loyalty to the sovereign.

British and Austrian reaction to the Italian insurgencies is quite interesting. Britain perceived the situation in 1798–99 as an opportunity to stop the French advance to the Orient. Austria considered these insurgencies an opportunity to reconquer northern Italy. Both powers supported these insurrections, and both provided money and weapons as well as officers and men to strengthen the resistance. The British viewed Naples as a good base for pushing the French back from the central Mediterranean. When the French seized Naples, Sicily served as another good base.

When Cardinal Ruffo landed in Calabria, he organized a large and effective resistance that destroyed the Neapolitan Republic and recaptured Naples. After the victory, Ruffo wanted to pardon some of the Italian revolutionaries, but the king and more so the queen and the British admiral Horatio Nelson wanted blood. In fact those men—the Jacobins, as they were improperly called—had betrayed their king, joined with the French, and accepted a puppet state; they had supported a foreign enemy army with money, supplies, and laws, so they were executed as traitors.

The reorganized Royal Neapolitan Army marched north for the second time. Some British and Turkish troops supported it. At the same time an Austro-Russian expeditionary force led by Russian field marshal Alexandre Suvorov invaded northern Italy and overran the French army and its republics. The coming of winter halted operations. Then, suddenly, Napoleon abandoned his army in Egypt and in November 1799 came back to Paris. The *coup d'état of 18 Brumaire* brought Napoleon to power as First Consul of the French Republic. He took command of a new Army of Italy, the Army of the Reserve, crossed the Alps, and, on June 14, 1800, defeated the Austrians at Marengo. France and Austria signed an armistice shortly thereafter. In autumn, when hostilities resumed, Brune passed the Mincio and marched to the Adige river, while Dupont deployed his men in three columns. The first column went from the Padana Plain to Leghorn to prevent the British fleet from supplying the Allies; a second under Mounier fought against the irregular bands from Arezzo and Romagna and forced them to retreat to the Apennines; and the last marched to Florence. Dupont defeated Tuscan general Spannocchi at Barberino on October 15, 1800, and entered Florence. Then on January 14, 10,000 Neapolitans under General Roger Damas left Rome and marched north along the Via Cassia. They took Siena and the bands from Arezzo as well as Spannocchi, and a few men joined them. But they were all discouraged by the bad news coming from Germany and were defeated in Monteriggioni, not far from Siena.

The Peace of Luneville ended the war in 1801. The Cisalpine Republic, destroyed by the Austrians, was reestablished as the Italian Republic. France absorbed Piedmont and later Parma. Tuscany became the Kingdom of Etruria under the former duke of Parma by 1803. Ferdinand IV and the new Pope Pius VII were restored to their thrones, while the House of Savoy remained confined on the island of Sardinia.

PART **IV**

THE NINETEENTH CENTURY

CHAPTER 13

Napoleon Emperor and King

In the Shadow of the Eagle: 1804–1807

The Cisalpine soldiers who escaped the disaster of 1799 fled to France. They were concentrated into an Italic Legion, which later returned to Italy in 1800. The legion fought well, capturing Varallo, Lecco, Bergamo, and Brescia, and advanced as far as Trente, Mantua, and Siena. French generals considered the legion effective, and it became the nucleus of the next Italian Army. Shortly there after, Italian revolutionaries in France proclaimed the restoration of an Italian Republic. They elected count Melzi d'Eril as president, but—after Tallyerand's suggestion—they changed their mind. Melzi was elected only vice president, with Napoleon as president of the republic.

After the Peace of Luneville in 1801, the republic was officially recognized and established its own army. According to the law issued on September 21, 1801, and modified the day after, it was composed of one Light Infantry Demi-Brigade (regiment) and four line infantry demi-brigades (regiments). Cavalry included four regiments—Mounted Chasseurs, Hussars, Polish Light Cavalry, and Gendarmerie—and the artillery had 32 companies. In 1802 a Presidential Guard was formed. The entire army was to field 22,000 men, with a reserve of 60,000. This was a five-year plan, which did not work, as the next war came only two and a half years later.

The *casus belli* was Britain's refusal to return Malta to the Neapolitan Bourbons when the French did not evacuate the Netherlands. Obviously, London preferred to have no French on the other side of the Channel and used Malta as leverage. Britain did not trust Napoleon's intentions and declared war on France in May 1803. Napoleon occupied Hanover—the personal possession of the king of England—and concentrated troops along the Channel coast, threatening an invasion. Britain responded by pursuing a coalition, composed of Austria, Russia, Sweden, and Naples. This was achieved by July 1805. According to their plans, two allied armies were to operate in Italy. An Austrian army had to advance from the Upper Adige to the Padana Plain, passing the Piedmontese Alps, and invade France. A

British and a Russian expeditionary corps was to land in Naples, then join the Neapolitan army to march north and link up with the Austrians.

Admiral Nelson destroyed the French and Spanish fleets at Trafalgar in October 1805 and prevented a French invasion of England. In Central Europe, however, things went poorly for the Third Coalition. Austrian and Russian armies were defeated at Austerlitz. The Habsburgs signed the Peace of Pressburg, ending the war. Soon after, Napoleon ordered the invasion of Naples.

The Italian Army—after 1805 the Army of the Kingdom of Italy—returned from southern Austria. Eugene de Beauharnais, viceroy of Italy and Napoleon's stepson, formally commanded 37,000 French and Italians. In January 1806 they invaded Naples. The 18,000 men of the Anglo-Russian Expeditionary Corps withdrew from the kingdom, leaving Ferdinand to his fate. The king of Naples was hopelessly outnumbered, 2.64 to 1, as his army numbered 12,000 infantry and 2,000 cavalry. As had happened seven years earlier, he fled to Sicily and left the kingdom under regency in Naples. The army resisted the French invasion, but was defeated. The regency surrendered on February 13, and Franco-Italian forces occupied Naples. Napoleon, however, gave the crown to his eldest brother, Joseph, establishing another Italian puppet state.

Despite the kingdom's surrender, Neapolitan troops continued to resist in the fortresses of Civitella del Tronto, on the Adriatic coast, until May 20, and in Gaeta on the Tyrrhenian coast until July 18. Thereafter, resistance emerged in mountainous Calabria. The insurgents were supplied from Sicily. Sicilian and British troops, supported by the population, fought the French in a long and exhausting guerrilla war. A little island near the Calabrian coast provided sanctuary for the rebels. The British and Neapolitan fleets controlled the sea; and the French were forced to concentrate their operations in the mountains.

Shortly after the conquest of Naples, Italian regiments from the Kingdom of Italy were dispatched to Germany, Poland, and Dalmatia. The 1806 campaign against Prussia saw a large number of Italians—Genoese, Piedmontese, etc.—fighting with the French-imperial armies. In fact, Genoa and the Ligurian republic were absorbed into the French empire shortly after 1804. The French-imperial army therefore included many all-Italian regiments, such as 7th, 17th, 26th, and 32nd Light Infantry Regiments, 103rd, 111th, and 113th Line Infantry, the Tirailleurs du Corses and du Po—and, among the cavalry, the 26th Chasseurs à Cheval, and the 21st Dragoons. These troops were dressed in blue instead of green, as the Italians, and they carried the French tricolor instead of the Italian green, white, and red. Some of these regiments fought at Jena and Auerstadt. Then, after the Prussian campaign, these regiments of Italians served in Poland. In 1806 an Italian-soldiered division under General Molitor occupied Dalmatia. The Italian division with the Grande Armée in Germany participated in the siege Colberg, defended by Prussian troops. After Napoleon's victory over the Russians at Friedland on June 14, 1807, Czar Alexander I of Russia signed the peace in Tilsit on July 7, 1807, ending the war.

Resistance in the South and the Battle of Maida: 1806–1809

Joseph Bonaparte's reign in Naples was all but tranquil. Ferdinand IV was in Sicily and wanted to regain his kingdom. Britain supported him and—more important—the people supported him as well. Popular resistance in Calabria began in March 1806, resulting in a harsh and bloody guerrilla war that left the province in ruins. French general Jean Reynier was charged with the repression of the resistance. He burned towns and killed civilians in Martorana and Confluenti.

A small allied division landed from Sicily to halt his advance. Under the command of General Charles Stuart, the Anglo-Sicilian force comprised 4,000 British and 1,200 Sicilian, Corsican, and Neapolitan troops. Reynier and Stuart clashed on July 4, 1806, in Maida. The French, 6,500 strong, attacked in columns. Stuart's battalions deployed in line, where firepower triumphed. Stuart lost 41 killed and 282 wounded. Reynier's casualties included 64 officers, 1,400 men killed, and 300 wounded. He also lost all his wagons and carts. His retreat was continually tormented by partisans.

By itself, Maida was a minor event but demonstrated the effectiveness of well-trained volley fire over column attacks. When Stuart's report was received in London, Wellington was aware of it and realized that these were the right tactics to defeat the French. In fact, a French column could fire only 132 muskets in its first line of the column, against some 600 British muskets. In effect, the French were outnumbered 4.5 to 1. Moreover, if one chose a position close to the top of a hill or of mountain, he could place his reserve on reverse slope. Terrain therefore protected the reserve from enemy fire. At the same time, the reserve was close at hand and could be dispatched to the front. As is well known, Wellington successfully used this tactic in Spain and, later, in Waterloo; and this came from Maida.[1]

The Calabrians had little idea of the importance of Maida. They continued to conduct ambushes and raids against French forces. Reynier appeared unable to resolve the problem. Joseph left the comfort of Naples to personally observe the situation. He deployed six thousand men to guard the lines communications and supply while the rest of the army destroyed the towns of Laurino, Rocca Gloriosa, Torraca, Sapri, Lagonegro, and Lauria, killing their inhabitants. The partisans launched a counteroffensive at Saracena, Terranova, and San Basilio, and then, overconfident, fought a field battle near Cosenza. The French won, but with no real strategic result. For this reason a second French army advanced down the Tyrrhenian coast under Massena. Despite reinforcements, Joseph and Massena found it very difficult to win a partisan war supported by Britain and Sicily. Ferdinand and the British continued to feed men and supplies to the peninsula. Although Massena returned to northern Italy in December 1806, it was only in February 1808 that Reynier claimed to have the control of the situation, but resistance continued in Calabria until 1815.

The Italians of Sardinia and Sicily

The situation in Calabria is not difficult to explain if one puts it in the strategic context of Italy. Napoleon wanted to use Italy as a stepping-stone toward the Middle East and India. Britain desperately wanted to prevent this, as Napoleon's Egyptian expedition had been a terrible threat in 1798–99. Britain surrounded Italy with an anti-French chain along the Mediterranean islands surrounding Italy, Corsica, Sardinia, Sicily, and the Ionian islands. Corsican insurgents were supported from London. Sardinia, still ruled by the House of Savoy, repelled all French amphibious assaults. Victor Emmanuel I, king after his eldest brother Charles Emmanuel IV left him the throne, had a great deal of trouble. The British wanted to extend their influence into Sardinia, transforming it into a sort of protectorate. Victor Emmanuel, however, rejected this idea. He maintained a small navy and standing army, mostly composed of militia. It was sufficient to defend against Barbary pirate raids, but the king could only hope Napoleon did not intend on making a large-scale invasion of the island. Victor Emmanuel, therefore, looked for political support in Saint Petersburg in order to balance the British diplomatic offensive. Generals Paolucci and Gianotti, formerly in Sardinian service, as well as many other officers served in the Russian army. Paolucci was aide de camp to the czar. Gianotti was the czarevich's teacher. But the most significant influence came from the personal prestige of the Sardinian ambassador to Russia: Count Joseph de Maistre, the well-known political writer and native of Savoy.

The Sicilian situation was quite different. Ferdinand needed the British because of the imminent threat of invasion. As Sicily was closer than Sardinia to continental Italy, it was easier to invade. Britain gladly aided Ferdinand, as it wanted to control Sicily, the center of the Mediterranean. Ferdinand reorganized his army and appointed General Filippo Cancellieri to direct operations in Calabria. The standing army increased from 14,000 men in 1809 to the 19,000 in 1812. The entire Royal Army was divided into two columns. The Standing Column composed some 10,000 men garrisoning fortresses. The Mobile Column included 7,000 to 9,000 men for combat operations.

Sicily suffered from similar problems as Sardinia, a lack of money. Sicily was richer and more populous than Sardinia, but Ferdinand could obtain money only by asking local feudatories for it. Obviously, nobles demanded increased political power and autonomy in exchange for revenue. Ferdinand refused, but the British delegate, Lord Bentinck, feared a pro–French movement among the Sicilian aristocracy. He forced Ferdinand to abdicate the throne in favor of a regent, the crown prince Francis. This compromise solved the situation in part. Although Ferdinand later regained the throne, his son was still the official ruler. When London asked Palermo for military support to Spain, Ferdinand agreed, as the king of Spain, Charles IV, was Ferdinand's eldest brother. On September 12, 1812, the Sicilian crown signed a treaty to dispatch soldiers to Spain. A two-thousand-man Sicilian expeditionary corps landed at Alicante. They fought at Valencia in February 1813, at Castalla on April 13, and landed near Tarragona in June. Later they served in General Clinton's division in Catalonia. In February 1814, Neapolitan troops were involved in the siege of Barcelona. In March they were again at Tarragona, and in April they sailed back to Italy, to Leghorn and then to Genoa, to fight against the Italian kingdom.

Napoleon's Italian Army

In 1808, Napoleon expanded his territorial possessions in Italy. The Kingdom of Etruria, the former Grand Duchy of Tuscany, was absorbed into the empire. The pope was deprived of Rome and exiled. The Papal States on the Tyrrhenian coast, including Rome, were annexed into the empire, while those along the Adriatic Sea became part of the Italian kingdom. Etruscan troops became part of the French army, and papal troops formed new Italian regiments.

By 1810, Dalmatia and Carnia, including Gorizia and Trieste, were part of the empire, as well as northwestern and central-western Italy, with the exception of Lucca and Piombino. The Kingdom of Italy comprised north and central-eastern Italy with Napoleon as its king. The Kingdom of Naples, now ruled by Napoleon's sister Caroline and her husband Marshal Joachim Murat, occupied all of southern Italy, with the exception of the principalities of Benevento and Pontecorvo. Napoleon had previously presented these former papal territories to his former foreign minister Talleyrand and to Marshal Bernadotte, the next king of Sweden. Sicily and Sardinia were still ruled by their kings, and the little Republic of San Marino still survived as an independent entity.

What was the military situation in Italy? Napoleon considered his Italian kingdom a reservoir for money, men, horses, oxen, and weapons. It served as a useful bastion against Austrian invasion. In this case, however, the Italians could play only an auxiliary role, while the major role was played by the imperial army. It was a reflection of the poor opinion Napoleon had for the kingdom and its inhabitants. If he officially praised Italian troops, in his private correspondences he was sometimes unsure of them. He knew he had little support for French rule in Italy. In fact, as he said, if the French reduced their military control in the peninsula or if they were defeated, the Italians would have joined the enemy.[2]

It is difficult to quantify the amount of money the French stole from Italy, although it is well known how many men the glorious first Empire took for its wars. General and compulsory orders fed the Italian army, which maintained more than 88,000 men, 15,000 horses, and 150 guns by 1812.[3] The Royal Italian Navy had 8,000 to 9,000 men and 125 light men-of-war. This was, however, of little or no consequence. Napoleon wanted to include it in any future expedition to the East and to India; but how could it effectively challenge the British with only frigates, and with its ports all in the easily blockaded Adriatic? In fact, the Italian ships were built in Venice arsenal. Being the Arsenal in the lagoon, that is to say in not deep waters, the old Republic of Venice normally launched its ships with no weapons to be as light-weight as needed to allow them to come out of the lagoon. They had just what they needed to sail to the other side of the Adriatic, where they received their full equipment and armament. As in the past, now new vessels would be completely rigged upon arriving in Dalmatia, but this was impossible because the British navy controlled the Adriatic. British also prevented the French from reaching Venice from Toulon. Thus, only frigates could be launched and rigged. The Italian navy was therefore incapable of successfully threatening the British at sea. When in 1811 the navy sortied against the British at Lissa, it was soundly defeated.

Napoleon focused his energy on building land forces in Italy instead of a navy. The total number of Italians who served under Italian colors exceeded 200,000. More than half of them never returned home. Reliable figures are not yet available for casualties in French regiments composed of Italians. Neapolitan casualties under Joseph and Murat are also obscure. Estimates place casualties at 100,000 dead.[4]

What about their effectiveness? The debate is still open. According to some sources they did not perform well in battle. For instance, Napoleon used Italians in Spain to guard his line of communications. This meant largely acting as a constabulary force. They were eventually, however, employed in the field. They fought at Barcelona, Gerona, and Hostalrich. Later, Lechi's Italian division repulsed several attempts by the British to land on the Spanish coast. In 1812 the Italians fought at Teruel and near Madrid. In 1813 the Italian Severoli Division remained in Aragon, while the Palombini Division was concentrated in Biscay, acting against the allied troops marching north. Later, both divisions were concentrated in one division, under General Filippo Severoli. They fought with the French at Tarragona and were defeated. They retreated to Tolouse and, later, in Decemeber 1813, to Italy, where they fought in 1814.

Looking at casualties, it appears that of the 30,000 Italians sent to Spain, only 8,958 returned; 14,000 were killed in action, and 7,000 died in captivity. For example by August 1809, Lechi's division in Spain was reduced to only 1,000 men. In that same period, after nine months of fighting, Italian casualties amounted to 3,255 dead and only 69 prisoners.

Between 1804 and 1809 the Italian army was employed as an auxiliary force in Italy and Austria in secondary operations against Austrian troops. In 1809 the Italian Army marched in four divisions and a detached corps including 24,000 men, 3,600 horses, and 32 guns. At Wagram, the decisive battle north of Vienna, the entire army of Italy was committed to battle. It is thus, quite difficult to understand whether the Italian army was effective or not. It is reasonable to assume that its effectiveness improved over time. Prior to 1801, Italians did not have conscription. Old armies were mostly, if not completely, professional. The militia was called in only a few cases.

On August 13, 1801, the first conscription law was decreed. The response is easy to divine. The law, issued by a foreign occupier in a country where general conscription was unknown, resulted in recalcitrance. In the first draft, 18,000 recruits were called and only 4,000 arrived at their depots. In the following years, the situation did change a little: 25 percent of conscripts could legally avoid military service; and a further 17 percent purposely avoided conscription. Moreover, after the Gendarmerie captured and brought them to their regiments, as many as one-third immediately deserted. For instance, in February 1804, 16,687 recruits reached their regiments, but 4,199 deserted soon after.

According to many experts, a recruit in these times needed two years' drilling before being considered combat-ready.[5] Napoleon's armies were generally involved in war every year. The Italians were no exception. They were involved in a war in the autumn of 1803, when only numbering 10,000 men—those belonging to the Italian army since the very beginning—but over 22,000 could be considered ready by 1805. One can also suppose that the Italian army in its early days had simply no time to drill. Its effectiveness improved with its combat experience. If it did not perform well in 1805, its participation in Germany, Poland, and Spain was better. Italian troops were at their best during the tragic Russian and German campaigns in 1812 and 1813.

From Moscow to Leipzig

Napoleon ordered Prince Eugene, viceroy of Italy, to lead the IV Corps of the Grande Armée for the Russian campaign. Forces of the Kingdom of Italy consisted of three French and Italian divisions, including the Italian Royal Guard, a light cavalry brigade and logistics corps. In all, 27,397 Italians served with IV Corps. Losses in Russia amounted to 93 percent of Italians, compared to 97 percent of the rest of the Grande Armée.

Italian troops marched in the rearguard during the advance. They did not participate in the Battle of Borodino. It was only during the retreat that IV Corps formed the vanguard of the entire army, and it did not lose a single battle. The first engagement occurred on October 24, 1812, at Maloyaroslavetz, when the Russians attempted to block the line of retreat. General Doctorov led 80,000 men against no more than 17,000 French and Italians of Delzons's and Pino's divisions. The town was captured and lost eleven times that day. After eighteen hours of fighting, the Russians were repulsed and Doctorov killed. The Russians lost 8,000 men; French and Italian casualties totaled 5,000. Russian general Bennigsen wrote that the Italian Royal Guard had been especially engaged, receiving terrible casualties. Colonel Buturlin, the czar's aide-de-camp, later wrote that Maloyaroslavetz gave the viceroy's troops the highest honor.

On November 3, in Vyazma, the Cossacks attacked stragglers. "Italian troops bravely resisted. But those of Davout . . . after Maloyaroslavez did not maintain the good attitude they had had during the whole campaign."[6] On November 18 the Italian Royal Guard took part in the Battle of Krasnoi against Kutusov's 90,000 men. Napoleon had only 42,000 combatants, and 30,000 dispersed and cut off from their units. He avoided defeat and marched to the Berezina river. The temperature dropped to 30 degrees below zero centigrade and the wounded and sick were left to the enemy. Italian troops crossed the river during the night of November 27 and 28. At dawn the Russians attacked, and the bridges crashed under the weight of the troops. Thousands of soldiers and civilians died in the frozen waters. All the baggage and wagons were lost; it was the greatest disaster of the retreat.

Napoleon left the army for Paris on December 5 to organize a new army. At the same time the Grand Armée, now reduced to only 7,300 combatants, marched to Vilna. Reinforcements were there, including 20,000 Neapolitans watching ordnances and depots. On December 9, 1812, they entered the city: "Only the Imperial and the Royal Guards still looked like organized troops."[7] The retreat stopped only in Marienwerder, Poland. Prince Eugene sadly wrote to his wife that of over 52,000 French and Italians that passed the Niemen in June, only 2,844 men—half of them wounded—returned.[8] The Italian army had lost 26,000 men; all the oxen and horses, all the guns, and all the wagons. The few survivors had lost everything "but no matter, because I saved my life and my liberty and I'm very happy"[9] as one of them wrote to his parents.

Napoleon gathered fresh troops in Germany. The Kingdom of Italy was ordered to send troops, too, and in late summer 1813 the Austrian threat appeared once more. All Italian troops were concentrated on the kingdom's eastern border. The Italian army fought then in Germany at Mockern, Nedlitz, Halle, Lützen, Gerdorf, Nutzen, Lahn, Nieder-Au, Dresden, Janowitz, Leipzig, Bautzen, and in many other places, as well as in Italy. The result was quite similar to that of Spain's: 28,400 men and 8,000 horses went to Germany from autumn 1812 to summer 1813; only 3,000 men and 500 horses came back.

The End of the Kingdom of Italy: 1814

In the autumn of 1813, 35,000 Austrians marched to Italy and Dalmatia. In a few months the number of Austrian troops increased, while French and Italian troops remained at around 40,000 men, divided into four French and three Italian divisions. Increasing Austrian pressure pushed the French and Italians back to the Padana Plain. Conscription and returning Italian troops from Spain and Germany allowed for the organization of a new Italian division under General Zucchi, who had recently fought in Germany. On January 15, 1814, Murat, king of Naples, made a separate peace with the Allies and declared war on Napoleon. This act destroyed the Italian kingdom. Murat's Neapolitan troops marched north. Ferdinand's Sicilian troops landed in Tuscany along with British troops. The Austrians advanced and, on April 16, 1814, Eugene signed the Peace of Schiarino Rizzino, ending the war. The remaining garrisons capitulated, as in Genoa and Savona or, in the case of Venice, were ordered by the viceroy to surrender. Italian soldiers burned their colors, then mixed the ashes to the wine they drank so no Italian colors could be left to the enemy. In the spring of 1814, the tyrant had been defeated. The empire ended, and the Restoration began.

14

From the Restoration to the First War of Independence: 1816–1847

The Italian Armies of the Restoration

The Restoration in Italy was celebrated with genuine joy by the people and the aristocracy, but less so among the middle class. "At the end it came, that blessed day of the great news that Napoleon was no more our master and that we were, or we were going to be, free and independent! Whoever did not see Turin on that day does not know the frenzied happiness of the people."[1] Victor Emmanuel I, by Grace of God King of Sardinia, Cyprus, and Jerusalem, landed in Genoa and returned to his capital after sixteen years.

> On May 20 finally came this so much announced and blessed king. I was in line in Castello Square and I perfectly remember the group of the King with his general staff. Dressed in the old way, with their powdered and tailed wigs and such hats in Frederick the Great's manner, they were, all together, rather amusing features; but they looked to me, as well as to everybody, wonderful and perfect; and the old "cris mille fois répétes"—one thousand times repeated cries—welcomed this good Prince in a way that he had no doubt of the love and sympathy of his very faithful Turineses.[2]

Apart from love and sympathy, the old kings experienced problems—a lot of problems. Most important, they wanted to secure their crowns. The Austrians garrisoned all of northern Italy. They organized an "urban Guard"—a sort of police and constabulary force—throughout, waiting for the return of the former sovereigns or the arrival of new ones. It was equally necessary to reorganize the armies. Money was desperately needed for this, but there was little available.

Italy was practically destroyed by the years of war. If the French had stolen and robbed during the 1796–99 period, their pillaging had been legally sanctioned after 1800. No one can fully compute what Italy lost under Napoleonic rule. Calabria was devastated, its villages burned by the French. Malta was gone. More than

100,000 young men lost their lives serving the Napoleon, emperor and king. Taking into account the civilian and military casualties of 1796–99, the total is approximately 1 million killed in the seventeen years of Napoleonic Wars. This was 6.45 percent of the Italian population at that time. Moreover, the livestock were decimated. Ten of thousands of horses and thousands of oxen had been lost in Spain, Germany, and Russia; and only the poorest or oldest beasts remained.

Commerce and industry had been damaged by the Continental blockade against Britain. Money had been lost for the same reason, and because of the exorbitant military expenses spent by Napoleon in war and peace. It is truly difficult to calculate in current terms the amount of money taken by the French and raised from Italy. Italian historian Cesare Cantù in nineteenth century estimated the total amount to be something less than 400 million *livres tournoises* of that time. A book published in Lausanne in 1799 calculated that French pillaging totaled 150 million livres; but this only applied to the 1796–99 period. The *Journal of the French Society for General Statistics* supposed the French rule cost the Cisalpine Republic alone—that is to say, to only a small part of Italy, from 1797 to 1804—288 million *livres tournoises*.

It is obviously hard to provide this economic impact in terms of current purchasing power, but we know that in the year 1800 the exchange rate was 3 francs and 30 cents to an American dollar. Therefore to provide a comparison in contemporary terms, the entire sum was greater than $120 million American dollars in 1802 currency; this can be placed in the context of the Louisiana Purchase, which was sold to the United States for $15 million. But 400 million livres was the amount for only 1796–99, the first three years of war. French rule lasted fourteen years more, until 1814. If one accepts an average of 399 million livres per three years, and of a similar economic impact in the following years, and then compare that to an annual fiscal income of 133 million livres per year, the total is 1,862,000,000 livres. In contemporary American currency it is some $560 million, that is to say 37 times the Louisiana Purchase. Thus, once upon a time Italy was a rich country. After the Napoleonic era, it was truly one of the poorest regions of Europe.

All the restored Italian sovereigns sent their ambassadors to Vienna in September 1814 to discuss the restoration of territory. They anticipated receiving restitution from France and land from the allied powers. Instead they received surprises. The major powers acted without consulting any of the minor states of Europe. Britain, Austria, Prussia, and Russia determined the fate of postwar Europe. France joined the four powers by November 1814, after the restoration of Louis XVIII and through the skilled diplomacy of Prince Talleyrand, now the royal foreign minister. According to Louis's instructions, Talleyrand suggested going back to the old system. Each sovereign would receive his former territories. The Congress agreed in general, but did what was convenient for them.

Venice therefore did not receive its independence, but became part of the Austrian kingdom of Lombardy-Venetia. The Ionian Islands were retained by Britain, to guard the mouth of the Adriatic and keep an eye on the Balkans. Genoa lost its independence and passed to the king of Piedmont-Sardinia. The duke of Parma lost his throne, and Austria gave it to Maria Louise, Napoleon's second wife and daughter of the emperor of Austria. The Bourbon-Parma family received the Duchy of Lucca as compensation. Parma would remain under Maria Louise until her death and then revert back to Bourbon-Parma while Lucca had to go to Tuscany. The pope was restored to Rome, but the king of Sardinia did not receive Nice and Savoy until after the summer 1815. Similarly, Ferdinand IV was not restored to Naples, but left to Napoleon's sister Caroline and King Joachim Murat. They had defected to the Allies in return for their thrones.

This was not a satisfying situation. Politics and power dictated the settlement.

The sovereigns faced another difficult problem in reorganizing the state administration. Illiteracy was prevalent; and literate persons who opposed the revolutionary and Napoleonic administration were hard to find. Even the French-backed administrations experienced similar problems: insufficient literacy for proper governance. Now, in the spring 1814, only the pope had no trouble employing bureaucrats, because he had many literate people—the priests—in his administration. All the old and new governments, however, had no choice but maintain the former administration, regardless of their political past.

Certainly, the most culpable collaborators lost their positions, but the majority remained entrenched in the bureaucracy. A similar situation occurred concerning the reorganization of Italian armies. Here, however, compromising the military could be fatal to monarchs. Each state then solved the problem in a different way. The duke of Modena simply swept away all who had served Napoleon. Ferdinand III, grand duke of Tuscany, established a small army composed of former Napoleonic soldiers, but they remained faithful in the following forty-five years.

The same happened in Parma as well in Lombardy and Venice. Austria united these two regions into the kingdom of Lombardy-Venetia and accepted all the former Napoleonic soldiers. They received the Austrian rank corresponding to their Italian or French ones; and few problems emerged in the following years.

Piedmont had a terribly difficult time. The king had only 2,500 men in Sardinia. He needed at least ten times more in Piedmont and, unfortunately, all the Piedmontese who had served under Napoleon had been in the French army. The former emperor was so hated that no one at court accepted the idea of employing in anyone who served him. It was, however, necessary to have an army as well as a state administration. The solution was quite strange. The court asked all who had served the king up to the last year of his reign—1798—to take their old places in the administration. The positions and ranks available because the previous administrators were dead, or too old, now were taken over by their sons or grandsons. Former Napoleonic soldiers were admitted, but at a reduced rank; a general became a colonel, a captain became a lieutenant, a sergeant became a corporal. Moreover, police control was required; and on July 13, 1814, Royal Patents established the new corps of Royal Carabineers.

Carabineers are traditionally considered an Italian legacy of the French gendarmerie. This is not really true and they should be more properly considered an evolution of the pre-Napoleonic Italian military constabulary forces. But the corps became a political police, strictly linked to the sovereign. In Italian terms *reale* and *regio* are normally translated in English as "royal," but there is a significant difference between them. *Regio* means "royal" as in English, that is in the sense of something belonging to the monarchical state. *Reale* means royal, too, but it should be more properly translated as "king's own." The army, the navy, the ambassadors, the ministries, the government itself were officially designated as *regio*. The household and the king's property were designated as *reali*: king's own. The role of the Carabineers was considered so important to Victor Emmanuel I that he declared them as "king's own," directly dependent on him. Unfortunately, a part from Carabineers, the overall transformation of the Piedmontese military reorganization was not successful.

The return of officers defeated by Napoleon eighteen years before pushed the army back two decades in terms of tactics and mentality. Furthermore, Piedmontese military experience gained through the Napoleonic Wars was dismissed because it originated with the French emperor. The best available military knowledge was rejected; and the army placed in the hands of an old general staff. The result was a ineffective army. It was extremely formal, well dressed, and drilled, but it was largely a parade ground force, not adequate for war. In the first clash between military effectiveness and political-reliability, priority was given to loyalty over experience. Looking at the general European situation, the kingdom's internal stability was most important, but this caused a lot of problems later. In fact, the 1815 cadets of Turin Military Academy became the 1848 colonels and generals. Most of the problems affecting the Piedmontese and then the Italian Royal Army have their origins in this era.

Murat's Attempt and the 1815 Piedmontese Expedition to France

Napoleon's "One Hundred Days" were a turning point in diplomatic negotiations. The Congress of Vienna was suspended. Napoleon prepared a new army, the Coalition, and the Italian sovereigns did, too. Joachim Murat made a terrible mistake, deciding to act according to Napoleon's actions. He issued a proclamation to all Italians, calling them to war. He wanted to establish an Italian kingdom under his leadership. He marched north with his army but was severely defeated at Tolentino by an Austrian army reinforced by Modena and Parma. The Austrians marched to Naples, while a second army of 85,000 men marched through the Piedmontese Alps accompanied by a Parmesan infantry regiment and a Modenese infantry battalion.

The Piedmontese army was still reorganizing, but Victor Emmanuel I ordered it to conduct an offensive into France, even though he possessed only 15,000 men with a few horses. The first skirmishes occurred at the end of March, but Napoleon concentrated his main army in Belgium, and not much happened on the Italian frontier. In June, after a march to the Padana Plain—in case Murat was victorious—the Piedmontese returned. They crossed the Alps and liberated Savoy. Soon afterward the Austro-Italian army, including Piedmontese, Parmesan, and Modenese, totaled 102,000 men. They invaded France and besieged Grenoble. The final French sortie was repulsed by a charge of the Royal Carabineers: it was their baptism of fire. Lyon, Gap, and many other French cities fell to the army before Napoleon's second abdication. At the conclusion of the 1815 Alpine campaign, Victor Emmanuel I signed a separate peace with France. He received Savoy and Nice, but the kingdom's political and diplomatic relevance was now reduced.

When the Congress of Vienna reconvened, heated arguments broke out. Talleyrand proposed legitimism as the best course for Europe. This meant going back to the political system prior to 1789, but—as we have seen—it did not happen. The Allies wanted a chain of buffer states surrounding France. It had to be composed of medium-sized states strong enough to contain France. The Netherlands received former imperial Flanders, later Belgium; Piedmont acquired Genoa; and Prussia appeared on the Rhine. Austria wanted to place a member of the Habsburg family on the throne in Turin. This would have given control of the Alps to Austria and eliminated any possibility of an Italian-born political power, but France could not accept it. Talleyrand and Joseph De Maistre influenced Czar Alexander I; and Victor Emmanuel remained on his throne.

Murat's foolhardy adventure allowed the Allies to remove the Bonapartists in Naples and restore the Bourbon king Ferdinand. The old king faced reality that his army was composed of Murat's former soldiers. To address this, he melded soldiers from Sicily and Naples in his new army. This seemed successful. When in October 1815, Murat landed in Calabria, trying to regain his kingdom, the troops arrested him. A military court judged him guilty and he was shot. With Murat's death, the Napoleonic period in Italy was at an end, but left a significant mark on the army and society.

The Congress of Vienna also addressed questions of compensation. All the European states demanded that France pay war reparations. Italy's damages could be assessed at 1.862 billion livres, with a contemporary value at $560 million. The Italian states asked the Congress of Vienna for only 120 million francs. It was ridiculous, but nobody at that time could compute the real damages. France objected to the sum total of amount, which came to 775,500,000 million francs. A compromise required France to pay all European states a portion of what they were asking for. The Italian states received only 40.5 million francs. Piedmont asked for 70 million: It received 30. The pope demanded 30 million: he was accorded 5. Parma, which paid its first tribute to the French in the summer of 1796, received only 1 million. Tuscany, may be because the grand duke was the brother of the emperor of Austria, wanted 4 million and received 4.5. Naples received nothing.

Revolutionary Attempts: 1820–1834

The Restoration deprived the bourgeoisie of its political power. All the Italian states went back to absolutism. The sovereign solely decided and issued laws, and only the aristocracy were admitted into the top ranks of governance. The former midlevel aristocracy and bourgeoisie hated this, as they were cut off from political power. Very shortly after the Restoration, political secret societies appeared. They were normally known as the Carboneria—the Coalmen—as all their members were known as *carbonari*: coalmen. But the *rivendite*—the "retailing shops"— were quite different each from the other. They had a generic mutual Masonic foundation. The *carbonari* were generally republicans, but some of them hoped for a new kingdom under Napoleon—still alive on Saint Helena—or in a confederacy of Italian states, or in early socialism, whose doctrine was then spreading from the ashes of the French Revolution. In any case, they acted against the rulers and demanded a constitution and called for a resurrection—a Risorgimento—of the nation. The first important *carbonari* revolt occurred in the Neapolitan army in July 1820. They demanded the Spanish constitution, that is to say, a constitution like that granted in Spain that same year. Soon after, Sicily revolted.

Revolution broke out throughout Italy. The Austrian foreign minister, Prince Clemens von Metternich, called for a conference of the major powers at Lubjiana (Laibach). Austria was granted permission to restore Ferdinand IV to the throne and crush revolutions throughout the peninsula. In March 1821, the Neapolitan *carbonari* were defeated. Ferdinand purged his army of all whose service did not appear perfectly loyal. He then reorganized the state. Sicily and Naples were no longer two separate kingdoms and the new Kingdom of the Two Sicilies appeared. Ferdinand changed his number from IV—as he was as the king of Naples—to I, because he was now Ferdinand I, the first king of the Two Sicilies.

In Piedmont the *carbonari* revolted as well. Many were former Napoleonic officers and noncommissioned officers now serving in the royal army and belonged to a *carbonari* group called Federati—the Federates. They wanted the "Spanish constitution" and asked the crown prince, Charles Albert, to help them, because in 1798 his family had chosen the Napoleonic side. Indeed, in spite of being a member of the royal house, Charles Albert's father, Charles of Savoy, prince of Carignano, was cut off from political power and hailed the arrival of the French as an opportunity to seize power, or save his revenue.

On the night of March 11–12, 1821, four infantry regiments and four cavalry regiments hoisted the sky blue, red, and black *carbonari* tricolor. Victor Emmanuel refused to accept a constitution. He abdicated the throne to his brother Charles Felix and went into exile. Charles Felix was in Modena at the time, so Charles Albert was appointed regent and issued the constitution. Unfortunately, Charles Felix rejected it. He ordered loyal troops to gather in Novara and, when joined by an Austrian army on April 8, they crushed the revolutionary regiments.

Charles Felix sent Charles Albert to France, where he served in the French army against the Spanish revolution in 1823. At the same time, the new king ordered his police and judges to take drastic action against the *carbonari*. Some escaped to Greece, where they participated in the Greek revolt, but the majority emigrated to Latin America. The language was similar to Italian and the existing commercial links between Genoa—recently annexed by Piedmont—and Latin America eased their transition. The very young Giuseppe Mazzini in Genoa saw many of them depart for the Americas.

Peace and order returned to Italy after this revolutionary interlude; and the Italian states attended to less urgent affairs, such as the perennial threat of the Barbary pirates of North Africa.

These pirates preyed on European shipping throughout the Napoleonic Wars. They continued their attacks into the Restoration, causing substantial losses to maritime commerce. Charles Felix expanded his navy to meet this threat. Ferdinand I did the same, and his merchant fleet in 1819 possessed the first steamboat in Italy. In 1825 the Royal Sardinian Navy raided Tripoli harbor. The Neapolitan navy did the same three years later. Then in 1830 the French intervened by invading Algeria, and piracy disappeared. As the Mediterranean was now calm, the Royal Sardinian Navy crossed the ocean and established a naval station in South America in Uruguay and at Rio de la Plata, to protect the commerce, properties, and activities of Piedmontese subjects.

In 1831 a new revolutionary wave reached Italy, inspired by the 1830 revolution in France. Giuseppe Mazzini—now a man—disseminated his ideas of a national union throughout the peninsula. Mazzini also advocated installing a republican government devoid of monarchy. His revolutionary movement, Giovane Italia—Young Italy—took the place of the *carbonari*. Furthermore, most revolutionaries accepted the notion of national unification and looked for historical and modern examples of Italian unity and independence to rally the people. The Napoleonic Kingdom of Italy fit the bill. The green, white, and red tricolor was now considered the national flag instead of the *carbonari* banner used in 1821.

Italian sovereigns were worried, as 1831 demonstrated that the previous 1821 revolts were merely a test. Former Napoleonic generals in 1821 had largely been neutral or supported their king. In 1831 the generals supported the revolutions. General Carlo Zucchi, for example, commanded a revolutionary army against the pope. This was a dramatic change from the past. The most important feature of *carbonari* or Liberal revolutionaries in 1821 hoped that their sovereigns would accept a democratic or constitutional evolution of their states. The sovereign had answered negatively, so no wonder if in 1831 revolutionaries were clearly against the sovereigns and clearly wanted national unification, which meant the end of the Italian dynasties.

Reaction was harsh and strong. Austrian troops entered the Papal States and disbanded Zucchi's army. A French expeditionary force landed in Ancona. In theory it was there to protect papal rule; in practice, it was there to establish a stepping-stone to the Middle and Far East, according to French imperialistic policy.[3] Although the Austrians withdrew their troops in 1831, the French corps remained in Ancona until 1838.

In the same year, 1831, Charles Felix I died and Charles Albert I came to the throne of Piedmont-Sardinia. He was not particularly supportive of the revolutionaries. The police repressed them, especially when, in 1834, Mazzini organized a plot against the monarchy. A great many revolutionaries were arrested or fled. One of them was a seaman in the Royal Navy, Giuseppe Garibaldi. He fled to Latin America, as many others did. There they found help and support from former Italian *carbonari* who had reached Latin America after 1821.

South American Training Ground: Garibaldi's Italian Legion

Garibaldi went to Latin America and took part in the Rio Grande do Sur Republican revolution against the Empire of Brazil.

"I learned fighting in Latin America" he wrote in his memoirs. His tactics were drawn from Latin American warfare. The main character of Brazilian forces was their extreme mobility. This was due to several factors. The first was their meat-based diet and the ease of finding large quantities of meat. Moreover, they had no carriages and baggage trains, which were useless in the jungles. Writing about his actions, Garibaldi attested that a European army would not have been able to fight as he did in Latin America, because it would have been slowed or stopped by baggage trains. As a consequence, this leads to the second factor: the absence of logistical equipment, as compared to European standards. No kettles, no mess tins, no packs or field tents and stakes; all the Latin Americans needed were a lance and a mantle as a shelter and a knife for their cooking, and accoutrements consisted of a cartridge belt and—if the soldier was rich—a bag. The third factor was the excellent adaptability to terrain. The European mentality wants to conquer environment; Latin Americans adapted to it.

Their maneuvering capability and extreme agility by taking advantage of terrain had baffled the Dutch army in the seventeenth century, whose units advanced in close battle order and found space in front of them; meanwhile a rain of bullets poured down on them. This later baffled the nineteenth-century Austrians, French, Neapolitans, and Germans more than it had the seventeenth-century Dutch.

Looking at the operations of the Garibaldini in Italy and France between 1849 and 1871, one notes two characteristics. First, the troops possessed extreme agility in advancing and retreating—often many times during the same battle—by taking advantage of terrain. They exploited the terrain and availed themselves of every opportunity to launch attack columns. This was not an exception, because the same flexible system was applied against the Austrians, the French, the Neapolitans, and the Germans. The second characteristic was the absence of cavalry. Garibaldi learned to fight effectively without cavalry in America where, every time infantry appeared on battlefield, it was able to prevail. The most extreme case was on February 8, 1846, in San Antonio. Garibaldi had 186 Italian Legionnaires[4] and about 100 Uruguayan cavalry. Argentinians attacked him in the open plain with 300 infantry and 900 cavalry. Garibaldi refused to retreat: All but six Uruguayans escaped. He fired a devastating point-blank fusillade into the enemy infantry and followed with a quick bayonet attack. He then resisted cavalry charges for the next eight hours. At the end of the day he retreated with all the wounded. This would be the same tactic later used in 1849 against the French in Rome and in 1859 against the Austrians.

On May 20, 1846, on the Daymàn river, Garibaldi used infantry to disorder enemy cavalry and protect and reorganize his own cavalry. When in Europe, Garibaldi preferred to use cavalry as a long-range reconnaissance force. All his battles were won with infantry, with the aid of artillery, but never using cavalry. Considering Latin American warfare was at the base of Garibaldi's victories and, looking at the fundamental role played by Garibaldi in Italian unification, we can affirm that Latin American warfare made Italian independence possible.

In the early days of 1848, Garibaldi received news about the Italian revolutions and decided to return to Europe: He had great expectations, and his great adventure was only beginning.

CHAPTER 15

The First War of Independence: 1848-1849

The 1848 Campaign

Since his accession to the throne, Charles Albert worked to restore Piedmont's political influence in Europe and its preeminence in Italy. In his mind, the enemy was Austria. Although Charles Felix increased the size of the Royal Navy, Austria was a Continental power. Therefore, Charles Albert pursued a substantial reorganization of the army in 1830s, in order to contend with them.[1] He halted their training for mountain warfare—that assumed war with France—and began to train on the plains, where they would face Austria. Despite army reforms, it suffered from the poor quality of its officer corps, a problem stemming from the internal political issues of the Restoration, exacerbated by the 1821 military revolt and subsequent purge of the army.

General Filippo Paulucci, back from Russian service, drafted the general plan. The result was—in 1839—a standing army based on general conscription and composed of eighteen infantry regiments, with two grenadier regiments and six cavalry regiments, and four artillery companies (including two horse artillery companies). The light infantry disappeared and in 1836, Grenadier Captain Alessandro La Marmora, proposed a new light infantry corps, the *Bersaglieri* (sharpshooters). Its distinctive symbol was a cock-tail–feathered plumed hat. Their role was to provide effective reconnaissance and rapid attacks. Therefore, the men were trained to move and fight only running, as they still do.

In the 1840s, the Royal Army appeared a solid and well-trained entity. Unfortunately, there were two main problems; an inadequate logistical system, and the general staff. The general staff did not command, it simply coordinated the movement of divisions, nothing more. According to state hierarchy, the king was the supreme commander of the army. The Chief of the General Staff was to provide him administrative support through the General Staff. The Guides, Royal Carabineers, Intendancy, Administration, Medical Corps, Artillery, and Engineer Corps all depended upon the General Staff. The staff, however, did not study or develop war plans. If the king was absent, then it was impossible to request orders, as the

General Staff only coordinated the institution. Unfortunately, the generals commanding corps or divisions tended to act autonomously and therefore did not coordinate their respective operations. This lack of coordination was at the root of defeat in 1848–49, and in 1866 and 1896. General Cadorna resolved it during the First World War only by consolidating the command function into the General Staff system based on the Prusso-German model.

No one in the 1840s could divine the future, and Charles Albert was waiting for an opportunity to strike at Austria. He instituted political reforms, succeeding in gaining the support of the Liberals and national patriots. In autumn 1844, Marquis Massimo d'Azeglio made a trip through Italy. When he returned to Turin: "I asked for an audience and I had it soon."[2] Charles Albert received him alone, on a dark and cold morning in January 1845, around six o'clock. D'Azeglio relayed to him all he had heard when talking to Liberals and patriots: "'Now your Majesty will tell me if he approves or disapproves of what I did and what I said.' Then I remained silent and I waited for the answer, that the King's face promised to be not harsh; but, about the main issue, I supposed it to be a 'ibis redibis',"[3] wrote D'Azeglio. "On the contrary, without hesitation and not avoiding my look, but looking right to my eyes the King said to me calmly and resolutely: 'Let those gentlemen know they must remain calm and they must not move, because by now there is nothing to do. But they must be sure that, when the opportunity arises, my life, the lives of my sons, my weapons, my treasures, my army will all be used for the Italian cause.'"[4]

These were revealing words. The Italian bourgeoisie made their first attempt to take power in 1821, and failed. The events of 1830–31 revealed that a successful revolution was impossible as long as Austria remained in Lombardy-Venetia. The Habsburgs possessed overwhelming force and used it to maintain order in Italy. Each time, Austrian intervention was swift and overturned the Italian revolutions. The Italian bourgeoisie decided it was necessary to seek assistance from a liberal-minded monarch with a powerful army. This is precisely what happened on a January morning in the Royal Palace in Turin in 1845. Charles Albert accepted a pact with the revolutionaries; his army for a constitution and a crown for a unified Italy. At that time, most nationalists advocated an Italian confederation, composed of all the Italian sovereigns with the pope as president. Charles Albert wanted to be the most powerful Italian sovereign, depriving Austria of Lombardy-Venetia as its Italian possessions. It was simply the traditional and historical policy of the House of Savoy. If by chance the entire peninsula could be gained, all the better, but the initial idea was of a confederation. In fact, when in late spring 1848 all appeared well, Charles Albert was acclaimed king of Northern Italy, nothing more. Republicans and Socialists rejected this agreement. Only a republic would be acceptable; but they were not the majority.

The opportunity Charles Albert had waited earnestly for came in 1848. In February, Parisians overthrew their king. Louis-Philippe escaped abroad, and the Second French Republic was established. Louis Napoleon Bonaparte became president in December. He was the son of Louis, brother of Napoleon and Hortense de

Beauharnais, and spent his youth exiled in Italy, where he joined the *carbonari*. The news from France about the clash between Parliament and king on electoral reform reached Italy, Germany, and Austria. The patriots demanded that the king of Naples, the young Ferdinand II, grandson of Ferdinand I, adopt a constitution. On January 29, he succumbed to popular pressures. On February 8, 1848, Charles Albert issued the Statute, the Piedmont Constitution. Pope Pius IX granted his own constitution on February 14, and Leopold II did the same in Florence three days later.

Riots in Vienna forced the prince of Metternich to resign on March 13. Five days later people in Milan revolted against the thirty-thousand-man Austrian garrison there commanded by Field Marshal Radetzky, a veteran of the Napoleonic Wars. Within five days, on March 22, the Milanese population forced the Austrians to withdraw. Charles Albert took this opportunity and declared war on Austria.

Radetzky was in a poor situation. Venice and Brescia also rose in revolt; and he could not get reinforcements from Austria because of the revolution in Vienna. Adding to the crisis, Hungary proclaimed its independence from the Habsburg Empire, requiring the attention of the Austrian army in Croatia. The old field marshal concentrated all troops in the so-called Quadrilateral: a portion of the Padana Plain protected by the four fortresses of Peschiera, Mantua, Verona, and Legnago. Standing in the Quadrilateral, Radetzky believed he could resist the Piedmontese along the Mincio river. This allowed him to secure his communications with Austria and prevented a possible surprise attack from Venice.

Charles Albert precipitously began the war. The dukes of Parma and of Modena had lost their thrones, and it was unclear whether Piedmont should act or wait and see. The Milanese aristocrats decided for him. The Milanese revolution could easily become a Republican, or even Socialist, revolution. The only way to avoid this risk was to channel the revolution in the direction of constitutional monarchy. That's why a delegation of Milanese nobles arrived at Turin and requested military intervention. Charles Albert accepted. Wanting to lead the nationalist movement for his own tasks, he adopted their colors, replacing the flag of the House of Savoy. The new flag included the crest of Savoy in the middle of the central white band; and this meant that the Royal House not only accepted and supported the revolution, but also directed it.

Piedmont's strategic situation was not good. Its army was scattered in garrisons and required fifteen days to concentrate on the border. The General Staff could only deploy 25,000 men on the Ticino river by March 30. By then it could be too late, so the king ordered an ill-prepared offensive. On March 26, General Michele Bes marched on Milan with 4,000 men, while his colleague Trotti passed the Ticino at Pavia with 4,000 more. The news of the war spread throughout Italy. The Italian population enthusiastically supported intervention. The grand duke of Tuscany sent his troops to join the Piedmont army. The pope, Pius IX, did the same. Naples sent two divisions to Lombardy and a fleet to the upper Adriatic. The Napoleonic general Lechi, former commander of the Napoleonic Italian Royal Guard, presented Charles Albert with the Eagles of the Italian regiments he had saved in his home since 1814. It was a changing of the Guard, the Italian leader committing to the the king of Piedmont the symbols and burden of the Italian revolutionary traditions.

In the early days of April 1848, Austria was racked by revolutions. There were no more than 90,000 men in Italy, including garrisons. Most of the navy had rebelled, as most of the sailors were Italians who joined the insurgents in Venice. The Piedmontese and Neapolitan navies were in the upper Adriatic, cutting any possible maritime line from Dalmatia to Venetia. On land, Charles Albert had commanded 100,000 men from all parts of Italy. Some 20,000 Italians volunteered, but their training and effectiveness was minimal. Moreover, the Italians were divided, because a portion—including papal troops—were camped near Venice, while the remaining forces were in Lombardy. The Austrian army was caught in the middle. Radetzsky could only receive reinforcements from Austria as long as he held Verona. The city guarded the entrance to the Trentino, the quickest route from Austria to Italy: it was the same route used by Prince Eugene in 1701.

Charles Albert swept away all the Austrian outposts. The strongest, in Pastrengo, was defeated on April 30. The king then marched to Verona but failed to seize the city. He decided then to besiege Peschiera. Strategically, this failure to take Verona decided the campaign. Radetzky maintained his lifeline to Austria. While Charles Albert methodically invested Peschiera, Radetzky assumed the initiative. He attacked and defeated the papal army, then on May 30 he attacked the Piedmontese at Goito, but was defeated. General Bava, however, did not take advantage of the victory and failed to pursue Radetsky to Mantua. The same day, Peschiera surrendered. Charles Albert's officers hailed his victories, but the tide soon turned.

The Austrian emperor and court fled to the Tyrol, where emperor Ferdinand was convinced to abdicate the throne. The court kept in close contact with the generals, and in any case a number of them acted without royal authority against the revolutionaries. It was clear by the end of August that Ferdinand would abdicate in favor of the eighteen-year-old Francis Joseph I. The young emperor was present when Vienna was besieged and seized by loyal troops at the end of October.

At the same time, Austria warned the pope that he was the chief of Christendom, not a simple Italian sovereign. If he did not remain neutral, Austria would separate the Catholic Church of the empire from Rome. The menace was considered; and the pope recalled his troops. The British, American, and French consuls in Trieste demanded the Piedmontese and Neapolitan fleets, that they lift the blockade against Austria. Austrian diplomatic pressure, Neapolitan troubles in Sicily, and King Ferdinand's desire to restore absolute power created a bevy of internal crises. He withdrew his forces.

The remaining 77,000 Italians in Lombardy held a long line from Peschiera to Mantua. A larger portion of the army was deployed around Mantua, preventing Charles Albert from taking the offensive. During the third week of July, Radtezky advanced from Verona with 56,000 men and attacked the Piedmontese army of 20,000 around the village of Custoza. After two days of hard fighting, he dislocated Charles Albert's army. Italian troops were too scattered to resist. Furthermore, supplies were late and soldiers ill fed. So, when 40,000 Austrians attacked, the first resistance was made by only 9,000 Piedmontese and, in the end, Radetzky's 50,000 men won against 20,000 Italians. The battle forced Charles Albert to retreat. He preferred to go to Milan instead of Pavia, "to help the brave Milanese,"[5] as he said. Nevertheless, his army was chased from Milan, too, and he signed an armistice lasting eight months.

The 1849 Campaign

The failure of the royal army stirred up republican revolution all over Italy. Venice declared itself a republic and was promptly besieged by Radetzky. The Austrian commander preferred to blockade the city by land and sea, waiting for the effects of starvation. At the same time, in November 1848, a political crisis in Rome forced the pope to flee to the kingdom of Naples, and he called upon all Catholic powers for help. On February 8, 1849, the Roman Republic was proclaimed. The revolutionaries formed a triumvirate, including Mazzini. The army was composed of papal troops and volunteers from northern Italy. Giuseppe Garibaldi was among them. He arrived in Italy just in time to fight during the last days of the 1848 campaign. He was called to Rome, but with little enthusiasm. Garibaldi was too important and too well known; and few among the revolutionary leaders, including Mazzini, really liked the idea of having him there. When he reached Rome, despite animosity, he was appointed deputy commander of the Republican army.

As Garibaldi and the triumvirate organized their defenses and set up Republican institutions, the armistice between Piedmont and Austria expired. On March 20, 1849, Charles Albert moved his troops. He had now 80,000 men, but Radetzky was waiting for him. Leaving 25,000 men to blockade Venice, he met Charles Albert with 70,000 men across the Ticino river. He lost a first battle at La Sforzesca, but won the second at Mortara and marched northward. Charles Albert counterattacked, and the two armies clashed outside of Novara on March 23, 1849. Radetzky won a decisive victory. Charles Albert realized the situation and abdicated the throne, leaving it to his son Victor Emmanuel. He went into exile in Portugal, where he died a few months later in Oporto.

The new king met Radetzky at Vignale, a little village not far from Novara. The conditions presented by the Austrian field marshal were hard to accept. The kingdom had to sign a ten-year truce, accept an Austrian garrison in the city of Alexandria, and pay 75 million lira in war damages. Radetzky suggested that these conditions could be mitigated if the king rescinded the constitution. Victor Emmanuel replied that he was an honest man who kept his House's word.[6] He was then known as the "honest man king." The pact between Charles Albert and the patriots remained. It was the definitive demonstration of the reliability of the House of Savoy. Republicans, however, proudly declared that they were still resisting Austria.

Italian freedom could be reached through a popular revolt. The people could fight and win a popular war to liberate their country.

When receiving news of Piedmont's defeat, Carlo Cattaneo, one of the most important political thinkers of that period wrote: "Good news: the Sardinians [Piedmontese] have been defeated. Now we shall be masters of ourselves. It will be us who will make a popular war. It will be us to drive the Austrians from Italy, and then we shall make the Federal republic."[7] In the best case, this could be considered total ignorance, political shortsightedness, and complete incomprehension of the nature of war. In the worst case, one could ask himself if this man was as smart as he supposed himself to be. Unfortunately, his words were taken to heart by the most consummate Republicans. For instance, Goffredo Mameli, a young patriot and author of a very popular song, which later became the Italian republic's national anthem, shared Cattaneo's revolutionary optimism.

The 1849 Repression

In the early days of spring 1849, Republican resistance was centered in Venice, Rome, Brescia, and Sicily. Austrian troops seized Brescia after a ten-day fight and forty-eight hours of shelling. Austrian general Julius Freiherr von Haynau was so ruthless that he was called by Italians "the hyena of Brescia," while they erected a monument to his colleague Nugent, who had been killed during the siege.[8]

Sicily had revolted against Naples, proclaiming its independence. It looked for a king from the House of Savoy, but its princes were forbidden to accept the invitation. In September 1848, Sicily was invaded by Neapolitan troops. King Ferdinand sent his best commander, the sixty-six-year-old general Carlo Filangieri, prince of Satriano. He was a veteran of the Napoleonic Wars and had fought at Austerlitz, Ulm, and in Spain. He was perhaps the best Italian general of his day after Garibaldi. He reached Sicily by sea with a fleet of eleven men-of-war and six transports, carrying 14,000 men. Their landing near Messina was a model operation. Despite the threat of a French-English diplomatic intervention, which delayed the operations several times, Filangieri defeated the Sicilian troops and entered Palermo on May 15, 1849. Nevertheless, he was considered too sympathetic to the revolution and was soon recalled.

By this time only Rome and Venice remained free. Naples, Spain, Austria, and France had answered Pius IX's plea for help. The French landed in Civitavecchia in April and marched to Rome, with General Oudinot commanding the seven-thousand-man expeditionary force. The son of a Napoleonic marshal, he was a Napoleonic veteran, too, having fought in Napoleon's last campaigns. Coming via Aurelia, on April 29, he was in front of the Roman walls, just outside the Vatican. Garibaldi, who was waiting for him, later wrote, "He attacked as if no walls existed and as if they were garrisoned by children."[9] The French presumption that the Italians were weak received the appropriate lesson. Garibaldi applied his Latin

American tactics for the first time in Europe, stopping the French with intensive fire and then destroying them with a rapid counterattack. They were completely beaten and retreated twelve miles from the city. Oudinot lost 300 dead, 150 wounded, and 365 prisoners, that is to say 11.6 percent of his forces. Garibaldi lost only 8 percent, that is to say, only 200 dead and wounded.

Oudinot requested reinforcements from France and a truce from the Roman triumvirate. Garibaldi advised the triumvirate not to accept. "We could drive the enemy into the sea: then we could talk."[10] The triumvirate, however, accepted. Later, Garibaldi sadly added: "If Mazzini—and no other is guilty—had practical capability, as well as he was verbose, in planning projects and enterprises; and if he then—as he always pretended—had the capability of managing military questions; if, moreover, he had listened to some of his men who, because of their records, could be supposed to be experts on something, he would have made less mistakes and, in the circumstance I'm reporting, he would have been able if not in saving Italy, at least indefinitely delaying the Roman catastrophe."[11]

In May, Mazzini sent Garibaldi south, because the king of Naples was advancing at the head of 16,000 men. Garibaldi attacked Ferdinand's troops near Palestrina and, ten days later, near Velletri, beating them both times. Then General Roselli, the supreme commander of Roman army, ordered Garibaldi to invade the kingdom before the Spanish landed an army. Mazzini, however, called him back to Rome. Oudinot had taken the offensive once more, with 30,000 men. The Republic had only 11,000 men available. Garibaldi wrote:

> Everything presaged a highly probable success going forward. Well: an order by the Roman Government called us back to Rome, which was threatened by the French once more. . . . If he who, after my advice, left me marching and winning in Palestrina, if he, then, I do not know for what reason, let me march to Velletri under General-in-Chief Roselli; if Mazzini, in the end, whose vote was absolutely incontestable in the Triumvirate, would have wanted to accept that I know something about warfare, he could have left the General-in-Chief in Rome, and charged me with the enterprise, leaving me to invade the Neapolitan Kingdom.[12]

The result was simple. The French kept their word, respecting the truce by launching a surprise attack twenty-four hours before it expired. Their assault overwhelmed the defenses. Garibaldi did all he could to delay the inevitable, but the French reached the height of Gianicolo hill. They sent an ultimatum to the triumvirate: if the Republic did not surrender, they would shell the city until it was destroyed. Mazzini and the triumvirate had little choice but to accept. Garibaldi left the city with his wife Anita and 4,000 men. He wanted to reach Venice, but the Spanish, French, and Neapolitans were on his heels, and the Austrians were coming from north. He escaped to San Marino along with 250 men and tried to reach Venice by sea. The Austrian fleet pursued, and he was forced to land near Ravenna. His wife died there. Garibaldi then escaped to Genoa. The Piedmontese government asked him to leave in order to avoid trouble with Austria and France.

Having lost his wife, Rome, and revolution, Garibaldi sailed for America. He stayed in New York, where he worked as a candle maker in the factory of Antonio Meucci, the Italian who invented the telephone.[13] After some time he went to South America as a sea captain and returned to Italy only in 1854.

At the same time as Garibaldi's defense of Rome, Venice resisted an Austrian siege. Daniel Manin, chief of the Republic, made a determined stand against the Austrians. They attempted to bomb the city from the air, using balloons, but this proved unsuccessful and the siege continued. In late summer the city ran out of food. Manin had no choice but surrender, on August 24, 1849. Radetzky did not take revenge on the rebellious city. He requested that they hand over their ordnance and weapons, and sent Manin and thirty-nine others into exile. The first war for Italian independence was over.

CHAPTER **16**

From the Peace to the Second War of Independence: 1849–1859

The Ten-Year Truce

The Austrian empire came out of the 1848 storm as the master of Italy. The reigning dynasties of Tuscany and Modena were both branches of the House of Habsburg, and Austrian troops garrisoned Tuscany, the papal city of Bologna in the Padana Plain, south of the Po river, and protected the duchies of Parma and Modena. Austrian influence was wider and more direct than before. In the south, Ferdinand II of Two Sicilies concentrated all his efforts on domestic affairs. The kingdom was under severe police control, and the army was now intended to be more of a large, well-armed constabulary force than a real army. By the way, he had the luxury of using his army in this manner as he often said that his kingdom was protected on three sides by saltwater and on the fourth by holy water, that is, the Papal States.

It was clear that no land attack could reach Naples without passing through the Papal States. Any invasion meant Austrian and French intervention. The Austrians garrisoned Bologna and the French Rome, in order to protect the Holy See. The king of the Two Sicilies could sleep safely. The Neapolitan Royal Navy was strong and modern enough to protect its coastline. Although their relations with the British were poor, the Two Sicilies had a strong relationship with Russia and Austria. As a consequence, Ferdinand simply froze the political climate in Naples. No significant technical progress was made under him after 1848, except for the navy. In 1839 the kingdom had been the first in Italy to possess a railroad, from Naples to Portici. In the following years, however, only two more railways were built, from Naples to Salerno and from Naples to Caserta.

The papal situation was quite similar. Pope Pius IX was a broad-minded man. When young, he had visited the United States and was considered a Liberal. Unfortunately, political considerations prevailed on his opinions. He was the pope. He had to support the Roman Catholic Church and its temporal power. Moreover, he had been threatened by an Austrian schism in 1848, and this was a lesson he could not forget. He disliked Austria, because of its oppression in Italy and, according to traditional papal foreign policy, he sought external support. He found French president Louis Napoleon Bonaparte receptive, although he was not a good Catholic. Louis Napoleon, however, needed the political support of the conservative Catholics in France. Backed by a conservative France in theory, and by a conservative Austria, Pius IX did not have much room to maneuver.

Piedmont was the only Italian state that had been able to escape Austrian pressure. Victor Emmanuel II experienced difficulties in his first year as king. The defeat led to rioting, especially in Genoa. Shortly after the Battle of Novara, in Parliament the extreme left cried for war, revolution, and a republic, against the king and the Church. The leftists were either former Jacobins who had cooperated with the French in 1798–1814, or their sons. It was a class composed of lawyers, notaries, attorneys, physicians, and merchants from small towns in the provinces. They had no experience in politics. They were certain that if France were now a republic, it would be similar to the republic that had preceded Napoleon. Surely it was the republic that had given the middle class political power. They were confident that France would intervene against Austria. They understood nothing. France was as conservative as Austria. In case of a local revolution, both nations could invade Piedmont as a "peace enforcing" operation.

Victor Emmanuel had few options. If he wanted to preserve the constitution, he had to act against political opposition and rioting. First, he gained the support of the Savoyard party, the most conservative in Parliament. Then he used the army to smash the riots and secure the state against internal disorders. This had two effects; France and Austria considered him a good, reliable, conservative king; and the ghost of intervention disappeared.

Militarily the war had been an unmitigated disaster. Piedmontese generals had proved terribly poor compared to their Austrian counterparts in the 1848 and 1849 campaigns. The narrow-minded cadets of 1815 made grave mistakes as generals. The battle at Verona had been lost because they did not to realize how strategically vital the city was to Radetzsky, and they showed incompetence at maneuvering the army in battle.

Victor Emmanuel was keenly aware of these problems. He had commanded a division during both campaigns. The victory of Goito on May 30 was due to his successful attack against the Austrian position. He fought well in the two-day battle of Custoza, and in the short campaign of 1849. He was not a great general, but he was clever and had good tactical sense. Although he wanted to shake up the General Staff, he could not. His generals were faithful and loyal, and he simply could not do that among the high command. Some of them were former Napoleonic sheep back in the king's fold—Bava, who commanded in Goito, was one— and that was a key reason not to cause disaffection among the senior officers. They could be as dangerous as the revolutionaries. Others belonged to families that had served the House of Savoy for many centuries: De Sonnaz, Della Rocca, La Marmora; and their families filled the highest ranks of the army, the navy, the diplomatic corps, and civil service. It was impossible to act without them, and it was better to leave them in their places.

In 1852, Camillo Benso, count of Cavour, was appointed premier. A former Engineering Corps officer, Cavour had visited France and Britain and was a strong supporter of liberalism. Once in office, he began a reform program. The army was reorganized, and new weapons were produced. In 1846, Piedmontese technician Ascanio Sobrero invented nytroglycerin. In the same year, artillery captain Giovanni Cavalli tested the first rifled cannon. It was a success, but the system needed improvements, delaying the adoption by the Piedmontese army until 1860. The army tested the model 1854 rifled musket, introduced in 1857, and changed its uniforms. Gradually the kingdom improved its armed forces. Further, railways were built throughout Piedmont and Liguria, connecting the sea to the Padana Plain. These changes came at a fortuitous moment, as the international situation offered the kingdom a peculiar opportunity.

The Crimean War

In 1854, Britain and France supported the Ottoman Empire in its war against Russia. Russia's strategic objective was to gain access to the Mediterranean.

A pillar of Britain's Mediterranean strategy was the securing of the route to India. If Russia achieved the liberty to move its Black Sea fleet into the Mediterranean, it would threaten Britain's position there. So, allied troops landed in the Crimea to neutralize the Russian fleet, at Sebastopol harbor. Allied casualties, however, were exceedingly high. Britain had difficulty replacing its losses quickly, as the distance from England was great and its army did not rely upon conscription. The military alliance between Britain and France bound them to maintain a certain quantity of troops in the war. As a consequence, in November 1854 the British foreign minister, Lord Clarendon, asked his ambassador in Turin if Piedmont would agree to send 10,000 to 15,000 men to the Crimea "at Great Britain's expense."[1] Piedmont agreed only if it were considered a full ally. This meant refusing British funding, in exchange for a loan. On January 10, 1855, Cavour signed a military convention with Britain and France. British loans amounted to 2 millions pounds, at 4 percent interest.

The Piedmontese Expeditionary Corps, commanded by General Alfonso La Marmora, was composed of 18,061 officers and included two and a half divisions, which included five infantry regiments, four *Bersaglieri* battalions, a cavalry regiment, three artillery groups, and an engineering battalion. The army landed in the Crimea on May 9, 1855. They occupied the town of Kamara, on the left bank of the Černaya river—the Black River—and took up position on the extreme wing of the allied line in front of Sebastopol.

Being far from the sea, they built with the allies a railway from Balaklava to Kamara, under the direction of Engineer Corps major Raffaele Cadorna. Horses were entrained, and it was one of the first military uses of a railway in a war. The heat more than the Russians became biggest obstacle for Piedmontese. Cholera, too, killed thousands of allied soldiers, and Piedmontese dead exceeded one thousand. Among them was General Alessandro La Marmora, brother of the commander in chief and founder of the *Bersaglieri*, who commanded a division.

Reinforcements reached the Crimea, replacing the casualties; and the total Piedmontese force employed by the end of the war totaled 24,082 men, including naval personnel. Losses due to combat were not as severe. The Piedmontese were involved in only one battle, on August 16, 1855, when 60,000 Russians sortied from Sebastapol against the French. The Piedmontese outpost, called Zig-Zag, stalled the Russian attack as its crooked line fortifications designed by Major Cadorna provided greater crossfire for the Italian soldiers. The 350 *Bersaglieri* and infantry in Zig-Zag resisted for an hour before withdrawing. The Russians then moved against the French, but the Piedmontese resistance had already warned them, and they pounded the Russians with a massive artillery barrage. Shortly thereafter, the entire Piedmontese expeditionary force attacked the Russian flank. By 8:00 a.m. the fighting was over. The Russians lost 2,273 dead and 1,742 missing in action. French casualties amounted to some 1,500 men, and Piedmontese losses totaled a mere 14 dead and 15 wounded, including General Roberto Gabrielli di Montevecchio, who died some two months later.

The Times war correspondent W. H. Russell wrote an account praising the Piedmontese action. It was the first Piedmontese victory since Goito, and a demonstration of the effectiveness of the new army. Having their baptism of fire, Piedmont could now be considered an ally in all aspects. After the conquest of Malakov Fort, Sebastopol surrendered. Russia agreed to negotiate and signed an armistice on September 8, 1855. A peace conference was called in Paris; and Louis Napoleon, now Emperor Napoleon III, and Lord Clarendon strongly supported Piedmont's seat at the table. Cavour fully participated, and this meant the kingdom was admitted to the restricted circle of major powers. It was the first step toward Italian unification.

Preparing a War

When in Paris, Cavour realized the extent to which Austria was diplomatically isolated. The Habsburg Empire remained neutral in the conflict. Both Russia and the Allies asked Francis Joseph to intervene. Helping Russia meant the destruction of the Ottoman Empire. This would create a political vacuum in the Balkans and provide the Russians with an opportunity to strengthen their cultural bonds with the Balkan Slavs. Austria could therefore not support Russia. But, unfortunately, it was impossible to join the Allies. In fact, the Austro-Russian frontier was in the large Hungarian, Polish, and Moravian plains. What could the imperial army do against a massive Russian attack?

Austria took the middle course. Francis Joseph, however, made a terrible mistake. He organized a large Observation Army and sent it to his eastern border, as close as possible to the theater of war. With the Allies in the Crimea, the Austrians were at Russia's back. Czar Nicolas I who expected Austrian aid as repayment for Russian military intervention against the Hungarian revolution in 1849, was forced to deploy another army on the Austrian side. This is why in 1856, Austria lost its previous good standing among the major powers. The Austrians were considered ungrateful traitors by Russia and unreliable by Britain and France. Austria's influence in Germany was going to be challenged by Prussia, which was looking for any possible opportunity to increase its position in Germany.

Cavour conversely had a much-improved diplomatic position. He demanded nothing. He simply made contacts and laid the groundwork for the future. He was confident that, without help, Piedmont could not defeat Austria. France now appeared a likely ally. He increased his direct contacts with Napoleon III and reached a compromise in July 1858 in Plombières. France would intervene in the case of Austrian aggression. In that case, after victory, Piedmont would gain Lombardy-Venetia, Parma, Modena, the papal portion of the Padana Plain, and the Adriatic coast, including Ancona. The remainder of central Italy would have to be given to the prince Napoleon Jerome, a cousin of the emperor, who would marry one of Victor Emmanuel's daughters. An Italian confederacy, including the Two Sicilies, would be established under the pope's presidency. For all of this, France would claim the duchy of Savoy and the county of Nice.

On the home front, Cavour gathered all the patriots in the Italian National Society. Daniel Manin, former ruler of the 1849 Venetian republic, was elected president and Garibaldi his vice president. The National Society's task was to achieve Italian unity, regardless of method. This meant that all the members accepted national unity and a kingdom under Victor Emmanuel. Mazzini rejected this, wanting a republic or nothing at all.

Cavour had simply to goad Austria into attacking Piedmont. Apart from speeches and indirect actions, Cavour's machinations centered on military conscription. As he told Count Cesare Giulini, he was looking for an agreement with the Lombard landowners. If they sent their peasants, who were liable for the 1859 Austrian conscription, to Piedmont, he said: "I'll enroll them in the Piedmontese regiments. . . . Austria will demand their extradition or their disarmament. . . . I'll refuse; then the Austrian army will invade Piedmont."[2] Annual Austrian conscription was conducted in the spring, that's why Cavour told British diplomat Odo Russel he was sure to force Austria to war in the second week of May 1859. It did not work very well with peasants, but it worked perfectly with the others: thousands of volunteers enrolled. Francis Joseph sent an ultimatum to Piedmont on April 19, 1859. Four days later the Piedmontese Parliament rejected it. "*Alea jacta est,*" Cavour said. "I come out from the session of the last Piedmontese Parliament; the next will be that of the Kingdom of Italy. We have made history." And then, as a good Italian, he added: "And now let's have our lunch."[3]

In Vienna, Francis Joseph worried that he had made a mistake. He visited his old teacher and political adviser, Prince Metternich. When he entered Metternich's house, the prince dispensed with etiquette for the first time in his life, and as soon as he saw the emperor, he shouted: "In heaven's name: No ultimatum to Piedmont."[4]

"It was sent yesterday,"[5] the emperor sadly replied. Austria's role in Italy was nearing its end.

The Second War of Independence of 1859

The Piedmontese army comprised 70,000 men and 120 guns.[6] Napoleon III brought to northern Italy an army of 108,000 men and 324 guns. Against the allied army stood Feldzeugmeister Franz Gyulai and an Austrian army of 160,000 men and 384 guns. Gyulai wanted to strike at the Piedmontese prior to the arrival of the French. The fastest invasion route was across Ticino and through the province of Vercelli, a flat land with extensive rice cultivation.

Cavour believed the Austrian invasion was imminent and ordered the flooding of the entire province, 175 square miles. The royal inspector of the canals was in charge of the work. His name was Carlo Noé—Noah—so, Cavour wrote him a letter saying: "Dear engineer Noè, your homonymous patriarch saved the Human race from the waters; please, save the Fatherland thanks to the waters."[7] The flooding stopped the Austrians after they reached Vercelli. Upon arriving, they discovered a large unexpected "lake" not on shown their maps.

At the same time, the French landed at Genoa and crossed the Alps. They found trains ready to move them to the front. This was the first time railroads played a basic and critical role in a war. On May 10, the concentration of allied armies was complete and Gyulai withdrew into Lombardy. Napoleon III and Victor Emmanuel pursued the Austrians along the same route Charles Albert had used ten years before. Austrian resistance at Montebello on May 20, was broken, at Palestro on May 30–31, and at Magenta on June 4.[8]

Gyulai retired to the east as the French and Piedmontese entered Milan on June 8. On that day a French corps engaged and defeated the Austrian rearguard at Melegnano, east of Milan.

At the same time, Garibaldi entered Lombardy. Victor Emmanuel had appointed him lieutenant-general, ordering him to attack the right wing of the Austrian army.[9] The king gave him complete autonomy of action. The generals opposed this, as they disliked this revolutionary. The king, however, confirmed the orders, and Garibaldi applied his Latin American warfare at the foot of the Alps. He had 3,000 men against Austrian general Urban's 40,000, but Garibaldi defeated him at Varese, and later at San Fermo. Then, on June 13, Garibaldi entered Brescia and Bergamo and forced the Austrians to retreat faster than anticipated.

Austria's situation was deteriorating rapidly. Piedmontese and French reinforcements arrived quickly via rail. The Austrians relied on the Lombardy-Venetia railway system, but it was not connected to Austria. The only line from Vienna to Italy reached Trieste. If one wanted to send troops to the Padana Plain, he had only two solutions: march across the Alps to Trente and south to Vicenza and

Verona, or send troops by rail to Trieste, then by sea from Trieste to Venice and by train from Venice west. As the French and Piedmontese fleets were in the Upper Adriatic, this trip was too dangerous. Austrian reinforcements therefore arrived slowly.

On June 18, Francis Joseph took personal command of the Austrian army in Lombardy. He had never commanded an army; his only previous experience was on the battlefield of Verona in 1848 as a spectator. Now he presumed to defeat the allied army. A few days later he received word that Prince Napoleon Jerome was coming north with a Tuscan-French corps. Tuscany, Modena, and Parma revolted against their Habsburg dynasties and were now gathering troops to march against the Austrians, whose intelligence, estimated the strength of the enemy corps at 60,000 men. Francis Joseph determined to attack it before they joined the 180,000 French and Piedmontese. He ordered his army across the Mincio.

On June 23, the French spotted Austrian troops on the hills along the right bank of the river. Napoleon assumed they were a rearguard. He could not imagine the Austrians to be so foolish to stand between the allied army and a major river such as the Mincio. He ordered the allies to advance the following morning. At dawn, 80,000 French marched on Solferino. They did not realize it was the center of the Austrian army, some 90,000 men. Some miles north, 60,000 Piedmontese were moving along the Milan-Venice railway, marching to the hill of San Martino, just south of Lake Garda. They did not know the entire Austrian VIII Corps, supported by two brigades from the V Corps, garrisoned it. On June 24, 1859, an unexpected battle occurred between 130,000 allies and 150,000 Austrians along an eight-mile front, from Solferino to San Martino hill.

The fight was terrible and bloody. Stormy weather disturbed operations. At sunset the Austrians were completely defeated. French casualties amounted to 12,700 men; the Austrians lost 23,300 and the Piedmontese 5,500. Thousands of wounded and dead covered the countryside. The Medical Corps was exhausted and overwhelmed by the work. All the field hospitals, churches, monasteries, villas, and houses were filled with wounded. Brescia, the nearest city, had no more room in its hospitals. Cemeteries were full and graves were dug everywhere, including along the railway. It was such a horrific sight that a Swiss observer, Henry Dunat, decided to do something to help the wounded and relieve their suffering. After his experience at Solferino, he established the Red Cross.

From the Villafranca Armistice to the League of Central Italy

After Solferino, Francis Joseph retreated to Verona. Allied troops advanced cautiously. Peschiera was besieged, while Garibaldi, whose forces increased to 12,000 men due to enthusiastic volunteers, approached the Trentino. On July 6 Napoleon offered an armistice to Francis Joseph, who readily agreed.

Despite the victory over the Austrians, the situation became rather difficult for the French emperor. In the early days of the war, Vienna had sought military assistance from Berlin, but Prussia demanded the supreme command of all German troops, including Austrians. This meant that Austria would have to give up its political influence in Germany, which the Habsburgs had jealously guarded for three centuries. Austria refused. But Austrian influence in northern Italy was waning with the retreat of the imperial army. Conversely, Napoleon feared Prussia. In fact, as soon as news of the first French-Piedmontese victories spread, the German states mobilized a 400,000-man army,[10] deployed on the right bank of the Rhine. Napoleon had only 180,000 men between Paris and the frontier. Domestic crises also emerged in the midst of the war. Napoleon's plans for Italy unraveled at the moment of victory.

Revolutionaries throughout the peninsula forced the Italian princes to flee. "Commissioners" then ruled these states in the name of Victor Emmanuel. No one, however, liked the idea of a Central Italian Kingdom under Prince Napoleon Jerome. The French public was asking why then had so many French lost their lives in Lombardy? And what about the pope? He had lost a remarkable portion of his states because of French intervention. A large part of the French public, including the empress Eugenie, questioned the logic of French involvement.

Under these circumstances both emperors came to an agreement. Piedmont would have Lombardy, but Austria could maintain Peschiera and Mantua, and the whole of Venetia. All the dethroned rulers could return to their thrones. Italy, however, had to be reorganized as a confederation, including Austria as the sovereign power of Venetia and Trentino. The pope would preside over the confederation as president. Victor Emmanuel realized when all was concluded that he had to be pragmatic. He could not continue the war against Austria without the French. He halfheartedly accepted the armistice.

Cavour resigned; but he quickly moved the National Society when the king's commissioners left Modena, Parma, Bologna, and Florence. They established local governments without monarchy. Tuscany, the duchies, and all the legations joined each other, forming a Central Italy League with an army of 60,000 men. They rejected the Austro-French treaty. This forced Austria and France to either accept the new situation or get involved in a new war against the League. London, however, stepped in and proposed a compromise. British policy did not appreciate the increasing French power in Italy, that is to say, in the middle of Mediterranean and linked to India through the Suez Isthmus. Britain suggested that France consent to the union of the Central Italy League in Piedmont in exchange for Savoy and the county of Nice. Napoleon III accepted, and on January 16, 1860, Cavour was reappointed premier. On March 11 and 12, after a plebiscite, a new state was born. It was clear that the next step was south toward Naples and Sicily.

CHAPTER **17**

Garibaldi in Sicily

From Sicily to Naples

On April 4, 1860, rioting broke out in Palermo. The Neapolitan police swiftly crushed it. Some revolutionaries, however, escaped to the mountains around Palermo. Sicilian liberals exiled to Piedmont realized that their plans had no prospects if it was left to the monarchy to alter the political institutions. Francesco Crispi, one of the revolutionaries, urged Garibaldi to intervene. The Republican general called to arms "the generous," that is to say, all the willing patriots. They concentrated in Quarto, near Genoa. On May 5, 1860, Garibaldi left Liguria with 1,089 men on two steamboats, the *Piemonte* and the *Lombardo*.

News of his trip soon arrived in Naples. The Bourbon fleet was dispatched but unable to locate Garibaldi. On May 11, in the early afternoon, the Garibaldini landed in Marsala, on the western coast of Sicily. The closest Bourbon man-of-war was ten miles away. Garibaldi and his "thousand" had only three cannon, some old rifles, and a few rounds. On May 15 they had their first victory, over 1,800 Sicilian troops and two guns commanded by Major Sforza at Calatafimi. They then marched on Palermo. Garibaldi attacked the city on May 27. After a three-day fight, the Bourbon garrison asked for a truce. Garibaldi agreed just in time to prevent his rearguard from being attacked by Major Beneventano del Bosco's column.

The new king of Naples, Francis II, had ordered the garrison and the fleet to shell the city. Luckily, he feared an interposition by U.S., French, and British vessels in Palermo harbor. So, no concrete orders for subsequent action came from Naples and, on June 7, the Bourbonian commander, General Lanza, evacuated the city. This was the signal for a general insurrection in southern and eastern Sicily. Neapolitan troops concentrated around Milazzo and Messina. After receiving reinforcements from northern Italy, Garibaldi attacked and seized Milazzo with 4,500 men on July 20. A week later the citadel capitulated. Then, Garibaldi's general Medici blockaded Messina, preparing the way for Garibaldi to land in Calabria.

Sliding between the Bourbon ships patrolling the Straits of Messina, Garibaldi's boats transported the army to the Calabrian shore. The Bourbons collapsed so quickly after the landing that there was little fighting en route to Naples. The Neapolitan generals surrendered, along with their 18,000 men, and Garibaldi's march continued unmolested.

The question about why the sudden collapse of Bourbon authority has been examined by historians. Some proposed the subtle and secret activity of Masonry. Some believe the Neapolitan generals and admirals were corrupted by the Piedmontese government. There is insufficient evidence to definitively support one or the other. It is highly probable that the senior Neapolitan officers acted in this manner because of the king's indecision. When they realized that Francis II was not strong enough to save his crown, they simply thought of themselves. The kingdom was at an end, and a new king was on the horizon; so why resist against the new state instead of looking to save their positions? This may explain why the Neapolitan army did not fight Garibaldi before Naples, but fought with determination in the following months, when only the true Bourbon supporters remained.

On September 6, King Francis II retired from Naples to Capua and Caserta with his remaining troops. He ordered his navy to sail to Gaeta, but only one ship obeyed. The other Neapolitan officers and crews secretly agreed with Admiral Persano's Piedmontese ships into Naples harbor, prior to Garibaldi's arrival—because Piedmont was formally neutral—and as soon as Garibaldi entered the city two days later, they hoisted the Piedmontese tricolor.

Garibaldi arrived in Naples by train with six companions and was received with great fanfare. The Garibaldini—now 20,000 men of the Southern Army—marched to the left bank of the Volturno River. The Bourbon army stood on the opposite bank with 25,000 men, preparing to recapture Naples.

Francis II still commanded 40,000 loyal men and looked for immediate assistance. This was not too difficult as Garibaldi, in a speech in Naples, announced his intentions to march on Rome, sweeping the French garrison out. This created a significant problem for Cavour. The French would intervene in such an event, and indeed, Austria could do the same. Franco-Austrian intervention would mean the end of the Italian Risorgimento. Cavour knew it and decided to prevent Garibaldi from fulfilling his pledge. As Cavour feared France more than he did Austria, he warned Napoleon III about a possible Mazzini initiative against the pope—Mazzini was in Naples—and told the French emperor that Piedmontese involvement was the best way to save the Papal States from the Republican menace.

Napoleon was not stupid and did not believe this story, but an extended and friendly Italian state would be better than nothing. Moreover, he was a former *carbonaro* who had spent his youth in Italy, and surely this played a role in his decision. He grumbled to the Piedmontese ambassador, *"Faites, mais faites vite!"* (*"Do, but do quickly!"*), and so the Piedmontese army intervened.

Castelfidardo, the Volturno, and the Siege of Gaeta

To reach Garibaldi, Piedmontese troops had to cross the Papal States, but Cavour needed a pretext. He demanded that the papal secretary of state, Cardinal Antonelli, disarm foreign units in papal service. On September 11, Rome responded in the negative, and Turin ordered the troops to move. Two corps, IV and V, crossed the border. As they were not at war strength, they consisted only of 30,000 men. French general Lamoricière commanded 20,000 papal soldiers, divided into three columns.

The Piedmontese acted quickly. V Corps crossed the Tuscan-Umbrian border and seized Perugia on September 14. It was defended by Swiss general Schmidt with 1,800 men. Then the corps marched to the Adriatic to join IV Corps. IV Army Corps, commanded by General Cialdini, marched down the Adriatic coast and on September 13 he defeated Swiss general De Courten's column. Five days later his 4,800 men of the vanguard beat papal troops near Castelfidardo. Of 6,800 papal soldiers, 88 died, 3,000 retreated to Loreto, 3,600 were captured, and the few remaining escaped to Ancona together with Lamoricière. Both Piedmontese corps met at Ancona. The city was besieged by land and sea and, after terrible shelling, the 350 officers and 7,000 men of the garrison surrendered on September 29.

On October 1, not far from Naples, the Garibaldini achieved their last victory. At dawn the Bourbon army attacked. Lamoricière coordinated the offensive, foreseeing a large encircling maneuver being made against the Garibaldini. Garibaldi had two advantages: He could move his troops faster than the enemy by using interior lines of operations, and he could receive reinforcements due to the railway connecting Naples to Caserta. The Bourbon generals employed merely 25,000 men, instead of the 40,000 they had at their disposal, and thereby lost their superiority in numbers. Garibaldi put 20,000 men in the field and gained the victory.

The failure of the Bourbon offensive meant the end of Neapolitan independence. The Piedmontese army was marching south. Victor Emmanuel had entered Abruzzo and, after a skirmish at Macerone, he met Garibaldi in Teano on October 26. Soon after this meeting, the regular army took over operations. Capua was besieged by V Corps and capitulated on November 2, while IV Corps marched to the Tyrrhenian coast. After crossing the Garigliano river on November 3, the 1st Infantry Division attacked and routed 20,000 soldiers at Mola di Gaeta, later known as Formia. A portion of them entered the southern Papal States and surrendered to the French troops watching the border. The others remained in Gaeta with Francis II, his court, and the foreign ambassadors.

Cialdini blockaded the city with 16,000 men, and Admiral Persano did the same by sea. The city, garrisoned by 12,000 men, was methodically shelled, day after day, by Piedmontese artillery, now using for the first time the Cavalli rifled cannons. On February 12, 1861, Francis II signed the capitulation and sailed to the papal port of Civitavecchia on a French ship. While Bourbon garrisons in Civitella del Tronto and Messina still resisted, the Parliament met at Turin on February 18, as the Parliament of the Kingdom of Italy. They proclaimed Victor Emmanuel II king of Italy "by the Grace of God and by the Will of the Nation."

"Brigands"

As all central and southern Italian states, the kingdom of Naples had brigands. Its poor roads, rough geography, steep mountains, and large and wild woods rendered brigands hard to find. After the defeat of the Bourbons, many soldiers joined the brigands and began a guerrilla war. The first skirmishes occurred in late 1860 and quickly increased in quality and quantity. It was at the same time that the new Kingdom of Italy faced social, political, and military problems. The Neapolitans perceived the Garibaldini as foreigners from other parts of Italy. It was analogous to the experience their grandparents had seen in the early days of that century. The majority of the southern population was illiterate and had never seen Garibaldini. In fact, because of their rapid advance, Garibaldi's troops had been seen in only a few towns and cities, mostly on the Tyrrhenian coast. People in the interior only received rumors about the coming soldiers of the "honest man–king."

As an Italian officer later remarked, this nickname created a terrible misunderstanding.[1] In fact, the worst social enemy of the southern commoners was not the aristocracy—usually referred to as "the lords," to which the "gentlemen" belonged—it was the middle class. This rural bourgeoisie, mostly composed of landowners, merchants, attorneys, physicians, land agents, low-ranking police officers, and judges, was normally referred to as the *galantuomini*—the "honest men"—just as was Victor Emmanuel's popular nickname. The officer wrote that the common people, who regarded the *galantuomini* as its worst enemies, simply thought of King Galantuomo as sovereign of the whole "honest men" class. As a consequence, they believed he would be the worst king. The countryside revolted, fearing a future of oppression and deeper poverty under the unlimited will and power of the *galantuomini* and their king.

As in all ancien régime societies, in the Two Sicilies the king was the only ally of the poor in the face of the aristocracy and bourgeoisie. Moreover, the common people had seen, or at least heard about, what happened in the past. In 1798 some of the lords and the most of the honest men revolted against the king, joining the French. Blood and violence spread, and less than a year later the dynasty returned. It happened once more in 1806. That time the dynasty was restored in 1815. And what about 1820–21, when the king disbanded the honest men at the head of the Austrian army? After every invasion or revolution occurred, the dynasty returned. If it had happened three times in the previous sixty years, why not this time, too? Obviously, common brigands profited from the situation, mixing their actions with those of the common people, killing and stealing.

Many brigands were supported by the former king, now exiled in Rome. He sent them money and recruited volunteers to increase their strength.

Victor Emmanuel's army was involved in real counterinsurgency operations. Light columns, mostly composed of cavalry, Royal Carabineers and *Bersaglieri*, supported by the National Guard, fought throughout the south. Fighting was harsh and bloody. Ambushes, attacks, and raids followed by retaliations were immediate and merciless. Some 90,000 men of the Royal Army, including the Royal Carabineers, were employed on campaign during those four years. Military courts worked hard. Summary executions were commonplace. Suspicion was enough to charge anyone with being a brigand.

The worst period of violence ran from late 1860 until early 1864. Once Royal Carabineers were posted in every town and village and made regular patrols, brigand strength gradually declined. The peasants and commoners soon realized they were supporting thieves and killers. The more they had contact with the new administration, the more they accepted the new kingdom.

The next step consisted of stopping popular support to the brigands. Peasants feared guilt by association and accusations of conspiracy. The penalties were harsh. The brigands were often worse, but troops eventually provided security; and, anyway their response was quick, effective, and decisive. The result was, in the early months of 1864, peasants and commoners began acting against the brigands. By early 1865 military actions decreased, allowing for normal policing by the Royal Carabineers. Only in 1870 did brigandage disappear from southern Italy. According to contemporary military and civil records, casualties on both sides are estimated at more than 20,000 men. Only in Sicily did local brigands remain, called *malandrini*—scoundrels—until the end of the last quarter of the century.

CHAPTER 18

The New State

Army and Navy in 1861

The new kingdom had to integrate and reorganize its entire military institution to accommodate its expanded role. The *Regia Marina Italiana*—the Royal Italian Navy—was now the third largest in the world after the British and French. It had 106 vessels and steamboats from the Piedmontese, Tuscan, and Neapolitan fleets; but after a few months, it was reduced to 97—112,726 metric tons and 1,166 guns—eliminating the oldest ships. The personnel, mostly belonging to *Corpo Reale Equipaggi*—the Crews Royal Corps—had some 10,000 men. Reorganizing the navy was quite simple. Ranks, uniforms, and discipline were modeled on the Piedmontese navy, but, Neapolitan operational rules were better, and were fully adopted.

It was not so easy for the army. Land forces had increased in size over the past months. Originally the Piedmontese army had ten infantry brigades, but absorbed five from Lombardy, four more from Tuscany, and seven from the Emilian duchies and legations. In 1861 the army absorbed a Garibaldini brigade and five Neapolitan brigades, and established five more completely new brigades. This gave the army 72 infantry regiments and 42 *Bersaglieri* battalions. Each regiment was composed of four battalions, of four companies. The cavalry had 19 regiments.

In 1862 the Italian Army—as it was officially called—was divided into six corps and twenty divisions. Each division had two line infantry or grenadier brigades, two *Bersaglieri* battalions, a cavalry regiment, artillery, an Engineer Corps unit, and supply and medical services.

Incorporating non-Piedmontese personnel was not easy. Former Garibaldini and Neapolitan personnel were carefully selected. Those who were accepted lost one rank, just as had happened to former Napoleonic soldiers in Piedmont fifty years earlier. Much of this applied to officers and noncommissioned officers, because Neapolitan privates generally refused to serve. They argued that they could not serve Victor Emmanuel because King Francis had not released them from their oath. Infantry and cavalry officer schools were established in Modena, in the ducal palace, while artillery and engineering schools remained in Turin. The national flag changed a little, as the royal crown was put over Savoy's coat of arms, in the center of the flag.[1] The army remained an enlarged version of the Piedmontese army for the moment.

From Turin to Florence

In 1861, soon after the proclamation establishing the Kingdom of Italy, Cavour died. Tuscan baron Ricasoli was appointed prime minister. In March 1862 he resigned and, since then, until 1996, practically no Italian government has lasted as long as constitutionally permitted. An intrusive crown, parliamentary fights between government and opposition, and wild press campaigns made Italian political life unstable. The ruling coalition was the so-called Right. It included conservatives, liberals, and moderates. The opposition composed the Left, including Republicans, Garibaldini, Nationalists, and so on. No Catholic party existed. In fact, in the 1850s, Cavour used legislation to deprive the Church of its monopoly on public instruction as well as its properties. His policy was clearly opposed to the Church's temporal power. The pope excommunicated him and prohibited Catholics from playing an active role in politics.[2] This caused a political vacuum, and in any case a lot of people simply did not vote. So, the Parliament represented a reduced portion of the electorate. Moreover, as it was, the right to vote depended on the census, and it would have been necessary to wait until the twentieth century for universal male suffrage.

Urbano Rattazzi served as prime minister after Cavour's death. In 1862, Garibaldi attempt once again to take Rome. He landed in Sicily, gathered 3,000 men, and crossed to Calabria. It is highly probable that this was akin to his actions in 1860, that is to say, he was acting according to an official government plan, "unofficially." French opposition, however, was swift; and Rattazzi needed to stop Garibaldi. *Bersaglieri* colonel Pallavicini engaged him at Aspromonte, in Calabria, on August 29. It was an unnecessary skirmish. The army lost five men killed and 23 wounded; the Garibaldini seven and 18 respectively, including Garibaldi.

Garibaldi was arrested for a short time and released. He spent much of his time thereafter in Caprera, except for a trip to London in 1864. Garibaldi's march resulted in Rattazzi's resignation because the army had shot the national hero. Domenico Farini replaced him, but after only three months he lost his mind. In the end, Marco Minghetti became the new premier. He had two central tasks: first and most important was Rome, the second was Venice. Both cities had enormous symbolic value, and both were still in foreign hands. Rome had been garrisoned by the French since 1849, and any move against the pope implied immediate French intervention. In September 1864, Minghetti promised Napoleon III that he would guarantee the independence of Rome in exchange for the withdrawal of French troops. Napoleon asked something more, and Minghetti showed his own goodwill by moving the capital from Turin to Florence. As Cavour had stated previously that the next capital should be Rome, this seemed the best way to resolve the situation with the French. After the French departure from Rome, the government had only to wait for an opportunity to seize the city. And Venice? Events in Germany would provide the solution to that problem

From the Third War of Independence to Rome: 1866–1870

In 1866, Prusso-Austrian competition for supremacy in Germany reached its zenith. Prussian chancellor Otto von Bismarck forced Austria to declare war on Prussia over disagreements concerning the former Danish duchies of Schleswig and Holstein. In this case, in Bismarck's opinion and that of the Prussian General Staff, it was better to have Italy as an ally, because it prevented Austria from concentrating its entire army against Prussia. The Italian Army had four of its six corps available, which meant 280,000 men, 36,000 horses, and 456 guns. Its Royal Navy had 103 men of war—186,869 metric tons and 1,398 guns—including seven modern battleships.[3] Berlin asked Florence for an alliance.

According to the pact, Italy would gain Venetia. Vienna anticipated the Italo-Prussian alliance and offered Venetia to Italy in exchange for its neutrality. The government foolishly refused. This was a great mistake: Why go to war to gain that which could be obtained by peace? The second mistake was the commanding general of the campaign. It was not Victor Emmanuel. He was a good division general, but no more. He knew it and looked for a capable chief of staff. Unfortunately, no general wanted the job with so intrusive a king as Victor Emmanuel. At last, Alfonso La Marmora accepted; but General Enrico Cialdini did not like the idea of serving under him. The king resolved this jealousy by dividing the Italian Army into two armies. La Marmora invaded Venetia from Lombardy with twelve infantry divisions and a cavalry division composing three corps—I, II, and III—grouped in the "Mincio army"; Cialdini with his "Po army," which on the eve of the war was composed of only one corps, marched from Emilia, across the Po, and into Venetia. Garibaldi received the rank of lieutenant-general, commanding the volunteers. The king recommended that he land in Dalmatia and march into Hungary, causing a revolt, but the generals rejected this plan; and Garibaldi crossed the Alps into the Trentino and marched on Trente.

On June 23, 1866, the Italian Army invaded Venetia. Archduke Albert commanded an Austrian army of only 80,000 men. He concentrated them in the Quadrilateral, as Radetzsky had done in 1848, anticipating La Marmora's eastward advance to join Cialdini coming from south. He was surprised when reconnaissance told him La Marmora was marching northeast, expanding his front. The archduke took advantage of this and attacked La Marmora on June 24, 1866. This encounter-battle was fought on an extended front around Custoza. La Marmora blundered. Ignoring the king's advice, and despite a superiority in cavalry, he did not conduct reconnaissance or establish outposts. Then, during the battle he failed to establish a central headquarters. Despite the construction of a telegraph line—the Engineering Corps had built a 201-mile transmission net, with 1,000 stations transmitting 12,000 telegrams during the entire month and a half 1866 campaign—it was quite difficult to locate the chief of staff. After an entire day of hard fighting, La Marmora retreated in good order. It had been an indecisive engagement, but news of the battle and the ensuing propaganda spread. The press did its best to portray the Battle of Custoza as a national tragedy. It was not. The battle was a draw, and the campaign was not yet over.

Garibaldi in the same period attacked and defeated Austrian forces six times in eighteen days. After his victory in Bezzecca on July 21, he practically controlled the region. He advanced on Trente as the Austrians dismantled their positions. By that time Italian mobilization had been completed. Cialdini received a portion of La Marmora's troops who placed Peschiera under siege with II and III corps and had the task of occupying Venetia in the rear of Cialdini's advancing troops. Cialdini marched north with 150,000 men composing the five corps: I, IV, V, VI, and VIII. The Austrians withdrew quickly to avoid being trapped. They were then engaged and defeated at Versa, on the right bank of the Isonzo, on July 26.

During the previous week the government had ordered the fleet into action. Admiral Persano moved to Lissa, a little island in a good strategic position. The Italian fleet, with 21 men-of-war, shelled the island at 11:00 a.m. on July 20. The Austrian navy, 26 men-of-war, sortied from Pola and attacked the Italians. It sank two vessels and after only forty minutes returned to port. Admiral Persano did not pursue, but simply declared he was maintaining control of the waters. As with Custoza, this minor engagement did not reduce Italian military power, but politics, the press, and Parliament portrayed it as another national tragedy.

Operations continued in Venetia when Prussia and Austria signed an armistice shortly after Prussia's victory at Sadowa-Koniggratz. Italy had no choice but accept it, or face Austria alone. Garibaldi had almost reached Trente when he received orders to stop. He simply replied: "I obey."[4] The war was over, and Venetia was annexed to the kingdom. Rome, however, remained separate and under papal rule. Garibaldi could not resist and in 1867, he attempted to seize Rome once more. He raised 6,000 volunteers for the enterprise. The French deployed troops to support the papal troops who, on November 3, 1867, defeated the Garibaldini in Mentana. The Italian government probably had a secret agreement with Garibaldi, who later significantly wrote: "I take upon myself . . . most of the responsibility."[5] The papal government received a new French garrison in Rome and proudly displayed Garibaldini weapons and uniforms taken on the battlefield. Above these trophies was written *Non praevalebunt*—"they will not prevail." Three years later they prevailed.

France declared war on Prussia in 1870, and the French garrison was withdrawn from Rome. This was the opportunity the Italian government had been waiting for. Italian troops crossed the border—after 1861 the Papal States were reduced to a region a little smaller than what is now Lazio—and marched to Rome. Garibaldi was not with them. He was en route to France with volunteers, wanting to save the new Third Republic against the Germans. He reached France in November and fought in the Vosges at the head of 20,000 volunteers. He was the only general to defeat the Germans in that campaign. In Dijon, on December 1, 1870, he applied his Latin American tactics and repelled German attacks. On January 21, 1871, he fought Prussian general von Kettler's troops. After three days of fighting, the Germans were repulsed again. They lost one of their colors, the only one lost by the Prussians in that war.

In the meantime, the pope refused to leave Rome to the king. Thus, on September 20, 1870, General Raffaele Cadorna attacked the city's defenses. A breach was opened on the left side of Porta Pia, the monumental gate by Michelangelo on the Nomentana route, the same one the Garibaldini had used three years earlier. Then, Italian troops entered the city. The papal garrison, including also Belgian, Irish, French, and Canadian volunteers, surrendered upon the pope's order, and the kingdom finally found its capital. The Italian Army had forced the Roman Catholic Church to abandon the temporal, by seizing it, and focus instead on the spiritual.

In His Majesty's Service

In 1861 the new kingdom had many problems. Victor Emmanuel ruled 27 million subjects, and most were illiterate. Public debt amounted to 2,450 million liras of that time.[6] It absorbed 30 percent of the annual budget. The armed forces required 25 percent, and the remaining 45 percent was used for everything else. Piedmontese standards were extended to the rest of Italy. Piedmontese laws superseded other legal systems, and the metric system replaced miles and feet, barrels and ounces. The north had most of the 973 miles of rail in the kingdom, practically all the factories, most of the schools, and a good road network. The south was largely agricultural. No real road system, little rail and industry. In fact, the Bourbon army had moved until 1861 from the west coast to the east coast by sea instead of land. Ports, however, were quite good but needed to be modernized.

Politicians and parliamentary debates were far removed from the situation surrounding the conditions of the new state. Parliament had two chambers. Senators were appointed by the king and served for life. Deputies were elected and came from the provinces. The largest city in the kingdom—Naples—had merely a half million inhabitants, and universities existed in several former capitals a few cities. So, "province" meant roughly 10,000 inhabitants per town, often less, with few educational institutions past high school. Many deputies lacked an appreciation of culture, knowledge of world affairs, and had little concept of European politics. A few of them spoke another language, normally French. Moreover, governments and political majorities were unstable. So, deputies focused their attention on their electoral colleges, to secure their own reelection. They had no time to focus on European affairs. That's why they responded to every international crisis as if it were a surprise; and many of them did not really understand the complexities of European affairs. Their solutions therefore were generally not appropriate. This is largely the reason for Italy's ineffective foreign policy, especially after 1876, when the so-called Historical Left, a strong nationalist coalition composed of Garibaldini and Republicans, took power.

Many Leftist nationalists simply did not understand that colonial empires originated with the expansion of traditional trading points and served as providers of raw materials and markets for industrial goods. They considered colonies only as symbols of national prestige. Accordingly, they believed that Italy, a great power, had to possess colonies, no matter if Portugal and Denmark—who had colonies—were not considered great powers while Austria and Russia, who had no colonies, were.

The deputies often came from families whose ancestors had been revolutionaries for generations, going back to the French Revolution and Napoleonic era. In fact, when the kingdom was established, southern and northern upper and middle classes had similar culture and language. But the lower classes in these areas had practically nothing in common except religion. Northern and southern dialects were quite different and more like different languages than dialects. A northern peasant in a Sicilian or a Calabrian town would be unable to fully understand the language. Indeed, the lower classes were very poor and had to satisfy their immediate needs; and this made it extremely difficult to educate them, because they all needed to work for food and to survive.

Lower classes needed just a few clear and simple symbols to allow them to develop a national consciousness. For the middle class, it was revolutionary liberal nationalism. The most clear and concrete symbols for the peasantry were the king, the flag, and the army. The king was often abstract. He was a sort of fabulous and distant figure. The flag and the army were something more tangible. When in the army, young Italian men saw everywhere the same uniforms, the same discipline, the same rules, the same tricolor flag. Italy was represented by the flag. It was honored by the entire regiment and by the army, and this gave it importance.

Only a few men could really see the king during their life, but all the soldiers could see the portrait of the king: Victor Emmanuel II until his death in 1878, and his eldest son Humbert I until 1900. The king wore the blue uniform as did the army. He became a concretely recognizable feature; an officer like all the officers of the regiment; a military man wearing the military uniform with the same little stars—symbol of the Italian military—on the collar.[7] The illiterate recruit could easily associate the king as soldier, too. Moreover, the flag had the royal coat of arms in its central band. As a result of this mixture of flag, coat of arms, king, and uniform, the worker, the peasant, the fisherman, and the shepherd found a mutual reference in the army. Through these references they accepted the concept of a nation.

The young conscript served four, later three, years, and in the early twentieth century, two years. He served in different regions and used railroads, often for the first time in his life. He saw new and unexpected places, large and ancient cities, the sea, the Alps, rivers and wonderful lakes, or wild mountains and dry plains in the south. All of these places were Italy, his country. Furthermore, the army gave him a bed, clothes, food three times per day, a little money, and free time each day; often this was more than he normally had at home. At last the army established compulsory education for recruits and taught reading and writing. In fact, soon after the establishment of general conscription, figures show a significant increase in literacy among the young male population.[8] So, the army became the symbolic embodiment of the country, cementing unity, the guardian and soul of the national spirit and—as the last phrase of the military oath said—"of the King's and Fatherland's inseparable Good."

CHAPTER 19

The Kingdom, Royal Policy, and the Colonies, from Rome to Peking: 1871–1900

The Royal Army in Italy and the Royal Navy Abroad

Soon after the conquest of Rome, Italy reorganized its army. General Cesare Ricotti-Magnani looked to the structure of the recently established and unified German army as an example. The Italian Army—now the *Regio Esercito*, the Royal Army—was rebuilt on an active army, or *Esercito di Campagna*, Campaign Army; a provincial, later mobile, militia, or *Milizia Mobile*; and a territorial militia, the *Milizia Territoriale*, which respectively formed the second and third line armies. All soldiers were dressed with the standard blue uniform, and different corps were distinguished only by their caps and colored collar patches.

After ten years of tests, according to the law issued on March 22, 1877, the Campaign Army had ten (twelve after July 8, 1883) corps, formed from twenty-four divisions. Each division was comprised of two infantry brigades, a cavalry regiment, *Bersaglieri*, artillery, an Engineering Corps unit, and services. Each infantry regiment in peacetime consisted of 61 officers and 1,280 men (to be doubled in war), divided into three battalions on four companies. Infantry had a grenadier brigade, 47 line brigades, 12 *Bersaglieri* regiments, and, after October 15, 1872, Alpine troops, which in 1883 consisted of six regiments. Artillery had ten regiments and, after 1877, a mountain artillery regiment. The Engineer Corps consisted of different specialized regiments: telegraphers, radiotelegraphers, pontooneers, miners, railwaymen, lagoonnaires (to be used only in marshes, deltas, and lagoons, as a sort of marines), and aerostatic, that is to say, the units using balloons, established in 1885.

Including Carabineers and services, the Royal Army had approximately 250,000 men in its peacetime complement. The Mobile Militia was organized into companies. The line infantry had 960 companies, the *Bersaglieri* 60, Engineers Corps sappers 10, and artillery 60. Territorial Militia had companies, too: line infantry 1,440, and fortress artillery had 100. This organization did not change until 1923.

The country—and the army, too—had a desperate need to expand track. At the end of 1861 the kingdom had 1,590 miles of line. Five years later railroads covered 3,100 miles and in 1876, 4,834 miles. It was not a great net, especially considering that Germany in the same year had 17,943 miles, France 13,700, and Austria-Hungary 10,759. Italy now ranked fourth in western and central Continental Europe, with Sweden fifth at 2,330 miles.

The real obstacle to surpass was not the poverty of the nation or its lack of money; it was its lack of industry. Italians possessed good technical know-how as inventors and technicians: the 7.96-mile-long Moncenisio railway tunnel inaugurated in September 1871 was a good demonstration of it. Unfortunately, they had a limited and weak industrial base and no raw materials. Native iron, copper, lead, and tin were all consumed during the Etruscan and Roman periods. Coal was far from the higher British quality. Moreover, no heavy industry existed. In fact, the first Italian battleships had been built in the United States, France, and the United Kingdom.

Now, in December 1873, the minister of the navy, Admiral Simon Pacoret de Saint Bon, a native of Savoy, warned the Parliament that the fleet—mostly wooden—was not too old, but the newly invented torpedo boat had introduced a revolution. A torpedo boat needed only half a million liras to be built and could easily sink a bigger and more expensive cruiser or battleship. So, de Saint Bon told the deputies, it was necessary to build a new fleet of iron ships. The 1873 navy budget had a little more than 33 million liras allocated to it. De Saint Bon proposed an extraordinary 12 million annual expenditure for the next four years. But, he warned: "If we would like to expend much more than this 12 million, we would not be able unless expending it abroad. The force of our national industry, the production capability of our arsenals and of the metallurgical factories existing in the country is not so wide to allow us to expend more than 12 million per year. I think, by the way, that if we shall not use great energy, we shall not be able to expend them."[1]

He was right. The lack of heavy industries was the first problem to solve. It was addressed by his successor, the next minister of the navy, Benedetto Brin, general of the Naval Engineer Corps.[2] Brin was a strong supporter of national heavy industry, and his support pushed the government toward protectionism. Italy needed weapons and ships to remain independent and a world power. Weapons and ships could only be produced by heavy industry. No country could leave its liberty in the hands of a foreign state or a foreign company. What if outside support and products were unavailable at the beginning or in the middle of a war? Italy needed its own heavy metallurgical industrial system, too, and, if money was lacking, the government could provide it; and, if the price of foreign products was lower, the government could protect Italian production by enforcing import duties. If coal was in short supply, well, waterpower and, later, electricity could be an answer.

Brin concentrated much of his energy into putting heavy metallurgical factories in the town of Terni. It was in Umbria, far from the sea, so no enemy landing or shelling could reach it. It had on one side the Marmore Falls, one of the highest waterfalls in Europe, whose energy could easily be exploited in place of coal. The result was quite good. In a few years, heavy industry was born. As a result the railway system increased in size, and at the end of the following thirty years, in 1905, it covered 6,978 miles and was served by 2,768 steam and electric locomotives. Subsequently, in the third quarter of the nineteenth century, the *Regia Marina* ranked third in the world for quantity and quality after the British and French navies.

With the development of domestic heavy industry, Brin was free to design a new type of battleship. The *Duilio* was a 12,265-metric-ton battleship whose fifteen-knot speed was provided by its 7,710 horsepower engines. It had four 17.7-inch Armstrong cannons and a lot of smaller guns. Moreover, it was heavily protected by 21.66 inches of armor made after a special Brin design. The best armor at that time was the "Sandwich system," used for the HMS *Inflexible*. It consisted of a wooden plate carrying 13.7 inches of iron plate and another wooden plate carrying another iron plate like the first. When tested at the Spezia Royal Arsenal, the sandwich armor was successfully punctured by 3.2-inch cannons, while the "Brin's 55 centimeters," as the new Italian-designed armor was called, resisted the 17.7-inch Armstrong guns, the most powerful in the world. Launched in 1876, the *Regia Nave*—Royal Ship—*Duilio* and its twin *Dandolo* came into service in 1880. They were considered the most powerful ships of their times.

Despite the development of a national navy and heavy industry, protectionism had two unfortunate effects. Italian companies considered government support as a matter of fact and expected to have it in the future. When they experienced economic difficulty in the following years, they cried for the government's help and lobbied the deputies to obtain what they desired. This allowed Italian companies to not worry about their future. They did not improve their production systems, preferring short-term gains instead of long-term investment and higher gains. This problem exploded for the first time in the early 1880s in relation to the condition of the merchant fleet, but it emerged again prior to the Second World War and a third time in the early twenty-first century, when unsolved industrial problems caused economic difficulties combined with those due to the new European common currency.

Second problem emerged after the Left took control of Parliament in March 1876. It developed its strong liberal-nationalist policy by supporting Brin's plans. Duties on imports were enforced on industrial products, largely from Britain and France. Britain did not react, but France answered by imposing import duties on Italian products. Being a nonindustrialized country, Italy exported mostly agricultural goods, mainly produced in the south. Duties reduced their market and ruined the southern Italian economy. The lack of market caused a lack of work, whose immediate effect was emigration. Hundreds of thousands of southern Italians left Italy, looking for work and a new life in a new country. America was the most attractive destination, but this time Italian emigrants were not the educated people coming from northern and central Italy as in 1821 and 1831. They were a massive movement of illiterates from poor little southern villages. It was not the best of Italy, and this poor, desperate, and ignorant people was what the Americans, the Germans, and the French saw coming to their countries, and what they saw became "the Italians" by definition.

Despite massive emigration and economic problems, from a military perspective Italy seemed to be growing stronger. This is one reason why in 1882, German chancellor Bismarck accepted Italy into the German-Austrian Dual Alliance. Bismarck wanted to keep France isolated after the Franco-Prussian War. His opinion about Italian military effectiveness did not matter. For what it was worth, it was suficient. In fact, as Bismarck said, he needed only "an Italian drummer on the Alps to attract a whole French Army Corps from the Rhine." Moreover, the *Regia Marina* was a real threat to the French Mediterranean fleet and empire. Brin had, in fact, optimized scarce Italian resources to have first-class battleships equivalent to the French. The 1866 Italian-Prussian alliance was still active in a certain sense. Prussia had supported Italian interests in Rome during the 1870 papal-Italian crisis. Italy had done the same for Prussia and Germany in some South American riots, and it had also officially ignored—that is to say, refused—appeals to support France in 1870.

Italy was isolated and had feared a French intervention since 1870 under the pretext of helping the pope. Furthermore, it was known in Rome that the French General Staff was studying the feasibility of an invasion of Italy and—as admiral de Sain Bon had remarked in 1873—it was impossible to defend the long Tyrrhenian coast. By 1882 the unnamed enemy was France, as Austria had ceased to be a threat.

Italy initially looked to Britain rather than Germany. There had been a long and positive historical relationship between Britain and the House of Savoy. The second half of nineteenth century, however, was a period of "golden isolation," and Britain simply did not care very much for alliances. Italy therefore accepted the German overtures, even if this meant making an alliance with the hereditary enemy, Austria. Such an alliance made it impossible for Italy to dream of taking Trente and Trieste, with their predominantly Italian populations. The Left, composed of former Garibaldini, continued to look for an opportunity to seize those lands, regardless of the complications that could emerge from such a policy. When Bismarck organized two conferences in Berlin to discuss and organize the European order and the colonial exploitation of the world, Italian prime minister Benedetto Cairoli—a former Garibaldino—remained out of the discussion.

The situation was complex. Several years prior to the German alliance, Bismarck had gathered the leaders of the major powers in Berlin to avoid a general European war stemming from the harsh Russian settlement of San Stefano, which was imposed on the Ottoman Empire after the war of 1877. The Vienna principle of territorial compensation was successfully applied. Austria wanted a protectorate over Bosnia-Herzegovina. Britain, Germany, and Russia supported this idea. The Austrian-German suggestion to Italy was not to ask for Italian territories still owned by Austria, but to look at Tunisia. France wanted Tunisia, and Britain needed French diplomatic support in order to secure Cyprus. Britain supported a French protectorate because it did not like the idea of Italy controlling Sicily and Tunisia, that is to say controlling the strategic center of the Mediterranean. Italy then requested Trieste and Trente, but was refused. This happened because Italian governments feared international crises. But it also reflected a rather naïve and poorly schooled understanding of global affairs.

Italy had no plans for Latin America. The Rio de la Plata Italian naval station soon increased to a naval division. But the *Regia Marina* only protected Italian citizens' local interests and acted as a peacekeeping force. As a result, it played a significant role in practically all the wars and revolutions in Latin America between 1861 and 1911, but no more. The *Regia Marina*, however, did not act only in Latin America. Since 1864, it sent its ships around the world. Ship commanders had diplomatic credentials and could sign agreements. Good relations with Japan and China were established during the later months of 1866. A few years afterward, similar agreements were made with Burma and Korea. In 1871 the Burmese king had explicitly asked for Italian involvement in his country to avoid complete British colonization and escape French attempts to overthrow his monarchy. His kingdom was caught between British India, independent Siam, and French Indochina. In the same period the Chinese government considered the possible Italian purchase of Taiwan, and in 1880, Korea pursued commercial treaties.

Unfortunately, the Italian government did not take advantage of its improved conditions in the Far East and did not support commercial initiatives. More simply, the government failed to exploit the remaining empty spaces in Asia with the same alacrity as the other powers. It was not the same for Africa; it was worse.

Africa and China

Initial contacts between Cavour and Africa occurred before the Second War of Independence. After the opening of Suez in 1869, the Italian shipping company Rubattino bought a little land in the Red Sea, on the Eritrean coast. In 1881, France seized Tunisia, in accordance with the provisions of the Congress of Berlin. Italian public opinion—voters were only 4 percent of the population at that time—were enraged, but the government had no international support. In 1882, Britain offered Italy shared governance in Egypt in exchange for Italian military participation in British operations against the Egyptian revolt. Italy refused. In 1885, Italy decided to expand its microscopic African possessions. The Eritrean seaport of Massawa was occupied, and the first colonial military unit was created. It soon proved to be so effective that France modeled its *Armée Coloniale* on the corps.[3] Its official designation after 1902 was the *Regio Corpo Truppe Coloniali*—the Royal Corps of Colonial Troops.

Italy also established commercial trading posts on the Somali coast. Further expansion in Eritrea was slow because of the government's fear of international implications. The first colonial war broke out in 1887 against Ethiopia. Italian troops enlarged the colony and built the first railway from Massawa to Keren. In 1890, Dervishes appeared from Sudan and attacked Italian possessions. Captain Fara's six officers and 230 colonial troopers defeated them at Agordat on June 27, 1890. After three years, 10,000 Dervishes raided from Cassala to Eritrea. Colonel Arimondi had 2,181 men, including officers, and was outnumbered 4.5 to one, but he defeated the raiding force and killed their chief. When back in Cassala, Dervishes tallied their casualties to more than 3,200 men. Arimondi had lost only 107 dead and 123 wounded. He was immediately reinforced by General Baratieri, the colonial governor. With more than 2,500 men, Arimondi seized Cassala on July 17, 1894.

Another war against Ethiopia broke out in 1895. After many successful skirmishes and engagements, Italian prime minister Crispi—the same who persuaded Garibaldi to go to Sicily in 1860—determined to end the war with an invasion and conquest of Ethiopia in 1896. Historian Bruce Vandervort wisely remarked in his book that telegraph links between Rome and the campaigning troops deprived Baratieri of the full decisional autonomy he had successfully used in previous operations.[4] The result was a defeat. On March 1, 1896, Baratieri ordered his 17,696 men and 56 cannons to attack no less than 80,000 Ethiopians and 46 cannons that Emperor Menelik had in the Adowa valley. All the Ethiopians had firearms. The Italians had no cavalry, and the Ethiopians fielded 8,600 on horseback.

Italian troops came down from their positions at dawn and, according to their orders, moved through the canyons to reach the valley. They had a poor knowledge of the terrain and lacked good maps. Instead of advancing like a fist, they advanced as the fingers of a fully open hand. The battle developed as three distinct clashes at the egress of three different canyons. The Italian troops were outnumbered 5 to 1 and, when considering only the infantry, it was 6 to 1. Moreover, the Italian columns could not support each other, so when ammunition ran low, Italian troops were overwhelmed. Casualties on both sides were quite high. The Italians lost some 5,700 men and 3,000 prisoners. Ethiopian casualties totaled 7,000 dead and no less than 10,000 wounded.[5] Then Italian press reacted as it had after Custoza thirty years earlier. It was a national tragedy: Crispi should disappear; it was the worst disaster Italy had ever seen: Crispi should disappear; it was a shame: Crispi should disappear; and Crispi disappeared.

Really, it was not the disaster often portrayed. From a strategic perspective, Adowa had been not too different from what the British had suffered at Ishandl-wana.[6] Moreover, 25,000 reinforcements were en route to Eritrea. In fact, within two weeks Italian troops reacted, repelling a new Dervish incursion in the north, against Cassala, and an Ethiopian attack around Adigrat. Regardless, in May 1896, Rome ordered a stop to all operations. Political propaganda successfully destroyed Crispi's premiership. Adowa thus remained in the national mind as a shame and a terrible disaster. And moreover in 1897 the Italian government gave Cassala to Britain, which had not asked for it. There was no public opposition, it happened because the government wanted no more involvement in African issues.

The next error in colonial policy came two years later. In 1899, while preparing the Kitchener Sudanese campaign, London offered Rome shared rule over Sudan in exchange for military intervention. Rome reacted as it had in 1882 over Egypt: it refused. Thus Italy lost three opportunities to expand its possessions in northeastern Africa. Political attitudes toward colonial policy were so irrational that, while ending their game in Africa, the Italians played it in China.

In 1898, Rome demanded that Peking accept San Mun Bay as an Italian-controlled port. It was the last of a long, long series of brutal foreign demands made on Imperial China. Peking refused. The *Regia Marina* dispatched a squadron to San Mun, but no further action was taken. The squadron remained and, when in the summer of 1900 the Boxer Rebellion exploded, Italian cruisers sent a detachment to Peking. A portion of it bravely helped the French defend the Pei Tang Catholic cathedral while the other defended the European Legations in Peking during the famous fifty-five-day siege.

More seamen took part in the Taku landing and, later, in conquering Tientsin. In August 1900 the 1,965 men composing Italian Royal Troops in China—as the Italian expeditionary force against the Boxers was officially referred—reached Peking. Italy now had seven cruisers and 2,543 men in China, including seamen.[7] They were involved in numerous operations along the coast and in the interior. When the war ended, Italy obtained a fort in Shan Hai Kwan and a 151-acre settlement at Tientsin. For the following forty-three years, Italy maintained a small naval squadron—the Naval Station of the Far East—and a naval garrison, increasing its presence with a settlement in Shanghai too in the 1930s. It cost much more than expected and Italy had little to gain from it, but political prestige prevented the abandonment of the Asian colonial policy. It took World War II to end the Italian presence in China.

Benedetto Brin—the man who created the modern Italian Navy. Courtesy of Italian Navy Historical Service.

Infantry barrack circa 1902. Author's personal collection.

7th Alpine Regiment descending a mountain. Author's personal collection.

Bersaglieri relieving guard, 1902. Author's personal collection.

Mounted Royal Carabineers in full dress, 1927. Author's personal collection.

Royal Navy, 1927. The commander of the port of Leghorn with his officers. Author's personal collection.

Airship n1—later, The Norge—out of its hangar near Rome. Author's personal collection.

Two famous pilots—De Pinedo and Italo Balbo, 1929. Author's personal collection.

Mussolini in Bologna, 1929. Author's personal collection.

King Victor Emmanuel III visiting Libya, escorted by carabineers, Spring 1933. Author's personal collection.

Italian veterans inspected by Hitler in Munich, June 25, 1939. Author's personal colledtion.

Heavy artilley leaving for Russia, parading in front of the king, 1942. Author's personal collection.

PART

THE TWENTIETH CENTURY

CHAPTER 20

Before the Great War: 1900–1912

The New King and His Kingdom

On July 29, 1900, an Italian anarchist back from America shot king Humbert I in Monza. Crown Prince Victor Emmanuel became the third king of Italy. His ascension to the throne marked a deep change in official policy. Victor Emmanuel III did not like Germans at all, especially Kaiser Wilhelm II. Moreover, he did not like his late father's domestic policy. Humbert had supported the nationalist Left's strongly reactionary policies. The Royal Army had been widely employed against workers, and there was no relief to social crises. There was a strong connection between policy and economy and, the ruling coalition would not act against the interests of its constituents. Moreover, many deputies and senators were landowners or owned factories and had a direct interest in maintaining the status quo.

The Italian Socialist Party was a heavily supported organization. It increased its activities in support of the working class. In 1900, industry in Italy was not as strong as in other Western European countries, but it had great significance. It was concentrated in several large cities, Milan, Turin, and Genoa, comprising the so called industrial triangle. It was also centered in towns, such as Leghorn, Terni, Piombino, and Brescia. Italy could produce all the goods it needed, if not at the same price and in the same quantity as some foreign producers. Technological improvement was remarkable as Italian industry kept pace with its European competitors. Technology also made its way to the armed forces. In 1896, Guglielmo Marconi had invented the radio-telegraph and, two years later, supported by the *Regia Marina*, he was able to receive signals sent from more than eleven miles away.

The *Regia Marina* think tank also produced something new in shipbuilding. In 1903, Naval Engineers Corps director Colonel Vittorio Cuniberti published in *Jane's*—at that time *All the World's Fighting Ships*—an interesting article about capital ships. According to him, capital ships should carry cannons of the same caliber—possibly 12-inch guns—to be most effective. His article was the birth of the modern Italian battleship.

Italy benefited from other technological inventions. In 1853, two Florentine physicists, Niccolò Barsanti and Felice Matteucci, made basic studies and experiments with engines. Within forty years, in 1892, German engineer Gottlieb Benz built the first four-wheeled automobile. In 1895 the Italian Royal Army staff asked the Ministry of War to develop this new technology and, in 1898, the *Regio Esercito* bought its first steam-automobile, a French-made De Dion–Bouton. It was given to the Engineers Corps Railway Detachment in Rome. Meanwhile, in 1899, FIAT—*Fabbrica Italiana Automobili Torino*—Italian Automobile Factory, Turin—began production. In 1901 the Royal Army bought its first gasoline-powered automobile. Tested in following years, automobiles were officially formed into a military unit in 1906 as a branch of the Engineers Corps.

In 1877, Enrico Forlanini, a former Engineers Corps officer, conducted his first experiments with the helicopter. He built a steam-powered 3.5-kilogram machine, which was moved by two coaxial helices. It achieved a height of thirteen meters, flying for twenty seconds, but no further development occurred. Forlanini later focused on airships and, in 1900, began building in Milan his first airship, but again development ceased, in 1909.

Anyway, Italy had a long tradition in flight. The first Italian balloon flew near Milan on February 25, 1784. It had been the fourth flight in the world and the first outside of France. The Royal Army had an Aerostatic Regiment, starting in 1885. But balloon trips depended on wind. It was necessary to develop something better, such as airships. The first Italian airship was designed and built by Engineers Corps captains Carlo Crocco and Ottavio Ricaldoni, who later reached the highest rank in the Royal Air Force Engineers Corps. Their Airship Number 1 flew for the first time in Vigna di Valle, a military base some twenty miles north of Rome, on October 1, 1908. In that same year, Leon Delagrange made the first airplane flight ever seen in Italy, and Wilbur Wright came to Europe.

Delagrange's flight was not a particularly great success, but it worked. An Aviators Club was established in Rome in February 1909, and its president, Major Massimo Mario Moris, chief of the Aeronautical Section of the Specialist Brigade of the Army Engineers Corps, went to France to meet Wright. Wright consented to come to Italy to teach flying to navy lieutenant Mario Calderara and Engineers Corps lieutenant Umberto Savoia and, moreover, to sell to Italy his airplane. On April 15, 1909, Wilbur and Orville Wright[1] made their first flight on the Centocelle military field, not far from Rome. When the Wright brothers left Italy on April 26, it was the dawn of the Italian air force. That same year the first Italian aircraft was built by the Faccioli SpA automobile factory.

Interest in new technologies made the Italian armed forces major investors in and clients for national industry and, sometimes, for foreign ones. For instance, Italian navy was the first European armed force to officially adopt the Maxim machine gun. Industrial development implied increasing social contrasts. Victor Emmanuel III soon changed his official policies. In November 1903 he appointed Giovanni Giolitti prime minister.[2] This sixty-one-year-old premier was from Piedmont. His grandfather on his mother's side had cooperated with the French before 1814, serving as the mayor of his town. He had been minister for a long time under King Humbert, who appointed him premier for the first time in 1892. Minister of the interior from February 1901 until June 1903, Giolitti ruled Italy as prime minister—apart from a short interregnum—until March 1914. He was a smart, quiet, and reflective man, just what Victor Emmanuel III and Italy needed.

Giolitti was able to listen to both the workers and the industrialists and pursue compromises and agreements. He did not fear socialism or revolutions, and balanced well between extreme political positions, using Catholics to limit socialists, so he permitted general strikes as a valve for social unrest and as an indicator of the political weight of socialists. Under his leadership Italy had a quiet period and could celebrate its first fifty years as a united nation.

Giolitti's Foreign and Colonial Policy, and the Italian-Turkish War: 1911–1912

In 1902, Italian foreign minister Prinetti told the French ambassador that Italy considered the Triple Alliance a defensive pact, so in the event of German aggression, France should not fear Italian intervention. Reactions in Vienna and in Berlin were strident. It was an important turning point. Inspired by the king, Italian foreign policy was slowly turning from the Central Powers and looking for new alliances and better diplomatic space. The British saw an opportunity in the growing rift between Italy and Austria. They too were concerned about Wilhelm's aggressive colonial policies. King Edward VII courted Victor Emmanuel, trying to facilitate the dismemberment of the Triple Alliance.

Italy's relationship with Austria declined after the turn of the century. This was particularly the case since the crown prince, the Archduke Francis Ferdinand, placed Franz Conrad von Hötzendorff as chief of the General Staff of the Austro-Hungarian army. The general saw a bleak future for Austria. He foresaw a war against Russia, Italy, Montenegro, and Serbia. These powers had strict links between them. Helen, queen of Italy, was the daughter of King Nicholas of Montenegro. She had been educated at the Russian court, and Italian Balkan policy was not too friendly toward Austria. The clash over the Balkans was similar to those of Venice and the Habsburg court centuries earlier. Conrad planned preventive wars to meet these perceived future crises. When a terrible earthquake destroyed Messina in 1908, Conrad asked the emperor for permission to attack Italy. It was a wonderful opportunity, he said, because practically the entire Italian armed forces were digging out the ruined city, where more than 100,000 people lost their lives. A horrified Francis Joseph rejected the proposal.[3] That same year, Austria ended its protectorate of Bosnia-Herzegovina and annexed both provinces. Italy protested. Rome claimed that Austria had broken existing mutual pacts in the Balkan political order, but Vienna rejected the charge. The *Regia Marina* prepared its first plan for a naval war against Austria.

In 1911 the Italian government wanted to expand in the Mediterranean to compensate for the changing situation in the Balkans. Italy had interests in Libya and, after reflection, decided to seize it. Libya was still part of the Ottoman Empire. The Turks, facing crises in the Balkans, too, could accept it as an Italian protectorate, but not full sovereignty. Sultan Abdul Hamid II rejected the Italian ultimatum and, on September 29, 1911, the war began.

Giolitti did not like wars. He considered them useless, especially when it was possible to negotiate. In this case a nationalist press campaign forced him to war. It was the fiftieth anniversary of Italian unification, and "the Nation" demanded a glorious victory to remove "the shame of Adowa."

The navy struck first. At 2:30 a.m. a Turkish torpedo boat was sunk by Italian destroyers near Prevesa, while Admiral Faravelli's 2nd Naval Squadron had appeared off the coast of Tripoli the previous night.[4] On October 3, Tripolitan coastal forts were shelled. Then a detachment of seamen landed and seized the city. The 10,000 men of the Army Expeditionary Force arrived on October 10. They arrived late because the government had reflected so much, it had failed to mention the possibility of war to the General Staff. This failure to communicate with the General Staff resulted in the normal discharge of conscripts whose term of service was over; and the army, now finding itself at war with insufficient troops, had to call back the reserves.

Chief of Staff General Alberto Pollio realized that he needed more than 20,000 men to seize Libya. The Turks proclaimed the Holy War (jihad) against the Christians coming from Italy, and a portion of Arabs took up arms. After a bloody surprise attack against the 11th *Bersaglieri* Regiment at Shara Shat, reinforcements arrived quickly. On October 26 the 3rd Infantry Division defeated the Turks at Henni. On December 4 the army gained another victory, at Ain Zara, and after a difficult but successful fight at Bir Tobras, a further victory was gained at Gargaresh on January 18, 1912. Despite these victories, the war went slowly. The entire Libyan coast was under Italian control, but the interior was difficult to maintain, requiring counterinsurgency warfare. The Royal Army used all possible weapons and technology in Libya. Trucks were used as well as armored cars. Radio was largely used, and airships bombed enemy troops. A real milestone was the employment of aircraft in a combat role, for the first time in the world.[5]

The Italian army tested the use of aircraft for reconnaissance in the 1911 summer exercises, using two sections of four planes. When the war began, the General Staff ordered the Airplanes Squadron to Libya. The 10 officers and 29-trooper unit had nine aircraft, each with its own hangar. First test flights occurred on October 22, but the first official flight happened the day after, when Captain Carlo Piazza made a short-range reconnaissance of sixty-one minutes. The first long-range (for that time) reconnaissance flight occurred on October 24. Captain Moizo spent two hours flying to Azizia and back to Tripoli. On November 1, 1911, 2nd Lieutenant Giulio Gavotti made the first bombing attack from a plane. He dropped a bomb on Ain Zara and three more on the Tajura oasis. In March 1912, Captain Piazza took the first photo by plane. On May 2, Captain Marengo conducted the first night action. He recognized Jok Kebir and, on the night of June 11 he made the first night bombing. Captain Moizo held another record he would have preferred to avoid; being the first pilot captured by the enemy. In fact, in the last days of the war, because of an engine breakdown, his plane landed near El Maya and he was taken prisoner. The Turks had their own records for the first antiaircraft artillery fire, on December 15, 1911, and on January 31, 1912, the first enemy pilot— Captain Carlo Montù—was wounded by antiaircraft fire. But, it was far too early in the century to see airpower providing troops with decisive tactical support.

In the summer of 1912 the Italian government decided to carry the war closer to Turkish territory. Libyan operations were not decisive. The *Regia Marina* had swept the Turkish navy from Mediterranean and the Red Sea, and Italian troops could easily move by sea. The Royal Army landed on Stampalia Island and then conquered the remaining Dodecanese Islands. The next step had to be against the Turkish fleet, which remained inactive in the Dardanelles. The last time Italian ships tried to enter the Dardanelles in pursuit of the Turkish fleet had been in 1657. Now the situation was a bit different. On the night of July 18–19, Vessel Captain Enrico Millo led his five-torpedo-boat squadron into the Dardanelles. He arrived in sight of Nagara, where the enemy fleet was located, but underwater iron chains, sea mines, and a strong artillery response did not allow him to go forward. He came out of the straits with no damage to his ships or crews. The Italian press acclaimed him as a hero. The French press announced that the Turks had sunk four Macaroni battleships.[6]

The extension and duration of the war led to complications in both Italy and the Ottoman Empire. Italy was spending a lot of money and, moreover, Conrad von Hötzendorff had asked Francis Joseph again for permission to launch a preventive attack on Italy.[7] The emperor rejected this proposal, too, but the discussion was known in Rome. No German diplomatic support had been given to the Libyan war, and strange rumors emerged in Eastern Europe. The same rumors worried Austria, Britain, and the Ottoman Empire. Russia was quite happy with the Italian attacks on the Ottomans. Russia hoped for a great Turkish defeat, opening the route to the Mediterranean. This was Britain's nightmare, but how could Britain intervene against Italy if they were trying to cut Italy from the German alliance? Indeed, even the small Balkan states were preparing to raise arms against Turkey. Bulgaria, Greece, Serbia, and Montenegro attacked European Turkey in the so-called First Balkan War. Both Italy and the Ottomans needed to end their war as soon as possible. On October 18, 1912, Turkey signed the Lausanne Treaty and gave Italy Libya, consenting to a provisional Italian occupation of the Dodecanese Islands, too.

CHAPTER 21

The Great War: 1915-1918

1914-1915

After the annexation of Bosnia through the Libyan war, Austrian attitudes were noticeably unfriendly toward Italy. Italian foreign policy began to shift as a consequence, and in the course of the Bosnian crisis, General Alberto Pollio was appointed chief of staff of the Royal Army. A convinced supporter of the Triple Alliance, Pollio was well considered in Germany, and his wife was from a noble Austrian family. This did not stop the Italian Army's intelligence from expanding its network in Austria-Hungary. In 1908 it was quite active, and its main task was assessing Austrian military movements by rail. The greatest results came in the next years, through the chief of Austrian counterespionage, Colonel Alfred Redl. Redl had been compromised by Russian agents, and he funneled information to Russia and later Italy. This intelligence coup lasted from 1910 to 1913, when Redl was discovered and shot himself.

The assassination of Austrian archduke Francis Ferdinand in Sarajevo and the subsequent Austro-Serbian crisis in June 1914 caused the Great War. According to Baron von Margutti, Francis Joseph "in July 1914 decided for war based upon the existing situation."[1] What happened in European chanceries from June 24 to August 12, 1914, when Britain declared war on Austria, is well known. Less well known are the events surrounding Italy's decisions in August 1914. On June 28, 1914, General Pollio died of a heart attack in Turin. A few days later the king appointed General Count Luigi Cadorna as his new chief of staff. It was a significant "Risorgimental" choice. The sixty-four-year-old Piedmontese general was the son of the man who seized Rome in 1870. On July 24, 1914, Italian premier Antonio Salandra and the foreign minister, the Marquis Antonino di San Giuliano, were spending their holidays at the hot springs in Fiuggi. When they received news of the Austrian ultimatum to Serbia, they summoned the German ambassador von Flotow, who was in Fiuggi for the same reason. They told the ambassador that as the Triple Alliance was a defensive pact, and as Austria is threatening war, Italy is not obligated and will not support Austria.

Italy would remain a neutral power, and when the war began the press was highly influenced by Allied propaganda. Italians were not anxious to enter the war, except for a very small political minority. Socialists disliked the idea, Giolitti did not consider war a good opportunity, and most of the members of Parliament had similar opinions. Most Italian assessments prefigured a quick German victory.[2] There were two very active political groups, however, that wanted Italy to enter the war, particularly when it became clear later that Germany would not achieve a rapid victory, if victory at all. The political group was not a party, but a sort of association composed of many Italians who were born as Austrian subjects in Trentino or Venezia Giulia and Dalmatia. These irredentists wanted their birthplaces united with Italy. They played a major role in lobbying the government to enter the conflict and were fully supported by another group of the same mind.

As all the Western countries, Italy has a long tradition of connections between culture and war, but the Risorgimento created a change in that correlation. Nationalist culture made policy and pushed for war. Italian Risorgimento authors depicted the sad situation of Italian history under foreign powers. Simply describing his prison experience in Spielberg Castle, Silvio Pellico savaged Austria in the public mind with his famous book *Le mie prigioni* (*My Prisons*). Count Alessandro Manzoni's romance, *I promessi sposi*—the only one of that period—showed what foreign rule, in that case the Spaniards in Milan, meant. National poet Giosué Carducci, a former *carbonaro* and a sort of Italian Tennyson, sang about war and the glory of the Piedmontese army and the Savoyard dynasty. The best-known and loved composer, Giuseppe Verdi, had his own troubles with Austrian censors concerning his operas. Thanks to his *Forza del destino* (*The Force of Destiny*), nobody could forget how the Austrians had been defeated in 1744 at Velletri by the Italians—no matter if they were Bourbon Neapolitans. On the walls of Italian cities and towns was scrawled *Viva Verdi* ("Long live Verdi!"). In appearance, it acclaimed the composer; in reality, it was an acronym meaning "Long Life to—*Viva*—**V**ittorio **E**mmanuele **Re D'I**talia—Victor Emmanuel, king of Italy. This was the past, but now something new appeared. The last quarter of the nineteenth century was the age of Decadence. One of its major features was Gabriele D'Annunzio, whose main interest was to taste everything just to experience new sensations. Decadence, however, produced a reaction. A not too brilliant poet, Filippo Tommaso Marinetti, wrote the "Manifesto dei Futuristi," inspiring a new cultural movement. Futurism stated that the old-fashioned, elegant, sophisticated Decadent world was over; and that humanity had to live in a new era: an era of progress, of activity, of real life. Technology was the best expression of this new life, and war was the purification that humanity had to experience in order to eliminate its worst members and ideas.

Activity and technology became the theme for futurist paintings and poems. Ardengo Soffici, Ottone Rosai, Giacomo Balla, and Umberto Boccioni filled their masterpieces with colors and movement. And what was faster than a car, a train, a plane? So cars, trains, and planes emerged in paintings on canvas and on walls.

Futurism acclaimed the Libyan War as the dawn of a new era, an era when Venice had to be a naval base instead of a romantic city for lovers; an era when Rome had to be the capital of a strong and powerful nation. And the coming of the glorious Third Rome arrived after the first, the ancient Imperial Rome; and the second, the center of Christendom and culture. It was not by chance that all of this peaked in 1911, during the fiftieth anniversary of the kingdom. A complex mixture of policy, Risorgimental heritage, national pride, culture, technology, big plans, and hopes for the future exploded. D'Annunzio soon became closer and closer to the futurists. He liked action, because action implied new sensations.

He wrote a poem about the royal seamen who died in China in 1900. He celebrated torpedo boats in the Adriatic and the glory of the navy before 1911. He supported intervention in the war in 1914. He spoke about intervention because he believed in it. He looked at the war as the greatest of man's adventures. His speeches and articles flooded Italy. As Rudyard Kipling later remarked it was "D'Annunzio's poetry that has literally helped to move mountains in this war."[3] This call for intervention happened while the most pacific party, the Socialists, had an internal crisis. The party's majority wanted to preserve neutrality. A minority, including the influential deputy Leonida Bissolati, and the director of the party's newspaper *L'Avanti!* (*The Forward!*), Benito Mussolini, supported Italian intervention. Cesare Battisti, a Socialist deputy from Trente in the Austrian Parliament, encouraged such activity in his Italian political compatriots.

Premier Salandra had clear ideas on Italy's role in the war from the very beginning. In fact, when in July 1914 the chief of staff, General Cadorna, was informed of Italian neutrality, he went to Salandra. "I say to him: 'Does the neutrality you have declared mean that the war against France will never be made?' He answered: 'Yes.' 'So'—I say—'what must I do?' He looks at me. 'Must I prepare the war against Austria?' 'This is evident.' He says to me: 'Yes, this is all right.'"[4]

Therefore, in July 1914 the premier already believed that intervention against Austria was the proper course. The French victory on the Marne and the Austrian failure in Serbia and against Russia improved his attitude. If the war was not over by Christmas, an Allied victory was possible. Gradually the king's cabinet moved away from the Triple Alliance to the sphere of the Triple Entente of Russia, France, and Britain.

The 1915 Campaign

In the spring of 1915 diplomatic talks with both alliances made it clear that Italy would benefit from joining the Entente. German pressure on Austria to give Italy Trente and Trieste in order to maintain its neutrality had failed. Vienna refused to consider any possible territorial cession to Rome. Conversely, the Allies desperately needed help to relieve German pressure on all fronts. The Russians could not expand their operations because its lack of weapons, and it had just suffered an egregious defeat at Tannenberg and at the Masurian Lakes as well as in Poland. The shortest route for supplies to Russia went through the Dardanelles, but this had been closed by the Turks since October 1914. Allied attempts to open the straits were bloodily failures at Gallipoli in 1915. Eventually, Allied negotiations with Italy succeeded and the Pact of London was signed.

Unfortunately, the Italian government played the negotiations poorly. Although the Pact of London included the annexation of the Trentino, Venezia Giulia, and Trieste, it did not take into consideration the city of Fiume. It made no clear mention of acquisitions in the Middle East. Moreover, it failed to include discussions on German colonies in Africa or the Far East. It only spoke of "border adjustments" and "equal compensation" in Africa: no more.

In nuce, Italy's troubles for the next twenty-five years were all prepared in London on April 26, 1915. The government simply did not inform the Parliament, the people, nor the armed forces. In fact, Cadorna was informed only in the early days of May 1915 of the government's formal promise to enter the war before May 26. Mobilization occurred in a hurry. Beginning on May 4, 2,500 trains carried mobilized troops and 4,500 more trains moved the army to the border through June 15. On May 24, 1915, the Royal Army moved across the border. One and a half million men and 150 ships were the sword of the House of Savoy in its fourth and final mortal duel in seventy years against the House of Habsburg.

The *Regio Esercito* entered the war with four armies and a reserve. They were composed of 14 corps divided into four cavalry divisions, 35 infantry divisions, one *Bersaglieri* division, and two Alpine groups. Dressed in gray-green uniforms[5] and using model 1891 rifles, Italians went to war with remarkable enthusiasm. Many of them hoped the war would be over quickly, despite what was happening in France. Furthermore, Austria was the hereditary enemy. It was the same empire their grandfathers had fought, that their fathers had called "the menace," and the sons now were going to fight in what was being defined—and it was truly considered by the soldiers—as the Fourth War of Independence.[6]

Not a single Italian intellectual stayed home. All answered the call, mostly as volunteers, and they all went to the trenches. Writers such as Soffici, Gadda, and Slataper; painters such as Boccioni, Balla, and Rosai; the poets D'Annunzio, Montale, Ungaretti, and Marinetti; politicians such as Mussolini, Bissolati, Corridoni, and Battisti; and millions of commoners came from Italy and from abroad. Millions of Italians, and hundreds of thousands of Italian immigrants returned, went to fight "for the King's and Fatherland's inseparable Good."

Cadorna took the offensive but faced serious difficulties. He had to organize the army and quickly transform it from a peacetime institution to wartime. Soldiers and reserve officers lacked adequate preparation and training. Italian generals moved slowly, and the Austrians had time to improve their defenses and transfer troops to the frontier. In Cadorna's mind the Italian army had to act fast, crossing the Carnatic Alps to reach the Lubjiana Valley. According to Franz Conrad von Hötzendorff, the Austrian chief of staff, the Lubjiana Valley was the perfect place for a battle of annihilation against the Italian army. Regardless of Conrad's predications and plans, the problem was that he lacked troops because of intensive Austrian involvement in the Balkans and on the Russian front. He requested German aid, but the Germans refused, having already dispatched an army to the Serbian border in 1915. Conrad therefore had to arrange his defense as best he could, by exploiting natural obstacles.

The Italian front ran from the Swiss border to the Adriatic Sea. It was like a sideways "S," or a sinusoid. The First and Fourth Italian Armies fought in the Trentino along a semicircle from the Swiss border to Dolomites. The Second and Third Armies fought on the next semicircle, from the Dolomites to the sea. Their front went across the Carso and the Friuli Plateau to Trieste and the Carnatic Alps. Many Austrian positions had been prepared since peacetime, but now they were improved. Long and deep caverns had been dug in the mountains and filled with artillery and machine guns. Alpine valleys from Venetia to Trente were as deep and large as American canyons. The mouths of the Austrian caverns were at least thirty or forty feet above the valley floors, and Austrians could shell the Italians from the safety of their positions. It was considered impossible to attack along the valley floors. All Italian attacks moved up the steep slopes, with troops climbing the mountains under intense enemy fire from Austrians who remained safely entrenched at the top. When, after a bloody battle, the top of one mountain was taken, the game started again with the next mountain.

> Up there, men fight with field guns, machine guns and rifles, and more deadly showers of stones heaped together and sent sliding down at the proper time. Up there if a man is wounded and bleeds only a little before he is found, the cold kills him in minutes, not hours. Whole companies can be frostbitten and crippled even while they lie taking cover in the pauses of a rush, and the wandering mountain just takes sentries from under the lip of their rock as they stand up to be relieved, and flick them into space.[7]

How did troops get up the mountain?

> You climb up a fissure of a rock chimney—by shoulder or knee work, such as mountaineers understand—and at night for choice, because by day the enemy drop stones down the chimney, . . . carry machine guns, and some other things with . . . and when you emerge from your chimney—which it is best to do in a storm of a gale, since nailed boots on rock make a noise—you find either that you command the enemy's post on the top, in which case you destroy him, or cut him off from supplies by firing down the only goat-path . . . ; or you find the enemy commands you from some unsuspected cornice or knob of rock. Then you go down again—if you can—and try elsewhere . . .
>
> Special work is somewhat different. You select a mountaintop which you have reason to believe is filled with the enemy and all his works. You effect a lodgment there with your teeth and toenails; you mine into the solid rock with compressed air drills for as many hundred yards as you calculate may be necessary. When you have finished, you fill your galleries with nitroglycerin and blow the top off the mountain. Then you occupy the crater with men and machine guns as fast as you can. Then you secure your dominating position from which you can gain other positions, by the same means.[8]

On the Carso Plateau the situation was the same. The Austrians possessed the heights of the hills separating the Italians from Gorizia and Trieste. "In its complex, the Carso was far easier to defend instead of attack. It stood perpendicular to the

Isonzo, the Vipacco river and Friuli plain, like a balcony from which one could shoot the attacking forces as if from ten-meter-high building. It was a natural fortress: a great bastion with a great moat: the Isonzo and the Dottori channel."[9] Italian infantry had to move from the bottom to the top; Austrian positions were well protected by lines of barbed wire swept by machine gun crossfire.

As soon as Italian infantry came out of its trenches, Austrian artillery conducted interdiction bombardment along with infantry fire. It was quite normal to see the first Italian wave completely killed within a couple of minutes before reaching the first line of wire. Italian artillery threw its preparatory fire onto Austrian positions, just as the Allies did on the Western Front, but it could shell as much as it wanted without really creating any exploitable holes in the Austrian defenses. Shelled barbed wire became just a more inextricable jungle of death. It was impossible to cut it with the special wire cutters provided by the army.

During the summer of 1915, Italian infantry sent out special patrols during the night. They had to creep toward enemy positions, carrying twenty- to twenty-six-foot-long metal pipes filled with high explosive. When they reached the enemy barbed wire, they lit the fuse using a cigar. The explosion generally opened good holes in the wire, but sometimes it did not reach the enemy trenches.

Due to the relative positions of the armies, Italian trenches were at lower elevations compared to the Austrians. Soldiers therefore had to remain under cover the entire day. As soon as one of them stretched out a portion of his body, he was immediately shot. The standard Austrian sharpshooter, called Cecchino—Little Francis, after Emperor Francis Joseph—had a seven-round rifle whose characteristic noise—rendered as *Tah poom* in a military song—allowed Italian soldiers to determine if the magazine was empty or not and if was it possible to safely rush out of a hole. For this reason all movements were conducted by night, and the Austrians responded by illuminating Italian positions with searchlights.

The trenches were terribly uncomfortable. They were muddy and enveloped in a loud atmosphere, with a terrible mix of smells, including feces and putrefication from dead bodies left on the field or lying under the earth and pushed up by the artillery fire. It was common to see bodies sticking out of the walls or out of the ground of the trenches and bunkers. Cold and rain were constant in the mountains, and in winter the snow added avalanches to all the other risks. The lack of grass and trees due to artillery fire rendered the plains a squalid sight of naked stone. In this situation, it is no wonder the Great War on the Italian front was anything but fast. Cadorna's tactics were the same as all his colleagues on other fronts, from the Channel to Gallipoli; massive frontal attacks preceded by a sustained artillery barrage.

The First Battle of the Isonzo ended on July 7, 1915. The Second Battle began immediately afterward and ended within a few days; 56,813 Italians and 57,038 Austrians died, for nothing. On October 13 the Allies urged Cadorna to attack and relieve pressure on the Russians. The French had tried on September 20 with the bloody Artois and Champagne offensives. The Russians, however, were defeated in the Tarnow-Gorlice offensive. Further, Bulgaria joined the Central Powers and

Serbia collapsed. Under these circumstances, on October 18, Cadorna launched the Third Battle of the Isonzo, which lasted through November 4, 1915. Using for the first time the Adrian steel helmet and supported by 1,363 guns, 290,000 Italians attacked 105,000 Austrians and their 625 guns. The strategic objective was Gorizia, as it had been for Venetian infantry three centuries earlier. On November 2, Italian casualties amounted to more than 67,000 men. Cadorna temporarily halted operations on November 4, only to order the fourth battle on November 10, with no result and heavy casualties.

The situation was no better at sea. The *Regia Marina* organized the rescue of the remaining Serbian army. It was the biggest logistical operation the *Regia Marina* had ever conducted. Fleet Admiral Louis Amadeus of Savoy, duke of the Abruzzi—the world-renowned polar explorer and mountain climber—planned and directed it. On November 22, Italian ships landed in the Albanian harbor of Durazzo with an expeditionary force. It was ordered to delay the Austrian advance to permit the Serbians to escape. Italian ships shuttled between Italy and Albania, carrying ordnance and supplies to the Serbians and returning with escaping troops, their Austrian prisoners, and civilian refugees. Despite the threat of the Austrian fleet, the *Regia Marina* made 584 supply cruises, evacuating 115,000 Serbians, over 175,000 civilians, and the survived 22,298 Austrian prisoners over the 70,000 they captured in origin.

Aside from this success, operations at sea suffered from the same problems they had on land. The Austrian fleet stayed in port at its major base in Pola, south of Trieste. The sea was filled of mines and submarines. Naval warfare was reduced to light ship raids, ambushes, and bluewaters patrols. Casualties were low, results were not exciting; and the Allied navies' task was to simply prevent Austrian ships and submarines from leaving the Adriatic Sea.

1916–1917

In 1916 the Italian military effort became increasingly effective. Logistics improved. More roads were built and railways were constantly active. The 372-mile-long front was now served by 4,000 miles of roads. Kipling remarked: "There was curiously little traffic by our standards, but all there was moved very swiftly. The perfectly made and tended roads do most of the motor's work. Where there are no bumps, there can be no strain, even under the maximum loads. The lorries glide from railhead to their destination, return and are off again without overhaul or delay."[10] Railway systems were as decisive as trucks. During the whole war, Italian rail moved 15 million men, 1.3 million horses, mules, and oxen, 350,000 vehicles and guns, 1,830,000 wounded and sick and 22 million metric tons of ordnance and supplies. It required 50,000 trains—that is to say 2 million cars—whose activities amounted to covering 18,641,000 miles in forty-one months.[11]

1916 also saw the first Italian air victories. Strangely, the Supreme Command had not learned any lessons from Libya or from the Western Front's skies. When the war began, Italy's aircraft—one hundred in all—were used only for reconnaissance. Slowly, the Italian air force improved. A first bombing run was made on August 20, 1915, by a 300-horsepower Caproni trimotor bomber against the Austrian airfield at Aidussina, near Gorizia. On April 6 the first Austrian plane was shot down by an Italian interceptor, Cavalry Captain Francesco Baracca, who later became the best Italian ace, with thirty-four kills. Italian aircraft factories improved production. During 1916 they produced 1,300 planes and 2,300 engines.[12] By the end of the year the Italian air force had forty-nine air squadrons and, after June 1917, it achieved air superiority through the end of the war.[13]

The year 1916 was also the most difficult in terms of land operations. The Austrians and Germans planned direct strong offensives to destroy enemy resistance. Luckily for the Allies, both Conrad and General Erich von Falkenhayn, chief of the German General Staff, demanded support for their own respective offensives but refused to help each other. As a result, the Austrians and Germans did not coordinate their operations.

Falkenhayn attacked at Verdun in February. Soon the French high command was calling for an Italian diversion on the Isonzo. On March 11, 1916, the Fifth Battle of the Isonzo began, lasting through the month for the first time. The Austrians used flamethrowers and iron-hammers to kill the Italian soldiers wounded or poisoned by gas and still lying on the ground. They lost practically no land, apart from Mount Adamello. Then, on May 15, Conrad launched his offensive: the so called Strafe Expedition, the "punitive expedition." Forty Austrian divisions—189 battalions and 18 *Standschützen* units—supported by 1,193 guns, came down from the Trentino to attack General Pecori Giraldi's First Army. Pecori Giraldi had 155 battalions and 775 guns. The Italian line was forced back in the center but resisted on the wings. Within five days the Austrian offensive looked like an inflating balloon, with a little mouth.

Cadorna had been taken by surprise. Despite clear warnings, he was confident that no Austrian attack would come from the Trentino. The desperate resistance of the reinforced First Army gave Cadorna time to organize an army in fifteen days. After only twelve days he concentrated 179,000 men and 35,600 horses in the triangle of Vicenza-Padova-Cittadella, creating the Fifth Army of four corps on eight divisions. The Austrians now found their strategic situation deteriorating rapidly. After Victor Emmanuel wrote a personal letter to Czar Nicholas II, Russian general Brusilov directed a massive offensive against the Austrians on June 4. The Fourth and Seventh Austrian Armies lost 186,000 dead and 80,000 prisoners within five days. Conrad, however, insisted on maintaining the impetus of his offensive in Italy until June 15. The Italian counterattack began the following day; by the end of that month the fighting ended. Austrian casualties amounted to 5,000 dead, 23,000 wounded, and 2,000 prisoners. Italy lost 6,187 dead, 28,544 wounded, and 41,401 prisoners and missing in action; too much for a defensive battle. Likewise, in the following counteroffensive, the Italians lost 72,000 more men; the Austrians some 50,000.

Conrad was confident he had so heavily damaged the Italians that they could do little harm. He was wrong. In the early days of July, Cadorna decided to exploit the situation with the Sixth Battle of the Isonzo. In only one week, 3,000 trains shuttled 302,884 men, 150 guns, ammunition, and 57,134 horses from the Venetian plain to the Isonzo Valley. The objective again was Gorizia.

The Third Army, commanded by the duke of Aosta, a cousin of the king, put on line six divisions and 1,329 guns along a seven-mile front. On July 4 an Italian attack against Monfalcone was so heavy that the Austrians did not realize it was a diversion. On July 6 at dawn, the VI Corps' 590 guns began their bombardment. An hour later, 390 "bombards" (special trench artillery) were added, to destroy the barbed wire. Their fire stopped every half hour to allow patrols to assess its effects. At 4:00 p.m. the infantry attacked. The barrage moved forward, according to the white plates the first wave of infantrymen carried on their backs. After only forty minutes mount Sabotino was taken. It had resisted fourteen brigades' efforts during previous nineteen months. A bridgehead was established on the left bank of the Isonzo. The following day, Italian troops established a second bridgehead and, on July 9, at six in the morning, the Italian vanguard raised a tricolor at the Gorizia railway station. Then, after having traversed these mountains to reach Gorizia, they found that the Austrians had established themselves on all the other mountains east of the town.

The Sixth Battle of the Isonzo was the only real Allied victory during 1916. It was exploited by Allied propaganda; and Romania joined the Allies, and was rapidly overrun by the Germans in 1917. Cadorna considered Gorizia a first step and subsequently launched three more battles on the Isonzo, but in two months his troops had advanced only three miles, losing 85,000 men. The Allies' situation continued to decline steadily. On April 9, 1917, British troops attacked the Germans along the Aisne River. In one month they lost hundreds of thousands of men. The French soldiers eventually responded to the high casualty rates by refusing to obey orders. The mutiny of the French army threatened the entire Western Front. In the East, the Russian army was thrown into disarray by the revolution in St. Petersburg. Although the United States declared war in April 1917, it was too early to see American troops in Europe. To discourage the Germans from taking advantage of the strategic crisis, the Italians inaugurated the Tenth Battle of the Isonzo, on May 12, 1917. The battle was over in less than a month, and the only result was a mountain of casualties: 133,757 Italians and "only" 75,700 Austrians.

The Italian offensive gave the Allies time to prepare their own operations. The British army attacked in Flanders on June 7 after a sixteen-day artillery preparation. The Russian army moved again, for its last battle, on July 1, and forced the Austrians out of Bukovina. The Germans, however, counterattacked and captured all their lost ground. The Germans had to stop, too, because of the bloody Franco-British offensive at Ypres: 450,000 more British soldiers died "in Flanders Fields."

Meanwhile, Italian troops fought on mount Ortigara. Then, on August 17, supported by 2,380 guns and 1,199 bombards, twenty-one Italian divisions attacked the Bainsizza Plateau and Ternova Wood. At dawn the following day, 1,368 guns and 638 bombards shelled the Austrians on the Carso. On the night of August

18, the Second Army victoriously crossed the Isonzo and took 20,000 prisoners, 125 guns, and more than 200 machine guns. When the battle ended, Cadorna had lost 18,794 dead, 89,193 wounded, and 35,087 missing in action. The Austrians lost 110,000 men and the Bainsizza.[14]

A Defeat and a Miracle: 1917-1918

By 1917, Austria faced a military crisis of its own. German field marshal von Hindenburg wrote that Austria declared it had no more force to resist to a twelfth attack on the Isonzo. The war had drained its resources and ability to adequately replace its enormous losses. According to General Eric Ludendorff, quartermaster general of the German army, German military analysis concluded that the Austrians could not survive another battle. In order to prevent the complete collapse of their ally, the Germans dispatched an army to the Italian frontier.

German troops had been on the Italian front since 1915, even though Italy did not declare war on Germany until the summer 1916. In late 1917, seven German divisions came from France; and seven Austrian divisions arrived from the east in preparation of a new offensive. The Central Powers disposed 37 divisions and 4,126 guns against Italy. On October 24, 1917, General von Below's Austro-German Fourteenth Army attacked at Caporetto with 248,000 men, comprising seven German and eight Austrian divisions. Facing them was the Italian Second Army with 117,000 men. The Austrian objectives were to force the Italians to retreat from the imperial border, relieving the pressure on Trieste. During the Austro-German war conference held in Maribor on September 15, 1917, between Archduke Eugene of Habsburg and German generals Krafft von Dellmensingen and Otto von Below, von Below had set the minimum goal as the Tagliamento river. Then he foresaw the possibility of crossing the Tagliamento, between Cornino and Pinzano, making the entire Italian line in Carniola, Cadore, and Trentino collapse, allowing the Austro-Germans to invade the Padana Plain and cross the western Alps, reaching Lyon. The attack was prepared by a short and intense artillery bombardment, including poison gas. The front collapsed.

According to plans, Austro-German units passed the first and the second Italian lines and, wasting no time in the mountains, they advanced along the valley floors. At 3:00 p.m. they were in Caporetto, and Italy faced a major disaster.

On October 25 the enemy smashed the last Italian defense lines around Mount Globokak and Kolovrat, and on October 26 they reached Monte Maggiore. The advance was so fast that the Italian Army had no idea of Austro-German positions. Roads were filled with refugees and retreating troops. The Italian Supreme Command received news of the breakthrough late and had little idea of events. Indeed, it did not know which units of the Second Army still existed and where they were. Chaos reigned. The only thing clear was that the Austro-Germans were coming down the Venetian plain to the sea. They bypassed a portion of the Second Army and the entire Third Army on their left flank. At the end of their advance, all these

Italian troops would have been encircled and trapped. Cadorna ordered a general withdrawal to the Tagliamento river. At the same time, he committed cavalry divisions to slow the enemy advance.

Cadorna thought of resisting on the Tagliamento, but was informed that enemy units had already crossed it. He then ordered a withdrawal to a defensive line he had studied since 1916, from Mount Grappa running along the Piave river to the sea. The Fourth Army left its mountain positions and crossed the Piave, as did the Third and remainder of the Second Army. After two weeks the retreat was completed. Of more than forty-five divisions in existence in October, only twenty-nine were still combat capable. The army had lost 20,000 dead, 40,000 wounded, and 350,000 prisoners. The enemy captured 3,152 guns; and the Italian army lost one-third of its portable weapons, all of its ordnance and supply depots and all airfields with their material. But, in spite of appearances, it was only an operational defeat.[15] What saved the Italian army from complete collapse was the speed of its railway movement. It enabled the entire Third Army to escape. There were a further 400,000 men available, once reorganized. Last, the Italian army fell back upon its supply lines, while Austrians had logistical difficulties keeping pace with the advance, because their rail lines stopped where the front had been during previous thirty months. So, Caporetto was a substantial defeat, but it was no worse than what happened a few months later to the British Fifth Army between Croisilles and La Fere.

Cadorna faced the responsibility of command at this time of national emergency. He was attacked in the national press by critics from all corners. It was a disaster, this was correct; it was the biggest disaster that had befallen Italy, this could be correct; it was an absolute tragedy, this was wrong; but it rendered Caporetto a still-used synonym for catastrophe. Cadorna had made mistakes, but he was no worse than his British and French colleagues. His greatest fault was losing miles in a war where advances were measured in yards.

The Allies agreed to send French and British reinforcements to Italy. But they halted at Brescia, waiting in reserve. Cadorna employed Italian troops to stop the subsequent enemy assaults. He was removed from command, however, for a variety of reasons, including politics and Allied pressure. The French were particularly pleased with the change in the General Staff. Cadorna had often refused to act as they wanted. Now they hoped to put a French general in charge of the Italian Army or, at least, to see the Italian headquarters accept directions from the French.

The king appointed General Armando Diaz as the new chief of staff on November 9, 1917. The day after, Conrad attacked the Asiago Plateau with seven divisions, but was repulsed. Another Austrian attempt cross the Piave failed, too, as well as attacks against Mount Grappa. Then Diaz asked the Allies for help for a counteroffensive. In spite of the existing written agreements, the Allies refused until the Italians demonstrated they were capable of maintaining the front by themselves. They did. In fact, on November 22, Austrian troops made their last attempt, which failed, too. The Italian Supreme Command directed the British troops to Montello hill, and the French were deployed in the Tomba-Monfenera sector.[16] The front held into 1918.

Forgotten Soldiers: TAIF, France, Palestine, Salonika, and Albania: 1916-1918

Many Italian soldiers fought outside of Italy, too. France received both the TAIF and the II Army Corps. TAIF—Auxiliary Italian Troops in France—consisted of 60,000 men not fit for combat, employed in the rear area. Later, in April 1918, the Italian II Corps arrived in France, consisting of two divisions. It fought in the Argonne. In June it passed to the British Fifth Army on the Ardre, west of Rheims. It played a distinguished role resisting the Germans along the Fifth British Army front between Croisilles and La Fere. In August, II Corps went back to the Argonne and then to the Aisne, along the Chemin des Dames. In November it reached the Meuse river. It lost 16,502 dead throughout its operations in France, whereas the French lost no more than 500 men in Italy.

Another small Italian expeditionary force was fighting in Palestine, in Allenby's army. It took part in the third battle for Gaza and entered Jerusalem on December 11, 1917. A third Italian expeditionary force had been in Albania since rescuing the Serbian army in 1915. Now constituted as the XVI Corps, it was concentrated around Valona. The fourth and last expeditionary force was in northern Greece, composed of an infantry division, which took part in all the operations in the Salonika sector.

"Three Centuries of Faith and a Victory!"[17] 1918

The Royal Army reorganized substantially during the winter 1917–18. The United States provided much needed financial support—$10 billion to the Allies—and horses, cattle, raw materials, and war material. Italy and the Allies could strengthen their military organization, whereas the Central Powers had no great industrial state to resupply and bolster their drained economies.

In the last days of April, the army established 471 new artillery batteries. Factories produced more than 4,000 guns between January to May 1918. The newly established Motor Corps consisted of 71,700 men and 25,000 cars by October 1917. In January, despite losses after the Caporetto and Isonzo retreats, the corps increased to 82,000 men and 25,800 cars; 102,500 men and 29,800 cars in June, and 180,000 men and 37,700 cars by the end of the war.[18] The infantry too had been reorganized. The army raised an additional 104 regiments, from units broken during Caporetto and by adding recruits. Firepower was improved, with more machine guns and flamethrowers; and each regiment received a four-gun artillery section. All of this compensated for the loss of ordnance and portable weapons during the Caporetto offensive.

The reorganization and resupply of the Italian Army worried the Austrians, who refused to give the Germans support for their coming offensive on the Western Front, but instead launched another offensive on the Piave. It was the same mistake as in 1916. This time it proved fatal. On March 21, sixty-three German divisions attacked the British on a fifty-mile front between Croisilles and La Fere. The British Third Army retreated. The Fifth collapsed. Its divisions were scattered worse than the Second Italian Army had been in Caporetto. The Germans opened a ten-mile-wide breach and advanced on Amiens, dividing the French and British fronts. Fifty French divisions rapidly reinforced the line to stem the German breakthrough. This set the stage for the Second Battle of the Somme, which had a high political price. French general Foch demanded and obtained the supreme allied command in France, including British troops.

Diaz waited and watched for any indication of an Austrian offensive. Intelligence had warned him about Austrian movements. The Italian Information Service had done a good job during the war. After two battleships were sabotaged and sunk at Taranto by Austrian secret agents, it had stolen the Austrian codes with a night raid on the Austrian consulate in Zurich. Then it had warned Cadorna in advance of both the date of the Strafe Expedition and Caporetto. Unfortunately, Cadorna did not act upon the information. Diaz, however, acted differently. He carefully listened to the Information Service and prepared the army for its first major battle in 1918.

In the spring, intelligence informed him that fifty-eight Austrian divisions were preparing to attack. They were supported by more than 7,000 guns and 540 planes. An army commanded by Conrad, who had been demoted from chief of staff to army command, was to advance down the Trentino while another army commanded by Field Marshal Boroevich von Bojna had to cross the Piave. Verona was their strategic objective, but Venice the prestigeous one. Medals celebrating Emperor Charles's entrance into Venice had already been struck in anticipation of victory.

Diaz had fifty-six divisions, some 7,000 guns, and 560 planes. He carefully planned for the forthcoming battle. Austrian land operations had to be supported by naval action. For the first time in the war, the entire Austrian fleet had to sail past the Allied blockade out of Otranto and at the same time raid the *Regia Marina* in Brindisi.

On June 9 the first Austrian squadron came out of Pola to join the fleet in Cattaro, and then moved south. On June 10 at dawn, two Austrian battleships and seven destroyers were spotted by corvette captain Luigi Rizzo. He attacked the Austrian squadron, although he commanded only a couple of motor torpedo boats. Amazingly, he sunk the Austrian battleship *Szent Istvan* and escaped the destroyers. The Austrians subsequently abandoned their entire operation.

Back on the Continent, General Foch was urging Diaz to attack. Diaz replied that the army was not yet prepared for offensive operations. Foch responded that he needed help, that the Germans had launched an attack on the Aisne, and their leading units were a mere thirty-seven miles from Paris. The Germans took 85,000 prisoners and 1,200 guns; and the French government was preparing to leave the city once again, as it had done in 1914. On June 3 the German advance stopped.

Six days later they renewed the offensive, gaining a further eight miles. Urged on by the situation, on June 12, Foch sent a third request to Diaz, while the president of the French republic summoned the king's ambassador, demanding help. Foch wrote, "As the Austrian offensive had not taken place, one could exclude it as a possibility. Therefore, the Italian offensive had to be launched as soon as possible."[19]

Diaz simply did not respond. On that same June 12, at dawn, Austrian artillery opened fire, inaugurating Operation Avalanche, the offensive Foch had ruled out. Italian artillery reacted quickly and effectively, silencing the Austrians with counter-battery fire within two hours. The day after, at 3:30 a.m., the Austrians bombarded the Italian front again, but when their infantry went "over the top," it was massacred by Italian artillery. This was the last charge of the Habsburg Empire. Colonels in full uniform were seen leading their regiments out of the trenches, only to be killed after a few steps. The fire was so terrible that routed Austrian troops fled as far as Trente, and some even farther. More than eight thousand deserters were found on the other side of the Alps, at Innsbruck. Having failed to cross the Piave, too, the Austrian attack halted on July 6. The battle was over, and the empire with it.

The Italian armed forces improved their performance in battle. Motor torpedo boats filled the sea. Italian planes, after their greatest victory in the dogfight above Istrana in January, flew over Vienna. It was D'Annunzio's idea. He had made his first flight as a passenger in 1909, with Glenn Curtiss as the pilot. He loved flying, and planned a raid on the enemy capital. Nine Italian planes reached the city and dropped thousands of leaflets, declaring that they were too civilized to drop bombs. They said they were just demonstrating what the Italians could do if desired.

Summer passed slowly. One million American soldiers were fighting in France, but only a regiment and a few good pilots were sent to Italy.[20] The Western Front was as active as the Italian front was calm. The Germans launched numerous offensives, pressing the front to the breaking point. Foch urged Diaz again to intervene against the Austrians, but Diaz refused. Cadorna's actions through 1917 had so weakened the army that when Diaz was ready to move, in October, he had 200,000 men fewer than in June, because of the lack of available recruits. On September 29, Diaz finally decided to attack. Bulgaria just surrendered; and Italian troops from Salonika joined the Italian XVI Corps in Albania. The Austrian army in the Balkans was on the verge of collapse, particularly because the Germans had recently withdrawn their forces to continue their own operations on the Western Front.

Austrian forces in Italy consisted now of fifty-seven divisions with 6,030 guns and 564 aircraft. Diaz disposed of fifty-seven divisions, with 4,150 guns and more than 600 bombards. The Italian air force had 1,683 aircraft.

Diaz planned to throw the Austrians out of Venetia. It centered on a battle across the Piave around a little village called Vittorio Veneto. The offensive was delayed until October 24, the first anniversary of Caporetto. The Austrian army buckled under the weight of the Italian attacks. On the fifth day an Austrian delegation including a German officer requested an armistice negotiation. Austrians were admitted, the German was sent back. By October 31 the enemy the Italians had fought for more than one hundred years, the Imperial and Royal Austro-Hungarian Army, collapsed.

On November 3, 1918, at 3:15 p.m., the First Italian Army entered Trente while Italian ships entered Trieste harbor, landing *Bersaglieri* battalions. Twenty-four hours later, on November 4, 1918, at 3:00 p.m., "The war against Austria-Hungary, that under the high direction of His Majesty the King, supreme commander, the Italian Army, inferior in numbers and means, began on May 24, 1915, and with indestructible faith and tenacious valor, managed uninterrupted and under enormous duress for forty-one months, is won."[21] But the war was not over for Italy. Diaz sent a telegram to Paris about Austria's collapse, adding that war was not over for Italy as Germany was still fighting. That was why the Italians had not accepted talks with the German delegate.

The *Regio Esercito* planned operations to strike at Germany, following Austria's armistice. The army intended to pass the Alps, attacking Bavaria and Saxony from Austria with twenty-nine divisions, divided into three armies.[22] In fact, thanks to an armistice clause, Diaz forced the Austrians to give him control of their roads, railways, and telephone systems. On October 28, German general Gallwitz warned: "If Austria would make a separate peace, the situation would be desperate."[23] Sadly, later Ludendorff wrote: "In Vittorio Veneto, Austria did not lose a battle, but lost the war and itself, dragging Germany in its fall. Without the destructive battle of Vittorio Veneto, we would have been able, in a military union with the Austrian-Hungarian monarchy, to continue the desperate resistance through the whole winter, in order to obtain a less harsh peace, because the Allies were very fatigued."[24]

Kaiser William II could continue the war or surrender, but he had no more soldiers. The German army could now only resist on the Western Front. There were no troops available to stand against the coming Italian offensive. They retained more than 2 million men in Russia after the Treaty of Brest-Litovsk in January 1918. Their unwillingness to end occupation in the east to transfer their army to the west was a strategic blunder. The Austrians had done the same, and the results were apparent. In order to prevent the *Regio Esercito* from capturing Munich, and the Western Front from falling apart in the face of renewed Allied operations, the German government pursued negotiations.

On November 9, William left the throne, being ousted by a parliamentary revolution. The provisional German government asked the Allies for an armistice. The German army was still abroad. It occupied large portions of the former Russian empire, practically the whole of Belgium, and a great portion of northern France. No enemy had entered Germany, so why an unconditional surrender? Nobody told them that the despised and militarily ineffective Macaronis were the real threat. And, who could believe it? The Italians!? Come on! The only possible answer was that someone had betrayed Germany. And when on the eleventh hour of the eleventh day of the eleventh month of 1918 the guns remained silent, all the seeds of the next war were planted.

From the Great War to the Ethiopian War

After the War

The war ended, and Italian society was quite different from 1914. The Italian industrial system experienced remarkable growth; and Italy could now be considered an industrialized country, although it was still far from British and French standards, and that of the United States. The most significant change was that women had been out of the home, working in factories and for the local administration. This implied a new role for women in Italian society, but the basic right, the vote, was still twenty-eight years away. Austro-Hungarian and German troops returned home, more or less in order. Allied troops advanced and occupied increasing amounts of territory. They had to secure parts of Central and Eastern Europe due to the collapse of the Central Powers and Russia, in addition to the political vacuum after the fracturing of the Ottoman Empire. New states emerged with their own demands. Problems arose like mushrooms after a hard rain; and it was quite difficult if not impossible to resolve them.

French, British, American, and Italian troops attempted to provide order in the growing geographic chaos that developed after the war. Allied help was provided to the White Russians during the Russian civil war. Allied expeditionary forces including Italian troops operated in Siberia and Europe, near Murmansk, and on the Black and Caspian Seas. The former Ottoman Middle East was free, and the Turks lost everything but Anatolia and a little land around Istanbul. Italians, French, and British, however, occupied the capital, while the Greeks demanded the right to occupy the entire Anatolian Coast.[1]

Discussions, debates, and arguments concerning new borders became commonplace, and a threat to any general peace. President Wilson proposed to solve the problems using his Fourteen Points as an outline. They worked well on paper. They did not work well in reality, because people of different ethnic and national origins were mixed and each determined to join their closest cultural neighbor or be independent altogether. It was impossible to satisfy everyone. Plebiscites were held to define borders, in Poland, Germany, Hungary, Austria, and other new states. Allied armies deployed provisional garrisons until the Paris Peace Conference decided the final course of action. It was here that Italy, an Allied power, found itself in a rather shocking situation.[2]

Georges Clemenceau, the French prime minister, wanted to establish French influence in Central and Eastern Europe to the exclusion of others. This caused the first diplomatic crisis between Rome and Paris. Britain and France were interested in mandates—that is to say, in provisional administrative control—over the former Turkish territories in the Middle East as well as the former German colonies in Africa and Asia. Neither ally wanted to share with Italy. Britain was also looking for deeper involvement in former Russian and Turkish territories because of oil. Italy was trapped between the extra-European focus of Britain and a European-focused France, while coping with the apparently neutral position of United States. The other allied powers cut Rome off from the diplomatic game.

In fact, Italy received no former German colonies, because France and Britain made it clear during the negotiations that renouncing territories in Africa and Asia may mean obtaining more land in Europe. When discussion over European territory began at Versailles, the British and French invoked the Pact of London regarding Italian acquisitions; that is to say, the cession of Istria to the line Monte Nevoso–Volosca, including the islands of Cherso, the Quarnarolo, and Pago, but not Fiume and the island of Veglia.

President Wilson supported Italian demands to extend the northern Italian border to the Alps, including the strategic Upper Adige. But when negotiations turned to Istria and Fiume, French premier Clemenceau became obstructionist. France and Britain seemed to consider Italy more a defeated power than an ally, even though Italy was expected by its allies to send troops everywhere, and half the Italian navy was in the Black Sea and along the Anatolian coast. Italian expeditionary forces were in Murmansk, in Siberia, and scattered throughout Central Europe, but Italian territorial interests were ignored. German colonies had already been divided, and Britain and France refused to reopen the matter. During the war Japan had lost 1,344 dead compared to 680,000 Italians, but Japan obtained former German colonies and Italy did not.

The Greeks demanded Rodi, owned by Italy, and large portions of Turkey. France and Britain backed Greece. Yugoslavia wanted Dalmatia and Fiume, historically part of the Republic of Venice, and France supported Yugoslav demands over Italian protests. Greece and Yugoslavia wanted Albania. Italy had promised independence to Albania, but France supported both Yugoslavia and Greece. The result of all of this on the ground was that Italy simply abandoned the Allies. Italian troops in Anatolia had an increasing friendly attitude toward the Turks and did not provide support to the Greeks during the War between Greece and Turkey. Anti-French and British attitudes led Italy to pursue a philo-Muslim policy in the Mediterranean and Middle East.

Fiume was the crucial point. Italians populated the city, as had been the case in Istria and Dalmatia since the Venetian era. Slavs lived in the countryside, Italians lived in cities and towns. Fiume was just beyond the line of demarcation decided in London in 1915, but since October 1918, Italians in Fiume had voted to join Italy. According to Wilson's Fourteen Points, this should be satisfied. France and Britain, however, did not consider Wilson's policy useful in this case. Frequent clashes between Italian and Yugoslavian troopers in Fiume were followed by a clash between citizens and a French outpost. In the end, French troops fired on the Italians; and personnel from the *Regia Marina* were sent to keep the two apart. They were fired by the French. Italian seamen responded and destroyed the French outpost, and a diplomatic storm broke in Paris.

The Italians were ordered to change their garrison and reduce their presence in Fiume. Britain offered to send police units. The Italian population in Fiume planned an uprising. A grenadier battalion joined the plot and had contacts with D'Annunzio, who accepted the invitation to be leader of the uprising. On September 12, 1919, he led a military column into Fiume. The Fiume question was critical for the Italians, and D'Annunzio's popularity was so great that the troops ordered to stop him not only disobeyed, most joined him. D'Annunzio entered Fiume under a rain of flowers.

The Italian government had to deal with this enormous crisis. The Allies did not want Italian sovereignty over the city. D'Annunzio declared, however, he would not accept any solution other than full annexation to Italy.

In June 1920, Giolitti began his last premiership. He signed an agreement with Yugoslavia making Fiume a free city. Then he tried to negotiate with D'Annunzio. When talks failed in December, Giolitti ordered the navy and loyal troops to eject D'Annunzio and his supporters from the city. They shelled Fiume by land and sea and, on the last day of the year, the city surrendered.

The crisis was over, but it was a portent of things to come. The government looked weak. It had taken no real action during the nine months prior to Giolitti's premiership, and many people were concerned about the possibility of a nationalist revolution led by D'Annunzio. Giolitti too seemed unable to act promptly. The message was clear: an armed group could act against government policy without a quick and strong government reaction.

Fascism and the March on Rome

Italy's economic situation soon after the war ended was rather poor. The war cost 148 billion liras, twice the entire state expenditure from 1861 through 1913. Lack of money induced the government to cancel factory contracts and release soldiers as soon as possible.

Italian industries reacted to the end of government contracts by dismissing workers. Unemployment increased and in a few months became an economic tragedy. The government then placed the army and navy on a peacetime footing, leading to rapid demobilization. According to official figures, the Italian armed forces had reached 5 million men under arms. Excluding the 680,000 who died, and those remaining in service, some 4 million young men were now looking for work, flooding the labor market by early 1919. Wages dropped, and bread prices were officially controlled. The dollar increased from 6.34 liras in 1918 to 18.46 during the first quarter of 1920, passing 26 by October 1922. Wages did not increase but prices did, and Italy went into a terrible recession.

Economic problems placed pressure upon the political situation. Riots and disorder occurred throughout the country. The lower classes asked for social and economic aid. The Socialist Party's power increased quickly, and fear of a Communist revolution as had occurred in Russia soon appeared. The main problem was that the government, during the worst period of the war, had promised former soldiers coming from the countryside agricultural reforms, including the division of large properties among peasants. After the war, none of these promises were kept, and the economic situation went from bad to worse. Workers protested, went on strike and insulted and beat officers in uniform, as they represented the government. They occupied factories and fields and organized armed groups, most of them having had forty-one months of job training on the Carso and Isonzo.

The government appeared weak and irresolute. When the Socialists, generally called "Reds," attempted a general uprising in Italy in 1920, they seemed able—and later declared themselves to have been able—to control all the cities, except for six, because the government failed to provide central direction.[3] The upper and middle classes worried about revolution. Refugees from Russia reached Italy with terrible stories of bloody massacres by the Reds, and radical Socialist programs were similar to the Bolsheviks' policies. In the context of 1919, the Spartacists, the German Communist movement, staged a revolution in January, which was crushed only after much turmoil by the spring. A Communist revolution in Hungary succeeded until 1921, and the Bolsheviks were winning their civil war. The threat of Communist revolution was not theoretical, but very real.

Fascism emerged in the context of this postwar political upheaval and fear of Communist insurrection; but what exactly was Fascism? Benito Mussolini was a former Socialist and a Republican. He actively supported Italian intervention in the Great War in May 1915. He enrolled in the *Bersaglieri* and was released after being severely wounded by a grenade during an exercise. He continued his journalistic activities and, after the war, he returned to policy-making. He once said he drew some of his ideas from Sorel and a bit from Blanqui, both French Socialist theoreticians, but Fascism came from deep and complex roots. It was a natural path from Futurism, from the nationalist extreme Left, from the Garibaldinian Left, and more. In 1920, workers felt betrayed by the government that had drafted them and for whom they had fought in the war. They did not love Fatherland, because the Fatherland had sent them to the trenches, giving them no better life after the war. They despised the victory, because it gave them no advantages. They disliked the armed forces, because the armed forces were the most concrete symbol of the state and the war. They did not love aristocrats and bourgeoisie, who, as the owners of land, farms, and factories, were their master and enemies. Above all, workers simply wanted to survive, to have a job to pay for a house and food for their families. Revolutionaries promised them a better future, if they joined the revolution.

Conversely, the bourgeoisie had seen most of its sons die as reserve officers during the war. How could one admit they died for nothing? Despising victory meant despising and insulting their memory. Moreover, strikes damaged the middle class—no services, no mail, no trolleys, no trains worked—and worker uprisings frightened them. The government did not react. Public order disappeared. What could one do?

Into this disorder came the Fascists. To the eyes of bourgeoisie, they were former combatants. In case of strike, they drove trains and trolleys, they swept dirty streets, they secured public order, they respected officers and the armed forces, and above all they fought against the Socialist and Communist armed groups. They raided the occupied countryside; they reacted against the so-called "Red violence." This was important, especially for the big landowners of the Padana Plain. They supported and cultivated Fascism in Emilia to protect themselves and their properties. The result was that by April 1921, Fascism appeared well organized and powerful. It had money, it had people, it had supporters and it could fight against the "Reds."[4]

Clashes using firearms generally occurred between Socialists and Fascists, and criminals and killers were on both sides. A standard Fascist group, a *Fascio*, was composed of a *Squadra d'Azione*—Action Squad—also defined as *Squadraccia*, the Naughty Squad, and the remaining members. The *Squadra* was composed of former combatants and employed in "punitive expeditions," that is to say, raids against their opponents. The remainder of the *Fascio* was composed of young men, mostly high school and university students, used only "for booing in front of the Prefecture."[5]

Clearly the situation was far different and changed depending on the part of Italy. Industrial cities did not suffer from the same problems as agricultural towns, and the countryside was not the same as the coastal towns. For the working class, Fascism was clearly allied to the "owners," or to the "masters," and therefore they placed it on the other side of the barricade. The middle-class vision of Fascism appears as too simplistic, naive and definitely insincere—and often it was—but nobody, Mussolini included, had an idea of Fascism's future plans. The bourgeoisie sought order and, possibly, business. The Fascists were looking for immediate results. Mussolini had no long-term political programs, as Hitler and the Nazis had. He wanted power, no more. His comrades had no more ideas about future than he did.[6] They were a mixed group, including Republicans and monarchists, former Socialists and Conservatives, nationalists and time-wasters. Their liturgy came directly from the Risorgimento. The *Fascio*—the bunch—was an ancient Etruscan and Roman symbol of justice and public authority. In the eighteenth century, the Enlightenment discovered Roman Republican virtues, and the *Fascio* became the symbol of unity and the people's strength. In this sense it was used in the United States, in this sense it was adopted as the Republican coat of arms in France, and in this same sense it reappeared in Italy. The Roman heritage came from the French Revolution and from the Risorgimento. The eagle was the imperial symbol of ancient Rome, so Fascism filled its monuments with eagles, and *Fascio*, as other countries had in the past. Emilia-Romagna day laborers used black shirts as a work suit. Later, *Regio Esercito*'s *Arditi*—special commando units during the Great War—adopted black shirts; and black was the color of anarchism. What a contradiction in terms for a movement that was the essence of authority.

"Giovinezza," the official "Fascist triumphal anthem," in origin was the song from the popular prewar light opera *A Farewell to Youth*, about Turin university students and their girlfriends. Then it became a students' song and—when the students, after a few years, were called to arms—it was adopted as the regimental song for the 8th *Alpini*. From there, through veterans, it passed to Fascism. Its first line read "tightly tightly arm-in-arm, to a humble nice dressmaker." It later became "Hail you people of Heroes, Hail you Fatherland of Immortals." Fascism invented nothing. It simply took from here and there.

Gradually Fascism increased its relevance in Italian politics and society. Within a few months Socialist groups were beaten and destroyed everywhere, with little or no intervention by the police or government. When in the summer of 1922 the Socialist Party tried to organize a general strike, it was a failure. In October, Mussolini played his cards, preparing the March on Rome and declaring himself a monarchist. Premier Luigi Facta—a Giolitti man who did not possess Giolitti's energy—was unable to resist the unarmed Fascist groups marching on Rome. When on October 28, 1922, in the very early morning, he asked the king to issue special orders, Victor Emmanuel III refused. Facta resigned. That same day the king summoned Mussolini and gave him the premiership.

From the March on Rome to the Ethiopian War

Mussolini's period was marked by many military innovations. As Fascism touted a military spirit, it possessed an accentuated military look. The first issue was the Fascist Militia. The *Milizia Volontaria per la Sicurezza Nazionale*—Voluntary Militia for National Security—established itself halfway between a party-owned police and an army. They organized the former *Squadre d'Azione* into a disciplined new armed force. Its military effectiveness was rather poor and it could only act as light infantry. It disappeared in July 1943 and soon reappeared a few months later as "M"—Mussolini—Battalions of the Fascist Social Republic.

The issue was the air force. After the Great War, it had been established as a part of the army, but on March 28, 1923, a royal decree established the *Regia Aeronautica* as an independent armed force.[7] *Regia Aeronautica* personnel established a number of important flying records. In 1919, Lieutenant Antonio Locatelli, a Great War ace, was the first to fly across the Andes. The next year Arturo Ferrarin and Masiero reached Japan from Italy. In 1925, Francesco de Pinedo made a 34,200-mile flight from Europe to Asia and Oceania and back. In 1928, Ferrarin and Carlo del Prete made the longest nonstop flight, from Rome to Touros, in Brazil. In 1926, the airship *Norge*—designed and built in Italy as N. 1 by General Umberto Nobile—flew from Europe to Alaska, passing above the North Pole. The next airship flight made by Nobile ended with the *Italia* airship crashing as it returned from the Pole in 1928. This was the end of airships. Previous military exercises demonstrated that they had an increasingly scarce military relevance; and they were abandoned.

The real organization of the *Regia Aeronautica* began after 1926, when Italo Balbo—one of the *quadrumviri*, the four highest-ranked Fascists—was appointed undersecretary of state for the air force.[8] The *Regia Aeronautica*, however, established its first operational doctrines in 1929.[9] General Giulio Dohuet's air warfare theories on the strategic importance of massive air bombing surely influenced these doctrines, but a further examination shows an influence by General Amedeo Mecozzi, who had unquestionably been influenced by American general Mitchell's theories, too.[10] Italian operational doctrine sought to employ a small number of aircraft. Anyway, the first combined exercise, made in the summer of 1929 with the army and navy, demonstrated it was impossible to act without an air force in a modern war.

De Pinedo and Balbo experimented with various flying formations. The results were the transoceanic flights. After a first flight to Brazil, in 1933, Italo Balbo's twenty-four amphibious planes flew from Orbetello through Chicago to New York City. It was considered one of the greatest aviation successes of that period. Balbo paraded triumphally in New York, and a street in Chicago was named after him.

This kind of response helped bolster the Fascist regime—"the Regime"—making it appear modern and technologically advanced. Technology, however, required money for research and development. The country was still poor, and the Regime preferred to concentrate its resources on results everyone could understand. Research on radar was put aside, as well as radio-piloted remote-controlled aircraft and jet propulsion.

Other achievements came quickly. For the first time, an Italian transatlantic ship—the *Rex*—won the blue ribbon, in 1934. That same year electric locomotives in Italy ran at 93 miles per hour, and in 1939 they established the world record—126.138 miles per hour—during a trip from Florence to Milan, with an average speed of 102.526 miles per hour. Railroads in Italy consisted of ten thousand miles of track, of which 25 percent was electrified. Few lessons, though, were learned from all of this technological hype. For instance, Italy participated in the Schneider Cup, a prize to the fastest seaplane flight. In 1934 military pilot Francesco Agello reached 440.678 miles per hour.[11] This is still the world record for a seaplane. It was achieved using an inline engine, but in the following years and until 1942, the *Regia Aeronautica* asked only for radial engined aircraft. Protectionism played a major role, but industrialists preferred to exploit their old production chains instead of invest money in new systems for better products, and decision makers at the top seemed unaware of technological improvements.

The next war is normally prepared for by studying the previous one. This happened to the Italian armed forces. According to the best Italian expert on weapons, Lieutenant Colonel Filippo Cappellano, the impact of the Great War on the generals in the interwar period led them to pursue weapons, from hand grenades to tanks, capable of fighting in the mountains, because the last war had been fought primarily in the mountains. As the air force had not been relevant in the Great War, it was possible that, in spite of what the *Regia Aeronautica* said, the *Regio Esercito* and the *Regia Marina* chiefs of staff did not listen. Moreover, the Direttive, the air operational doctrine, if accepted, would give the *Regia Aeronautica* strategic management of the war, and both the army and navy did not like it.

Anyway, the *Regia Aeronautica* soon demonstrated its tactical and strategic importance. Since 1923, Mussolini had wanted to secure colonies. Somali Colonial Infantry quickly secured Somalia in 1926–27. Italian control of Libya needed to be expanded. During the Great War, Italy had lost positions in Libya, and its rule was reduced to some coastal towns like Tripoli, Homs, and Benghazi. Operations began in 1922 and ended ten years later, when all the territory was conquered and local resistance destroyed. The *Regia Aeronautica* effectively supported these land operations. Reconnaissance, supply, and medical evacuations were conducted by air with good results. Bombing proved to be basic for winning. It is still unclear exactly if poison gas was used. What is clear is that in 1929, *Regia Aeronautica*'s poison gas was over but the reason for this is still obscure.[12]

Colonial operations in Libya succeeded largely because of a young general, Rodolfo Graziani. A former grenadier officer, he had substantial colonial experience. He was promoted numerous times for his distinguished service on the Carso during the Great War and, when back in Libya in the early twenties, he immediately appeared as the best colonial operations officer. He used air reconnaissance to direct his fast-moving columns composed of trucks, armored cars, and even camels.[13] He gained such fame that, when asked about the best generals of his time, French marshal Lyautey included him. Of course, Graziani was not gentle and kind. His operations were rough and his behavior brutal, but he succeeded despite the cost in human lives.[14] This was the contemporary European way of acting in the colonies, and this was the policy in Ethiopia when war exploded there in 1935.

The Italo-Ethiopian War: 1935–1936 and 1936–1939

The *Regio Esercito* was reorganized in 1926 with the addition of the Tank Corps—*Corpo dei Carristi*. It was attached to the infantry, but in 1934, General Federico Baistrocchi reformed the entire army. The *Regio Esercito* fielded thirty-one infantry divisions, three *Celeri*—"Swift"—Divisions, and many Alpine Superior Commands. Light tanks appeared in cavalry regiments, too. Infantry firepower increased with the addition of a regimental artillery battery, mortars, and antitank units, new machine guns, new hand grenades, and the new "Model 33" steel helmet.

In 1934, Italy stopped the German attempt to seize Austria. Hitler had become Reich chancellor the previous year. He declared himself to be a pupil of Mussolini, but Mussolini did not have a great opinion of him, or of Nazism. Moreover, Italian policy protected Austria, and Austrian chancellor Döllfuss was Mussolini's close friend. When Döllfuss was killed by Nazis and Hitler prepared an invasion of Austria, Mussolini ordered three divisions to the Brenner Pass for a counterinvasion. Hitler abandoned his plans. France and Britain appreciated it, especially because Italy allowed them to avoid war. Hitler perceived Italy as the only reactive power among the European Allies of the Great War. He believed it would be a good idea to neutralize Italy by making it an ally.[15] A good opportunity appeared in 1934. After Adowa in 1896, the Ethiopians remained quiet until 1912. During the Italo-Turkish War and the Great War, they attempted to invade Italian colonies on six separate occasions, using up to fifty thousand men. For this reason, on June 4, 1930, the War Ministry prepared a plan for a war against Ethiopia.[16] When another border skirmish occurred in 1934, and after a British topographical expedition supported Ethiopians attacking an Italian outpost at Ual-Ual, Mussolini decided to act by October 1935.

The governor-general of Eritrea, Emilio De Bono, was placed in charge of organizing the next campaign. While Graziani stood in Somalia waiting for an opportunity, De Bono's troops crossed the Eritrean border on October 3, 1935. It was the worst possible terrain for a modern campaign; a dry, rough landscape, with rigid mountains and no roads. No less than 100,000 soldiers and workers had to build roads for the advancing army of 197,000 men with 700 guns and 200 tanks and armored cars. No fewer than 10,000 trucks shuttled supplies along hundreds of miles between the advancing army and the port of Massawa. According to all observers, the Italians were going to be defeated because of terrain and logistical problems.

The greatest problem was not the terrain, but a clash between policy and military-technical exigencies; and policy won. The sixty-nine-year-old marshal De Bono knew Eritrea and northern Ethiopia quite well. A former *Bersaglieri* officer, he had fought there beginning in 1887. He advanced slowly, securing his supply lines. Mussolini needed victories and ordered him to move faster. De Bono refused. He was forced to resign, and Marshal Pietro Badoglio replaced him. Badoglio was an artillery officer from Piedmont. During the Great War he had commanded the XVII Corps, which was smashed at Caporetto because he had directed his artillery not to fire without his personal orders. Then he disappeared, and no artillery fired on the German first wave. After Diaz's appointment as the new chief of staff, Badoglio was appointed deputy chief of staff to the surprise of many. He did not like Mussolini—in fact, as the army chief of staff in October 1922, he planned a military resistance against the March on Rome, but he made his career under his rule. As a governor in Libya, he oversaw final combat operations. Now he told Mussolini that the war in Ethiopia was progressing too slowly, and Mussolini appointed him governor of Eritrea.

Badoglio obeyed Mussolini and sped up the campaign. He did what De Bono refused to do. He advanced to the Uarieu Pass, beyond his logistical limit. Supplies now required a 125-mile trip from the logistical center of Senafé, instead of the previous 50 miles, and Italian deployment was unbalanced on its left wing. The Ethiopians observed these strategic problems, taking advantage of them to attack in January. Their offensive almost completely unraveled Italian operations, but the XXVIII October Blackshirt Division held on tenaciously, and the *Regia Aeronautica* dropped poison gas on the Ethiopian troops.[17] The clash between policy and the military ended with a quasi-defeat on the field. It would have direct consequences within four years.

The following months of war went quickly. Mussolini favored the northern front because he wanted to win on the same battlefields as the 1896 war. Nobody could deny that the terrain was useless for war, when compared to the flat southern front in Somalia. Graziani exploited it. He obtained Mussolini's permission to attack across the desert. He bought Caterpillars and Ford heavy trucks in United States for carrying supplies. Then he advanced with his 50,000 men against 70,000 Ethiopians. Graziani intercepted their radio communications, altered their messages, controlled their movements by air reconnaissance, and, in January, engaged them. While Badoglio was in crisis around Uarieu Pass, Graziani occupied the whole of southern Ethiopia. He was 275 miles from Addis Ababa, the Ethiopian capital, when Mussolini ordered him to move east; Addis Ababa was for Badoglio.

Supply problems were solved thanks to air transport. This allowed Badoglio to move faster and repeatedly defeat the Ethiopians around the Amba Aradam, the Amba Uorc—the Golden Mountain—and in the Sciré, until their final collapse at the battle of the Ahshahngi Lake. Then he advanced with a motorized column composed of 1,870 trucks and cars. He was stopped at Termaber Pass, as 650 cubic yards of mountain route had been blown up by the Ethiopians' Swedish military advisers. It was repaired within twenty-four hours, and Badoglio entered Addis Ababa on May 5, 1936, as he had promised Mussolini.[18] That same evening Mussolini announced the victory to Italy and the world. Four days later he proclaimed the Italian Empire, composed of Eritrea, Somalia, and Ethiopia. Victor Emmanuel III became *il Re Imperatore*, the king-emperor, but the war was not over. Badoglio knew it and did all he could to leave Ethiopia as soon as possible.

On May 20, Graziani took the office of viceroy and was immediately occupied fighting guerrillas. In fact, the rapid Italian victory had involved no more than a quarter of Ethiopia in the theater of war. Lack of roads and rough terrain made the Ethiopians hard to find and defeat. Moreover, Ethiopians resisted Italian authority, and the scattered Italian garrisons were easy to attack or besiege. Graziani applied the same system he had employed in Libya, including poison gas; but success eluded him. The Libyan desert had been easily controlled by air; Ethiopia's wooded terrain was difficult.

Increasing violence in Italian operations pushed the Ethiopians to make an attempt on Graziani's life in February 1937 in Addis Ababa. He was severely wounded. He ordered a bloody massacre in the city as retaliation. A few months later Mussolini recalled him and appointed Amadeus of Savoy, duke of Aosta, the new viceroy. Amadeus—eldest son of the commander of the Third Army in the Great War—ruled well. He improved the military situation, but as a *Regia Aeronautica* general, he was not in charge of land warfare. General Ugo Cavallero was given that responsibility. Cavallero began operations in January 1938. He had no light hand, but his large-scale operations succeeded. As the British Foreign Office remarked in 1939, there was no doubt that Ethiopia was now fully controlled by Italian forces.[19]

CHAPTER **23**

"Overseas Spain" and "Overseas Tirana": 1936–1939

Ethiopia's Consequences

The Ethiopian war caused more trouble for Italy than one could imagine. As soon as the 1934 Ual Ual clash ended, a nasty debate occurred between Italy and Ethiopia at the League of Nations, the international league born after the Great War. France and Britain supported Ethiopia and charged Italy with aggression against another member of the League. Mussolini reacted poorly and refused to stop his military action. The League imposed "sanctions," that is to say, commercial restrictions on Italy. Mussolini declared that Italy was under siege by the League and proclaimed the so-called "autarchia," a form of national economic self-sufficiency. The nation responded enthusiastically. France and Britain were still perceived as rich countries forbidding proletarian Italy from finding "a place in the sun."

Once again, for the second time, Italians recalled how poorly they were treated by Britain and France in the treaty negotiations after the Great War, when no former German colonies had been given to Italy. "Sanctions" were the worst mistake from a propaganda perspective, and Mussolini's popularity soared. By stepping back, however, the whole situation appeared quite differently. London and Paris were in trouble. They needed Italian military support to prevent any possible further German initiatives; but it was impossible not to take a strong stance against Italian aggression toward another member of the League. Both governments therefore imposed sanctions, but excluded oil from the embargo. Italian military vehicles received all the gasoline they needed to win in Ethiopia, and it was not by chance.

Britain and France—especially Britain—looked at the issue as a problem to be concluded as quickly as possible. If Italy lost the war, the question was over. If Italy won, the only possible solution would be to look "officially angry" at Italy. Then, after a few years, when diplomatic waters calmed, an agreement could be made. In fact, in the spring of 1938 the British government officially recognized the Italian empire, including its possession of Ethiopia. Unfortunately, Mussolini assumed this was a sign of weakness.

Shortly after sanctions were imposed, Mussolini left the League of Nations and moved closer and closer to Germany. He gave his assent for Hitler to seize Austria. By a diplomatic and commercial perspective, leaving the League did not result in isolation. The United States, Germany, and Japan were not members of the League; and trade with them was possible. Unfortunately, thanks to traditional Italian provincial shortsightedness, Mussolini looked to Europe instead of the world. He did not pursue President Roosevelt's formal and informal offers for talks, and slowly he fell into Hitler's trap.[1]

"Overseas Spain"

In the summer of 1936, many Spanish generals revolted against the country's Republican government. They asked Italy and Germany for military support. Mussolini did not like the idea very much, but he saw it as an opportunity to outmaneuver France. From the Italian point of view, France appeared to have a peculiar ability to act in a way that drew the ire of other countries. In those years, not only did Italians view French attitudes as hostile toward Italy, but also premier Leon Blum made two policy errors, which further alienated Italy. The first was a Franco-Spanish pact. Spain allowed French troops transit through Spanish territory to reach North Africa in case of war against Italy. The second was his announcement of sending weapons, ordnance, and men to support the Spanish Republic.

Mussolini did not care about Spanish affairs, but if French intervention rendered Spain a sort of French protectorate, or strategic ally, Italy could find both the exits from Mediterranean closed to Italian shipping. Suez was owned by a French-British company. The Straits of Gibraltar were passable because Spain owned the African side, despite British possession of Gibraltar. What if France indirectly controlled that side as Britain controlled the European one? This could pose a threat to Mussolini's strategic interests. Italian foreign minister Galeazzo Ciano convinced Mussolini to commit the *Regio Esercito* for the OMS—*Oltre Mare Spagna* (Overseas Spain)—operation.

The Italian Military Mission arrived first in Spain to coordinate with General Francisco Franco. Then the *Regia Aeronautica* sent him a squadron of twelve bombers. On August 4, 1936, Italian aircraft attacked and swept the loyal Republican Spanish fleet out of the Straits of Gibraltar. Then Italian and recently arrived German aircraft transported Spanish colonial troops from Africa to Spain.[2] Italian military support gradually increased. Technicians, tanks, and specialists were sent to Franco as volunteers. He lacked modern weapons and used them not for training his troops, but directly in combat. Italian light tanks played a basic role in smashing the enemy front at Navalcarnero, on October 21. Three days later, Italian military advisers had to fight in Borox. Italian light tanks met Russian-made tanks for the first time and won. Just as the Spanish nationalists and Falange (the Spanish conservative-right party) received support from Italy and Germany, the Republic, which was dominated by Socialists, Communists, and anarchists, received substantial aid from the Soviet Union.

Italian armored forces acted as the Spanish Nationalists' vanguard and reached Madrid University during the tenacious battle for the capital. The Italian General Staff realized this was no more matter of training the Spanish and, with Mussolini's direction, increased its military involvement by committing forty thousand more men. "Who asked for it?"[3] Franco curtly asked Lieutenant Colonel Emilio Faldella, chief of the Italian Military Mission, although he did not refuse them.

The CTV—*Corpo Truppe Volontarie* (Corps of Voluntary Troops)—arrived in Spain. It was composed of four light divisions supported by a large heavy artillery contingent—the *Artiglieria Legionaria* (Legionnaire Artillery)—and an air component, the *Aviazione Legionaria*.

Thousands of pages have been written to demonstrate that the CTV were anything but volunteers and that Italy's involvement in the Spanish Civil War was unpopular; they are largely wrong. Although it is true that the first three thousand men sent to Spain in December originally applied to go to Ethiopia as civil laborers, it is also true that, according to archival documents, a lot of people asked to volunteer for Spain. The Army Archive contains many reports about it. For instance, L'Aquila Military District received hundreds and hundreds of applications. Campobasso Military District suddenly received more than one thousands volunteers.[4]

Why such large participation in this civil war? There were two central reasons. The first was propaganda. News from Spain, more or less enhanced by state propaganda, depicted a terrible situation in Spain. The horror of the war being waged against the clergy, with monks and priests being tortured and shot, nuns raped, churches destroyed, and sacrilege committed, all played upon the Italian public. For a Catholic country such as Italy, these horrors were enough to encourage a sort of "crusade," as the Nationalists called the war. The second reason was money. Each volunteer received a 300-lira enlistment bonus, 20 liras daily pay, and an additional 3 pesetas daily pay from the Spanish Nationalist government. It was a lot of money for the lower classes, especially in a period of high unemployment, even if the Fascist government did not admit it.[5]

General Mario Roatta commanded the CTV—under the name Mancini, because officially Italy was not involved. They fought successfully at Malaga and Motril in February 1937.

On the Republican side, a lot of volunteers were coming from everywhere to fight Fascism. George Orwell from England, Ernest Hemingway from the United States, and, incidentally many Italians, too, who composed a battalion. Italians were present on both sides, but Franco did not like it. When he thought that strategic suggestions from Rome were becoming too intrusive, he sought to reduce their presence, yet events convinced him otherwise. On February 15, 1937, he asked the CTV to launch an offensive on Guadalajara within a month. Three days later, however, after a victorious Republican counterattack, Franco asked Roatta for immediate intervention. It was the turning point.

On March 8, 1937, Italian troops attacked along the Carretera de Francia, the route from the south to Madrid, Saragossa, and France. Snow and ice pelted the advancing troops, and bad weather over Nationalist airfields prevented any air support for the Italian offensive. On the Republican side, good weather did not restrict Republican aircraft from providing air cover. Moreover, when the Republicans counterattacked, the Nationalists gave no support to the Italians. Despite these circumstances the CTV initially advanced 22 miles, lost 12, and then held the remaining 10 miles. But they failed to reach their objectives, and the battle had to be considered a loss. After this, Franco did not accept Italian strategic advice.

Republican propaganda exploited this victory: *No pasaràn*—They will not pass! Mussolini was so angered by this propaganda that he determined to commit greater forces to the war. Italian troops increased in quality and quantity and Mussolini finally admitted official involvement on October 20, 1937. His admission also ended the grotesque "piracy" in the Mediterranean. Since the early days of the civil war, merchant ships en route to Spain had been sunk by "mysterious" submarines. The *Regia Marina*, did not admit responsibility, but it was well known. After a League of Nations initiative, the *Regia Marina* together with German *Kriegsmarine*, the British Royal Navy, and French *Marine Nationale* participated in antipiracy control in the Mediterranean and along Spanish coasts.

The Italian and German secret services in the Black Sea and Dardanelles observed Soviet ships carrying supplies and ordnance to Spain. Italian submarines acted accordingly and "pirates" sank the ships. But it was thanks to the operations against piracy that the Royal Navy was able to decipher the *Regia Marina*'s secret codes. This would become a problem for the Italian navy in a few years.[6]

On land, Italian forces fought on all Spanish fronts. The Legionnaire Air Force, as the *Regia Aeronautica* was called in Spain, lost 175 pilots in combat. Troops were used in the north; and Legionnaire Artillery support played a fundamental role in the campaign in the north. Italian troops took part in seizing Bilbao, and the following battle of Brunete was won with the decisive role of the *Aviazione Legionaria*: It destroyed 100 enemy aircraft, and its close air support halted enemy counterattacks. Italian troops later attacked and, on August 26, seized Santander. When Italian tanks reached the center of the city, Nationalist supporters acclaimed them, crying, *"Han pasado! Han pasado!"*—they passed! After that battle, General Ettore Bastico was recalled to Rome. In fact, Franco protested because Bastico allowed many military and local civilian Republican officers to seek refuge on British ships. It was not the first time Italians acted differently from Spaniards. Italian troops considered Republicans as prisoners of war. The Nationalists did not. In the early days of the war their military courts sentenced prisoners to death. A first Italian formal protest made little impact. When Italian headquarters protested again, the Nationalists replied that they were being more careful about who was sentenced to death: they acquitted up to 30 percent of the total!

Further operations proved decisive for the war in northern Spain. Franco's troops were hard-pressed near Huesca in December and were saved by the Legionnaire Artillery and Air Force. In March, Italian troops fought in Catalonia. They took Huesca and marched to the mouth of the Ebro. By the time they reached the sea they had lost 3,000 men, taken 10,000 prisoners, and captured three cities and fifty towns. The Spanish Republic was now cut in two.

The war ended on April 1, 1939. Italian support had clearly been decisive. The CTV lost 6,000 dead and 16,000 wounded, but further support was given Spain. Mussolini presented Franco with all the vehicles and heavy weapons used by the CTV. He did so because it was cheaper to leave them instead of shipping them back to Italy, but as it was the spring 1939, it was the worst possible time to give such a present to anyone. Italy would sorely miss the heavy equipment.

"Overseas Tirana"

Hitler was slowly moving Europe to the brink of war. French and British appeasement and Italian diplomatic support allowed Hitler in 1938 to acquire part of Czechoslovakia. He pursued a closer friendship with Italy in order to achieve an alliance. Mussolini did not like Germans very much, but Germany seemed powerful and impossible to stop, while Britain and France appeared weak and uncertain and the United States was far away and not interested in European affairs.

Mussolini believed the "young peoples"—Italy, Germany, and Japan—were ready to seize world leadership through a war against Britain and France. The last diplomatic conflict over Ethiopia and the Spanish Civil War had demonstrated how far Italy was from Britain and France. Moreover, French attitudes were all but friendly. Mussolini then moved Italy toward a military alliance with Japan and Germany.

Mussolini decided to secure Italy's strategic position first in the Adriatic. He wanted to close the Channel of Otranto, and the easiest thing to do was seize the Albanian harbor of Valona, key to the eastern side of the Adriatic. Albania had been essentially an Italian protectorate since the 1926 Treaty of Tirana, which established Italian-Albanian friendship. Nobody, however, could divine the future, and Mussolini decided that Albania had to be conquered.

On April 4, 1939, the *Regia Aeronautica* deployed on the airfields of Grottaglie, Brindisi, and Lecce its Squadron A, while the *Regia Marina* concentrated its ships for transporting the *Regio Esercito* expeditionary force: 22,000 men, 125 tanks, 860 vehicles, 1,200 motorcycles, and 64 cannons for operation "Overseas Tirana."

Convoys left Italy on April 6, and troops landed the next morning. The Italian advance guard entered Tirana on April 9 at 10:10 a.m. Soon after, Italian S. 81 aircraft landed in Tirana carrying a grenadier regiment. By April 10, Overseas Tirana was over. Italy had lost 12 dead and 81 wounded to conquer what the king defined as "a land containing four stones." On April 12, Albania offered its crown to Victor Emmanuel III, who now was "king of Italy and of Albania and emperor of Ethiopia."

The War with the Germans: 1940–1943

How Not to Prepare for a War: 1937–1939

Libya, Ethiopia, Spain, Albania, and the Italian armed forces had been at war since 1923, apart from a short interruption between 1933 and 1935. In the spring of 1939 their situation was poor, and it was poor at the moment the biggest war the world had ever seen was on the horizon. The first problem was the lack of a central state policy. What was Mussolini's foreign policy? It was unclear. He changed it so frequently that it was really hard to make concrete military plans. Current war plans included an anticipated intervention against France, or Yugoslavia, or both. A further likelihood was a conflict with Britain, but in that case the land war would be fought in the African colonies and naval engagements in the Mediterranean.

The question remained: could Italian armed forces face a war on that scale? The answer was clear: not at this time. The standard interpretation concerning the state of the Italian armed forces in 1939 is that they possessed old equipment that would be useless in a modern war. This is a fallacy. Their equipment was as good as the other European armed forces in 1939, except perhaps the Germans. The problem was that the Italian armed forces lacked sufficient equipment to carry out the operations with which they were tasked. They did not have enough vehicles, weapons, and ammunition. It was something one could expect after fifteen years of war in Africa and Europe, including intervention in China.

The Italian armed forces could not acquire the material it needed in sufficient quantities because Italy lacked an effective industrial system.[1] Italian industry's traditional attitude did not change after the Great War. The 1936 League of Nations sanctions improved it slightly because the lack of foreign products forced Italians to buy domestic goods despite their high price and lower quality. In terms of military value this was not a terrible problem prior to 1939. When World War II, however, sped up the pace of technological advances, the weakness of Italian industry became all too apparent and the production gap increased compared to other nations. Comparative figures for war production of high-technological production such as aircraft are quite revealing. In 1939, Italy produced 1,750 aircraft; in 1940, 3,250. The next year, 1941, marked the highest point of production with 3,503. Then Italian production slowly decreased: 2,813 in 1942, and 1,930 in 1943, for a total of 13,523 planes throughout the entire conflict. In 1942, Japan made 9,300 planes, the Soviet Union 8,000, Britain 23,671, the United States 47,859, and Germany made 15,596; that is to say, in only one year Germany produced more aircraft than Italy did in four years of war. German aircraft were faster, more effective, and more powerful and modern than Italian ones. In the period 1939–45, Japan produced 64,800 aircraft, the Soviet Union 99,500, Germany 125,072, Britain 125,254, and United States more than 300,000.[2]

The same happened for other weapons. Italy could produce good material, but their quantity was insufficient to manage a modern war; and industrial cartels were able to impose their products despite their quality.

Coordination of war production was also severely lacking. General Cavallero, who left the army just after the Great War,[3] became general director of Pirelli, the well-known Italian producer of tires and rubber products established by a former Garibaldino. The Pirelli Company was involved in the Credito Italiano banking group. Cavallero left his position in 1925 when Mussolini appointed him as war undersecretary. He directed the 1926 military reform together with Badoglio, who at that time was chief of the General Staff. After three years, Cavallero left the ministry to return to Credito Italiano. With Mussolini's influence, he was appointed president of Ansaldo, the heavy industry conglomerate specializing in steel, armor, guns, tanks, and naval engineering. Through Cavallero's military contacts, Ansaldo soon had a monopoly to supply the armed forces. In 1933, Ansaldo passed to IRI, the national Institute for Industrial Reconstruction. IRI rescued and reorganized a significant number of Italian companies in trouble. In that same year Ansaldo produced the little L3 light tank; and Cavallero made a ten-year contract with Ansaldo and Fiat to build tanks. The two companies practically established a monopoly. After the 1933 "armor scandal" about poorly made armor, less effective and resistant than needed but made for military purposes, due to a possible collusion among Ansaldo, Terni, and San Giorgio, Cavallero left Ansaldo[4] and, as discussed in the preceding chapter, returned to the army for East African operations. In 1941 he was appointed chief of staff of the *Regio Esercito* after Graziani resigned.

As a result of the virtual monopoly and because of the old-fashioned mind-set among industrial leaders, the Italian armed forces received up-to-date weapons only until 1938. Then the industrialists prevailed. Factories did not improve their production systems and preferred to exploit what they had in spite of the desire for new technologically improved products. Moreover, the monopoly prevented competitors from entering the market with new and innovative war material. For example, in 1941, Fiat and Ansaldo canceled contracts for producing German Panzer III and IV tanks under license; furthermore, they decided not to develop the Skoda 21 tank, also under license because it would have been impossible to produce without involving other companies such as Alfa Romeo, Reggiane, OTO, and Lancia. The Italian Army was interested in producing the German designed Maybach engine for tanks. It did not happen, because it preferred to introduce the Ansaldo engine for the Italian P 40 heavy tank. The P 40 was available in the autumn of 1943 and was used by the Germans after the Italian armistice.[5]

It was the same during the Russian campaign. The *Regio Esercito* staff realized the *valenki*, the winter boots used by the Soviets, were very good for Russia's winter weather. It called for bids from national companies to produce them. One company proposed production. The others did not try to compete for the contract through a competitive offer; they simply did what they could to prevent the first company from obtaining the contract. No company prevailed. The result was simple, Italian soldiers kept their old shoes.[6]

This industrial mentality explains why the *Regio Esercito* began the war with useless tanks. The L3 light tanks were equipped with a couple of machine guns and thin armor. The L6 were not much more effective. The M 11/39 had two machine guns in its 360-degree rotating turret and a gun fixed in the front; contrary to what was needed. The M 13/40 was better, but its speed was slow, its armor thin—in fact, crews improved it with sandbags—and its cannon was a simple 1.8-inch gun. During the war Ansaldo made the 3-inch self-propelled howitzer using the M 13 body. It was sent to Northern Africa and was a surprise for British tanks. As a tank officer later wrote, nobody ever understood why the army and Ansaldo respectively continued ask for and to produce the M 13 tanks and its improvement M 15/42.[7] It would have been better to produce the more powerful 3-inch self-propelled howitzer. In fact, it was more effective, faster, and cheaper to build, because it was an M 13 deprived of the turret.

According to General Carlo Favagrossa, who on May 23, 1940, read in a newspaper that he had been appointed undersecretary of state for war production, the situation was poor for the army and air force, but good for the navy. In autumn 1939 the *Regia Aeronautica* had 2,856 aircraft, but only 1,190 were combat-ready. Flight schools had 218 additional planes. No heavy bombers existed and no Italian aircraft had as powerful engines and weapons as the foreign equivalents. In 1918 the Italian air force had 1,683 modern aircraft.

The *Regia Marina* had no aircraft carriers, but the capital ships were quite good and modern, other than submarines. Ammunition and ordnance were good, too, as well as sufficient fuel supplies.

The *Regio Esercito* experienced the worst situation. According to the report presented by Graziani on May 25, 1940, its divisions were too lightly armed. It had 23,000 vehicles, 8,700 special vehicles, 4,400 cars, and 12,500 motorcycles. Tanks numbered some 1,500 useless light tanks and merely 70 medium battle tanks.

The *Regio Esercito* possessed only half the number of vehicles it needed to manage something similar to the German "Blitzkrieg." It was impossible—as Graziani said—to fill the gap, because the country simply did not have enough cars and trucks. Artillery was old and had little ammunition. Fuel was sufficient for only a few months. Italy produced 15,000 metric tons of crude oil annually. Albania provided 100,000 more metric tons. Normal armed forces consumption was 3 million tons in peacetime; in war it increased to 8 million.[8] Libyan petrol had been discovered, but it was too deep to exploit.

The *Regio Esercito* fielded 93 divisions in 1939. After the so-called 1938 "Pariani reform," an infantry division had two infantry regiments, an artillery regiment, a mortar battalion of two companies, an antitank company, and a Blackshirt Legion, which was essentially an infantry regiment of two battalions instead of three. Each infantry regiment had 1,650 men, as did the artillery. The Legion had 1,200 men, and each company 150. An infantry division therefore had no more than 7,000 men.

How could Italy wage a global war with armed forces under these conditions? Millions of pages from diaries, memories, articles, archives, and histories overwhelm the historian who seeks to explore this issue. There is a great need for further detailed study. Italian historians are expected to cull their own archives, but there remains a lot of work to do and, very often, these historians do not consult foreign archives and research in Britain, France, Germany, and the United States.

On the other hand, most foreign researchers generally do not know Italian, therefore, Italian documents and histories cannot be consulted. The Italian Armed Forces Historical Office published official histories of virtually all the campaigns. While there lacks a general interservice official history, one can still gain a good and complete perspective of Italian operations. Official and unofficial accounts are detailed, but a historian absolutely needs to consult contemporary documents, too, otherwise it is impossible to understand what happened and why.

What comes out of this sea of papers, when digested, is that Mussolini did not like Germans, but he was sure that France and Britain did not like him. The Germans seemed more powerful and friendly than France and Britain, and they desired a military alliance with Italy. They signed the Pact of Steel, forming the so called Rome-Berlin Axis. According to the pact, in subsequent negotiations and agreements, a division of the world was foreseen. Germany would expand eastward, that is to say, against Russia. Japan would expand in Far East; and Italy would expand in the Mediterranean basin, including the Balkans and the Black Sea. Conquests in Africa were to be divided between Italy and Germany.

When Germany attacked Poland, Mussolini proclaimed Italian neutrality. No matter. Hitler did not need an Italian intervention. He looked only to deprive the former Great War allies of Italy, and he succeeded. Mussolini—as all Italians—was shocked by the Nazi-Soviet pact in August 1939. He had not been informed of it and this was enough to compel him to renounce the German alliance in favor of Britain and France.[9] But no French or British offer was made. Moreover, the Germans quickly seized Denmark, Norway, the Netherlands, and Belgium and, in May 1940 they attacked France in an impressive succession of great victories. In a few weeks the supposedly most powerful army in Europe, the French, collapsed. The British Expeditionary Force was cut off and surrounded at Dunkirk. American intervention was practically impossible and the Soviet Union was neutral. The end of the war appeared to be on the horizon.

Mussolini concluded that the best choice was to join the Germans in their war against France and Britain, in order to seize territory in the Mediterranean. Malta, Corsica, Savoy, and Nice—the Italian territories possessed by foreign powers—and Tunis along with other African lands were meant to compensate Italy for the "disloyal behavior" London and Paris had exhibited in 1919.

Mussolini imagined that peace talks would begin shortly, after only a few weeks of war and a few casualties. The few casualties, however, had their own political and military impact. Mussolini distrusted the Germans. He feared a German-Italian conflict after the war. Hitler could be magnetically fascinating, but he was an unreliable ally and his men were corrupt criminals.[10] Moreover, as Marshal Enrico Caviglia wrote in his journal, Italy had practically no money, as the competent minister admitted in front of the Chamber of the *Fasci* and Corporations, the new name of the Chamber of Deputies. The situation remained critical; and Mussolini decided to preserve Italian military power in case of a German-Italian clash in the postwar era. In the best case, the current war would weaken Germany so much that Hitler would prefer not to attack Italy. In the worst case, Italy would at least have the power to resist.[11] Conversely, the Germans looked with suspicion and derision at Italy.[12]

Marshal Caviglia wrote that under these circumstances, Italy decided on a very strange strategy. Declare war on France and Britain, but only move forces when the end of the war was near. Mussolini could then demonstrate his troops were fighting; and this would be sufficient to claim territory as compensation for participation. This was not a strategy, but a shortsighted political trick, and it ultimately led to the collapse of Italy.

Italy declared war on France and Britain on June 10, 1940. Army Group West, composed of the First and the Fourth Armies, attacked France on June 21, the day after the French requested an armistice with Italy. The attack was a failure; and Mussolini asked for only a thirty-one-mile-deep occupation zone on the French side of the Alps. Then, an air expeditionary force was sent to Belgium to support German air operations against England. A submarine base was established in Bordeaux for transoceanic operations in the Atlantic against Britain and, later, the United States. After the armistice with France, then, the only active Italian front remained in eastern Africa.

East Africa: 1940–1941

The Italian Army in East Africa consisted of 280,000 men, largely colonial troops. After the declaration of war in June 1940, the number increased to 324,000 by conscripting local Italians. Unfortunately, they had old weapons and practically no ammunition. In fact, when excluding no more than 200 rounds for each machine gun, each soldier had exactly three hand grenades and 45 rounds for his rifle. There was one truck for every 190 men, and no supplies reached Italian East Africa during the war, except for a little arriving via air from Libya across the desert. Italian forces had 200 planes, a light tank squadron, a medium tank company, 984 guns, and 275 mortars for operations.[13]

The British and French had no such a forces available, despite the lack of adequate logistics, thus the Italian offensives into Somaliland and Kenya were successful. The Italians followed up by seizing the shore of Lake Rudolph and Kurmuk, Gallabat, and Cassala in Sudan. The British reacted on November 6, 1940, when British, Sudanese, and Indian troops supported by a twenty-six-gun artillery unit and a tank squadron attacked the Italian garrison at Gallabat and Metemma. Colonel Ezio Castagnola had only three battalions, no tanks, and a bit of air support, but he repelled the British attack and destroyed half of their tanks. According to the standards of the war in Africa, this was an enormous victory, but it was not exploited. Italian East Africa chief of staff General Claudio Trezzani decided to maintain a defensive posture after the initial successes. Italian troops stood until the British and South Africans counterattacked the following year. In January 1941, after Graziani's retreat in Libya, British troops came down from the Sudan and up from Kenya. In a few months the Italian position collapsed. Italian resistance in Keren was marvelous; Generals Carnimeo and Lorenzini directed it very well from February 3 until March 27, 1941, but it was not enough.

In the south, the British troops studied Graziani's previous campaign. They came from Kenya along the same route Graziani had used in 1936 to seize Ethiopia. The Italians' lack of ordnance, trucks, tires, and fuel made the rest rather easy. On April 6 the South Africans entered Addis Ababa. Two days later, British troops coming from the north captured Massawa after desperate Italian resistance. *Regia Marina* units suffered a different fate. Some scuttled their ships. Submarines escaped by circumnavigating Africa; and the colonial ship *Eritrea* reached Indonesia and joined the Far East Italian Squadron. On May 19, 1941, after a seventeen-day-long, 35,000-round bombardment, the duke of Aosta surrendered with his 5,000 soldiers on Amba Alagi.

Italian resistance continued in Gimma and Gondar. General Gazzera evacuated Gimma on June 21, and retired west, finally surrendering with all his remaining troops to the Belgians coming from the Congo, on 3 July. General Nasi continued to resist in Gondar. After a terrible aerial bombing and artillery shelling, on November 28, 1941, the twentieth year of the Fascist era, the last garrison of the Italian empire surrendered.

Guerrilla operations continued as small groups scattered throughout Ethiopia and Somalia attacked British troops. Some them received money from the Imperial Treasury the duke of Aosta had left to the Italian Committee in Addis Ababa. The chief of the same Committee, Angiolino Savelli, a civilian in charge of the administration under British supervision, was in contact by radio with the *Regia Marina* headquarters in Rome. This situation lasted until 1946, when the last resistance group, commanded by Royal Carabineers African corporal Alì Gabré surrendered to British authorities. At the end of 1942, however, most activity ended because of a lack of ammunition and weapons.

Greece

While British troops seized Keren and Massawa in East Africa, in the spring of 1941 the bloody Grecian campaign ended in Europe.

Mussolini attacked Greece on the eighteenth anniversary of the March on Rome, October 28, 1940. He authorized the war because Greece, in spite of its neutrality, allowed the Royal Navy to refuel in its national waters. Second, after the Nazi-Soviet Pact in 1939, Stalin was free to move against Romania by occupying Bessarabia (Moldova). In late summer 1940, Moscow presented Bucharest with an ultimatum. Romania had little choice but to accept it. Although this was not perceived as a problem when Hitler agreed to the pact in 1939, the speed of conquest pushed up his war schedule and it became apparent that with the invasion of the Soviet Union on the horizon, the Soviet air force could now reach the Ploesti oil fields within thirty minutes from their bases in Bessarabia and Germany acquired practically all of its oil from Romania.

In order to secure Romania, Hitler sent a German military mission to Bucharest. Mussolini was informed of this on October 12, 1940. He reacted badly. According to existing Italian-German agreements, after the war, Romania and the Balkans were to be in the Italian zone. If the Germans entered Romania, Italy needed to consolidate its position, and the best way was to secure control of the Black Sea egress by seizing Greece. Greece could be easily attacked from Albania; and Mussolini ordered his chiefs of staff to plan accordingly.

Meeting on October 17, 1940, the *Regio Esercito* told Badoglio, chief of the general staff, that the lack of railways and the poor road system in Albania required 500 trucks to keep materials moving from the ports and 1,250 more trucks to supply the army in the interior. Moreover, Italian troops in Albania were outnumbered in case they had to act against the whole Greek army. Badoglio asked the *Regia Marina* for support. Despite optimistic reports coming from Albania about the enthusiastic Greek welcome to the Italian invaders, Admiral Cavagnari said that the lack of good ports on Greek and Albanian shores in the Adriatic created a logistical nightmare. Badoglio asked the *Regia Aeronautica* to provide air transport. General Pricolo declared that he had sufficient aircraft to fight, but none capable of transporting supplies. Badoglio cut off the discussion and arguments, stating, "The Duce has judged and declared that for him the occupation of Greece is of major importance. So no more discussion."[14]

On October 28, 1940, 105,000 Italians of the XXV and XXVI Corps and the "Littoral Group" crossed the Greek frontier. Within two weeks their advance was stopped by a lack of supplies; and the Greeks counterattacked. The Italian front collapsed. Italy had the Eleventh and Ninth Armies in Albania. They had nine divisions and could receive no more than two additional divisions per month because of the poor capacity of the Albanian ports. These reinforcements could do no more than replace the casualties taken, but not increase overall Italian strength. The Greek army, however, deployed no fewer than thirteen divisions, three brigades; and a task force. Moreover, Greek divisions had more soldiers than Italian divisions. Finally, when the Greek government realized it did not have to fear Bulgarian or Turkish intervention, it concentrated the entire army against the Italian invasion. Shortly thereafter, a British Expeditionary Force landed in Greece from North Africa. Overwhelmed by enemies, and not adequately supplied because of logistical problems, the Italian troops fought a terrible campaign. The terrain added further difficulties to Italian operations. Albania and northern Greece have mountain chains running from north to south. The front ran from west to east, perpendicularly cut by the mountains. Due to the lack of personnel, the *Regio Esercito* concentrated its divisions in the valleys to stop Greek attacks on the valley floors, along the roads. The Greeks, however, attacked along the ridgelines and prevailed on the local small garrisons. If the Italians garrisoned the ridges, the Greeks concentrated troops in the valleys and smashed the front.

By December the Italian Army had been ejected from Greece and lost one-third of Albania, too. As soon as reinforcements landed in Durazzo or Valona, troops were sent here and there to fill new gaps in the line, even if they were only company or platoon strength. Complete regiments were dismembered after landing; and colonels simply did not know where army headquarters had sent their soldiers. In horrible conditions, lacking uniforms, food, and ordnance, Italian troops were able to stop the Greeks only during the Christmas period. Between January 26 and February 12, 1941, the situation improved. The Greeks and Italians reached a stalemate. A first Italian counteroffensive on March 9 ended with no result after five days. The strategic situation in the Balkans, however, was changing. Bulgaria and Yugoslavia joined the German-Italian alliance when, on March 27, a British-supported plot upset the philo-Axis Yugoslavian government. This opened a new front to the rear of the Italian troops in Albania and rendered Hitler furious. On March 27, Hitler ordered his generals to attack Yugoslavia. On April 6, German troops entered northeastern Greece, too. The invasion went smoothly, because the Greek army was concentrated against the Italians. In only fifteen days the Germans defeated both the British and Greek forces and reached the rear area of the Greek army fighting the Italians. The Italians attacked on April 15 and were able to reach the old Albanian-Greek border before the end of operations.

On April 21 the war in Greece was over. Mussolini's criminal improvidence cost the *Regio Esercito* 13,755 dead, 25,067 missing in action, 50,784 wounded, 13,368 frostbitten, and 52,108 ill. Total casualties were 155,172 men, the strength of an army. On June 25, after seizing Crete, too—with a little Italian support from the Dodecanese—the Germans left the Italians in command of occupied Greece. It lasted until September 8, 1943.

Yugoslavia: 1941-1943

After March 27, 1941, Belgrade had an anti-Axis government. The Germans reacted quickly. The Italians were not as fast as the Germans, but they too prepared an offensive against Yugoslavia. On April 6, 1941, operations against the 1.4 million men of the Yugoslavian army began. The Germans entered Yugoslavia from Austria, Bulgaria, and Hungary, together with Hungarian troops. The Italian Second Army crossed the border and divided in two. The first group moved east, seized Ljubiana, and met German forces in Karlovac. The main part of the army—the king present—marched south, along the Dalmatian coast, to meet Italian units coming north from Albania.

The small garrison of Zara sortied from the city and swept away the local Yugoslav units. Then General Giglioli marched south and east, reaching Knin before the Germans. The Second Army's divisions Torino and Littorio respectively captured Ragusa (Dubrovnik) on the coast, and Mostar and Trebinje in the interior, where they met Infantry Divison Marche coming from Albania.

On the Yugoslav-Albanian border operations had been incredible. The *Regio Esercito* had only the 31st Tank Regiment and some Blackshirt units facing 130,000 Yugoslav soldiers. The SIM—*Servizio Informazioni Militari*—Italian Military Intelligence, knew the Yugoslavian code and broadcast false orders to Yugoslav units. As a result, the Yugoslavs delayed their offensive against Albania. When they made a first attempt, Italian tanks successfully repulsed it and, when they realized the trick and tried to react, Italian divisions Centauro and Messina defeated and destroyed them. On April 17, 1941, the Yugoslav campaign was over, with a complete Axis victory; 6,028 officers and 337,684 men surrendered to Axis forces. Unfortunately, operations went so fast that some 300,000 men had been cut off. They escaped and quickly formed partisan units.

Yugoslavia was divided between Italy, Germany, Hungary, and Bulgaria. The rump formed a kingdom of Croatia, whose crown was offered to Aimone of Savoy, the youngest brother of the duke of Aosta. Italy held the coastal region and Germany the interior. A demilitarized zone from 31 to 62 miles in length remained between them. As in Ethiopia in 1936, the real war was only beginning. The newly born partisan units, organized by Colonel Mihailovic, attacked the Axis-allied Croatian government, whose chief was Ante Pavelic. Croatians—Roman Catholics—hated Serbians—Orthodox—Jews, and Muslims, mostly living in the south. The Serbians living in the Lika zone reacted against the Croats. Germans supported the Croats and attacked the Jews. The Italians protected the Jews against the Germans, disliked Croats, and disapproved of their persecution of the Serbians.[15]

Until the fall of 1941, Mihailovic's partisans fought against the Germans; Serbs fought against Croats; Italians stood by and observed the whole situation. Of course, things changed when Tito appeared. Italians scattered their garrisons throughout their occupied zone; and General Roatta conducted numerous and successful counterinsurgency operations, but the situation did not change very much. Partisan activity continued until the end of Italian occupation on September 8, 1943.

The CSIR and the ARMIR, Russia: 1941–1943

Hitler ordered planning for the invasion of Russia in the autumn of 1940. It was originally intended for the spring of 1941, but was postponed for operations in Greece and Yugoslavia. The German invasion, code named Barbarossa, began on June 22, 1941. As it was, the Germans blamed the Italians for the delay, but the arrival of British troops in Greece and the anti-Axis stance of the Yugoslav government were all contributing factors in Hitler's decision to delay the offensive. According to them, if they would not have needed to help the Italians in Greece, they surely would have entered Moscow before Christmas 1941. They lied. Basil Liddell Hart implicitly demonstrated it[16] when speaking about 1941 late spring's rainy and muddy weather, preventing any offensive before the last week of June.

Hitler informed Mussolini of the German offensive only on June 21, 1941, in the evening. This was not part of the Pact of Steel, but Mussolini offered, and Hitler accepted, Italian military support. In July, the XXXV Corps left Italy under the name CSIR—*Corpo di Spedizione Italiano in Russia*—the Italian Expeditionary Corps to Russia. The CSIR included three divisions, a cavalry group, and a Blackshirt Legion. It consisted of 60,900 men, 5,500 vehicles, and 4,600 horses. Air support was provided by 89 planes belonging to the XXII Hunter Group and the LXI Reconnaissance Group.

Commanded by General Giovanni Messe, CSIR fought well. It was in Ukraine and took part in the victories of Dnepropetrovsk, in September, and Kiev. In October, Italians seized Stalino and, on November 2, Gorlovka.

After these results, Mussolini increased Italian participation. Mussolini pledged an entire army. Messe disagreed. As he told Cavallero on May 30, 1942, and Mussolini on June 2, CSIR had suffered a high number of casualties, relations with the Germans were poor, especially concerning the treatment of Russian civilians and Jews; Italian tanks were useless, and vehicles were lacking. Mussolini did not care. He simply answered that Italy could not send less soldiers than Slovakia. When negotiating peace, he said, "ARMIR's 200,000 men will weigh more than CSIR's 60,000."[17]

In the late spring of 1942, the Eighth Italian Army, now called ARMIR—*Armata Italiana in Russia* (Italian Army in Russia)—commanded by General Italo Gariboldi, arrived in Russia. It included 227,000 men, 16,700 vehicles, 960 guns, 380 1.8-inch antitank guns, 19 self-propelled light guns, and 55 light tanks. It was sent to the Don river, northwest of Stalingrad. In July, ARMIR took part in operations against Krasniy Lutsch—taken by the 53rd Infantry Regiment—and in the subsequent battle of Serafimovich. The first Soviet counteroffensive began on August 12, 1942, and is referred to in Italy as the the First Battle of the Don. Three Soviet divisions crossed the river. Infantry Division Sforzesca was outnumbered 4 to 1 and had no tanks. It resisted as best as it could. When it collapsed, Italian survivors held two strong points: Yagodny and Chebotarewsky. Chebotarewsky was overwhelmed, but Yagodny resisted. While the breach in the Italian front widened, the Yagodny garrison was attacked on August 20. It held and counterattacked from August 21–24, until ammunition ran out; and then the Italians faced the last Soviet attack with bayonets. *Bersaglieri* reinforcements arrived just in time and repelled the enemy. That same day, Italian cavalry charged near Isbushensky,[18] repelling a couple of Soviet battalions.

The Soviets stretched the Italian line on the Don like a rubber balloon, but they could not break it. At the end of August they withdrew, having lost 50 percent of their troops. On September 10, the Soviets made a further attempt. They crossed the river near Dubowikof, but the Ravenna Infantry Division threw them back. All these operations were tied to Soviet efforts to stop the German Fourth and Sixth Panzer Armies' drive on Stalingrad.

When the Soviets launched their great Operation Uranus to relieve Stalingrad, on November 19, 1942, Italians were marginally involved. Stalingrad—today Volgagrad—is on the Volga river. The Don flows perpendicular to the Volga from north. It turns east a bit and south of Rossosh, making a loop to the Sea of Azov. ARMIR was in the great Don Bend. It had the Second Hungarian Army on its left and the Third Romanian Army on its right. The first phase of Uranus smashed the Third and the Fourth Romanian Armies and enveloped the 250,000 Germans fighting in Stalingrad. On December 16, 1942, the Soviets began Operation Saturn, with Rostov as its objective. They had to overrun Hungarian and Italian troops. It was not too hard. From the Soviet bridgehead at Mamon, fifteen divisions supported by no less than one hundred tanks attacked Italian Infantry Divisions Cosseria and Ravenna and advanced against Sforzesca, too. Outnumbered 9 to 1, the Italian line resisted for two days. On December 19, ARMIR headquarters ordered the remaining troops to withdraw. Italian soldiers moved west on foot, trying to escape the Soviet tanks. Their casualties were terribly high. Italian Divisions Torino, Cosseria, Pasubio, and Ravenna marched one hundred miles in the harsh Russian winter. Temperatures dipped from 10 to 35 degrees Centigrade below zero. They escaped encirclement on December 25, 1942, while the Sforzesca and Celere Divisions together with remaining Romanians retreated under the protection of the Alpine Army Corps, composed of three Alpine divisions and Infantry Division Vicenza.

When Italian retreat ended, on January 17, 1943, the Alpine troops withdrew. The corps had few trucks and cars, and a mad crowd of half-disbanded Romanians, Hungarians, Germans, and Spaniards with them for the 140-mile march to the new Axis line. Temperatures reached 45 below zero. In spite of cold, snow, ice, and a lack of food and ammunition, Alpine troops continued their retreat. It was an epic tragedy, worse and greater than in 1812. Soviet tanks appeared here and there. They attacked and shelled, but all their attempts to encircle the Italians failed. On January 26 the Alpine Corps reached Nikolayewka, but the Soviets were already there. Alpine Division Tridentina threw its last three battalions and its last mountain artillery group with only a few rounds against the Soviet positions. Under the eyes of the unarmed and disordered column, they attacked Nikolayewka throughout the day. At sunset, their attacks had failed. Then, Tridentina commander General Reverberi jumped on the last still movable German halftrack. "Tridentina forward," he shouted. The entire desperate column followed him and crashed through the Soviet positions. Soviet Official Bulletin Number 630, announcing the total defeat of Axis forces, admitted, "Only the Italian Alpine Army Corps must be considered undefeated on Russian soil."[19]

On January 30 the first survivors reached the Axis line. By February 3 the last arrived. ARMIR had lost 84,830 men; 29,690 more were wounded, ill, or horribly frostbitten. Total losses amounted to 114,520. The Soviets declared they took 80,000 prisoners, but after the war only 10,000 returned home from Soviet prisons. In March, the Eighth Army was sent back to Italy. As a corporal later wrote, his battalion:

> drew toward the steppe where the ARMIR left 85,000 dead and missing soldiers, . . . We remained silent for five minutes presenting our arms, in honor of the fallen. Then, by company, we boarded the trucks to Gomel. From Gomel, by train, we crossed Poland, Germany, Hungary and, through Tarvis Pass, we reached Udine. The first shock I had was that as soon as we left the cars, a desperate crowd assailed us. They were the relatives of the ARMIR missing. Having photos in their hands, they asked us if we had seen this or that man. I escaped to the barracks because I could not stand so great a despair.[20]

Alexandria 68 Miles: North African Campaigns and the Mediterranean Maritime War

In June 1940, Libyan governor General Air Marshal Balbo prepared for an attack in Egypt. After his plane was shot down on June 26, 1940, Graziani was appointed his successor. Badoglio ordered him to commence operations before July 15. Graziani did not like the idea; although he had a lot of men and guns, he lacked adequate trucks and vehicles. He did not move. Badoglio ordered him again to attack before September 10. On the twelfth, Graziani moved. He commanded three corps, a Libyan Division Group and a Motorized Group. In spite of the lack of vehicles, the minefields, and the extremely hot temperature—56 degrees Centigrade—he advanced twelve miles per day in the desert. On September 18 his vanguard reached sixty-two miles into Egyptian territory, when the need for water and gasoline dictated a halt to operations.

British general Richard O'Connor was waiting for him in Marsa Matruh, eighty miles east. He had prepared an armor counteroffensive. Graziani held his positions through December 9, when O'Connor attacked. The Italians were completely surprised. According to British historian Correlli Barnett, the *Regio Esercito* in general fought well, but its old light tanks could not stand up to British ones, and their hand grenades and antitank guns proved ineffective against British armored vehicles. Italian artillerymen fired all they had until they were either killed or wounded.[21] O'Connor moved rapidly due to his superiority in vehicles and armor, and completely defeated Graziani. In a few days he advanced 620 miles, conquering half of Libya. It was the first British victory of the Second World War.

By February 1941, when Gariboldi took command, Graziani had lost 134,000 men killed, wounded, and prisoner, and 360 light and medium tanks captured or destroyed. On February 12 the German Afrika Korps arrived. General Erwin Rommel took operational command under Gariboldi's supervision and launched an unexpected and incredibly successful offensive, but was stopped due to fuel and supply shortages. The continuation of the Libyan war depended entirely on supplying Axis forces from Italy through the Mediterranean. Poor preparation and planning and North African ports' little capacity affected operations terribly. Italy did not seize the British base of Malta in the early days of the conflict, when the island contained few troops and merely three aircraft. The *Regia Marina* was in charge of maintaining communications between Libya and Italy. It had to escort convoys and contend with the Royal Navy.

The first days of the war had been not too good to the *Regia Marina*. Italian submarines in the Red Sea concerned the British. They feared an Italian naval blockade of the Suez Canal, in case Italians would sink a ship into the canal. The *Regia Marina* Red Sea Squadron was, however, light, composed of seven submarines and a few destroyers.

The strategic situation in the Mediterranean was quite different. The *Regia Marina* maintained the preponderance of its strength there and was very effective. But Naval headquarters in Rome was disinclined to commit its battle fleet to achieve naval superiority in the Mediterranean. Instead, it was largely employed to protect convoys and maritime supply routes. This was not a good idea. Frederick the Great once said the best strategy consisted of three principles: attack, attack, and always attack. This was precisely what was required. Admiral Luigi Rizzo, the famous Great War sinker, suggested many offensive operations, but they were not approved. Defense and, above all, ship preservation was the order of the day.

Submarines operated successfully on both sides, but the first naval engagement occurred on July 9 near Punta Stilo, off Calabrian shores, with no real result. *Regia Aeronautica* conducted thirty-one air attacks against British ships that day, also with no result. So, British admiral Andrew Cunningham concluded that the Italian navy was incapable of preventing the Royal Navy from entering the Mediterranean from Gibraltar. A second engagement ten days later confirmed Cunningham's conclusion. Several months passed with no action until the night of November 11–12, when twelve Royal Navy torpedo bombers attacked the Italian naval base at Taranto and sank three battleships. Luckily the ships were not in deep water, and in a few weeks they were repaired. The Taranto raid was the first demonstration of the utility of using aircraft against ships; and the Japanese navy was said to have carefully studied it, learned the lesson, and used it when planning Pearl Harbor.

Mediterranean maritime warfare thereafter consisted of attempts to deny the enemy the ability to supply their armies in North Africa. The Royal Navy escorted convoys to Egypt and Malta. At the same time the *Regia Marina* had the same responsibilities to supply North Africa, passing just off Malta. Both routes crossed between Italy and Libya, and both navies tried to destroy the other and failed; and sea-lanes remained open on both sides.

If the Royal Navy had damaged the *Regia Marina* in battles such as Capo Matapan, off Greek shores, the *Regia Marina* responded with equal effectiveness raiding British ports. The X MAS Flotilla grouped all the Italian special forces.

They raided Malta, Suda, Gibraltar and, above all, Alexandria, where in December 1941 six men sank two battleships and a tanker on the same night. If Italo-German operations in North Africa depended mostly on supply and supply depended on shuttling cargo, whose trips depended on the ability of the *Regia Marina* to keep routes open, then it succeeded in its objectives.

The *Regia Aeronautica* did not adequately support the *Regia Marina*. Their aircraft were ineffective against the Royal Air Force. Malta was normally bombed, but according to the old air doctrine *"Direttive per l'impiego dell'Armata aerea"* (Directive for the Employment of the Air Force), Italian aircraft did not conduct massive bombing raids. Results were clearly poor, and continued in this manner until the German X *Fliegerkorps* was deployed in Sicily. But by the time German aircraft arrived, it was too late to seize Malta. The feasibility of a landing was studied. Operation C 3—a landing in Malta—foresaw sea and air operations using paratroopers. By the time the new paratroopers of Division "Folgore" were ready, the desperate need for men in the Sahara led Italian headquarters to deploy them in that theater as an infantry division.[22]

The war in North Africa continued in a peculiar way. The desert theater provided no opportunity to arrange a terrain-supported defense. In case of defeat, the loser could only retreat quickly along hundreds and hundreds of miles of coastal road, or through the desert. That's why in 1941, Rommel's offensive easily reached the Egyptian desert on April 15. Two months later the British Eighth Army attacked around Halfaya Pass. In a few hours Eighth Army lost 99 of its 104 tanks. Rommel did not exploit his success, because of a lack of supplies. In fact, because of Royal Navy activity, that month he received from Italy only 8,000 metric tons, as opposed to the 60,000 he needed.

In November 1941 his Italian-German Army had only 438 tanks and 490 planes compared to 724 British tanks and 1,311 aircraft. On November 18, 1941, Gen. Alan Cunningham, a brother of the admiral, launched his "Crusader" offensive. He wanted to reinforce Tobruk, a strategic Libyan coastal town seized by the British in 1940; and Rommel had been unable to recapture it. Cunningham had 118,000 men. Rommel had 100,000. The British 22nd Tank Brigade achieved initial success against the Germans at Sidi Rezegh, but when it encountered the Italian Ariete Tank Division near Bir el Gobi, it lost 52 tanks in a few minutes and stopped. On November 22, Rommel's tanks joined the Ariete and took Sidi Rezegh. The next morning Cunningham was informed he had lost 18,000 men. His tanks numbered only 257, and only 30 were still combat-ready. British general Sir Claude Auchinleck took personal command of forces. He reinforced British troops and immediately counterattacked. Rommel retreated to El Agheila, in Tripolitania, Western Libya. On January 6, 1942, he halted, resupplied, and sixteen days later, on January 22, the Italo-German units attacked.

Within a few days the British army was completely beaten. They lost 370 tanks and the whole of Cyrenaica—eastern Libya. The British now lacked supplies because of temporary Italian naval superiority due to the Alexandria raid. Moreover, Rommel received two complete convoys. On May 26, 1942, his 90,000 Italians and

Germans, with 560 tanks and 704 planes, began their last offensive. British general Neil Ritchie now commanded the Eighth Army. On May 26 he had 100,000 men, 849 tanks, and 320 aircraft. He was utterly defeated. On June 19, Tobruk was surrounded. Two days later, after a hard shelling, South African general Klopper surrendered with 33,000 British, Indian, and South African troops to General Navarrini, commanding the Italian XXI Corps. Ritchie had lost some 45,000 men and 400 guns. He had only 100 tanks remaining.

On that same June 21, 1942, Rommel engaged and defeated Ritchie once more around Marsa Matruh. The British escaped to the east and halted in Egypt. They chose a vertical defensive line from Mediterranean to the El Qattara depression. Australian and Indian reinforcements arrived in time to reinforce the line. In fact, on July 1, the Axis vanguard reached "Heaven's doors," a place whose Arabic name was going to remain in history: El Alamein. By this time the Italo-German vanguard had only 4,400 men, with 41 tanks and 71 guns. They attacked and were repulsed. On July 7, Rommel had no more than 5,000 men in front of the British army. Ten days later, when the whole ACIT—*Armata Corazzata Italo-Tedesca* (Italian-German Armored Army)—was on line, his four tank divisions totaled exactly 58 tanks. Alexandria and the delta of the Nile were only sixty-eight miles away.

Axis troops had poor quality food and lacked gasoline and water. Supply was difficult because the depots were 250 miles away. Heat, dysentery, fevers, and clouds of flies tortured the troops. Moreover, they all knew that the longer they waited, the more the enemy was reinforcing its position. In August, Rommel was informed by SIM, the Italian intelligence, that the next British attack was foreseen coming after October 20. The new British commander, General Montgomery, was perfectly aware of the forthcoming American-British landing in Morocco in November. Under these circumstances Axis forces had clearly to retreat. It was not necessary to lose lives and materiel in a battle. It was worth the wait, but Montgomery decided Britain had to demonstrate its ability to defeat the Germans and, on October 23, 1942, he launched Operation Lightfoot.

The first British action was against the southern flank of the Axis forces. The Italians repelled the attack. The British lost 600 men and 120 tanks. Montgomery did not stop. He slowly increased pressure and widened the front. On November 1, however, he launched Operation Supercharge. It practically destroyed the Littorio and German 15th Tank Divisions. The Ariete and German 21st Tank Divisions arrived, halting the British advance, but in the evening the Axis possessed only 187 tanks; and 155 of them were the little ineffective Italian ones.

On November 3, Rommel ordered the retreat. Germans troops withdrew, using all the former British vehicles taken at Tobruk. The four German divisions were near the coast road, enabling them to escape. The Italian divisions moved through the desert, with British tanks on their heels. They were destroyed. The Brescia, Bologna, Pavia, and Trento Infantry Divisions and the Littorio Tank Division simply disappeared in a hail of fire and shelling. The Ariete had to protect them. It still had 111 tanks and 12 self-propelled howitzers. On November 3, Eighth Army continued the attack. Ariete counterattacked; and the fight was scattered throughout the desert. At 3:30 p.m., Rommel received its farewell: "Enemy tanks made a breakthrough south of Ariete. With this, Ariete is surrounded. It is some five kilometers northwest of Bir el Abd. Ariete tanks fight."[23]

In the night, the XIII Tank Battalion continued fighting. Its last six tanks aggressively defended Fuka station on November 6 against the 1st, 7th, and 10th British armored divisions. They were ultimately destroyed. The same day the Folgore Division surrendered. After having shot literally all its rounds, despite the paratroopers asking to fight with bayonets and hand grenades, the commander ordered them to lay down their arms. The surviving 34 officers and 272 men received British military honors. They had arrived from Italy with 5,000 men.

The Allied landing in Morocco meant the end of the French government established after the 1940 armistice. Germany and Italy occupied Vichy-owned territories, including Algeria, Tunisia, and Corsica. Despite Italian pleas not to leave Tripoli, Rommel ordered his troops to Tunisia. Then he moved west. On February 14 he attacked and defeated the Americans at Kasserine Pass. At the same time, beginning in January 1943, the Italians began to establish a defensive line on the Tunisian-Libyan border, using the existing French fortifications. On February 20, 1943, General Messe, former commander of the CSIR, took charge of the First Italian Army in Tunisia.

The following months saw the desperate Axis forces attempting to prevent the Allied eastern and western fronts from joining. Rommel was recalled to Germany and left General von Arnim in his place.

In the last days of April, Montgomery took Takruna and Enfidaville, the last Axis outposts on the road to Tunis. Messe concentrated his troops in the Gebel Garci mountains and prevented him from advancing any farther. Montgomery waited until Allied forces coming from the west broke von Arnim's troops on May 6 and 7. They then captured Tunis and Bizerte. On May 11 the Afrika Korps was reduced to scattered units while the XXI Italian Corps surrendered. Von Arnim sent Messe his farewell. The XX Italian Corps continued to resist till the day after, May 12, while Rome authorized it to surrender: "Today it has been a splendid day for our artillery. They shot all they still had. Then, before evening, we have heard different detonations. It was ammunition used to blow up the guns."[24] The following day, May 13, 1943, Italy's war in North Africa ended.

The War Against the Germans: 1943-1945

From the Landing in Sicily to the Fall of Fascism: July 1943

Invasion was imminent in the summer 1943. Although the situation was bad, it was not yet considered desperate. Colonies were lost, but the *Regio Esercito* still occupied Greece, western Yugoslavia, Montenegro, Albania, southeastern France, and Corsica. Indeed, Italian troops were in Russia and on the shores of the Baltic. The *Regia Marina* had submarines operating in Atlantic and against the Soviets in the Black Sea, but its strength was reduced significantly. It had lost 35,000 men, 87 ships, and 85 submarines; and the scarcity of fuel had put three battleships out of order.

The Allies conducted strategic bombing raids on Italy, but damage had been minor, especially when compared to Germany. Allied bombers were at their extended range as their bases were too far from the Italian mainland. The war was going poorly for Mussolini, but defeat appeared far off, or at least not too close. In spite of what the Allied chiefs had declared at the Casablanca Conference, that they would only accept the unconditional surrender of Axis powers, some within the Fascist government assumed they had the option of negotiating a separate peace if necessary. This was wrong. Italian politicians were completely blind to the Allies' attitudes and the general strategic situation. Regardless, it was clear that Mussolini was the greatest obstacle to pulling Italy out of the war. Members of the Fascist Party and the armed forces began to explore the possibility of removing Mussolini from power.

When the Allies landed in Sicily (Operation Husky), it was one in a series of events that led to a plot that hatched on the night of July 25, 1943. Allied troops in Sicily consisted of the British Eighth Army and the U.S. Seventh Army. The Allied operation was enormous; 2,500 transport ships escorted by 750 warships, with 400 landing craft and ultimately 478,000 men, 14,000 vehicles, 600 tanks, and 1,800 guns. The Italian Sixth Army, commanded by General Alfredo Guzzoni, defended Sicily. Including navy and air force personnel, Guzzoni had 315,000 men and 40,000 Germans. Unfortunately, his troops were primarily composed of coastal divisions—five of the nine—and he had only a few old tanks. After considering his options, he concentrated his forces in the southeastern sector, Husky's territorial objective. SIM was sure that the Allies were going to land in Sicily, after precise information coming from its agents in Lisbon, while German intelligence believed the Allies would land either in Sardinia or Greece. Kesselring disregarded the Italian intelligence reports and deployed German tank units to concentrate in central and western Sicily.

In late June, SIM information from Lisbon warned that the landing was imminent. On July 7, the *Regio Esercito* staff warned Guzzoni that the landing was expected within two or three days. Despite these warnings and the Allied seizure of Pantelleria Island, Kesselring kept his troops in the interior and did not defend the coast. It was one of the major reasons for the failure of the Axis to defend Sicily. On July 10, 1943, at a quarter past midnight, Guzzoni was informed of the forthcoming landing. Within fort-five minutes all Italian units moved to the coast between Gela, Licata, and Syracuse. Italian troops blew up much of the Gela and Licata ports, to deny them to the Allies. The question was whether they could offer adequate resistance.

Allied headquarters had organized the landing in detail, including making contact with local Mafia, which was expected to help Allied forces.[1] Italians resisted, but they were overwhelmed. For example, when the Eighth Army landed, that part of the coast was defended by the 206th Coastal Division, scattered along 82 miles of shoreline. The British first wave alone outnumbered the Italian defenders, who had no tanks, 3 to 1: they were annihilated. Then Montgomery moved to Catania. But it took twenty-three days of hard fighting before it entered the city, defended by General Passalacqua.

The American Seventh Army landed south of Gela. Italian coastal units resisted as best they could, but suffered high casualties. The 429th Coastal Battalion lost 45 percent of its men. Then the Livorno Division counterattacked, supported by fifty old tanks. Guzzoni's orders were obeyed quickly and efficiently, but German tanks were too far away, and the attack was not as impressive as desired.[2] In spite of the German absence, General Chirieleison conducted the attack while Italian planes bombed the beachhead.[3] He lost 50 percent of his men. When German tanks finally arrived, the attack was renewed. It advanced so far that at 11:30 a.m., Guzzoni's headquarters intercepted an American message ordering the landing troops to prepare to reembark. Supported by naval fire, however, American troops fought bravely and enlarged their beachhead.

General George S. Patton, commanding Seventh Army, reviewed the strategic situation. Montgomery had been stopped in front of Catania and there was no reason to lose time. He deviated from the original Allied plans and moved north, to Palermo. From Palermo he could reach Messina in order to cut off any retreat by Axis forces.

The Seventh Army advanced through central Sicily. The Assietta Infantry Division tried to stop it, but, outnumbered 20 to 1, it was clearly impossible. It was destroyed and Patton quickly entered Palermo, and took 10,000 prisoners. Then the Americans moved east to Messina. They were delayed at Troina, where, on

August 4, the Aosta Infantry Division and German 15th Panzer Division made twenty-four counterattacks, but Patton eventually reached Messina.

Axis units abandoned Sicily and withdrew to Calabria across the Straits of Messina. In seven days, despite Allied air superiority, 39,956 Germans with 9,605 vehicles, 47 tanks, and 94 guns, and 62,000 Italians with 227 vehicles and 41 guns, were ferried to Calabria. The Sicilian campaign was over. Axis losses totaled 8,603 dead, 260 tanks, 500 guns, and 132,000 prisoners. Allied casualties consisted of 4,299 dead and 3,242 missing in action.

The Allies moved on to the Italian mainland with a landing in Calabria. British troops first arrived on September 3, while Allied headquarters prepared the next landing, for Salerno on September 9.

The loss of Sicily and the invasion of Italy made the end inevitable; and the Fascist and military plot to overthrow Mussolini developed with great speed. The Fascist and military hierarchy turned to the king, but he seemed reluctant. Victor Emmanuel did not like the idea of losing the crown because of a false step. In 1925 he did not intervene during Matteotti crisis, which ended the constitutional government. He decided to wait. He knew Fascist leadership was disappointed with Mussolini, and in theory the king could ask Mussolini to resign; but what if Mussolini refused? What if he resisted and caused a civil war while a war was still in progress? The problem here is one often forgotten. At that time everyone in Italy feared Fascism, because they did not know it was weak. Twenty years of uncontested propaganda had succeeded in creating a submissive society. Later, the joyous reaction after Mussolini's resignation was something no one anticipated and a complete surprise.

From the king's point of view there was a large and apparently strong party. Millions of Italians belonged to it. The armed forces were filled with Fascists. Although professional officers considered that their loyalty to the king came first, the crown prince Humbert second, and the Duce a distant third, what about reserve officers and the rank and file? Furthermore, the party had its own army—the Militia—dispersed throughout the state and society. It appeared well organized and faithful; nobody realized that this was largely propaganda, too. The only force the king had to could counter the Fascists was the *Regio Esercito*, which was scattered across Europe. It was a risk. Victor Emmanuel understood that in case of an Axis victory, Mussolini would have transformed Italy into a personal dictatorship, eventually abolishing the monarchy.[4]

All of the king's concerns changed when a number of important Fascist leaders maintained separate contacts with the crown. They prepared to force Mussolini to leave the premiership. According to them, it was the only possible way to abandon the German alliance and negotiate with the Allies. On Saturday, July 24, 1943, at 5:00 p.m., the Grand Council of Fascism met in Rome. It concluded the following morning at 2:00 a.m.; of 28 members, 19 voted against Mussolini, one did not vote; and only eight supported him. At 6:00 a.m. the king was informed. At 5:00 p.m. the Duce met the king at Villa Savoia and, surprised, was told he must resign. Twenty minutes later, when leaving the meeting, he was arrested by the Royal Carabineers. At 10:45 p.m. the radio announced Mussolini's resignation and Marshal Badoglio's acceptance of the premiership. Soon after, mad and joyous crowds filled the streets of Italian cities and towns, cheering the king. Fascism fell; and the Fascists disappeared. On the morning of July 26, magically, a majority of Italians no longer admitted to having ever been a member of the Fascist National Party. Shortly thereafter, in the following forty-five days, the king's government began negotiating an armistice with Allies. Hitler, however, did not intend to observe all of this from a distance. He ordered Kesselring to seize control of Italy in case of an armistice.

September 8, 1943

Italian-Allied talks quickly reached a conclusion. General Giuseppe Castellano signed the armistice in Cassibile. But the army and civilian population were not informed immediately. This part of Italian history has been widely described. There are probably more accounts, memoirs, diaries, books, and articles concerning the Italian armistice and the following days than about any other period of Italian history. This does not mean that there is a clear understanding of the events that transpired. In a certain way we know how it happened, but we do not exactly know why and, moreover, why in that way.

Italian headquarters in France, Italy, the Balkans, and Eastern Europe appear not to have been informed by the Supreme Headquarters in Rome of the armistice and subsequent events. It is unclear, because while some units were aware, others were not. A complete assessment of the situation is difficult, if not impossible. According to evidence, one can only say that, in the late afternoon of September 8, 1943, Allied headquarters announced Italy's surrender. Two hours later, at 7:45 p.m., Marshal Badoglio's message was broadcast on EIAR, the Italian broadcasting system. Badoglio simply stated that Italy had signed an armistice, but he did not mention what to do with the Germans. He only spoke of reacting to unspecified attacks. At the same time, the Germans broadcast the code word for their operation in reaction to the Italian armistice—it was ironically *Achse*, "Axis." Marshal Kesselring assumed that all German troops south of Rome would be lost, but when the next morning he received initial reports, he realized that the Italians were not moving to neutralize German forces. He moved quickly, before they or the Allies had time to realize their grave strategic error.

From their perspective, Italian troops remained inactive because they had not received orders. The armistice meant no more fighting against the Allies, but did not imply joining the Allies against the Germans. No contingency plans existed to contend with a German attack. There was no declaration of war on Germany. That is to say: Italy could be at the same time not completely at peace with Allies but at war with the Germans. It is no wonder that armed forces headquarters began calling the General Staff in Rome from France, from the Balkans, from Corsica, from Russia and Greece, from Italy, and from the city itself. General headquarters had no answer, because Badoglio had left Rome with the king, the court, and most of the General Staff without informing anyone. They went by car to the port of

Pescara, on the Adriatic and, during the night, sailed to Brindisi in Apulia, which was under Allied control.[5] Badoglio left no orders, just as he had done at Caporetto twent-six years earlier.

Catastrophe struck on the night of September 8. The responses of the Italian troops differed, depending on their circumstances. The little *Regia Marina* squadron in China scuttled all its ships, and its men were imprisoned by the Japanese.[6] The Italian Eleventh Army in Greece was scattered in small coastal garrisons, while the Germans were grouped as the Axis operational maneuvering group, and no resistance was possible. Its headquarters agreed to the German offer to be sent to Italy by train in exchange for leaving their heavy weapons. But as soon as they left Greece, they were completely disarmed and sent to prison camps in Poland and Germany. Many other units in Greece and the Balkans immediately reacted to the Germans. Infantry Division Pinerolo together with units from other divisions resisted in the Thessalian Mountains and escaped capture. Troops from the Second and the Nineth Army joined the Yugoslav and Albanian partisans. They later formed partisan divisions and fought until the end of the war. Infantry Division Emilia, garrisoning Cattaro, swept away local German units. Then, when they realized after a few days that no reinforcements were forthcoming, its men boarded ships, crossed the Adriatic, and landed in Apulia. The Germans were pushed out of Apulia, Sardinia, and Basilicata. The rest of Italy as well as all other Italian occupied zones, except Corsica, were seized by the Germans. Italian units disbanded, sometimes after a long resistance, sometimes after no resistance. The Germans rounded up all the Italians they could and proposed that they join the Reich to fight, or be sent to prison. A few units chose the Reich, the large majority accepted prison.[7]

Corsica was a remarkable exception, because its Italian garrison was able to resist until Allied troops landed. Then, Italian units were ordered to leave their heavy weapons and vehicles and were ferried to Sardinia. The Aegean Islands were cleared by Infantry Divisions Cuneo and Regina until the Allied landing, but the German counteroffensive by air, sea, and land destroyed them as well as the British forces landing to help. After a long resistance until November 18, the garrison at Lero was massacred by the Germans, as was the Acqui Infantry Division on Cefalonia.

Carabineers and *Guardia di Finanza* were ordered to remain in place.[8] Being both military and civil police, their headquarters had decided that their primary mission was to maintain public order.

Most of the *Regia Aeronautica*'s planes flew south to Allied or Italian airfields. The *Regia Marina* left its ports and reached Malta, according to the terms of the armistice. The German Luftwaffe chased Italian ships and sank several, including the battleship *Roma* off the Sardinian coast.

The Remains of an Army: Fall 1943

In the last days of September 1943, Italy's situation was tragic. The *Regia Marina* saved 64.74 percent of its tonnage; 24.57 percent was scuttled, and the remaining 10.68 percent had been sunk by the Germans en route to Malta. The

Regia Aeronautica saved 246 aircraft and 1,200 men. Some 100 aircraft were combat-ready. They began cooperating with Allied air forces after September 11, 1943, in the Aegean Sea and, after the twelfth, in Italy, from Apulia.

On September 8 the *Regio Esercito* numbered 3.7 million men. The Germans subsequently captured 820,000 of them. Some 2 million were missing; at home, fighting as partisans, or dead.

The SMRE—the *Regio Esercito* staff—controlled Seventh Army, composed of the IX and XXXI Corps, the Sardinian garrison consisting of the XIII and XXX Corps, and the VII Corps arriving from Corsica. They lacked everything, from shoes to ordnance, to vehicles, to gasoline and uniforms. The king's government tried to reorganize the remnants in Apulia into the LI Corps. It comprised two infantry divisions, a couple of coastal divisions, a coastal brigade, and the garrisons of Taranto and Brindisi. It was definitely ineffective and quite far from Allied standards. Moreover, the Allies seemed to have no intention of sending Italians to the front. They did not like the idea of a potential Italian collapse threatening the Allied front. They asked the Italian government to declare war on Germany and prepare their soldiers for rear-area operations similar to work generally left to prisoners of war. Italian divisions therefore, were organized as rear-area units. Their soldiers carried only personal light weapons. In 1944 some divisions were reorganized as constabulary forces.

While the chaos of the Italian armed forces was sorted out, the Germans moved swiftly. On September 12, 1943, Mussolini was rescued on Mount Gran Sasso by German commandos and flown to Germany. Hitler put him in charge of a puppet government, the Italian Social Republic at Salò.[9] The Germans needed it to maintain order among Italians in occupied territory, and to act against partisans. Mussolini's republic was exploited by German propaganda as the expression of Italian resistance against "Anglo-Saxon" invaders. On September 18, Mussolini spoke from Radio Münich. He said Italy should continue the fight, with Hitler's support; and Graziani was appointed to command the Republican Army.

Enlistment began and units were formed. It had a great influence on events in the south. It is no wonder that after the birth of the Social Republic and its army on October 13, 1943, the king's government declared war on Germany. A few weeks later, on November 4, Allied authorities ordered that the SMRE the Italian General Staff command that the Italian 1st Motorized Group, established on September 26, to move north.[10]

Mussolini's Republic and the Resistance

Mussolini's republic at Salò was short lived. In its early days the Republican Army included 62,000 officers, including 300 generals. Only in the following months did the Republican army change, as most officers were dismissed, and in 1944 it numbered 9,000 officers and 245,000 men. Land units included the National Republican Guard, Black brigades, and the X MAS Flotilla. The Black brigades were the Republican version of the Voluntary Militia for National Security.

It included former members of the Militia and was simply the militarized version of the *Fasci*, that is to say, the territorial political organization of the Fascist Party. Their reliability was as poor, as was their military effectiveness. The National Republican Guard included Carabineers and the Italian Africa Police, composed of members of the Colonial Police, whose deployment to Africa had been prevented by the fall of the empire.

The X MAS Flotilla had simply remained in place. Its commander, Frigate Captain Junio Valerio Borghese, became a German ally. He looked to the Italian people as the only really reliable and independent entity. He attracted many volunteers and, in spite of later propaganda, it achieved a strength of 6,000 men, divided into six battalions. All of these men chose Fascist Republican units for different reasons. Soon after September 8, many military men had to face a difficult question: was it right to fight against a former ally along with former enemies? Some of them simply obeyed the king's orders, and some did not.

Those who obeyed the king remained in the armed forces; many who belonged to a disbanded unit joined the partisans; and those who had been captured, suffered cold, illness, and starvation in German prison camps. There were also a large number of Italians who disobeyed the king. It would be too easy to say they did so because they were Fascists. There was no general rule. For example, Italian prisoners in India, the United States, Canada, and other countries had to choose between considering their guardians as friends or enemies. The situation of a prisoner is quite different from that of a free combatant. A prisoner who did not choose to cooperate with Allied forces was sent generally to a special Criminal Fascist Camp.[11] Some decided that the king had betrayed the country; and they did not want to be involved in such an action. Thus, they joined the Germans. Some had no money and needed it, and when the Social Republican officers offered them higher pay, they joined the Republic.[12] Finally, some remained in their place through the continually changing situation. In a certain sense, this was what happened to the X MAS Flotilla.

Many of Mussolini's new soldiers escaped starvation in German POW camps by joining one of the four Republican divisions being trained in Germany. Some of those people chose this course because it was the only way to return to Italy and, as soon as they arrived, they deserted and joined the partisans, or went home. Many served for a combination of all of these reasons.

Social Republic units, mostly from the X MAS, were employed by the Germans against the Allied beachheads at Anzio and Nettuno, south of Rome, through the winter and spring of 1944. At the same time, the National Republican Air Force units—three fighters groups, one torpedo bomber group, and two air transport groups—made several successful raids against Allied positions while the National Republican Navy performed poorly, because of a dearth of ships.

Of the 57,498 men belonging to the four divisions, only a few were used against Allied troops, such as in Garfagnana against the Brazilian expeditionary force. In fact, the republic, that is to say the German headquarters, employed most of them in antipartisan warfare.

The Social Republic largely succeeded in maintaining control of territory and communications under German occupation. Partisans were divided into many groups, depending on their political affiliation. There were units composed of military men—normally apolitical—there were Communists composing the Garibaldi brigades, Socialists composing the Matteotti brigades, and members of the so-called Action Party originated the "Justice and Liberty" units. Republicans formed the Mazzini brigades, while Christian-Democrats, liberals, and others composed the *Brigate autonome*. All the partisans depended upon the CLN—Committee for National Liberation—and, later, from 1944—from the CLNAI—Committee for National Liberation Alta Italia (Upper Italy). Partisans were daring and active, but they lacked heavy weapons, and the terrain did not provide good protection. Although they succeeded in liberating regions for a few days, German and Fascist reactions eventually regained control. Partisans knew that, in case of capture, torture would be followed by execution, but this did not deter them from operations against bridges, roads, troops, and railways throughout Italy.

Regardless, they depended on the *Regio Esercito* staff for supply and direction. In fact, the army was divided in two, the regular and the partisan branches. As Allied troops advanced, the more partisan units joined the regular army. Some Partisan units were inserted into the line as regular units, such as the Maiella or the Mario Gordini Partisan Brigades, which were integrated into the British Eighth Army.

The Liberation War: 1943-1945

The Italian Liberation Corps (CIL), formed in Apulia, was directed north by Allied Headquarters in October 1943. It first saw action on December 8, 1943. American headquarters ordered it to seize Monte Lungo and Monte Sammucro. The initial attempt failed. The second, on December 16, succeeded. The CIL was then sent to the rear and remained inactive and in very poor condition until February 1944. In January 1944, Marshal Giovanni Messe, former commander of Italian troops in Tunisia, was permitted to return to Italy from British internment, as chief of staff. He appointed General Umberto Utili commander of CIL. Utili completely reorganized CIL; and it returned to the front in March 1944 in the Mainarde Mountains sector. After several engagements, CIL was increased to 25,000 men.[13] Allied headquarters dispatched it to Abruzzo, and from there it gradually fought its way to the to Marche. Alongside British and Polish units, it faced the German LXXVI Corps. On September 24, 1944, it was dissolved. Why?

After liberating Rome on June 4, 1944, and following the landings in Normandy and Provence, Allied troops needed as many men as possible in France. Approximately 43,000 Italian prisoners had been shipped from North African camps to southern France to provide rear-area support. Free French forces had also been moved from Italy to France, and Allied operations in Italy needed to fill gaps in the front. On July 23, 1944, the *Regio Esercito* was ordered to provide two Italian combat groups. They were organized and equipped along British lines. Demand for troops quickly resulted in the expansion of the Italian combat groups to four, with a fifth as a training unit. Each combat group had 8,758 men, British equipment, and British inspectors.

The Allied headquarters perceived the situation as problematic. The CIL was growing. It had no British inspectors but was fighting very well. Its strength was going to be equivalent to an Allied corps, but this would have meant permitting the Italian Army to act as an ally. This had to remain impossible. Italy was a defeated enemy and only necessity led the Allies to give the Italians the honor of cobelligerent status, a newly invented term, which did not imply alliance. Combat groups meant Italian forces now increased from 25,000 to 50,000 men. But the doubling of combat strength did not translate into the establishment of an Italian army operating on its own front. In fact, each combat group, equal to a division, was scattered among British and American armies. So the Italian General Staff and the group commanders had no role in planning operations, they could merely carry out their orders. Thus they could not ask for being considered real Allies.

Combat groups fought in the last campaigns of the war and, in April 1945, took part in the final Allied offensive in Italy. Field Marshal Alexander had twenty-two divisions and seven brigades at his disposal. In the early days of April he engaged Kesselring's Armies Group C with twenty divisions and the National Republican Armed Forces. While the Germans surrendered, Italian Republican units fought to their last round against the Yugoslavs and the French.

Italy's odd political situation led to significant fighting by partisan together with Fascist units against French troops coming through the Alps to seize the Aosta Valley. On the other side of Italy, Fascist Republican units fought in Friuli, Istria, Dalmatia, and Carniola, against Yugoslav partisans. Italians succeeded in the west thanks to American pressure on the French government. They failed, however, in Friuli, because the Eighth Army moved too slowly and, due to the agreements at Yalta in February 1945, Istria and Dalmatia were lost to Yugoslavia.

During the last days of war, on April 25, 1945, partisans captured and killed Mussolini and all the Fascist hierarchs they could find. The Duce's body was promptly displayed hanging by his feet in Milan, while his documents disappeared.[14] Republican troops disbanded. Most of the soldiers were massacred by partisans. According to reliable figures, of the 25,000 dead belonging to the Republican armed forces, some 15,000 were killed after April 25, 1945, that is to say, after the official conclusion of the war.

CHAPTER 26

Italian Armed Forces from World War II to the End of the Cold War: 1946-1988

After World War II

The first day of peace began a dramatic period in Italian history. It is true that Italy was in a far better situation than Germany, but it was still quite bad. The king's government had to face all the problems of a defeated country with the few organized institutions it still possessed. In spite of the armistice and of the subsequent difficulties, civil life in 1943 did not change very much. Only the armed forces disappeared, but all the services, including the police, worked as well as before. Then they had been divided by the front. In northern Italy civil service formally passed to the Social Republic, while the south remained under the king's control.

Step by step, as each portion of Italy was liberated, the Allied Military Government (AMG) took control. Then, when the situation was stable, the AMG transferred power to the Italian authorities; but Allied supervision continued. At the end of the war the bureaucracy tried to rebuild its component parts. The lack of communications made it extremely difficult, the Allies still controlled movement of resources and, of course there was a severe lack of money and goods. The new government in consultation with the Allies introduced the equivalent of a de-Nazification program in Italy. Special commissions were sent north to review what each member of the military or civil service had done in the past twenty months, that is to say, from September 12, 1943, until April 25, 1945. Casualties from the war totaled an estimated 470,000, including civilians. It was less than after World War I, but damage at that time affected only a small portion of Italian territory. After the Second World War the entire country experienced substantial material loss. Factories were heavily damaged, even if both partisans and secret services cooperated to save plants and rescue machinery. No less than 60 percent of the railways had been destroyed, and damages amounted to 900 billion lira. Roads were heavily damaged, and bridges had been destroyed by both Allied air forces and the retreating Germans. Millions were unemployed and had no money and no food. Hundreds of thousands of refugees escaped to Italy from Istria and Dalmatia, because of the Yugoslavs, who were killing Italians. Hundreds of thousands of prisoners were still far away in Allied prison camps, in India, the Soviet Union, the United States, Africa, Australia, and in Japan, too, waiting for their freedom.

All the colonies were gone as well as Albania and the Dodecanese Islands. The Yugoslavs occupied a portion of the northeast, including Istria and Zara in Dalmatia. American and British troops controlled the remainder of the country. The king's government ruled only two-thirds of the territory; and that was under Allied control. A Sicilian separatist movement supported by the Mafia sought British backing.

The government could be supported only by armed forces, but the armed forces were in poor shape. On May 8, 1945, the *Regia Marina* consisted of 64,000 men, five battleships—it had eight when the war began—19 cruisers, 11 destroyers, 39 submarines, 22 escort ships, 19 corvettes, 44 coastal units, 56 minesweepers, 19 landing craft, two training ships, one support ship, and approximately 140 coastal and support units. The *Regia Aeronautica* came out of the war with three air groups, the three *Raggruppamenti Aerei*—which had fifteen groups. The *Regio Esercito* had still combat groups, auxiliary units, and troops for internal security. The internal security forces consisted of four light infantry divisions deprived of heavy weapons. They acted as a constabulary force, mainly in Sicily, and resolved the separatist crisis there.

The situation in the north was equally critical. There were a high number of deaths due to the so called "flying red squads," which were intimidating and killing, especially in the so-called "death triangle" in Emilia Romagna, despite increased control by the Royal Carabineers and police. The Communists comprised the strongest component of the partisan movement. They were backed by the Soviet Union and hoped to achieve political power, changing Italy into a Communist republic during the next plebiscite and following elections. The plebiscite centered on the question of whether to maintain the monarchy or abolish it. The *vote* was held in June 1946, and women voted for the first time.

After the armistice, Victor Emmanuel III appointed his son Humbert as a lieutenant-general of the kingdom. In May 1946 he formally abdicated the throne in favor of his son and went into exile in Egypt, where he died in December 1947.

Humbert declared that, in case of an electoral victory with a reduced majority, the plebiscite would be repeated within a year. The plebiscite was held on June 2, 1946, despite the fact that no prisoners of war had yet returned home from Allied camps, preventing a half million voters from voting.

For the first and only time in Italian history, results from the south arrived faster than from the north. They indicated a monarchist victory, but when the following day results from the north were tallied, the Republic won by 10 to 12 million votes. Humbert accepted his fate. He released the armed forces from their oath and went into exile in Portugal as his ancestor Charles Albert had done in

1849. Enrico De Nicola, a well-known attorney and the former president of the Chamber of Deputies in 1922, was elected as provisional chief of the state.

The new Italian Republic had to address all the problems linked to the Treaty of Peace and to the new world reorganization. On February 10, 1947, the treaty was signed in Paris. The Allies abandoned all the promises made in 1943. Italy lost all its colonies and gave Greece the Dodecanese Islands. Yugoslavia obtained Istria and Zara, that is to say, what the Yalta Conference had agreed upon. France demanded territory on the western slope of the Alps. They had been specifically chosen because they controlled the sources of Italy's hydroelectric energy. Fortunately, other Allied powers soon rejected this agreement, and Italy lost only a few small towns dominating a couple of Alpine passes.

From a military perspective the treaty was a tragedy. Italy had already started to reorganize its armed forces in the fall of 1945. The army released its conscripts, reducing its strength to 140,000 men, as anticipated by the Allied powers. The navy was supposed to maintain two battleships, seven cruisers, nine destroyers, all its light ships, and submarines. The air force too was to be allowed to keep its structure and increase its strength. All of this changed with the treaty.

The army—now the *Esercito Italiano*, as it had been in 1861—could have no more than 185,000 men, including 65,000 Carabineers. They were prohibited from possessing missiles and bazookas. No cannon with a range of nineteen miles was permitted, and the entire army could have no more than 200 medium tanks. The air force—the *Aeronautica Militare*—was permitted to have 25,000 men, no more than 200 interceptors and reconnaissance planes, only 150 unarmed cargo planes, and no bombers. The *Marina Militare* was reduced the most. It could maintain 25,000 men, and ships of less than 67,000 metric tons. It could maintain the two oldest battleships, four cruisers, four destroyers, 16 torpedo boats, 20 corvettes, 15 minesweepers, eight antisubmarine units, and 74 auxiliary ships. Submarines were forbidden. All ships above these limits had to be destroyed or left to the Allies. The navy revolted. It threatened a general scuttling; and the government did what it could to save the ships. They were unsuccessful; and the treaty left Italy a sort of convoy-escorting force as a navy. The Italian armed forces, however, did their best to find ways around the treaty restrictions. A submarine training school was unofficially maintained; and the air force increased its number of heavy aircraft by simply putting on their wings the cockade of the Order of Malta instead of keeping the Italian insignias.

1948–1988

The Italian armed forces were promptly rebuilt after 1948. The growing tensions between the Soviet Union and the United States, as witnessed during the Berlin blockade, made it clear to the United States and Britain that Italy would play a key and strategic role in any future conflict. In the same year that they combined their German zones of occupation into West Germany, the Allies changed their attitude toward Italy. The army reorganized the combat groups into normal divisions. Then in 1948, it reestablished other infantry divisions. In 1951 it had ten infantry divisions,[1] two tank brigades,[2] and two Alpine brigades.[3] In the same year it established the Army Light Air Corps, to be used for reconnaissance, while the Lagunari Regiment passed from the Engineers Corps to the infantry, focusing on landing operations and amphibious warfare more than before. Three additional Alpine brigades[4] were organized in the subsequent two years, while the tank brigades were increased to divisional strength, and a third division was created. By 1953 the army had thirteen divisions and five Alpine brigades.

The navy had 178 ships, equal to 125,000 metric tons of fighting tonnage and 50,000 more of auxiliary tonnage, supported by 48 antisub aircraft and 30 helicopters in the early 1960s. At he end of 1971 the *Marina Militare* ranked fifth in the world after United States, the Soviet Union, Britain, and France, with 44,000 men and 144 fighting ships divided into four naval divisions, a Minesweeper Command, a Submarine Command, an Undersea Raiders Command, and three Helicopter Centers. In the same year the air force had 70,000 men divided into 35 Flying Groups on 22 airbases, and supported 13 Missile Groups.

What did not change after the war, or, if we prefer, since the days of the 1814 Restoration, was the General Staff. A substantial reorganization of the armed forces from top to bottom was carried out between 1962 and 1965. The new NATO views about nuclear weapons foresaw a reduced use of tactical weapons, so the major plan against a possible Soviet invasion was based on conventional weapons. The 1963-issued doctrine Series 700 "Employment of the Great Complex Units"[5] focused on the renovated importance of classical weapons; and this implied a wide change in portable weapons, mortars, and above all tanks, including the M-47, M-60, the Leopard 1, and the newly introduced M-113 armored vehicle. The Defense General Staff was established, but it simply coordinated the army, navy, and air force staffs, with no real commanding authority. It needed thirty more years to receive full authority over the entire system.

Italy committed its armed forces abroad for much of the postwar era. An Italian Red Cross field unit was sent to Korea, and that same year the United Nations gave Italy a temporary mandate over Somalia, until 1960. Italy organized the AFIS—*Amministrazione Fiduciaria Italiana*—in Somalia, and sent 5,700 men from the armed forces to organize Somali troops. They returned in 1955, leaving only a few advisers until 1959.

Italy was admitted to United Nations only in 1955. Italian troops began participating to UN peacekeeping operations beginning in 1960. The first was ONUC in Congo—the former Belgian Congo—where, in Kindu, thirteen men of the Italian air force were massacred by Congolese who thought they were Belgians. In the following years Italian military personnel were involved in some United Nations operations, such as in Yemen in 1963–64, on the Pakistani-Indian border in Kashmir since 1959 for UNMOGIP, in Jordan since 1958 for UNTSO and Lebanon, and, briefly, in 1965–66, for UNIPOM.

Lebanon saw a remarkable Italian involvement. In fact, after their first short six months' participation to UNOGIL in 1958, in 1979 Italy sent a helicopter squadron for the still-working UNIFIL operation. Then in 1982, an American-French-Italian expeditionary force landed in Beirut. Its role was to evacuate Palestinians from Beirut to Cyprus and Syria. Soon after the expeditionary force departure, Lebanese militias massacred Palestinians in the refugee camps of Sabra and Shatila, and the MNF, Multinational Force, came back and remained in Lebanon until early March 1984.

Italy acted outside of the United Nations as well. In fact, the MNF was not a United Nations operation. It was not the first time. In 1973 the Italian navy reacted against a Libyan intrusion in blue waters near Malta. This began a still-active Italian-Maltese military agreement. Later, in 1979, the navy sent a squadron—two cruisers and a support ship—to the South China Sea to rescue the so-called Vietnamese "boat people," South Vietnamese escaping by sea after the North Vietnamese victory. This was possible only thanks to the naval law issued some years before. In 1973, Admiral De Giorgi had been appointed as navy chief of staff. According to him, a Soviet-American conflict was improbable, but local low-intensity conflicts such as the Yom Kippur War were very likely, especially in the Mediterranean and other close theaters, such as the Marmara Sea, the Red and Black Seas, the Persian Gulf, and the Indian Ocean. According to his vision, the navy had to be ready to intervene, and it needed 160,000 metric tons of ships to do so. At that time it had only 105,000 and initially planned to reduce its size to merely 41,000 in 1984.

Admiral De Giorgi and the navy staff prepared the "White Book," proposing to expand the navy for such contingencies. On March 22, 1975, the Parliament approved the Naval Law. It gave 1,000 billion liras, some $2 billion, for a ten-year expansion to purchase thirty-two new ships and new helicopters and weapons. The navy acted quite quickly. By 1977 it had already spent three-quarters of the money, and within a few years the goal was reached. Suddenly the navy began testing its projection capabilities. The "boat people" rescue was also a test of projection. It worked, but demonstrated that the navy needed more logistics ships and a stronger aviation component.

From 1981 to 1984 the navy was involved in many international peacekeeping and security missions. According to MFO—Multinational Force and Observers—operations established by the 1979 Israeli-Egyptian peace agreement, minesweepers were sent to Sharm el Sheik in 1981 to patrol the Gulf of Aqaba and Straits of Tiran. They are still employed in these operations today.

Another minesweeper squadron was sent to Egypt in 1984 to sweep a large area south of Suez. Then in 1988, three frigates, three minesweepers, and a support ship composing the 18th Naval Group were sent to the Persian Gulf to protect Italian merchantmen during the last period of Iran-Iraq War. This last operation demonstrated the necessity of air cover for naval operations. The *Regia Marina* had abandoned the idea of a naval air force in 1929. Italy never had an aircraft carrier. Politicians did not like the idea of a big and expensive ship, while the opposition rejected the notion out of hand. In theory the opposition claimed they supported disarmament and world peace. The other aspect of their opposition was aimed at weakening NATO Mediterranean forces against the Soviets. The Italian Left supported—and still supports—Palestinians against Israel and Cuba against United States, opposing in all possible ways United States foreign policy. So, for instance, somebody spoke from the left benches of the Parliament against the navy expedition to rescue boat people, because they were abandoning Vietnam after the North Vietnamese victory. Then nobody reacted against the expeditionary force to Lebanon, because it was to rescue Palestinians, especially after the massacres in Sabra and Shatila. But when the ships were sent to the Persian Gulf, Leftist groups reacted. They supported in all the possible ways nonintervention. The mass media were clearly against it, and the government faced a really bad spell.

The Left spoke loudly against any intervention abroad. This was due to the desire to weaken NATO, to present strong opposition to any aspect of direct or indirect U.S. policy in the world; in this case, to rescue people from Vietnam implicitly meant that the U.S. had fought on the right side and Vietnamese Communists were wrong. The same happened in Lebabon, because since Palestinians were perceived as enemies of Israel and Israel was perceived as a close ally of the United States, supporting the Palestinians meant weakening Israel and weakening the United States and their world policy. This same attitude based on anti-Americanism gave the ground to oppose the expedition to the Gulf the first time, in the eighties, the first Gulf War, and the operation in Somalia in 1991–95.

CHAPTER 27

Italy and NATO until the End of the Cold War

Soon after the signing of the Treaty of Paris, Italy realized it was isolated between two blocs. When in 1948 the Communists lost the first Republican general elections, Italy avoided Soviet influence, but it feared the risk of a Yugoslav attack, or, after the establishment of the Iron Curtain, to be the battlefield between the Soviets and Western Europe. What would happen under those circumstances? The Italian government, led by Alcide De Gasperi, believed the best solution was foreign protection, and looked to the United States. General Efisio Marras was sent to Berlin, where he met with General Lucius Clay. The Italian government dispatched Marras to discuss a military agreement, but Clay responded that the whole issue had to first be decided politically; no military talks before a general political agreement.

De Gasperi pursued a bilateral agreement with the United States. Washington was not particularly interested in his proposal. There were more pressing issues and, in any case, they could not sign an agreement with a defeated enemy. When later in 1948, General George C. Marshall came to Italy in his new role as secretary of state, he declared he was in Rome to listen to Italian offers. Unfortunately, Italian politicians presumptuously supposed they could negotiate as if the United States wanted Italy as an ally. This was still not the case. Washington could provide assistance, but surely it was not a priority.

According to their old-fashioned mentality, Italian politicians believed they would find France more receptive. This attitude directly stemmed from the historical memory of the 1796 cooperation between the Italian bourgeoisie and their French "liberators." It had survived the tumultuous nineteenth century, and it survived the Fascist period because of the great number of antifascist refugees in France. The hope of a friendly France, of the friendly and lovely Latin sister, was dashed when the French coldly invited Italy to join the Council of Europe, a political entity with no military relevance.

The international situation deteriorated steadily. The Soviet blockade of Berlin marked the beginning of the Cold War. In Rome, politicians realized that Italy could very well be the next battlefield between East and West. They desperately tried to find a way to gain American confidence and subsequent support. The Treaty of Paris truly weakened Italy, but one must also understand that the new Italian government considered defense a secondary issue. Politicians who won in the 1948 elections belonged to the old bourgeoisie. This was the same group that had led Parliament prior to the Great War, but the country now had less money and the strongest Communist Party in Western Europe. The government's biggest concern was, in fact, domestic security. Virtually all state resources were spent maintaining control of the country. Police control and welfare were the equivalent of Roman "bread and circuses." Welfare kept the people calm. Police prevented insurrection. The army could be useful as a constabulary force, too, but the country lacked sufficient revenue and therefore could not afford to spend it on a larger army.

Before 1948, De Gasperi included the Communists in his coalition government. Communist Party secretary Palmiro Togliatti had been appointed minister of justice, and he granted amnesty to all who had murdered someone after April 1945 for political reasons. This meant that a lot of dangerous Communists were freed. They still possessed weapons and were committed to an armed revolution, as was demonstrated by their reaction when a student wounded Togliatti. This meant above all that an incredible number of former Fascists were free; and nobody could charge them; moreover, many joined the Communists![1] The government had to address this problem, and more money was needed to increase the numbers and effectiveness of police and Carabineers. The government had to find revenue to pay war damages, pay salaries, keep the police and armed Forces, and rebuild the whole country.

In order to protect Western Europe against the Soviet threat, the Western countries developed an Atlantic Alliance. It was a political alliance whose military organization—the North Atlantic Treaty Organization, NATO—included a mutual defense pact for its members. Italy was clearly cut off it, especially after mistakes made by the new politicians. Ironically enough, France came to the rescue. France had been invited to join the Atlantic Alliance. Paris wanted NATO protection to be extended to its North African colonies, particularly Algeria. The United States and Britain disliked this idea. In response, France demanded that Italy be permitted to join the Alliance. This would push the southern border of NATO to the geographical parallel including Sicily. Defense up to the 35th Parallel and north would have included northern Algeria—that is to say, all of Algeria—too.

London definitely rejected this; and President Harry S. Truman was not terribly enthusiastic. The French, however, left him no choice; if Italy was not invited to join NATO, France would veto the admission of Norway. Norway was absolutely vital to protecting the North Atlantic maritime routes from America to Europe. President Truman was a pragmatic man. The Atlantic Alliance absolutely needed Norway, and it needed France as a major beachhead in Continental Europe. He therefore accepted Italy's admission.

Italian accession to NATO implied large-scale and full military support by the United States. The Italian armed forces were substantially reorganized and, as soon as possible, the limiting clauses of the Treaty of Paris were abandoned. Italy's role in NATO was simple; it had to provide the Alliance with strategic bases for operations in southern Europe. Its position in the central Mediterranean allowed the Allies to control any Soviet attempts to move from the Black Sea and eastern Mediterranean to the west.

In terms of land operations, Italy was marginal. The main Soviet penetration line was through Germany, to the Rhine. Italy was partially covered by three neutral nations—Switzerland, Austria, and Yugoslavia—and this gave at least a little time for an alarm in case of Soviet attack. In fact, throughout the Cold War, NATO strategy foresaw no special role for the Italian armed forces. In case of an invasion, the Italian air force had to place all its aircraft in Sicily and Sardinia to react to the fighting in Continental Italy. The navy had to do the same, because its main task was escorting convoys and supporting the U.S. 6th Fleet, based in Naples.

In case of limited actions by a special enemy corps, the army had to fight according to counterinsurgency doctrine. In the event of an invasion through the so-called Gorizia Gate, that is to say, through northern Yugoslavia—Slovenia—or Austria, the army was supposed to resist for two days, then it was to conduct a guerrilla war against the Warsaw Pact. A part of the army, a special secret organization known as "Gladius," or "stay behind," was organized and prepared to react against a possible invasion, while the government was supposed to flee abroad.

The Soviet Union too defined Italy as a secondary front. Soviet plans revealed after the dissolution of the Warsaw Pact determined that Italy had to be attacked and seized by Hungarian and Soviet troops, but the main Soviet objective would be an advance through Germany. Anyway, the Soviets did their best to prepare for a possible invasion by secretly mining Italian waters after 1949.

Regardless of military preparations and planning, the major Soviet task was to foster a Communist political victory in Italy. This would have meant, in the worst case for the Soviets, a neutral Italy with no more NATO bases on its territory. In the best case, Italy would join the Warsaw Pact. The Italian Communist Party did its best to achieve political power. After 1948, the Italian Parliament was dominated by Christian Democracy, the Catholic party established in the early 1920s by Don Luigi Sturzo, a Catholic priest. It was heavily influenced by the Church.

The government's power was based upon two main pillars, the police and the judges. The armed forces became third.

Communist policy was quite interesting. Initially they knew they were too weak to prevail, so they decided to establish a coalition of the Left. Leadership had to be maintained internally by the strongest, which were the Communists. This was the same policy of the Popular Front in Spain during its civil war. It proved effective for twenty years. Then, during the terrorism of the 1970s, the Socialist Party moved to the center and in the early 1980s made a strong alliance with Christian Democracy, gaining the premiership.[2]

The second step was Communist cultural policy. It was impossible to have an armed revolution because of the American presence in Italy, and because of the impossibility of direct Soviet involvement. The Communist Party's basic strategy was to conquer "the hearts and minds" of Italians. It had to be achieved by establishing a deep and complete Communist presence where minds were educated, in the schools and in the universities. It needed time, of course, but at the end of the process, the entire Italian ruling class, or—in the worst case—its majority, would be composed of Communists, and power would be achieved. The Communists established a presence at universities—normally among nonscientific faculty—and in the cultural world, and the result was a fracture between a majority composed of roughly two-thirds of the country and a minority including 100,000 to 200,000 people who spoke through mass media, such as journalists, writers, actors, art directors, painters, and so on.

This explains why Italian intellectuals are mainly on the Left. The gap existing between the Left and the majority has often been demonstrated by the vote. The Left won a general election only twice, in 1996 and in 2006. The same gap existed between popular patriotism and national spirit on one side and the Leftist accusations equating patriotism with Fascism. For instance, displaying a national flag— something that normally happens in the United States—was considered a dangerous nationalist or crypto-Fascist demonstration. The national anthem was sung less because nobody learned it in the schools; and the flag was displayed daily only in the barracks, at the airports, or at the border or on ships. The only place where one could fly his own flag without risk of being labeled a "Fascist" was the stadium. Things changed only when Carlo Azeglio Ciampi became president in 1999.

In the 1950s and '60s the Communists had two more tasks: to weaken the justice system and the police. The police system included police, Carabineers and the *Guardia di Finanza*. The first step of the Communist program consisted of depriving the police of its military character, in order to control it through unions. The Radical Party, a small progressive Leftist party, was used as the battering ram and, in the 1970s, the police became a civilian body. The Carabineers and the *Guardia di Finanza* refused to abandon their military status. The Communists suggested a new organization for the security system. The police would remain in the cities and the Carabineers would move to the towns and countryside, but it was not accepted.

The Justice Department was very hard to subvert. So, the Communist Party did all it could to support judges and their desire for increased autonomy.

In the early1960s the Italian economy grew significantly. The Christian Democrats proposed a welfare program. It was based on a dream, as the funds needed were supposed to come from national economic growth. The Italian growth rate of that time was quite high, but it was hard to predict a similar growth rate in the coming years. Then in 1968, riots and violence occurred throughout Europe, but in Italy they were the origins of terrorism. The situation was quite complex and difficult to explain. It is still unclear if terrorism was organized by a foreign power or if it developed domestically and was later supported by a foreign country. What is clear is that Italy suffered from Leftist terrorism supported by the Soviet Union and a Fascist terrorism supported by unknown forces. The first terrorist actions occurred in the very early 1970s and soon increased with incredible efficiency and violence. Fascist terrorism was violent, but it was never perceived by the population as a real menace against the state because their activity was not as frequent as that of Communist terrorists. Marxist terrorism was considered the greater risk. The Communist Party officially disapproved of Marxist terrorism, but, luckily for them, the party and its members were never hurt by Marxist terrorists, apart from a couple of cases. The main objective was Christian Democracy. More than two hundred of its members were killed or wounded, not to mention *Carabinieri*, judges, policemen, journalists, industrial managers, and relevant officers of state administration. Communist terrorism was perceived as a real threat for Italian policy and for NATO, while in that same period Germany fought against RAF (Red Army Faction) Communist terrorists, and the IRA attacked Britain.

Month by month, terrorist actions increased in quantity and quality. No less than three different Marxist terrorist groups operated in Italy; and the government needed all its resources to face the threat. The easiest answer was to increase the entire police apparatus. Security expenditures increased, and most of the police were employed in antiterrorist activities. Unfortunately, this provided an opportunity for the Mafia and other similar criminal organizations to expand. When in the early eighties the war against terror was won, organized crime had enlarged its activities. Moreover, in that same period the Left proposed and supported many laws to reduce penalties and periods of imprisonment, as well as grant amnesties. The police had to increase their activity. At the same time the weekly service was reduced to thirty-six hours for civil policemen, but these conditions were extended to Carabineers and *Guardia di Finanza*, too. This meant that if daily service previously needed three men, now it needed four. In other words, the police system had to be increased in men and money to achieve the same results as before.

The Leftist campaign for freeing light drugs increased their abuse and rendered criminals stronger. The police had to face increasing crime; and in 2006 the annual murder rate reached 580–600 out of 59 million inhabitants. Expenditure for police forces increased. The oil crisis of the early seventies joined to financial and economical crises, causing additional problems. Italy obtained very good results in the eighties, ranking as the fourth nation in the world economy, at the same level of France; but in that same period its industrial system had problems.

In the early fifties, Italy, France, Germany, Belgium, the Netherlands, and Luxembourg formed the European Common Market. It could be a good resource for a country with a decisive policy. But thanks to the proportional vote, Italy was in the same situation it was in the nineteenth century: Governements had insecure political majorities scattered into five or six different parties, all demanding more power, all threatening a crisis in case of rejection. Politicians looked more at local quarrels than at major issues and simply looked to avoid international problems, acting as the Allied countries did. Sometimes they agreed to international agreements at any cost, in spite of whether it was good or not for Italy.

Moreover, France looked for a strict agreement with Germany. Italy remained cut out, and the problem increased as the European community widened. On

European issues, Italy was often beaten and, when agreements about opening European markets were discussed, Italian industry received a real knock. In fact, it had wasted its time according to its traditional short-term policy. No real reorganization was made. Few invested in research and development; and most industrialists cried for the state's help. Italy's financial situation grew worse.

The republic had to pay for its welfare system, for its security, and for the crude oil needed by industry and daily life. The money supply was insufficient, and the deficit increased. Something had to be cut, and members of Parliament suggested cutting military expenditures.

Things in policy did not change so much in the 1980s. The attitude of Italians during the late Cold War was marked by philo-Americanism and anti-Sovietism. Italians normally preferred and supported center and moderate coalitions. It was as conservative as needed and as progressive as required to maintain social progress and welfare. This is why at the end of the 1970s the Italian Socialist Party abandoned its alliance with the Communists and moved to the center, closer to Christian Democrats. They formed a coalition that included the Republican, Social Democratic, and Liberal Parties. It was called "the Pentaparty" after the five parties composing it. It was during this coalition's tenure that Italian foreign policy became more active.

It acted with more energy than in the past and with a remarkable loyalty to NATO. Soon after the beginning of the Cold War, the clash between NATO and the Warsaw Pact was indirect and based mostly on nuclear dissuasion. As the U.S. and USSR increased their nuclear arsenal, the situation eventually stabilized. Soviet strategy during the 1970s centered around the Brezhnev Doctrine, surrounding the West by supporting Marxist revolutions throughout the world. The regions specifically affected were Africa, Asia, and Latin America, where the Soviets and their allies provided military and material aid to the new Marxist regimes.

At the same time the Soviets possessed a clear numerical superiority in conventional weapons. In the early 1970s, NATO maintained only naval and nuclear superiority, but appeared unable to repel a conventional Soviet ground attack in Europe. When, after the conference held in Havana in 1979, nonaligned countries basically decided to stand equally distant from both the West and the East, the Soviet Union announced it was going to deploy SS-20 missiles in Europe. People wondered whether, in case of nuclear attack in Europe, the United States would really have reacted using their own nuclear weapons and exposing their metroplitan territory to a Soviet nuclear reappraisal. German chancellor Helmut Schmidt asked for a clear and concrete NATO initiative. Negotiations in Geneva between American delegate Paul Nitze and Soviet Juli Kvjtsinsky began. They aimed to reach a compromise based on so called "zero options," that is to say the mutual and contemporary removal of all the Pershing, Cruise, and SS-20 missiles from Europe. Unfortunately they failed. The Soviets stood on their position. The only alternative for NATO was to deploy Cruise missiles. Germany agreed to have Cruise missiles on its own territory only if another "great nation in continental Europe" agreed, too.[3]

The United States was ready to deploy its best midrange and tactical nuclear missiles.[4] Missiles, however, were relatively short-ranged and necessarily required launch bases on the European Continent. The German position forbade for the moment the use of bases in Germany, leaving only Belgium, the Netherlands, Denmark, and Italy. The Italian government ensured a positive parliamentary vote. This was quite important, because the Italian Parliament was the first to decide in Continental Europe. The Communists rejected this vote and began a "pro-peace" campaign in Europe against the Cruise missiles. Mass media heavily supported the anti-Cruise front. Then in a memorable session, ignoring the Leftist demonstrations and the press, the Italian Parliament accepted Cruise missiles on Italian territory. Now, Moscow was within range. The Italian vote satisfied Germany and led other NATO members to accept U.S. missiles. In response the Soviets increased their missile system. By the 1980s the United States announced the "Star Wars" system. The Soviets feared this would negate their missile effectiveness and, moreover, it was losing money and resources supporting its gigantic military institution as well as all the Third World Marxist countries. This was the background when in the 1980s, Mikhail Gorbachev became the Soviet leader and announced the end of the Warsaw Pact. Soviet troops left Eastern Europe. Communist regimes collapsed, and the Soviet Union disbanded in 1989, dividing into fifteen independent countries. The Cold War was over.

From the Cold War to the War on Terror: 1989–2005

Armed Forces Reorganization after Cold War and Peacekeeping: 1989–2001

Not caring that history was at an end, as someone just wrote, in 1989 the eastern system collapsed. When the Berlin Wall came down and the Warsaw Pact disbanded, all the Western countries believed that there would be a "peace dividend," and the cost of maintaining large armed forces could be reduced drastically. It was abundantly clear they had not learned from the past. A long period of crises and instability followed both the world wars, and one could reasonably expect something similar in the wake of the Cold War. Shortly thereafter, low-intensity conflicts and civil wars necessitated the deployment of U.S. and NATO forces in places unimagined in the past.

Italy was not an exception. In 1980 the Italian Army had 270,000 men, divided into 4 divisions and 13 additional brigades, supported by 1,200 main battle tanks, 5,000 armored vehicles, and 57 artillery and missile groups. As a result of the combined effects of a state deficit and of illusions stemming from the end of the Cold War, in 1991 the army was severely reduced to only 19 brigades and its strength was decreasing.

As with all Western countries, Italy moved toward a professional army. Comparative studies on Italian, German, and French armed forces were published concerning the merits of a professional versus a conscripted army, but the problem was considered more political than military in nature. Italian politicians were divided. The Right liked the idea of a professional army. It had supported it since the seventies, believing it more effective than one composed of conscripts. The Left did not like this idea. It feared a professional army as a tool for a conservative national agenda. Many groups on the Left rejected the concept of armed forces altogether. They advocated abandoning NATO and refusing to United States permission to use Italian bases.

The clergy also supported a progressive reduction of military power. After Vatican Council II, contemporary issues, including peace at any cost, banning weapons and nuclear disarmament, attracted large parts of the Catholic clergy. Even if the Church never officially supported these issues, many priests and religious groups advocated conscientious objection. They achieved a certain level of success, because of their relevance in a Catholic country and because a greater portion of the population looked at military service as at a waste of time. Gradually military service had been reduced from 18 to 15 months. Then, in the eighties it was reduced to 12 months for soldiers and 15 for officers and, in the nineties, no more than 10 months for soldiers. Conscientious objectors could now choose civil as opposed to military service.

This reduction had a negative impact on the armed forces' effectiveness. For example, when the new armored car Centauro appeared, crews needed ten months' training to be combat ready; but how could conscripts be trained properly if their service concluded at the moment they were combat-ready? This is essentially the reason why the government supported professionalization of the armed forces when the Cold War ended. A mixed system of professionals and conscripts continued through the second half of the 1990s, with the end of conscription in the spring 2005.

Professionalization had its problems; also if serving in the Carabineers and the *Guardia di Finanza* was considered separate from military service, because it was police service. Military recruitment did not go well. Women were admitted to the armed forces only in 2000, and this helped fill the units. But it was not until 2004 that the armed forces achieved their recruitment goals; and, at that time, the strength of Italian armed forces' had decreased dramatically. If in 1991 the army had only 19 brigades, according to the "New Defense Model;" in 1995 the armed forces should have mustered 320,354 men. According to plans, however, the number decreased to 185,750 in 1998 and later down to a 128,000 "all-professional" army. By 2005 there were 250,000 men and women for the three branches of the Italian armed forces.

The impact of the military transformation became apparent with the crises in Somalia, Kuwait, Kurdistan, the Persian Gulf and the former Yugoslavia—that is to say Bosnia, Kosovo, and Macedonia and Albania. All needed long-term and expensive peacekeeping operations. Short-term similar operations involved Italian troops in Angola, Mozambique, and East Timor. Smaller units, sometimes consisting of no more than ten or twelve men, were sent to Cambodia, Congo, the Ivory Coast, Kenya, Kashmir, Namibia, Eritrea, Ethiopia, the Palestinian Authority, Rwanda, El Salvador, Guatemala, and Yemen. When later the War on Terror began, a considerable effort was made in Afghanistan and Iraq, and later more troops were sent to the Sudan, too.

The armed forces reacted as best they could to these increasing demands. On February 11, 1997, Parliament approved Law No. 25. It gave the defense chief of staff united command of all armed forces. Then, each branch conducted a long and extensive reorganization. At the end, all units in metropolitan territory were subordinate to a permanent Superior Command, such as the army, air force, and navy commands. These were subordinate to a high command, the *Comando Operativo di Vertice Interforze*—Joint Service High Operational Command—or COI. All branch Superior Commands were planning staffs and did not directly control military units, but, when ordered to enact their plans, those units earmarked for operations were subordinated to their command. This finally created a system where the planning staff achieved command powers for military operations after 150 years.

The army had a *Comando Forze Terrestri*—Land Forces Command, or Com-FoTer, which had three branches: schools, logistics, support—and the operational branch. This was divided into four different groups: a *Comando Forze di Proiezione*—Projection Forces Command; a *Comando Truppe Alpine*—Alpine Troops Command; and two *Comandi delle Forze di Difesa*—1st and 2nd Defense Forces Commands.

The *Aeronautica Militare* developed something similar. Its General Staff was reduced. The previous organization of the three air regions became a single Air Squadron Command. Air bases decreased from 20 to 10, flying groups from 38 to 32, and personnel from 63,747 in 1998 to 55,000 in 2005.

The *Marina Militare* significantly altered its structure. It used peacekeeping operations as tests, just as the other branches did. The navy, however, had a major interest, because of the increasing overseas involvement of the armed forces. It was clear that only a few peacekeeping operations could be conducted without naval support. The *Marina Militare*, then, developed and expanded its projectability and sustainability. The 1991 Gulf War demonstrated it was time for the navy to establish air protection. The navy sent a squadron: the 20th Naval Group composed of frigates and logistical ships, tasked to protect U.S. carriers and supply the Allied fleet. There was no Italian carrier at that time, so the air force sent Task Group "Locusta" composed of ten "Tornado" multi-role aircraft[1] and some air cargo planes to cooperate with the UN offensive to free Kuwait and provide air support for Italian ships. But transferring land-based Italian aircraft to the Gulf was quite expensive. Moreover, the land-basing—in Abu Dhabi and the United Arab Emirates—was far from the operational theater and proved that air intervention was not as flexible as required.

The navy tested its air capability in the operation in Somalia. At that time, in the early nineties the navy built its first aircraft carrier, the *Garibaldi*. It was originally designed as a helicopter carrier, but could easily be used by VTOL (**V**ertical **T**ake-**O**ff and **L**anding) planes. After the Gulf and the first Somali intervention, the *Marina Militare* decided upon full air capability. Its naval air force—an antisubmarine one, including both planes and helicopters—could not provide such support. In 1995 the "On Board Naval Air Squadron" was established. It was composed of VTOL Harriers AV-8B and received its eighteenth and last plane in 1997.

This gave the Italian armed forces a solid projection and sustainability for peacekeeping and "low-intensity" operations. The navy experimented with possible kinds of naval squadrons. Lessons were learned in Lebanon, the Gulf and, above all, Somalia about landing from sea and air, sea-air, sea-land, air-land, and three dimensional combined operations. Air force cargo, armored, and protected vehicles, and personal and support weapons and equipment were improved. Satellite communications provided by the SICRAL system and an expanded satellite surveillance by National system Cosmo SkyMed were also available to the Italian armed forces. When the most distant intervention was conducted in East Timor, the results were quite good. By the time this occurred, in 2004, many things had changed at home since the first Gulf War in 1991.

Second Time: Peacekeeping and Foreign and Domestic Affairs

Pentaparty rule ended in the early nineties when the Justice Department began inquiring about its funding. Files were opened about practically every important Pentaparty politician. This inquiry period, known as *Mani Pulite*—"Clean Hands"— quickly dissolved the ruling coalition and weakened policies and Parliament's position before the magistrates. Curiously, other than a couple of soon-abandoned and archived inquiries, no party and practically no politician of the opposition front was prosecuted by the law, as well as no one from the Italian Social Movement—heir of the Fascist Party—which never had power in the central administration and, at that time, none in the local administration, too, other than some towns.

The Socialist Party was destroyed by the entire affair and, in the approaching 1994 general election, the situation was odd. The majority of voters clearly disliked the Left, but there were no organized parties to take advantage of the situation. At this time the well-known television tycoon Silvio Berlusconi organized a new party and easily won the 1994 election. In no more than six months he gathered practically all the former members and voters of the Pentaparty and reached an agreement with the newly reformed Social Movement, and the autonomous party called Lega, and won.

Not long after the elections, United States policy was coping with the post–Cold War era. United States foreign policy was clearly exposed in the spring of 1995 by State Secretary Warren Christopher in an article in *Foreign Policy*. According to Christopher, the fall of Soviet Union presented the United States with an exceptional opportunity for modeling the world according to American values and mind. There were four major strategic goals: preserving United States world supremacy, keeping productive political-economic relations with the most powerful countries, establishing new international institutions or improving existing ones, and supporting democracy and human rights according to American ideals and interests. Republican senator Robert Dole substantially agreed with Christopher.

In fact, in his article "Shaping America's Global Future,"[2] he practically said that after the end of the Cold War the United States could build a durable peace based on preserving America's interests and supremacy.

Consequently, Christopher wrote that there were five intervention sectors. America should: strengthen a global and free market commercial system. Europe needed a better security system. The Middle East needed a durable and firmly established peace. Weapons of mass destruction had to be reduced. Finally, terrorists and drugs traders had to be destroyed.

It was a quite fine program. Unfortunately, Rome soon realized there was no role foreseen for Italy. In fact, the United States improved its relations with Japan and Germany. On April 17, 1996, Japan signed the Twenty-first Century Treaty. It was a closer alliance between Japan and the United States, and China saw it as a mechanism for their isolation. In Europe, the United States largely supported German foreign policy in the Balkans and Eastern Europe. At the global level the United States suggested a reorganization of the United Nations. According to them, Germany and Japan—the defeated enemies of World War II—could now enter the Security Council. No mention was made of Italy. At the same time, when preparing the G7 meeting for Denver in June 1996, sources at the United States Department of State asked to reduce the meeting from seven to only the economically most important countries on the three concerned continents. This implicitly meant that only the United States, Japan, and Germany would have met in Denver. Britain, France, Italy, and Canada rejected this idea, but the threat to Italy's position was clear.

When the civil war in Yugoslavia exploded in 1990, not caring about Italian national interest and supporting a wider Western political plan, Rome recognized the newly established Slovenia and Croatia in spite of Belgrade's offer to return the land Italy had lost in 1945. Then, when trouble in Somalia developed the following year and the United Nations decided on intervention, Rome was completely cut off. Washington clearly supported, if not suggested it, and Rome was offended, especially when remembering that Somalia was a former Italian colony with a large diffusion of the Italian language.

Furthermore, when an Italian peacekeeping force reached Mogadishu in March 1993, a new problem emerged. The Italian command normally looked to negotiate with Somali warlords; Americans preferred direct military action. The difference between Italians and Americans became so deep that Italian headquarters asked the United Nations command for permission to leave Mogadishu. Italian troops were moved to other Somali towns. The U.S. command insisted in action, and the result was a bloody ambush and an escalation of fighting. The American press then admitted that the Italian way was not wrong and suggested that United States troops to do the same.

After the peacekeeping mandate expired in March 1994, Italian forces left Somalia. When the whole UN-Somali operation failed, a complete withdrawal was decided for the end of 1994. The United Nations asked the United States and

Italy for support, and the 26th Italian Naval Group returned to Mogadishu for the joint U.S.—Italian "United Shield" operation.

Military action could not compensate for a cold political evaluation. When assessing the situation from Washington, an observer could only define Italy as a deeply troubled and disturbed country. Its economy was not good. The Italian deficit was one of the largest in the world. Domestic political affairs were chaotic thanks to the "clean-hands" inquiries. Moreover, Italy had contacts with Arabs, including terrorists, and disagreed with American perspectives about the Mediterranean and Middle East. No change was in sight. How then could an American observer at that time consider Italy a reliable country supporting American policy?

For these reasons it is no wonder President Clinton went forward with his proposal to reorganize the United Nations. And it is no wonder that Italy reacted against this reform program. Much of it happened during Silvio Berlusconi's first premiership. It first came in the form of Italian opposition to the Security Council reorganization. Then Rome vetoed Slovenian and Croatian admission to the European Union. This weakened German foreign policy; and Berlin did not like it. The next step was in Egypt. The United Nations held its conference on birth control and family planning in Cairo. Italy was the only industrialized country that did not support it. Moreover, it acted as a link between the Third World's Christian and Moslem countries; and the plan was fully defeated. As last, the Italian ambassador to the United Nations gained a nonpermanent seat in the next Security Council. After this, Berlusconi resigned due to unrelated events; and a Leftist coalition that supported Lamberto Dini's premiership came to power.

The former governor of the Bank of Italy, Dini, had a problem. His supporters united against Berlusconi but had very different points of view about practically every other issue. The coalition was weak and the old game began again. Italian politicians were so worried about domestic affairs that they had no time for foreign policy. In 1996, for the first time, a Leftist coalition won a general election. Unfortunately, the main issue of the coalition was about stopping Berlusconi, and the parties still had quite different ideas about everything.

When the Yugoslav crisis over Kosovo developed, the Italian premiership faced coalition troubles. In fact, the majority of people supporting the coalition were Communists or former Communists. Since the fifties their party had told them to act against aggressive United States "imperialistic policy." Now the United States was going to war against Yugoslavia, the former Communist—and by definition democratic—Yugoslavia, still ruled by former Communists—but, by definition, still Democratic. Reaction in the streets and in the press was quite harsh. It were particularly nasty because the majority, who now rejected their policies, chose the government. The government responded by simply not publicizing Italian involvement in the war, at least not for the first days.

After the first NATO air operations in the Adriatic and against Yugoslavia in

March 1999, the Italian press asked why Italian airspace needed to be protected by foreign countries against possible Yugoslav intrusion. Two days later the *Aeronautica Militare* officially announced that Italian aircraft had been in action against the Yugoslavs on the Adriatic and in Yugoslavia since the eve of the war. The parliamentary Leftist majority was astonished. The opposition was quite amused. When officially asked, the government admitted that the armed forces were not fighting a war, they were merely conducting "long-range defensive actions." Then, the government admitted forty-two Italian aircraft, that is to say, 10 percent of all Allied forces, were involved in the war, as well as two frigates. Moreover, twelve Italian air bases were used by Allied aircraft, not to mention the ports and infrastructure provided for logistical support.

The longer the air campaign lasted, the more the Leftists grumbled against their government. In May, 54 Italian aircraft were involved in a total NATO force of 780. Luckily the war ended before a land attack started. Italian peacekeeping troops in Albania, Macedonia, and Bosnia were ordered to Kosovo along with other NATO troops. The Italian peacekeeping presence in the Balkans was not too unusual. Italian troops had landed in Albania as a peacekeeping force three years after the collapse of the Communist regime, in 1993. After a few years, a larger Italian Force returned to Albania in 1997 to stop clandestine immigration across the Adriatic to Italy. Strict naval control was established in the Otranto Channel. Italian light ships were based at Saseno Island, in the middle of Valona Bay, and Italy took care to assist Albania.

The Italian presence in Bosnia and Macedonia had begun earlier. After the collapse of Yugoslavia in the early nineties, a civil war broke out in Bosnia-Herzegovina. People acted just as their grandfathers had fifty years before. They considered those who had a different religion as enemies, and as the population was a mix of Catholic Croats, Orthodox Serbs, and Muslim Bosniacs, terrible massacres began. United Nations forces completely failed. The worst case occurred in Srebrenica. Unable to find a solution, the United Nations committed NATO to garrison Bosnia. Italian units went there as a part of NATO's interposition and constabulary force. They did the same when, later, Macedonia seceded from Yugoslavia.

Italian involvement in these operations was not simply a manifestation of strategic interest to maintain peace on their national borders but of their willingness to participate in UN operations and gain relevance in UN affairs. In June 1998, Italy achieved success when a large majority of countries declared that they preferred to take their own time to review the future of the Security Council. The American plan was slowed. Italy had time to prevent German and Japanese admission to the UN's most important committee. This implied, however, a deeper Italian participation in United Nations peacekeeping operations. Rome committed no less than two infantry regiments, a logistical battalion, related supporting units from the Engineers Corps and Army Light Air Corps, two frigates, amphibious ships, six to eight air force cargo planes, and eight to ten helicopters for United Nations operations.

Third Time: From September 11th to Iraq: 2001-2005

In spring 2001 the Leftist coalition was badly defeated, and Silvio Berlusconi became premier for the second time. He had to decide whether Italy would support U.S. military operations after the September 11th terrorist attack. United Nations resolution 1386 issued on December 20, 2001, allowed for military intervention against terrorist bases in Afghanistan. The United States asked for international support.

Italian domestic affairs were problematic for Berlusconi. The Left accused him of supporting American imperialist policy, saying more or less: "Let us fight for peace and down with Berlusconi and down with the Americans." The premier easily demonstrated that Italy was answering a United Nations' issue. No real opposition existed when Rear Adm. Maurizio Gemignani led an Italian squadron to the Indian Ocean, taking part in Operation Enduring Freedom in Afghanistan. Italian Naval Group—GrupNavIt—was composed of the *Garibaldi* aircraft carrier, two additional ships, support vessels, and the refueling ship *Etna*. They were included in the Allied naval forces as Task Group 620.01. The ships patrolled assigned areas in the Indian Ocean, while Italian aircraft operated in conjunction with U.S. Marine Corps aircraft in Afghanistan. GrupNavIt returned to Taranto naval base in March 2002.

More Italian ships were then sent on patrol in the Indian Ocean in the following years. At the same time, an Italian peacekeeping force was sent to Afghanistan, supporting UN operations there and, when the whole activity passed to NATO, the Italian presence continued.

The next crisis developed when President George W. Bush prepared to invade Iraq. This caused a deep fracture between the United States and some European allies. France and Germany refused any kind of support and spoke against United States intervention. Britain actively supported it, sending troops and participating in the war. Italy refused to participate in the war but offered peacekeeping forces afterward. The operation in Iraq went quickly. The war was over by Easter and in the late spring 2003 an Italian peacekeeping force arrived in southern Iraq. Leftist parties both in and out of Parliament opposed this operation.

Italian involvement in Iraq ran from the spring of 2003 to the autumn of 2006, when troops were withdrawn at a cost of twenty-five dead and as many wounded. Considering that Italy had only a very few casualties in Lebanon, only one dead after the 1991 Gulf War, and few casualties in Somalia, it was a hard knock when in late autumn 2003 terrorists destroyed a Carabineer barracks in Nasiriyah, killing nineteen Italians.

The next Italian intervention was in the summer of 2006, when the new Italian government led by Professor Romano Prodi strongly supported a peacekeeping interposition force in Lebanon, to stop the war between Israel and Hezbollah. An international force, mainly composed of 2,500 Italians and a few less French, with a large air and naval contingent, landed in Lebanon.

After reviewing the whole situation, in his five years from 2001 to spring 2006, Berlusconi had not acted poorly. It was clear that his main task was linked to the reform of the United Nations Security Council. He acted, looking for a space where Italy could exploit divisions between concerned countries. He fully advocated Russia's partnership with NATO in the summer of 2002, at the NATO summit at Pratica di Mare Air Force base, near Rome. These initiated good relations between Italy and Russia; and Berlusconi could act also as a link between the United States and Russia. This gave him leverage to modify the UN reform program, whose original plans foresaw only admitting Germany and Japan.

The Italian-proposed plan was quite different and included wide participation from Third World countries. In order to gain a greater support for their initiative, Germany, Japan, and their supporters were forced to suggest additional admissions to the Security Council. At first they looked to India and Brazil, increasing the Council from five to nine instead of the foreseen seven countries. This caused a reaction in South America and Asia, especially in Argentina and Pakistan. Then, a conference hosted by the Italians demonstrated that a majority did not like this plan. The Germans and Japanese then proposed a wider admission, permitting two African countries to join the Security Council as standing members.

According to President Clinton's original plan, the Security Council should have been composed of seven countries, and four of them—United States, Britain, Germany, and Japan—had to be strictly linked. The United States would have achieved the majority they did not have in a Security Council composed only of five members and containing Russia, China, and France. But in 2005 the situation completely changed. The Security Council was going to have no less than nine members. The intention was to prevent the U.S. plan from being implemented, if Italy could not have its own seat on the council.

The European powers had put Italians in a corner in 1613–17, and Venetian and Piedmontese—that is to say, Italians—reacted by giving decisive support at the beginning of the Thirty Years' War. They tried to do the same in 1696 and failed in the War of the Great Alliance. They did the same in 1719 when not considering Savoy's rights to Sicily and the indirect result was the emergence of the Mafia, spreading to America and Oceania, too. They did it in 1796, ignoring Piedmontese issues and resulting in Napoleon and twenty years of war. They did the same at Versailles in 1919, and Mussolini emerged and later Hitler. If history exists to teach lessons, it would be useful to see which ones Italian military history can teach.

Notes

Chapter 2

1. Desjardins, *Négociations diplomatiques de la France avec la Toscane* (Paris, 1861), II, 119.

2. Ciro Paoletti, *Gli Italiani in Armi—cinque secoli di storia militare nazionale, 1494–2000* (Rome, 2001), 38.

3. Ibid., 39.

4. Donato Tamblé, *Michelangelo e il Forte di Civitavecchia : analisi di una tradizione*, in "Studi Vetrallesi," IV, 8 (luglio-dicembre 2001).

5. Contemporary painting, oil on canvas, *Museo Storico Navale* (Naval Historical Museum), Venice.

6. Soldiers dressed in yellow and red are shown in a fresco representing a papal ceremony. It lies in San Pietro Church, in the ancient town of Tuscania, some fifty miles north of Rome. Soldiers dressed in white and red are frescoed in the cloister of the former monastery now hosting the Etruscan Museum in the same town.

7. Paoletti, *Gli Italiani in Armi,* 18–19.

8. Quoted in ibid., 74.

Chapter 3

1. Quoted in Georges Grente, "Lepanto salva l'Occidente," *Historia*, III, 16 (March 1959): 64.

Chapter 4

1. According to Count Capponi's family tradition, it was Cavalier Capponi from Florence who mortally shot Gustavus Adolphus, king of Sweden, with his pistol.

2. C. V. Wedgwood, *The Thirty Years War* (London, 1944), 247.

Chapter 5

1. Carlo Botta gives in his *History of Italy*—book twenty-seven, year 1669—a figure of 69 general assaults, 80 sorties, and 1,364 exploded mines. Kohlhaas in his *Candia: Die tragoedie einer abendländischen Verteidigung und ihr Nachspiel in Morea, 1645–1714*, gives a figure of 2,781 engagements. The best and most up-to-date figures on naval strength for both Venice and the Ottomans from the early seventeenth century to the second Morea War are in Luca Lo Basso, *Uomini da remo—galee e galeotti nel Mediterraneo in età moderna* (Milan, 2004).

2. There are few works on Italian militias. The only good recent works include Niccolò Capponi, "Le palle di Marte: Military Strategy and Diplomacy in the Grand Duchy of Tuscany under Ferdinand II de'Medici (1621–1670)," *Journal of Military History* 68, 4 (October 2004), which is the only work in English on this subject, and Claudio De Consoli's *Al soldo del duca: l'amministrazione delle armate sabaude (1560–1630)* (Turin, 1999).

Chapter 6

1. The best work in English about this and other aspects of the Maritime Powers' support for Savoy in the 1690–1713 period is Christopher Storrs, *War, Diplomacy, and the Rise of Savoy, 1690–1720* (London: Cambridge University Press, 1999).

2. Ruggero Moscati, *Direttive della politica estera sabauda da Vittorio Amedeo II a Carlo Emanuele III* (Milano, ISPI, 1941).

Chapter 7

1. Anne Stuart, sister of Mary Stuart and sister-in-law of William III, accessed the British throne after William's death in 1702. She died in 1714, leaving the throne to the House of Hanover, whose first British king was George I.

2. The Treaty of Utrecht stated that where the water flowed from the top of the Alps westward, was France; and where it went eastward was Savoy's. This part of the Treaty of Utrecht was never abolished and it is still active. After the cession of Savoy to France in 1861, the same conditions were applied to the new French-Italian border. This means that the top of Monte Bianco, the White Mountain, the highest mountain of Europe, is half French and half Italian. French maps—and others maps copied from the French ones—show the top as owned by France; and are completely wrong.

Chapter 8

1. This is clearly said in the Duke's letters to Alberoni still existing in Collegio Alberoni Archive in Piacenza. They have been extensively published in Giovan Felice Rossi's essay *La guerra iniziata in Italia nel 1717 dalla Spagna contro l'Austria fu voluta dal Duca di Parma che indusse a usare per l'impresa la flotta già allestita dall'Alberoni per la crociata contro il Turco*, in *Cento studi sul Cardinale Alberoni*, 4 vols. (Piacenza, Collegio Alberoni, 1978), 1, 242–262.

Chapter 10

1. Figures are taken by the Piedmontese official relation, whose text in Italian—*Relazione della difesa de Trinceramenti del Colle dell'Assietta fatta dalle truppe Piemontesi ed Austriache li 19 luglio 1747 (Relation of the Defense of Assietta Hill Entrenchments Made by the Piedmontese and Austrian Troops on July 19, 1747)*, lies in the Archive of the Historical Office of the Italian Army General Staff (since now AUSSME) Fondo antico (previously in Fondo L 3, lavori svolti, Stati Preunitari, Piemonte), last page. Among the French wounded was Marquis de Montcalm, who later commanded French troops in Canada in the Seven Years' War and was killed by the British at Québec in 1759.

2. In Italy, it is known as the Peace of Aquisgrana, Aix-la-Chapelle's Latin and Italian name.

Chapter 11

1. Letter of general Walsegg to Marshal Kevenhuller, on July 9, 1741, in V. Ilari, G. Boeri, C. Paoletti, *La corona di Lombardia—guerre ed eserciti nell'Italia del medio Settecento (1733–1763)* (Ancona: Nuove Ricerche, 1997), 84.

2. The Earl Philip Stanhope, Lord Chesterfield, *Letters to His Son*, London, November 18, 1748: "It is certain that in all the Courts and the Conferences where different foreign ministers are, those of the King of Sardinia are, generally, the ablest, the most courteous, the most délies."

3. All published in English in Vincenzo Giura, Gigliola Pagano de Divitiis, *L'Italia del secondo Settecento nelle relazioni segrete di William Hamilton, Horace Mann e John Murray* (Napoli: Edizioni Scientifiche Italiane, 1997).

4. Jean-Baptiste Labat, *Voyage en Espagne et en Italie* (Tivoli: Chicca, 1951), 148.

5. Du Paty, *Lettres sur l'Italie en 1785*, 2 vols. (Lausanne: Jean Mourer, 1796), I, 92.

6. Cesare Beccaria, *Dei delitti e delle pene (About Crimes and Penalties)* (Leghorn, 1764); Pietro Verri, *Osservazioni sulla tortura (Observations on Torture)* (Milan, 1768).

7. A very good overview of this period in British foreign policy is given by Jeremy Black, *Pitt the Elder* (Melksham: Cambridge University Press, 1992).

8. For the concept of this *ante litteram* cold war, see Virgilio Ilari, Piero Crociani, Ciro Paoletti, *Bell'Italia militar* (Roma: USSME, 2001), cf. C. Paoletti, *Gli Italiani in armi*. For the American posture in this struggle, idem., *America's Posture in the French-British Struggle for Supremacy: 1690–1815*, a paper in Proceedings of the XXVIII Conference of the International Commission for Military History, Norfolk, 2003.

Chapter 12

1. They were the future kings of France, Louis XVIII and Charles X.

2. After his marriage to Maria Theresa, Francis of Lorraine stayed in Vienna and left Tuscany to a governor. When his first son Joseph II became emperor, Tuscany was left to his second son: Peter Leopold. When Joseph died without heirs, Peter Leopold became Emperor Leopold II. He went to Vienna along with his oldest son Francis, later Emperor

Francis II, leaving the Tuscan throne to his second male son, who became Grand Duke Ferdinand III.

3. Lazare Carnot, in Michael Howard, *War in European History* (Oxford: Oxford University Press, 1976), 151.

4. L. Carnot, in M. Howard, vi.

5. There are only two books in Italian literature about this. The first was written by Guglielmo Ferrero. Its first edition appeared in 1936; the second in 1996 in Milan, published by "Il Corbaccio." It was entitled *Avventura (Adventure)*. The second and more detailed book is *La Guerra delle Alpi (The War of the Alps)*, by Ciro Paoletti, Virgilio Ilari, and Piero Crociani. It was published in Rome, by USSME, in 2000.

6. For specific sources supporting this argument see ibid., 261 passim; cf. See Alberto Costa de Beauregard, *Un uomo d'altri tempi* (Torino: Tipografia e libreria San Giuseppe degli artigianelli, 1897); Guglielmo Ferrero, *Avventura: Bonaparte in Italia (1796–1797)* (Milan: Corbaccio, 1996).; Ilari, Virgilio – Crociani, Piero – Paoletti, Ciro, *La Guerra delle Alpi (1792–1796)*, Roma, USSME, 2000; Ilari, Virgilio – Crociani, Piero – Paoletti, Ciro, *Storia militare dell'Italia giacobina, (1796–1802)*, Roma, USSME, 2001. Ilari, Virgilio, *La Guerra delle Alpi: le ragioni di una rimozione storica*, in Barberis, Valentina—Del Monte, Dario—Sconfienza, Roberto (a cura di), *Le truppe leggere nella Guerra delle Alpi*, Torino, Gioventura Piemonteisa, 2006. Las Cases, Emanuel de, *Memoriale di Sant'Elena*, Roma, Casini, 1969. Paoletti, Ciro, *Gli Italiani in armi – cinque secoli di storia militare nazionale 1494–2000*, Roma, USSME, 2001. Segre, Arturo, *Vittorio Emanuele I*, Torino, Paravia, 1935.

7. All these documents were quoted for the first time by Ferrero. They were in Public Record Office, F.O. 67, 20, and 21.

8. Guglielmo Ferrero, *Avventura*, Milan, Il Corbaccio, 1996, page 24.

9. Quoted in Las Cases, *Memoriale di Sant'Elena*, Firenze, Casini, 1987, page 79.

10. Napoleon to the Directory, on October 11th 1796, rip. in Oreste Bovio, *Due secoli di tricolore*, Roma, USSME, 1996, page 19.

11. The Neapolitan fleet was a very good second-rank one. Unfortunately, to save money, it was only half crewed. The remaining crews were called only in case of need. In 1798–99 the French advance was so fast that the fleet lacked the time to gather the crews. Nelson promptly ordered the ships uncrewed to be burned instead of being towed to Palermo. Britain preferred Naples, linked to Spain by the Bourbon family pact, to have no fleet at all.

Chapter 13

1. In Spain, Wellington had in his Peninsular Army at least three veterans of Maida, that is to say: Lt. Gen. Sir Lowry Cole, Maj. Gen. Sir James Kempt, and Lt. Col. John Colborne; so also if he had not previously noticed, he surely was perfectly aware of Maida on the eve of the campaign.

2. E.g., when he wrote to Eugene of Beauharnais on August 23, 1810: "If I would lose a great battle, one, two million soldiers will rush under the flags of my old France, whilst my Kingdom of Italy would stand me up."

3. In 1812, just before the Russian campaign, the Italian army had 88,935 men, 14,951 horses, and 150 guns divided into 48,560 infantrymen and 815 horse for 11 infantry regi-

ments and two Dalmatian battalions, 5,275 artillerymen with 2,850 horses, 6,576 cavalrymen using 5,976 horses, divided in six regiments. The Royal Guard had 6,192 men and 1,670 horses. The Engineer Corps had 1,400 men and 265 horses. Gendarmerie, of three regiments, had 1,908 men and 1,030 horses. The Royal Navy had some as 9,000 men. The remaining belonged to logistical, administrative, and medical corps, to the military schools, local and general staffs, and so on.

4. Studies are still going on, anyway good figures can be found in Cappello, Girolamo, *Gli Italiani in Russia nel 1812*, Città di Castello, Comando del Corpo di Stato Maggiore del Regio Esercito—Ufficio Storico, Memorie Storiche Militari, Vol. VII, Fascicolo IV del 1912, 1912. Assereto, Giovanni, *Coscrizione e politica militare nella Liguria napoleonica*, in *All'ombra dell'aquila imperiale*, Atti del convegno di Torino del 15–18 ottobre 1990, Roma, Ministero per i beni culturali e ambientali, Ufficio centrale per i beni archivistici, saggi, 28, 2 voll., 1994. Carillo, Maria Margherita, *La coscrizione nel Mezzogiorno d'Italia nel decennio francese*, in *Studi storico-militari 2002*, Roma, Stato Maggiore dell'Esercito – Ufficio Storico, 2004. Crociani, Piero – Ilari, Virgilio—Paoletti, Ciro, *Storia militare del Regno Italico (1802–1814)*, Vol 1 tomi I e II, Vol 2, Roma, USSME, 2004. Della Peruta, Franco, *L'armata del napoleonico Regno d'Italia* in *All'ombra dell'aquila imperiale*, Atti del convegno di Torino del 15–18 ottobre 1990, Roma, Ministero per i beni culturali e ambientali, Ufficio centrale per i beni archivistici, saggi, 28, 2 voll., 1994. Ferrari, G. – Giacchi, N., *Gli Italiani in Germania nel 1813*, Città di Castello, C.do del Corpo di Stato Maggiore del Regio Esercito—Ufficio Storico, 1914.

5. Discussion with Professor Greg Urwin, Temple University, May 2003.

6. General Buturlin, quoted in Ambrogio Bollati, *Gli Italiani nelle armate napoleoniche* (Bologna, 1938), 111.

7. Captain Baggi, quoted in Girolamo Cappello, *Gli Italiani in Russia nel 1812* (Città di Castello, SMRE—Ufficio Storico, Memorie Storiche Militari, Vol. VII, Fascicolo IV of 1912, 1912), 209.

8. Eugéne de Beauharnais to his wife, quoted in Cappello, *Gli Italiani in Russia nel 1812*, 316.

9. Italian Engineers Corp captain Belcredi to his relatives, quoted in Ibid., 318.

Chapter 14

1. Massimo D'Azeglio, *I miei ricordi (My remembrances)* (Varese: Feltrinelli, 1963), 110.
2. Ibid., 116.
3. For these aspects of French policy in Italy since 1796 see Giuseppe Brizzolara, *La Francia dalla Restaurazione alla fondazione della Terza Repubblica, 1814–1870* (Milano, Hoepli, 1903). Ciro Paoletti, *Gli Italiani in armi – cinque secoli di storia militare nazionale 1494–2000* (Roma, USSME, 2001). Ilari, Virgilio – Crociani, Piero – Paoletti, Ciro, *Storia militare dell'Italia giacobina, (1796–1802)*, (Roma, USSME, 2001). Crociani, Piero – Ilari, Virgilio—Paoletti, Ciro, *Storia militare del Regno Italico (1802–1814)*, Vol. 1 tomi I e II, Vol 2, (Roma, USSME, 2004). Radogna, Lamberto, *Storia della Marina Militare delle Due Sicilie 1734–1860* (Milano, Mursia, 1978). Randaccio, C., *Storia delle Marine militari italiane dal 1750 al 1860* (Roma, Forzani & Co., 1886). Pier Paolo Ramoino, *La Marina Italica*, a paper presented to the conference *La Legione Italica e la situazione italiana fra il 1800 e il 1806* (Brescia, Palazzo Bonoris, 6 ottobre 2006). Paoletti, Ciro, *La situación estratégica en el*

mar Adriático y la Marina italiana de 1798 a 1814, in *Poder terrestre y poder naval en la época de la batalla de Trafalgar*, Acts of the International Conference of Military History, Madrid, CEHM, 2005.

4. On April 1, 1843, Garibaldi organized an Italian Legion, about 500 men, in Montevideo to fight for Uruguay against Argentina. The Legionnaires were dressed with the later world-famous red shirts. They were prepared for the butchers of Montevideo (beasts' blood spots were supposedly less remarkable on red than on any other color). They could be a cheap and good uniform.

Chapter 15

1. Just that year Giuseppe Gabetti, bandleader of the 1st Infantry Regiment Savoia, composed the "Marcia Reale"—the "Royal March." In a short time it became the national anthem instead of the Sardinian anthem. It was officially accepted as the Italian national anthem until the end of the kingdom of Italy in 1946. The only place were it is still officially played in public is New York City. In fact, this is the traditional piece played in Little Italy during the Saint Gennaro Feast and during Columbus Day ceremonies.

2. Massimo D'Azeglio, cit. 539.

3. Ibid.

4. Ibid., 540.

5. Charles Albert, quoted in Ciro Paoletti, *Gli Italiani in Armi*, 402.

6. The Italian word the king used was *galantuomo*. It may be translated as gentleman as well as honest man. But in Italian the word *gentiluomo*—the perfect translation of the English word "gentleman"—has an aristocratic implicit meaning, which *galantuomo* does not. In this case, Victor Emmanuel, whose house had ruled Savoy since the year 998 and was the oldest ruling house of Europe, explicitly defined himself as a bourgeois would do.

7. Carlo Cattaneo to F. Arrivabene, in Paolo Pinto, *Carlo Alberto* (Milano: Rizzoli, 1990), 294.

8. The monument still lies in the monumental cemetery of Brescia. The inscription says: "Beyond the urn, no enemy anger survives."

9. Garibaldi, *Memorie* (Torino: Einaudi, 1972), 222.

10. Ibid., 223.

11. Ibid., 234.

12. Ibid., 227.

13. The United States Supreme Court recognized him as the father of the telephone in 1886, but he did not have a patent after 1873; by a legal point of view it was Alexander Graham Bell, who registered it in 1876 and was the owner of all the related rights.

Chapter 16

1. Lord Clarendon to Sir James Hudson, British ambassador in Turin, London, November 29, 1854, quoted in Pier Giusto Jaeger, *Le mura di Sebastopoli* (Milano, Mondadori, 1991), 125.

2. Cavour, quoted in G. Visconti Venosta, *Ricordi di gioventù* (*Memoirs of Youth*) (Milan, Rizzoli, 1959), 283.

3. Cavour, quoted in Ibid., 285.

4. Quoted in Franz Herre, *Kaiser Franz Joseph von Österreich* (Köln, Verlag Kiepenheuer & Witsch, 1978), 151.

5. Ibid.

6. They composed five ordinary divisions, a cavalry division and the Cacciatori delle Alpi—Chasseurs of the Alps—Brigade commanded by Garibaldi.

7. Cavour to Engineer Carlo Noè, quoted in Amedeo Ademollo, *L'allagamento del Vercellese nell'aprile 1859*, in *Studi storico-militari 2002* (Roma, USSME, 2004), 350.

8. Victor Emmanuel fought so bravely that the French Zouaves acclaimed him a corporal in their 1st Regiment. Then, every evening until his death, when calling "Caporal Savoye Victor Emmanuel" for the roll-call, another corporal answered "absent, because he is king in Italy."

9. According to the Piedmontese and later Italian ranks, a Brigadier was a colonel temporarily commanding a Brigade; but a Brigade was normally commanded by a Major General (one star), while a Division was commanded by a Lieutenant General. Army Corps and Armies were commanded by Lieutenant Generals "designated of Army Corp" and "designated of Army." After World War I, Great Units were respectively commanded by Brigade Generals, Division Generals, Army Corp Generals (three stars), and Army Generals, while the ranks of Major General and Lieutenant Generals were used only for Generals of non-combattant Corps, which were not composed of Regiments, like Medical Corp, Supply Corp, Administration, and so on.

10. See Jean Bérenger, *Storia dell'impero asburgico 1700–1918* (Bologna, Il Mulino, 2003). Brizzolara, Giuseppe, *La Francia dalla Restaurazione alla fondazione della Terza Repubblica, 1814–1870* (Milano, Hoepli, 1903). Herre, Franz, *Francesco Giuseppe* (Milano, Rizzoli, 1980). Herre, Franz, *Prussia* (Milano, Rizzoli, 1985). Mola, Aldo Alessandro, *Storia della monarchia in Italia* (Milano, Bompiani, 2002). Paoletti, Ciro, *Gli Italiani in armi – cinque secoli di storia militare nazionale 1494–2000* (Roma, USSME, 2001). von Naso, Eckahrt, *Moltke Mensch und Feldherr* (Berlin, Krueger Verlag, 1943). Pieri, Piero, *Storia militare del Risorgimento*, 2 vol. (Milano, Il Giornale, 2003), 2nd volume. Pinto, Paolo, *Vittorio Emanuele II* (Milano, Mondadori, 1997). Flaviani, Francesco, *Due imperatori a colloquio*, su "Historia," n. 14, genn.1959.

Chapter 17

1. Report in AUSSME, Fondo Brigantaggio, still reorganizing when this book was written.

Chapter 18

1. Obviously it was the so-called little coat of arms, the white cross in a red field bordered in blue (the border was used just to remember the traditional color of Savoy, in spite of the pure heraldic tradition, which does not use it for reigning houses. By the way, the

great coat of arms of the House of Savoy is so complicated that it would have been really very hard to put it on a flag.

2. As a Catholic, in his last moments Cavour was assisted by a priest, who absolved him and later had a lot of trouble with Church hierarchy.

3. Two of them had been built by Webb in New York.

4. Quoted in Ciro Paoletti, *Gli Italiani in armi* cit, 438. The exact text was: "I have received dispatch number 1073. I obey."

5. Garibaldi, *Memoirs*, 400.

6. The 1861 Italian Lira was officially equal to 4.5 grams of silver (0.158 oz) or to 0.2903225 grams of gold (0.010 oz).

7. They appeared after the December 13, 1871, Royal Decree, which ordered the army and the fleet to wear, as a characteristic symbol of military, little five pointed white metal stars on the collars of uniforms. Still in use, they are worn by all and only the military personnel on land, air, and sea. So, if one wants to understand if the Italian uniform in front of him is a military one or not, he needs only to look for the little stars on the collar.

8. The issue was discussed in the late seventies, by Lucio Ceva, *Le Forze Armate*, Torino, Utet, 1981 and Piero Del Negro, *Esercito, Stato e società*, Bologna, Cappelli, 1979. Whilst marshall Emilio De Bono, in his book *Nell'esercito nostro prima della guerra*, Milano, Mondadori, 1931, told that no real result had been obtained by the army, Ceva and Del Negro agreed that it could be reliable the officially admitted figure of a 15–20% reduction of illiteracy. The most recent and probably the best work was the paper presented by the late Alberto Arpino during an Italian-Spanish symposium in 1994. Arpino had compared figures about illitterate people resulting from the 1861, 1871, 1881, 1891, and 1901 census. He took in exam how many people could have passed through the new school system before going in the army, how many of them did not, how many of them went in the army after the introduction of the regimental primary school. Then he compared related ages and the illitteracy average per age. His data basically confirmed the abovesaid 20% figure and increased it to 22 or 25%. Unfortunately, he died two years later, his work was never published and was lost.

Chapter 19

1. Simone Pacoret Di Saint-Bon, *Discorso pronunziato alla Camera dei Deputati nella tornata del 6 dicembre 1873—(speech pronounced in front of the Chamber of Deputies in the December 6 1873 sitting)*—reported in *Rivista Marittima*, VII, 1 (January 1874): 34–35.

2. The Royal Navy gave vessel ranks only to the staff officers. All the officers belonging to Engineer, Medical and Administrative Corps had the same ranks as in the army. They could easily be distinguished by chevrons. In fact vessel officers had chevrons as in the British navy, other corps had like in the US Navy. De Saint Bon and Brin had the same rank, but being first a staff officer who commanded large naval units, he was an admiral, whilst the other came from the Naval Engineers Corps and he was a general. Vessel ranks were unified for the Navy Corps only after World War II.

3. As demonstrated by Bruce Vandervort, *War of Imperial Conquest in Africa, 1830–1914* (London: University College London Press, 1998)

4. Ibid. It is probably the best essay I have read about this topic and probably the only real objective analysis on Italian colonial wars.

5. See, Franco Bandini, *Gli Italiani in Africa* (Milan: Longanesi, 1971); Baratieri,

Oreste, *Memorie d'Africa* (Trento: F.lli Melita Editori, 1988); Bourelly, G., *La battaglia di Abba Garima* (Milan: Cogliati, 1901); Ceva, Lucio, *Le Forze Armate* (Torino: Utet), 1981; Paoletti, Ciro, *Gli Italiani in armi – cinque secoli di storia militare nazionale 1494–2000* (Roma: USSME, 2001); Rochat, Giorgio, *Adua, analisi di una sconfitta*, in *Ufficiali e soldati: l'Esercito Italiano dalla Prima alla Seconda Guerra Mondiale* (Udine, Gaspari, 20000; Di Ferdinando, Roberto, *La sconfitta di Adua*, on "Rivista Italiana Difesa," year XXII, n. 6, giugno 2004; Governale, Giulio, *Adua: i perché di una sconfitta*, on "Rassegna dell'Arma dei Carabinieri," anno LIII, n. 2, aprile – giugno 2005; Montanari, Mario, *Adua 1896*, on "Storia Militare," n. 32, mag. 1996; Rovighi, Alberto, *La battaglia di Adua*, on "Rivista Militare," n. 4, 1996; Zamorani, Massimo, *La Battaglia di Adua*, on "Rivista Italiana Difesa," anno, XV, n. 4, aprile 1997.

6. See the comments by sir Michael Howard about Adowa and Ishandlwana in his *War in European History* (Oxford, 1976), chapter VII, note 2 and the opinion of Bruce Vandervort, in cit. p. 29, 40, 153–164.

7. The International Expeditionary Force was composed of more than 61,000 men. Japan sent two divisions, Britain an Anglo-Indian division, France two brigades, Germany three. Russia sent 4,000 men, United States 6,000, Italy, as said some 2,000. Austria-Hungary sent only five small ships.

Chapter 20

1. Still suffering after the crash that occurred in Fort Myers on September 18, 1908.

2. Aldo Alessandro Mola, *Giolitti: lo statista della nuova Italia* (Cles, Mondadori, 2003); Aldo Alessandro Mola, *Storia della monarchia in Italia* (Milano, Bompiani, 2002).

3. As clearly explained by Francis Joseph's aide de camp Alberto di Margutti, in his, *L'Imperatore Francesco Giuseppe* (Milano, Agnelli, 1931).

4. The Italian navy was divided into naval divisions, commanded by a vice-admiral, corresponding to a division general in the army. Two or more naval divisions composed literally a "squad," that is to say a squadron, commanded by an "admiral."

5. Alderotti, Enrico – Lombardo, Alessandro, *Ansaldo* (Roma: Rivista Marittima, 2005). Ceva, Lucio, *Le Forze Armate* (Torino: Utet, 1981). Fatutta, Francesco, *Cento anni per l'Oto Melara*, on "Rivista Marittima," CXXXIX, gennaio 2006. *I "camions" della F.I.A.T. in Tripolitania*, on "L'Illustrazione Italiana" XXXIX, n. 4, 28 gennaio 1912, 74. Pignato, Nicola – Cappellano, Filippo, *Gli autoveicoli da combattimento dell'Esercito Italiano*, 2 vols. (Roma, USSME, 2002).

6. As it is well known, Macaroni is an ironic nickname normally used in Europe and in the Anglo-Saxon world for the Italians. What is less known is that it is very ancient. One of the oldest uses of this term in English is in a sixteenth-century version of "Yankee Doodle." *At that time* – I quote from *The World Book Encyclopedia*, 1975 edition, volume 21, 458, voice "Yankee Doodle," by Raymond Kendall – *"the word macaroni was used to mean the young men of London who dressed in odd Italian styles."* Of course, being "macaroni" equal to Italy, it was soon used by Europeans and Americans to mean the Italian soldiers, too. But this is improper. In fact, Italy has its own version of the standard private's nickname. An American private is "Johnny" especially when coming back home marching again. A British one is "Tommy," or "Tommy Atkins," a German is a "Fritz" after Frederick the Great's—der alte Fritz (the old Freddy)—family nickname and an Italian private is "Ciccillo Cacace" (pronounce "Chychylloh Kakacheh." Ciccillo is a southern Italy diminutive for

Ciccio, which on his side is a diminutive for Francis and may also mean "fatty." So, the closest translation in English would be "Little Fatty Frankie Cacace"). In fact, every time an officer (generals included), a noncommissioned officer, or a corporal must give his men an example of right or wrong, he speaks about what "Private Ciccillo Cacace" must do or not do in that case.

7. Margutti, quoted, 137.

Chapter 21

1. Prince Montenuovo, quoted by Baron Alberto di Margutti in, *L'imperatore Francesco Giuseppe*, (Milan: Agnelli,1931), 221.

2. A family memory: in August 1914, my great-great-grandfather was an 83-year-old retired infantry general. Enrolled as a private in 1848, he fought against the Austrians in 1859 and 1866. The day he found in his newspaper news of the war, he curtly commented: "*Germany wins.*" He died in 1921, after having seen his false prediction and his youth's dream realized with the definitive destruction of Austria.

3. Rudyard Kipling, *The New Italy*. This article, as the others here quoted, appeared in *Daily Telegraph* and *New York Tribune* in 1917. Quotations here refer to the last Italian edition in English, *The War in the Mountains—Impressions from Italian Front* (Rome: Rivista Militare Europea, 1990), 53.

4. Cadorna, cited in Gianni Rocca, *Cadorna* (Milano: Mondadori, 1985), 47.

5. The gray-green uniform had been tested in 1905 and adopted in 1908.

6. See for the opinions of contemporaries, written while combatants or written later, when they were veterans: Alessi, Rino, *Dall'Isonzo al Piave* (Milano, Longanesi, 1966); Caccia Dominioni, Paolo *1915–1919* (Treviso, Longanesi, 1979); Comisso, Giovanni, *Giorni di guerra* (Milano, Mondadori, 1930); de Rossi, Enrico, *La vita di un ufficiale italiano fino alla guerra* (Milano, Mondadori, 1927); Frescura, Attilio, *Diario di un imboscato – dall'intervento all'armistizio* (Bologna, Cappelli, 1934); Milanesi, Guido, *Fiamme dell'ara* (Milano,Ceschina, 1942); Monelli, Paolo, *Le scarpe al sole* (Milano, Mondadori, 1971); Prezzolini, Giuseppe (edited by) *Tutta la guerra* (Milano, Longanesi, 1968); Salsa, Carlo, *Trincee* (Milano, Sonzogno, 1934); Sangiorgi, Giorgio Maria, *75 m/m* (Milano, Agnelli, 1931); Sillani, Tomaso (edited by), *Lettere di Enrico Toti* (Firenze, Bemporad & figlio editori, 1924). See also contemporary weekly magazines such as *Il diario della nostra guerra – bollettini ufficiali dell'Esercito e della Marina* (Milano, different publishers, 1915–1918); *L'Illustrazione Italiana* (Milano, F.lli Treves Editori, 1915–1918); *La Domenica del Corriere* (Milano, Corriere della Sera, 1915–1918). Works written by others than veterans include: Bandini, Franco, *Il Piave mormorava*, (Milano, Longanesi, 1968); Gabriele, Mariano—Friz, Giuliano, *La politica navale italiana dal 1885 al 1915* (Roma, USSMM, 1982); Cedroni, Lorella, *La funzione dell' opinione pubblica italiana dal primo dopoguerra all'avvento del Fascismo*, in, Alberini, Paolo—Rainero, Romain H. (editors) *Le Forze Armate e la Nazione italiana (1915–1943)*, Proceedings of the conference held in Rome 22–24 October 2003 (Roma, CISM, 2004); Cuomo, Vincenzo, *Il volontariato militare italiano nella storia d'Italia*, in *Studi storico-militari 2001*, Roma, Stato Maggiore dell'Esercito – Ufficio Storico, 2004; Del Negro, Piero, *La Grande Guerra, elemento unificatore del popolo italiano ?*, in Alberini, Paolo—Rainero, Romain H., *Le Forze Armate e la Nazione italiana (1915–1943)*, Proceedings of the conference held in Rome 22–24 October 2003 (Roma, CISM, 2004); Del Negro, Piero, *La prima Guerra Mondiale e l'identità nazionale*, in "Studi storico-militari 2000," Roma, USSME, 2002;

PAPA, Catia, *Volontari della Terza Italia: i battaglioni studenteschi d'età giolittiana*, su "Rassegna Storica del Risorgimento," anno XCI, fascicolo IV, ottobre-dicembre 2004; Ansaldo, Giovanni, *Quel 24 maggio*, su "Storia Illustrata," anno II, n. 5, maggio 1958; Murialdi, Paolo, *La grande stampa è tutta interventista*, su "Storia Illustrata," anno XXVII, n. 330, maggio 1985; Tranfaglia, Nicola, *Piazza e Corona condizionano il Parlamento*, su "Storia Illustrata," anno XXVII, n. 330, maggio 1985.

7. Kipling, *A Pass, a King and a Mountain*, in *The War in the Mountains*, cited p. 33.

8. Kipling, *Only a Few Steps Higher Up*, in *The War . . .* cited, 45–46.

9. Enrico Cernigoi, *Le ultime battaglie del Carso e la conquista dell'altopiano di Comeno*, su "Studi Storico-Militari 2005," Roma, USSME, 2007, 329.

10. Kipling, *Only a few . . .* cited, 46.

11. A part Italian Official Relation on WW I – *L'Esercito Italiano nella Grande Guerra (1915–1918)*, see specifically, Jannattoni, Livio, *Il treno in Italia* (Roma: Editalia, 1980) and Monti, Enrico, *Il problema ferroviario militare in relazione alle operazioni di guerra*, su "Rivista Militare italiana," anno II, n. 8, agosto 1928, VI E.F.

12. Italian industrial system produced 11,537 planes and some 30,000 engines. By the way, figures show the Italian industrial system's weakness compared to France which in 1914–1918 produced 41,500 planes, while Germany made 48,000 and Britain a little less than 55,000.

13. Figures too show it. In fact, from May 24th 1915 until November 4th 1918, the Italian Air Force destroyed 643 Austrian aircraft and balloons, while Austrians destroyed only 128 Italian aircraft.

14. For all the figures, see the related tome in the Italian Official Relation on World War I (divided in 37 volumes) – *L'Esercito Italiano nella Grande Guerra (1915–1918)*, VII Volume

15. According to the operational doctrine, one wins a battle when he reaches the objective he has previously defined in his plans as "his objective." There are strategic victories—those allowing a side to win the war, and tactical victories, allowing a side to gain a great success but not necessarily a strategically significant one. This was the case; we know the Austro-German objectives: they were reached only for their original part of the plan but the Austro-Germans failed to destroy the Italian army. So, they gained a great victory, but the real strategic success was lacking. In fact, the Italian army remained active and able to defend the country; as it clearly demonstrated on the Piave, within one month. The problem for the Austro-Germans was that they reached what is defined as the " Zone of strategic exhaustion," that is to say: each army may advance as far as it can; but, at a certain distance, it can not receive supplies and reinforcements as it needs to feed the attack; when this happens the Army must go slowly or must stop. This is precisely what happened to the Austrians and to the Germans: they simply could advance anymore. The interruption of the roads and railways in Friuli where the war had been fought in the previous two years forbade any fast movement of needed supplies in the needed quantity.

16. Allied troops sent to Italy were only a French division and two British divisions. This did not prevent some author—e.g., British general Fraser in his Rommel biography—of speaking of the following Vittorio Veneto battle as of a "victory of British-Italian Army."

17. This verse by D'Annunzio is from the dedication of the *Leda senza Cigno* to the Grenadiers Brigade. The original Italian text, referring to the long wars against Austria and to the then 250 years old brigade, says: *Di noi/ tremò/ la nostra vecchia gloria/ tre secoli di fede/ e una/ vi-ttoria – Of us/ trembled/ our old glory/ three centuries of faith/ and a/ vic-tory.*

18. *Il Corpo Automobilistico dell'Esercito* (Roma, Rivista Militare, 1980), p. 10–12.

19. Emilio Faldella, *La grande guerra*, 2 vol. (Milano, Longanesi, 1978), II, 346.

20. They included Lieutenant Fiorello La Guardia, who later was a very popular mayor of New York City.

21. War Bulletin number 1268, issued on November 4th 1918, at noon.

22. A part Italian Official Relation on WW I – *L'Esercito Italiano nella Grande Guerra (1915–1918)*, 37 tomes (Rome, USSME, ended in 1985), Volume V: *Operazioni del 1918*, tome 2 bis, *Luglio-Novembre* – a detailed account is given by Francesco, Fatutta, *La ventilata operazione contro la Baviera del dicembre 1918* (*The foreseen operation against Bavaria of December 1918*) on "Rivista Italiana Difesa," Year XX, no. 3, March 2002, 92–97.

23. Quoted in Colonel Mario Caracciolo, *Sintesi storico-politica della guerra mondiale 1914–1918* (Torino, Schioppo, 1930), 187.

24. Quoted in General Emilio Faldella, *La grande guerra*, 2 vols. (Milano, Longanesi, 1978), II, 376.

Chapter 22

1. Cernigoi, Enrico, *Dalla guerra di Libia alla missione militare in Anatolia*, su "Rivista Italiana Difesa," XXI, n. 9 (September. 2003). Magnani, Enrico, *Il mantenimento della pace dal XIX al XXI secolo* (Roma, Rivista Marittima, 1998). Oşca, Alexander, *La politique de la France et de l'Italie au sud-est de l'Europe pendant les premières années après la Première Guerre Mondiale*, su "Revue internationale d'histoire militaire," n. 83 (Paris, Comission Française d'Historie Militaire, 2003). Paoletti, Ciro, *La Marina italiana in Estremo Oriente 1866–2000* (Roma, USSMM, 2000). Salimbeni, Fulvio, *Il confine orientale*, in Mola, Aldo Alessandro (a cura di), *Il marchesato di Saluzzo – da Stato di confine a confine di Stato a Europa*, atti del convegno per il IV centenario della pace di Lione, Saluzzo, 30 novembre -1° dicembre 2001 (Foggia, Bastogi, 2003).

2. For a general overview Duroselle, Jean Baptiste, *Storia diplomatica dal 1919 al 1970*, (Roma, Edizione dell'Ateneo, 1972). On the specific aspects concerning Austria the most recent work is Fiorentino, Waldimaro, *Il confine con l'Austria*, in Mola, Aldo Alessandro (a cura di), *Il marchesato di Saluzzo – da Stato di confine a confine di Stato a Europa*, atti del convegno per il IV centenario della pace di Lione, Saluzzo, 30 novembre -1° dicembre 2001 (Foggia, Bastogi, 2003). Salimbeni, Fulvio, *Il confine orientale*, in Mola, Aldo Alessandro (a cura di), *Il marchesato di Saluzzo – da Stato di confine a confine di Stato a Europa*, atti del convegno per il IV centenario della pace di Lione, Saluzzo, 30 novembre -1° dicembre 2001, (Foggia, Bastogi, 2003).

3. Local authorities had to decide on their own initiative. An additional family memoir: my great-grandfather was at that time the lieutenant colonel commanding the Royal Carabineers Group in Mantua. He reacted on his own initiative against the riots ordering 20 Carabineers he had in the city to fire. According to the law, the first volley had to be shot in the air; the second against the people. After the first volley, when watching the Carabineers' carabines lowering for the second, the people fled: There were no dead.

4. Probably the best book ever written about this period is Longanesi, Leo, *In piedi e seduti* (Milano, Longanesi, 1968).

5. Interview of Professor Aldo Ademollo, on March 12, 1985. Professor Ademollo was a founding member of the *Fascio* of Mantua in 1919. He later belonged to that of Florence and marched on Rome in October 1922.

6. Another problem with English translations. In English the word "comrade" is used to define both Fascist and Socialist/Communist party members. In Italian there is a difference, Camerata—literally comrade—was used by Fascists to define their comrades, while Compagno—literally companion—was, and still is, used by Socialists and Communists to define their own.

7. At this point in the narrative, the Italian Armed Forces will be mentioned using their Italian name, just to prevent the reader from mistaking them for the British ones.

8. The Quadrumviri—from Latin, literally meaning "four men"—were Emilio De Bono, a general of the Bersaglieri, later Marshal of Italy; Michele Bianchi, the Fascist party administrator; Italo Balbo, a former Alpini Officer during the war and later Air Marshal; Count Cesare Maria de Vecchi di Val Cismon. They ranked just under Mussolini. By the way, just to give an idea of what Italians now think of Fascism, all their sons, grandsons and nephews live quietly in Italy. Countess de Vecchi lives in Rome, De Bono's nephews in Cassano d'Adda near Milan; advocate Balbo works in Rome. Bianchi had no relatives. A granddaughter of Mussolini—the daughter of Mussolini's youngest son Romano and of a sister of the world known actress Sophia Loren—seats in the Italian Parliament as a deputy, thus it is still possible to see "vote for Mussolini" scrawled on Italian walls before an election.

9. The most important was the *Directives for the Coordinated Employment of the Army Air Units.* "Directives" were divided into three main parts. The first contained general issues and orders for actions above the ground. The second was about fighting above the sea; the third concerned antiaircraft defense, reconnaissance, emergency airfields, emergency places and so on. The only known copies are those owned by De Pinedo himself, at that time Deputy Chief of Staff of the *Regia Aeronautica.* I found it in a very strange way. It now lies in Rome, AUSSME, *fondi acquisiti, non catalogato.* The other is the "*Ipotesi Ovest, Ipotesi Est, Ipotesi doppia, considerazioni generali.*" An incomplete copy of it is in AUSSME, *fondi acquisiti, non catalogato*; a complete copy has been found by Professor John Gooch in AUSSME too; a third copy is in AUSSMM (Archivio Ufficio Storico Stato Maggiore Marina Militare—Archive of the Navy Historical Office), *Documentazione di base, busta* 1725, but it is the new and modified version written in 1933. The only study existing about the Directives is Ciro Paoletti, *The first air war doctrine of the Italian Royal Air Force, 1929*, a paper presented to the 67° annual conference of the American Society for Military History—Quantico (Virginia), the U.S. Marines Corp University, April 28th 2000.

10. See, Mecozzi, Amedeo: *Scritti scelti sul potere aereo e l'aviazione d'assalto (1920–1970)* (edited by Ferruccio Botti), 2 vols. (Roma, Stato Maggiore dell'Aeronautica—Ufficio Storico, 2007).

11. 709.202 kilometers per hour.

12. As clearly said in Francesco De Pinedo, *Promemoria per il Sig. Generale Giuseppe Valle, oggetto: passaggio di consegne della carica di Sottocapo di Stato Maggiore della R. Aeronautica* riservatissimo personale—(Memorandum for General Giuseppe Valle handing over the office of Assistant Chief of Staff of the R. Air Force; top secret and personal)" annexe number 4, "Ammonitions." Rome, typewritten, undated, but August 24, 1929, AUSSME, *fondi acquisiti, non catalogato.* The only published source is Ciro Paoletti, *Le risorse materiali della Regia Aeronautica nel 1929*, in "Rivista Italiana Difesa," XXIII, issue n. 4 (April 2005).

13. Italian Camel Corps was considered very effective, It was officially called Meharists, after the Mehara camel it used.

14. According to General Baron Amedeo Guillet, who knew the story directly from the captain commanding the Spahis squadron, when Italian Spahis—Libyan colonial light cavalry—took Omar-el-Muktar, who was considered the chief of the Libyan rebellion, and

presented him to Graziani, Graziani asked him: "*So, you would be Omar-el-Muktar?*" "*I AM Omar-el-Muktar.*" "*Yes YOU ARE Omar el Muktar and tomorrow YOU WILL BE dead.*" The day after Muktar was hanged.

15. Duroselle, Jean Baptiste, *Storia diplomatica dal 1919 al 1970*, Luciolli, Mario, *Palazzo Chigi: anni roventi – ricordi di vita diplomatica italiana dal 1933 al 1948*, (Milano, Rusconi, 1976). Pelagalli, Sergio, *Il generale Efisio Marras addetto militare a Berlino (1936–1943)*, Roma, USSME, 1994. Perna, Valerio, *Galeazzo Ciano: operazione Polonia* (Milano, Luni, 1999). Rainero, Romain H., *Il nuovo ordine mondiale: ambizioni e realtà dell'Italia fascista*, in, Alberini, Paolo—Rainero, Romain H., *Le Forze Armate e la Nazione italiana (1915– 1943)*, Atti del convegno tenuto a Roma dal 22 al 24 ottobre 2003 (Roma, CISM, 2004).

16. His Excellence the Minister of War general Gazzera to the Chief of the Governement, "Predisposizione per l'eventuale costituzione di grandi unità O.M.," on June 4, 1930, in Rome, State Central Archive, Presidenza Consiglio dei Ministri, 1928–30, Fasc. 1, sotto-fasc 2–2, prot. 8717. I found it by chance—as normally happen to historians—looking in a folder when preparing my book about the Italian Navy in China. If I wanted it, I probably would still be looking.

17. The complete and detailed account of air operations over Ethiopia, including which poison gas was used, when and in which quantity is in Ferdinando Pedriali, *L'Aeronautica italiana nelle guerre coloniali – Africa Orientale Italiana 1936–40: dalla proclamazione dell'impero alla Seconda Guerra Mondiale*, (*Air Force in Colonial wars—Italian Eastern Africa 1936– 1940 since the Empire proclamation to World War Two*) (Rome, Air Force General Staff Historical Service, 2000).

18. Another family memoir: uncle Guido—the brother of my great-grandfather on my mother's side—was lieutenant colonel Guido Lami. He commanded the Engineers Corps battalion of the Sabauda Infantry Division, composing the Badoglio column. When in front of Termaber, Badoglio called him: "*how long do you need to repair it?*" "*Twenty-four hours.*" "*Are you sure?*" "*Yes*" "*All right; I'll remember it.*" Then uncle Guido and his men worked hard the whole day and the whole night with no problems, a part—as he said later to my grandmother—all the Staff officers and generals coming to see the work and shake their heads. The next morning the Pass was repaired. So, uncle Guido took the heaviest truck he had and drove it, leading the column, to test the route until Addis Ababa. He was promoted colonel because of war merit and this did not render him more popular among his oldest colleagues.

19. Foreign Office Egyptian Department Memorandum to Lord Halifax, on February 9, 1939, cited in Alvin Mockler, *The return of Haile Selasse*, 270.

Chapter 23

1. See also, Carlo de Risio, *E Mussolini non incontrò Roseevelt*, (*And Mussolini did not meet Roosevelt*) in de Risio, Carlo, *Gli Italiani in guerra*, Rome, "Il Tempo," XLV (November 1989): 5. By the way, this was confirmed by what Mussolini's second son Vittorio personally revealed in a TV interview a bit later. When he visited the United States in 1937, Vittorio had to see Hollywood because he was the manager of Cinecittà, the Cinema studios in Rome, He established a production company together with Hal Roach. Then, he was received by F. D. Roosevelt. The president asked him to ask Mussolini for a visit or a meeting, just to see if the United States could balance Italian pretension toward Germany. When back in Rome, Vittorio referred to his father Roosevelt's proposal, but Mussolini did not

care for it. In February 1940, Sumner Welles came to Rome. On February 26 he met Mussolini and gave him a letter from Roosevelt for a sort of agreement. Unfortunately Mussolini was angry with France and Britain for the undeclared blockade of Italian Merchant ships—847 ships stopped and their goods confiscated since August 1939, for a damage of more than a billion liras of that time. Moreover, Hitler ensured Germany would have provided Italy the needed coal and crude oil. Three months later, the German offensive against France began and there was no more time to talk.

2. *Regia Aeronautica*'s previous experience included similar operations. In 1923 it evacuated civilians from Azizia, in Libya; and in 1936 infantry units had been air transported to Addis Ababa just after the end of the war. So, this Spanish operation was its first troop air transport in wartime.

3. Quoted in Sergio Attanasio, *Gli Italiani e la guerra di Spagna* (Milano, Mursia, 1974), 107.

4. In F 6, Fondo *Oltremare Spagna*, 336 folders. From 1 to 82 Comando Corpo Truppe Volontarie, 83–189 Intendenza CTV, 119–142 Artillery; 143–145 Commissariato; 146-148 Trasporti e tappe; 149–214 Units, 214 Drilling, 215 miscellanea, 216–236 Mobilization, 217–336 miscellanea.

5. Studies about this aspect are still rare and very rarely published and one is tempted to ask himself how much Fascist propaganda had the late effect to convince people that all worked well. Anyway, one can find something in Cernigoi, Enrico – Giovanetti, Massimo, *Ricordati degli uomini in mare* (Bassano del Grappa, Itinera Progetti, 2005); the book is about the submarine crews and it is a collection of interviews with survivors. When answering the question why did they enroll, most of the answers are more or less "because of the lack of work in the thirties." Something similar can be found in personal accounts or memoirs of people who did not have important positions at that time who were interviewed, or it is indirectly admitted in some contemporary document.

6. See the Italian Navy official relation: Bargoni, Franco, *L'impegno navale italiano durante la Guerra civile Spagnola (1936–1939)* (Roma, Ufficio Storico della Marina, 1998).

Chapter 24

1. Valguarnera, Giuseppe, *Seconda guerra mondiale: la struttura economica italiana alla vigilia del secondo conflitto*, su "Rivista marittima," CXL (maggio 2007). Alderotti, Enrico – Lombardo, Alessandro, *Ansaldo* (Roma, Rivista Marittima, 2005). Barlozzetti, Ugo—Pirella, Alberto, *Mezzi dell'esercito italiano 1933–1945* (Firenze, Editoriale Olimpia, 1986). Botti, Ferruccio, *Come non ci si prepara a una guerra*, su "Storia militare," n. 4 (genn. 1994). Botti, Ferruccio, *Il problema logistico italiano nella seconda guerra mondiale*, su "Informazioni della Difesa," n. 6 (1992). Fatutta, Francesco, *Cento anni per l'Oto Melara*, su "Rivista Marittima," anno CXXXIX (gennaio 2006). Ferrari, Paolo – Massignani, Alessandro, *Economia e guerra in Italia 1943/1945* su "Storia Militare," n. 73 (ottobre 1999). Ferrari, Paolo – Massignani, Alessandro, *Economia e guerra in Italia 1943—1945*, su "Storia Militare," n. 72 (sett. 1999). Luciani, Luciano, *L'economia e la finanza di un paese in guerra – l'esperienza italiana del 1940–1945*, su "Rivista della Guardia di Finanza," n. 4, (luglio-agosto 2000).

2. Figures officially published by the Italian Air Force in Gentile, Rodolfo, *Storia dell'Aeronautica dalle origini ai giorni nostri* (Firenze, Scuola di Guerra Aerea, 1967) and in Lioy, Vincenzo, *Cinquantennio dell'Aviazione italiana*, (Roma, Rivista Aeronautica, 1959).

3. For all concerning Marshal Cavallero, the best source is Ceva, Lucio, *Il maresciallo Cavallero*, su "Storia Militare," anno III, n. 19 (1995).

4. See Ceva, Lucio, *Il maresciallo Cavallero*, on "Storia Militare," anno III, n 19, 1995, p. 6, and Ceva, Lucio – Curami, Andrea, *La meccanizzazione dell'Esercito Italiano dalle origini al 1943* (2 vols., Roma, USSME, 1989), vol. I, chapters 4, 5, 8 and especially 9, and, in vol. 2, attached documents, especially document n. 23.

5. Barlozzetti, Ugo—Pirella, Alberto, *Mezzi dell'esercito italiano 1933–1945* (Firenze, Editoriale Olimpia, 1986). Ceva, Lucio – Curami, Andrea, *La meccanizzazione dell'Esercito Italiano dalle origini al 1943* (2 vols., Roma, USSME, 1989); Pignato, Nicola – Cappellano, Filippo, *Gli autoveicoli da combattimento dell'Esercito Italiano*, 2 vols. (Roma, USSME, 2002). Pignato, Nicola – Cappellano, Filippo, *Gli autoveicoli tattici e logistici del R. Esercito Italiano fino al 1943*, 2 vol., (Roma, USSME, 2005).

6. Lualdi, Aldo, *Nudi alla meta* (Milano, Longanesi, 1970).

7. Raffaele Campini, *Nei giardini del diavolo (In the devil's gardens)* (Milano, Longanesi, 1969).

8. Figures are taken from general Carlo Favagrossa's *Come abbiamo perduto la guerra (How we lost the war)*, Milano, Longanesi, 1962. Graziani's official report is completely published in Mario Montanari, *L'Esercito Italiano alla vigilia della 2ᵃ Guerra Mondiale (The Italian Army at the eve of WW II)* (Roma, USSME, 1982), 503–504.

9. Ciano, Galeazzo, *Diario* (Milano, Rizzoli, 1990); Pelagalli, Sergio, *Il generale Efisio Marras addetto militare a Berlino (1936–1943)*, (Roma, USSME, 1994); Perna, Valerio, *Galeazzo Ciano: operazione Polonia* (Milano, Luni, 1999); Kuby, Erich, *Il tradimento tedesco* (Milano, BUR, 1990). Plehwe, Friederich Karl von, *Il patto d'acciaio* (Roma, USSME, 1978).

10. According to reserved reports by OVRA to Mussolini, Italian Fascist "Hierarchs"—as they were officially called—admitted to corruption, because, for instance, as some of them said, they owned "the" car, that is to say one personal car. This revealed them as poor little chicken-thieves compared to their Nazi counterparts. What was this in comparison of what Goering or Goebbels had stolen?

11. See Enrico Caviglia, *Diario* (Roma, Casini, 1953). The conclusion reached by Pierpaolo Battistelli, briefly and completely exposed in his *L'evoluzione del Regio Esercito nella seconda guerra mondiale*, su "Storia Militare," n. 36 (1996) is the same.

12. See Erich Kuby, *Il tradimento tedesco*, (Milano, BUR, 1990).

13. See for instance Virgilio Ilari, *Storia del servizio militare in Italia*, De Biase, *L'aquila d'oro*, and my *Gli Italiani in Armi*, cit.

14. Badoglio, quoted in *Verbali delle riunioni tenute dal Capo di Stato Maggiore Generale (Minutes of the meetings at the Chief of General Staff's)* (Rome, USSME, 1983), Vol. I, years 1939–1940, meeting on October 17, 1940, 101.

15. A detailed account of Italian Army's actions in favor of Jews is given by Menachem Shelah, *un debito di gratitudine: storia dei rapporti fra l'Esercito Italiano e gli Ebrei in Dalmazia 1941–1943* (Roma, USSME, 1991).

16. See Basil Liddel Hart's, *History of Second World War*, London, Pan Books, 1970, chapter 11, 140.

17. Quoted in Benedetto Palmiro Boschesi, *L'Italia nella II Guerra Mondiale. 10-VI-40, 25-VII-43 (Italy in WW II. June 10th 1940– July 25th 1943)* (Milano, Mondadori, 1971), 109.

18. Apart some little tank units, the Italian Cavalry operated mainly on horses during all of World War II. In 1940 in Keru, Erythrea, Lieutenant Amedeo Guillet led his mounted

Gruppo Bande Amhara in a desperate and tactically successfully charge against British troops. Savoia Cavalleria Regiment charged in Isbushensky. The last Italian charge occurred in Poloy, Croatia, in Spring 1943.

19. Quoted in Paoletti, *Gli Italiani in armi . . .* , 581.

20. Bruno Berini, *La 121ª compagnia cannoni da 47/32 Granatieri di Sardegna* (*The 121st 47/32 Grenadiers of Sardinia guns company*), (Rome, published by the Grenadiers Historical Museum, 1984), 48. The 47/32 millimetres gun were normally used Italian antitank weapon.

21. See Correlli Barnett's description in his *The Desert Generals* (London, 1960), chapter 2.

22. Balbo established first Italian paratroopers in 1938 in Libya as a Colonial unit. In spring 1939 the first paratrooper school was established in Tarquinia, some as 50 miles north from Rome. In 1941 Italian paratroopers were launched on Cefalonia, Zante, Itaca and Ionian islands. Then, two Paratrooper Divisions were established: Folgore was the first, Nembo the other.

23. Cited in Paolo Caccia Dominioni, *El Alamein 1933–1962* (Milano, Longanesi,1964), 251.

24. Giuseppe Berto, *Guerra in camicia nera,* (*War in black shirt*) (Milano, Longanesi, 1967), 211.

Chapter 25

1. This story has not yet been clearly written and may never be. What is clear is that many officers commanding smaller units were shot by local members of the Mafia because they wanted to resist the Allies. Many American units were guided or informed by Mafiosi. It is hard to determine how effective Mafia aid had been. It is clear that after the Americans captured Palermo, of the newly appointed 82 mayors in the whole province of Palermo, 76 belonged to Mafia.

2. See, Hugh Pound's opinion in his *Sicily!*, chapter 4, published in 1962.

3. A family name tragically suitable for the situation: Chirieleison in ancient Greek means literally "*Oh Lord have mercy on us*" and it is used as an invocation of mercy in the first part of the Catholic Mass in Latin.

4. Mureddu, Matteo, *Il Quirinale del Re* (Milano, Feltrinelli, 1977).

5. Many authors suspect a secret agreement between the Court and the Germans to leave alone the long column carrying all the state officials. As a matter of fact, the vehicles were stopped many times by German checkpoints, but they were allowed to proceed. How could it happen? Simply, since the early days of the German presence in Italy, there was a password indicating a superior inspection. All the Italian and German patrols knew it, as well as they knew that, in case of that password, they were facing an allied general to be permitted to pass without controls.

6. Apart from the *Eritrea*, which was able to escaping the Japanese in India.

7. That's why, for instance, a little Italian coastal artillery unit fought against the Allies on D-Day resisting on the Ile de Cèzembre, off the Normandy coast, and a small motorized antitank unit serving in Russia later fought on the German side in Arnhem in 1944.

8. The *Guardia di Finanza* (Finance Guard)—*Regia Guardia di Finanza* at that time—is a military corps (in fact, its men have the little stars on the collar) subordinate to

the Ministry of Finance, instead of the Ministry of Defence. It is in charge of police survey on financial activities. It acts as a Customs guard, and as a Treasury special agency, as a coast guard, and as normal police. It is very proud of its old military traditions. It comes from similar corps existing in the old Italian States, as well as the Light Troops Legion of the Kingdom of Sardinia. That's why the Guard dates its origin to 1775. It was a nonmilitary corps until July 19, 1906. It received the little stars the following year and it had its colors on June 2, 1911; its baptism of fire as a military unit in Libya in 1911. A "Finanziere" was the first Italian soldier who fired the first shot in the Great War, preventing an Austrian attempt to destroy a bridge.

9. It is quite funny to note that the Italian Social Republic's national anthem was the *Inno di Mameli* and its national flag the Italian tricolor deprived of the crowned crest of Savoy. The Fascist Republic had the same national symbols of the democratic Italian Republic born in 1946.

10. The unit comprised the 67° Inf. Reg. Legnano on two battalions, LI Battalion Bersaglieri Allievi Ufficiali, V Battaglione Controcarri—on one hq platoon and 2 companies—Field Artillery Regiment, XII Artillery Group, Howitzer Group, minor units of the Engineers Corps and of Supply Corp, 51ª Section of the Medical Corp, total: 5,500 men

11. According to the late Leonida Fazi, a Bersaglieri second lieutenant, he was kept alive by British troops in Libya in 1941 after having lost his entire antitank platoon. He ironically remarked that in India after September 8, 1943, in the Yol Criminal Fascist Camp were he remained (he told me he could not consider the British who killed his platoon as friends) flew the Union Jack while the normal Italian POW Camp flew the Italian tricolor, and—he said—"This was the only difference. So, why cooperate?"

12. My grandfather, the one whose name I have, belonged to the 2nd Grenadiers Regiment. He was in the Army since 1913 and this allowed him to not join the Fascist Party. On September 10, 1943, the Grenadier Division was disbanded. He went home. After a few days, a general he knew very well came to visit and offered him a post in the army of the Republic in exchange for a higher pay. My grandfather had a family depending on him, no savings, and no good perspectives for the future: he refused, because he had sworn an oath to the king, not to the Duce. A captain in his regiment, however, who lived on the same block, accepted because of the lack of money. Both were not peculiar cases.

13. CIL at that time was composed of the Paratrooper Division Nembo and a couple of Infantry Brigades including Alpini, Infantry, San Marco (Marines) Regiment, a Cavalry squadron, Artillery, Engineer Corp and supply and supporting units.

14. Mussolini had a lot of documents with him. He took them from his secretariat archive. We have eyewitnesses who looked at them and who partially read some. For instance Silvio Bertoldi reported on two of these witnesses in his, *La guerra parallela* (Verona, Longanesi, 1966). We know these papers existed, we know partisans seized them and took photos before giving them to authorities; but we do not know if these documents still exist and where they are located.

Chapter 26

1. Folgore (infantry), Friuli, Cremona, Legnano, Mantova, Aosta, Avellino, Trieste, Pinerolo, Granatieri di Sardegna.
2. Ariete and Centauro, the former Littorio.
3. Tridentina and Julia.

4. Orobica, Taurinense, and Cadore.

5. According to the classical italian *organica*, that is to say, military organization, the words "great units" include units commanded by a general, from brigade up to army (brigade, division, army corps, army). Great units are divided into Elementary Great Units and Complex Great Units. The first units are those whose composition is fixed, that is to say, for instance: two regiments compose a brigade and two brigades compose a division; while the army corps and the army are defined Complex Great Units, because their composition is not rigidly foreseen. An army corps is composed of an undefined number of divisions, depending by the moments, as well as an army may be composed of a number of army corps, varying depending by the case.

Chapter 27

1. There are only a couple of very recent studies about it: Buchignani, Paolo, *Fascisti rossi: da Salò al PCI, la storia sconosciuta di una migrazione politica 1943–53*—Red Fascists: from Salò to the Italian Communist Party, the unknown story of a political emigration (Cles, Mondadori, 1998); and Franzinelli, Mimmo, *L'amnistia Togliatti – 22 giugno 1946: colpo di spugna sui crimini fascisti*—Togliatti's Amnesty – 22 June 1946: erasing the fascist crimes, Cles, Mondadori, 2006.

2. During the middle of the war, after El Alamein and the American landing in Northwest Africa it was clear in Italy that the war was lost. There appeared a small political organization, Partito d'Azione—Action Party. It grouped many young intellectuals, with a humanistic background. The organizer of the Action Party, Professor Guido Calogero, had a reformist and progressive program. He declared that all the disasters were due to Mussolini. The only solution consisted of going back to that purity of ideas. (I know it, because I personally listened to one of the first members of that party, professor Giuseppe Recuperati, remembering it, in Spring 1997, during a Conference of the Italian Society for the Studies about Eighteenth Century held in Rome, at the Faculty of Lingue of the first Università degli Studi di Roma La Sapienza, villa Torlonia, May 2, 1997, afternoon session.) Recuperati, now one of the most important Italian historians, an internationally well known authority about the second half of the Eighteenth century, told us that Professor Calogero stated the Action Party considered the 1799 Jacobins as its ancestors. So, the Party inspired its action to their ideas and named itself the preserver of their heritage.

The Action Party in 1946 sat on the left of the new Italian Republican Parliament. Its members were clever, highly educated and sometimes important. Ferruccio Parri, the chief of the National Liberation Movement belonged to the Action Party.

As often it happens, being composed of intellectuals, the Action Party was too small to survive. It soon disappeared—in the Fifties—and its members looked for other parties. They were welcomed everywhere. Even if the Party no longer existed, its influence grew thanks to its old members and, the more they made their careers—as an extreme example: one of them became Governor of the Bank of Italy, then was appointed Prime minister and later was elected as the President of the Republic, Carlo Azeglio Ciampi—the more their power increased, the more some of the Actionist ideas gained ground.

3. Cit. in Frescobaldi, Dino, *Quando L'Italia è stata determinante*, su "Nuova Antologia," anno 134°, fasc. 2209, ottobre – dicembre 1998, p. 36.

4. For a general overview, one can see: Ilari, Virgilio, *Storia Militare della Prima Repubblica, 1943–1993* (Ancona, Nuove Ricerche, 1994); Frescobaldi, Dino, *Quando L'Italia è*

stata determinante, su "Nuova Antologia," anno 134°, fasc. 2209, ottobre – dicembre 1998. Incisa di Camerana, Ludovico, *La vittoria dell'Italia nella terza guerra mondiale* (Roma, 1998); Lagorio, Lelio, *Problemi militari e internazionali: la posizione dell'Italia*, su "Quadrante," n. 16/17, ott. 1981. Luraghi, Raimondo, *La vulnerabile alleanza – la NATO dal 1949 a oggi*, su "Storia Illustrata," anno XXX, n. 352, marzo 1987; Minardi, Salvatore, *Il dibattito nazionale sugli Euromissili in Italia*, in *Le Forze Armate e la nazione italiana (1944–1989)* (Roma, CISM, 2005). The most important works about this issue are by the contemproray Italian Defense minister Lelio Lagorio and they are: Lagorio, Lelio *L'ultima sfida: gli euromissili* (Firenze, Loggia de'Lanzi editrice, 1998); Lagorio, Lelio, *Euromissili e dissuasione: le motivazioni tecnico-operative della scelta di Comiso*, su "Quadrante," n. 14/15, sett. 1981. Lagorio, Lelio, *L'ultima sfida: gli euromissili*, su "Nuova Antologia," n. 2205, genn-marzo 1998.

Chapter 28

1. "Locusta" lost a plane because of Iraqi antiaircraft fire, but the two pilots saved their lives, and spent the remainder of the war in Iraqi hands as POWs, along with other allied pilots.

2. Robert Dole, "Shaping America's Global Future," in *Foreign Policy* 98 (Spring 1995).

Bibliography

While preparing this Bibliography, the main problem was what to write here. A reduced space did not allow me to put all the 8,323 titles I used (not to mention archival documents from Rome, Milan, Cagliari, Turin, Florence, Parma, Mantova, Brescia, Genoa, and Naples State Archives as well as the State Central Archive in Rome, and the Army, Navy and Air Force Archives) to prepare this book, after thirty years of dedicated reading. It could be a good idea just mentioning works in English; but, unfortunately, apart from this one, practically nothing exists about Italian military history in the early modern era. The situation is not better about the following periods, that is to say the Risorgimento and colonial operations. Thanks to Frederick C. Schneid, there's good coverage of the Napoleonic era in Italy. The twentieth century also may be considered in a good situation because of the works by John Gooch, even if it is not exaustive due to its focus on the Fascist period. By the way, the situation in Italian literature is quite similar to this. Italian books are useless for an English-speaking reader who does not know Italian. I did not use texts in English, apart from some marginal exceptions, because they normally don't give more information than Italian books. So, what to do ? That's why I decided to mention only a few Italian books among the thousands I used.

The most complete, and the only existing general account is my: PAOLETTI, Ciro, *Gli Italiani in armi, cinque secoli di storia militare nazionale 1494–2000*, Roma, Ufficio Storico dello Stato Maggiore Esercito (Historical Service of the Army General Staff, since now USSME), 2001.

It must be considered useful for all the topics and all the periods from 1494 up to the end of the twentieth century. Its 652 pages cover the whole five centuries with as much detail as it was possible to put in only one volume.

For general accounts about the sixteenth through eighteenth centuries I used: BOTTA, Carlo, *Storia d'Italia continuata da quella del Guicciardini sino al 1789*, 10 voll., Parigi, Baudry, 1832; MURATORI, Lodovico Antonio, *Annali d'Italia dal principio dell'era volgare sino all'anno 1750*, 13 voll., Napoli, Lombardi, 1870.

Good sources about **Italian ancient States** are: CACIAGLI, Giuseppe, *Lo Stato dei Presidi*, Pontedera, Arnera, 1992; COLLETTA, Pietro, *Storia del reame di Napoli*, Milano, Casini, 1989; ACTON, Harold, *I Borboni di Napoli*, Firenze, Giunti, 1985; CONIGLIO, Giuseppe, *I Vicerè spagnoli di Napoli*, Napoli, Fiorentino, 1967; COSTANTINI, Claudio, *La Repubblica di Genova nell'età moderna*, Torino, UTET, 1991; DIAZ, Furio, *Il Granducato di Toscana – I Medici*, Torino, Utet, 1987; DUBOIN, Carlo, *Raccolta per ordine di materia delle leggi, cioè editti, patenti, manifesti ecc. emanati negli stati Sardi sino all'8 dicembre 1798*, 23 voll., Torino, 1816 – 1869; GALASSO, Giuseppe, a cura di *Il Piemonte Sabaudo – stato e territori in età moderna*, Torino, UTET, 1994; GIANNONE, Pietro, *Storia civile del Regno di Napoli*, 5 Voll., Milano, Borroni e Scotti, 1844; MACHIAVELLI, Niccolò, *Le Istorie Fiorentine*, Firenze, Barbera, 1899; PASTOR, Ludwig von, *Storia dei Papi*, 17 Vols., Roma, Desclée, 1961; SELLA, Domenico – CAPRA, Carlo, *Il Ducato di Milano*, Torino, UTET, 1984; SOLARO DELLA MARGARITA (edited by), *Traités publics de la Royale Maison de Savoie avec les puissances étrangères depuis la paix de Chateau Cambresis jusqu'à nos jours*, 5 vols., Torino, Stamperia Reale, 1836; TABACCO, Giovanni, *Lo stato sabaudo nel Sacro Romano Impero*, Torino, Paravia, 1939; BULFERETTI, Lugi – COSTANTINI, Claudio, *Industria e commercio in Liguria nell'età del Risorgimento 1700–1861*, Milano, B.C.I., 1961; DAL PANE, Luigi, *La finanza toscana dagli inizi del secolo XVIII alla caduta del Granducato*, Milano, B.C.I., 1965; MOLA, Aldo Alessandro, *Storia della monarchia in Italia*, Milano, Bompiani, 2002; **about the military in general:** PIERI, Piero, *L'evoluzione dell'arte militare nei secoli XV,XVI,XVII e la guerra del secolo XVIII*, in *Nuove questioni di storia moderna*, Milano, Marzorati, 1966; PIERI, Piero, *Storia militare del Risorgimento*, 2 voll., Milano, Il Giornale, 2003; ILARI, Virgilio, *Storia del servizio militare in Italia*, Roma, Ce.Mi.S.S.—Riv.Mil., 1991.

Good accounts about the **Italian Corps** are: **Air Force,** LODI, Angelo, *Il periodo pionieristico dell'Aeronautica Militare Italiana: 1884 – 1915*, Roma, Rivista Aeronautica, 1962; GENTILE, Rodolfo, *Storia dell'Aeronautica dalle origini ai giorni nostri*, Firenze, Scuola di Guerra Aerea, 1967; LIOY, Vincenzo, *Cinquantennio dell'Aviazione italiana*, Roma, Rivista Aeronautica, 1959; VALLE, Giuseppe, *Uomini nei cieli – storia dell'Aeronautica italiana*, Roma, Centro Editoriale Nazionale, 1958; **Armies of the Ancient States,** ALES, Stefano, *Le regie truppe sarde 1773–1814*, Roma, USSME,1989; ALES, Stefano, *L'Armata Sarda della Restaurazione 1814–1831*, Roma, USSME, 1987; ALES, Stefano, *L'Armata Sarda e le riforme albertine 1831–1842*, Roma, USSME 1987; BOERI, Giancarlo – CROCIANI, Piero, *L'esercito borbonico dal 1789 al 1815,* Roma, USSME, 1989; BOERI, Giancarlo – CROCIANI, Piero, *L'esercito borbonico dal 1815 al 1830,* Roma, USSME, 1995; BOERI, Giancarlo – CROCIANI, Piero, *L'esercito borbonico dal 1830 al 1861,* 2 tomes, Roma, USSME, 1997; CESARI, Cesare, *Milizie estensi (1814–1859),* in "Memorie Storiche Militari," Città di Castello, USSMRE, 1914.

CONCINA, Ennio, *Le trionfanti armate venete*, Venezia, Filippi, 1972; DA MOSTO, Andrea, *Milizie dello Stato Romano, 1600–1797*, in "Memorie Storiche

Militari," Roma, Vol. X, 1914; DE CONSOLI, Claudio, *Al soldo del duca: l'amministrazione delle armate sabaude (1560–1630)*, Torino, Paravia, 1999; GIACOMONE PIANA, Paolo – DELLEPIANE, Riccardo, *Militarium – fonti archivistiche e bibliografia per la storia militare della Repubblica di Genova (1528–1797), della Repubblica Ligure (1797–1805) e della Liguria napoleonica (1805–1814)*, Genova, Brigati, 2004; MUGNAI, Bruno, *Soldati e milizie lucchesi dell'Ottocento (1799–1847)*, Roma, USSME, 2005; PRELLI, Alberto, *L'esercito veneto nel primo '600*, Venezia, Filippi, 1993; ZANNONI, Mario – FIORENTINO, Massimo, *Le Reali Truppe Parmensi. Da Carlo III a Luisa Maria di Borbone: 1849–1859*, Parma, Albertelli, 1984; **Italian Army,** ALES, Stefano, *Dall'Armata Sarda all'Esercito Italiano 1843–1861*, Roma, USSME, 1990; ASCOLI, Massimo, *La Guardia alla Frontiera*, Roma, USSME, 2003; AUDITORE, Amedeo, *Il segno crociato del bene*, Roma, Au. De., 1956; BECHI LUSERNA, Alberto – CACCIA DOMINIONI, Paolo, *I ragazzi della Folgore*, Milano, Longanesi, 1970; Carabinieri, C.do Gen.le., *I Carabinieri 1814–1980*, Roma, Edizioni del Comando Generale dell'Arma dei Carabinieri, 1980; CEVA, Lucio, *Le Forze Armate*, Torino, UTET, 1981; *Cronaca e storia del Corpo dei Bersaglieri*, Torino, Daniela Piazza, 1986; *Genio—Trasmissioni*, Roma, Rivista Militare, 1980; GUERRINI, Domenico, *I Granatieri di Sardegna 1659–1900*, Roma, Comando Divisione Granatieri, 1962; *Il Corpo di Commissariato dell'Esercito*, Roma, Rivista Militare, 1990; ILARI, Virgilio – CARBONE, Flavio, *Elementi storici dell'Ordine Militare d'Italia*, Roma, Gruppo Decorati dell'Ordine Militare d'Italia, 2003; MECCARIELLO, Pierpaolo, *Storia della Guardia di Finanza*, Firenze, Le Monnier, 2003; MONTù, Cesare Maria, *Storia dell'Artiglieria Italiana*, Roma, tipografia d'Artiglieria e Genio, 1934; TEODORANI, Vanni, *Milizia Volontaria – Armata di popolo*, Roma, Rivista Romana, 1961; VIAZZI, Luciano, *Gli Alpini*, Roma, Ciarrapico, 1978; **Navies,** LO BASSO, Luca, *Uomini da remo – galee e galeotti nel Mediterraneo in età moderna*, Milano, Selene Edizioni, 2004; GUARNIERI, Gino, *I Cavalieri di Santo Stefano*, Pisa, Nistri—Lischi, 1960; NANI MOCENIGO, Mario, *Storia della Marina veneziana, da Lepanto alla caduta della Repubblica*, Roma, Ufficio Storico della Regia Marina, (Since now USSRM), 1935; CANOSA, Romano, *Storia del Mediterraneo nel Seicento*, Roma, Sapere, 1997; RADOGNA, Lamberto, *Storia della Marina Militare delle Due Sicilie 1734—1860*, Milano, Mursia, 1978; RANDACCIO, C., *Storia delle Marine militari italiane dal 1750 al 1860*, Forzani & Co., Roma, 1886; *Lista di tutti i bastimenti della marina dell'ex-reame delle Due Sicilie costruiti o acquistati dall'anno 1779 , epoca del suo incremento, sino all'aprile del 1815*, su "Rivista Marittima," anno XII, fascicolo I, Roma, Cotta & comp. Tipografi del Senato del Regno, 1878; **Italian Navy,** GABRIELE, Mariano—FRIZ, Giuliano, *La flotta come strumento di politica nei primi decenni dello stato unitario italiano 1861–1881*, Roma, USSMM, 1973; FULVI, Luigi – MARCON, Tullio – MIOZZI, Ottorino, *Le fanterie di Marina italiane*, Roma, Ufficio Storico Marina Militare (since now USSMM), 1988; *Il Corpo di Commissariato Militare Marittimo 1876–2001*, Roma, Rivista Marittima, 2001

Useful texts in English concerning the world global situation I used are: PAR-

KER, Geoffrey, *The grand strategy of Philip II*, New Haven, Yale University Press, 1998 and KENNEDY, Paul, *The rise and fall of the great powers – economic change and military conflict from 1500 to 2000*, New York, Random House, 1988.

All the aforesaid texts are useful for the military history of the whole sixteenth and the very early seventeenth century. For what concerns the seventeenth century: **about the Thirty Years War,** any good biography of Cardinal Richelieu may be useful. I used mostly BURCKARDT, Karl, *Richelieu*, Torino, Einaudi, 1945; As a general overview of the War, WEDGWOOD, C.V., *The Thirty Years War*, London 1944, italian translation as *La guerra dei Trent'Anni*, Milano, Mondadori, 1995; As a general overview of Italy in that period, a part my *Gli Italiani in Armi* there are only: PAOLETTI, Ciro, *Il Corpo di spedizione napoletano in Brasile*, su "Panoplia," year IX, n. 33, 1998; PAOLETTI, Ciro, *L'Italia e la Guerra dei Trent'anni*, in "Studi Storico-Militari 1997," Roma, USSME, 2000; PAOLETTI, Ciro, *La successione di Mantova: 1628 – 1630*, su "Panoplia," Anno IX, n. 34, 1998; PAOLETTI, Ciro, *Principisti e Madamisti*, su "Panoplia," Anno VIII, n. 31/32, 1997; PAOLETTI, Ciro, *La frontiera padana dello Stato pontificio nel secolo XVII*, in *Frontiere e fortificazioni di frontiera*, Firenze, EDIFIR, 2001; the best text about Italian officers in Imperial service is THIRIET, Jean Michel, *Gli ufficiali italiani al servizio degli Asburgo durante la guerra dei Trent'anni: identità e integrazione di una aristocrazia militare*, in "Quaderni della Società Italiana di Storia Militare" 1996–1997, Napoli, ESI, 2001; CAPPONI, Niccolò, *Le palle di Marte: Military Strategy and Diplomacy in the Grand Duchy of Tuscany under Ferdinand II de'Medici (1621–1670)*, in "Journal of Military History," Vol. 68. n. 4, oct. 2004; PAOLETTI, Ciro, *La prima guerra di Castro (1640–1644)*, su "Rivista Marittima," n.4, 1998; Coeval accounts: SIRI, Vittorio, *Del Mercurio, overo Historia dei correnti tempi*, Cuneo, 1642.

Other seventeenth-century wars include: Candia War; The basic work about the Ottoman army is MUGNAI, Bruno, *L'esercito ottomano da Candia a Passarowitz (1645 – 1718)*, 2 vols., Venezia, Filippi, 1998; the history of the Venitian Navy by NANI MOCENIGO, Mario, *Storia della Marina veneziana, da Lepanto alla caduta della Repubblica*, Roma, USSMRM, 1935 is still the best printed source. I used many coeval-printed relations about the main battles; **Piedmontese-Genoese War,** The only existing printed work is *Carlo Emanuele II e la guerra del Piemonte contro Genova nell'anno 1672*, in Ministero della Guerra – Comando del Corpo di Stato Maggiore, *Bollettino dell'Ufficio Storico*, Roma, CCSM, 1933; **Uprising of Messina,** Coeval sources as the ANONYMOUS, *Relazione di Messina*, s. i., but July 1674, and SAITTA, Antonio, *Messina antispagnola*, Messina, Niccolò Giannotta Editore, 1974.

The late seventeenth and first half of the eighteenth century: for a general overview, one needs a good biography of Louis XIV – in English I used BLUCHE, François, *Louis XIV*, New York, Franklin Watts, 1999 – and something about military evolution and increasing British power. I used: WHEELER, James Scott, *The making of a world power: war and the military revolution in seventeenth century England*, Phoenix Mill, Sutton, 1999; BLACK, Jeremy, *Britain as a military power*

1688–1815, London, UCL, 1999. About **The War of the Holy League or the First Morea War and the Second Morea War,** which other unconsidered wars, the most important works are: CACCAMO, Domenico, *Venezia e la Lega Santa. Disimpegno in Italia ed espansione nel Levante (1682–1686)*, in "Atti e memorie della Società Dalmata di Storia patria," Vol. XII, N.S. I, Roma, Società Dalmata di Storia patria, 1987; CASSELS, Lavender, *The struggle for the ottoman empire 1717 – 1740*, London, Murray, 1966; NANI MOCENIGO, Mario, *Storia della Marina veneziana, da Lepanto alla caduta della Repubblica*, Roma, Ufficio Storico della Regia Marina, 1935; PAOLETTI, Ciro, *La prima guerra di Morea 1684–1699*, su "Rivista Italiana Difesa," Anno XV, n. 12, December 1997; PAOLETTI, Ciro, *Il principe Eugenio di Savoia*, Roma, USSME, 2001. This last is one of the books concerning the **period between 1688 and 1748**. It is useful along with some other works for this and the following wars, that is to say: CARUTTI, Domenico, *Storia del regno di Vittorio Amedeo II*, Firenze, Le Monnier, 1863; STORRS, Christopher, *War, diplomacy and the rise of Savoy, 1690–1720*, London, Cambridge University Press, 1999; SYMCOX, Charles, *Vittorio Amedeo II e l'assolutismo sabaudo 1675–1730*, Torino, SEI, 1989; VOLTAIRE, *Le siécle de Louis XIV*, Paris, Stoupe, 1792; WILLIAMS, Henry Noel, *A rose of Savoy*, London, Methuen & co., 1910; or this and the **Spanish Succession**; ANONYMOUS (possibly Guido FERRARI) *Vita e campeggiamenti del Serenissimo Principe Francesco Eugenio di Savoja, supremo comandante degli eserciti Cesarei, e dell'Impero*, Napoli, appresso Domenico Lanciano, 1754, for the Nine Years War or the War of the Greta Alliance (or of the League of Augsburg), the next **War of the Spanish Succession**, the **1718 Savoy-Spanish war in Sicily** and the following **Polish Succession**.

MOSCATI, Ruggero, *Direttive della politica estera sabauda da Vittorio Amedeo II a Carlo Emanuele III*, Milano, ISPI, 1941 is about diplomatical aspects till 1748, that is to say till the end of the **Austrian Succession**. BAUDRILLART, Alfred, *Philippe V et la cour d'Espagne*, 5 vols., Paris, 1890–1901 covers the period of the three Succession wars and the 1718 war in Sicily.

Specific works on the Great Alliance or the Nine Years War include: AA.VV., *La guerra della Lega di Augusta fino alla battaglia di Orbassano*, Torino, Accademia di San Marciano, 1993; DE RIENCOURT, *Histoire de Louis XIV*, Paris, Barbin, 1695; ROWLANDS, Guy, *Louis XIV, Vittorio Amedeo II and French Military Failure in Italy, 1689–96*, su "English Historical Review," Oxford University Press, June 2000. **Specific works on the Spanish Succession** are a problem. In fact, practically nothing exists in English about the Spanish Succession in Italy. For a general overview see: BARNETT, Correlli, *The first Churchill: Marlborough soldier and statesman*, New York, G. Putnam's sons, 1974; BLACK, Jeremy, *Britain as a military power 1688–1815*, London, UCL, 1999; CHURCHILL, Winston Spencer, *Marlborough*, Verona, Mondadori, 1973; KAMEN, Henry, *Philip V of Spain*, New York – London, Yale University Press, 2001. Anyway, a part the previously mentioned ones, the most useful Italian books I used are: ASSUM, Clemente, *L'assedio e la battaglia di Torino (1706)*, Torino, Giani, 1926; ILARI, Virgilio—Boeri, Gian Carlo—PAOLETTI, Ciro, *Tra i Borboni e gli Asburgo: le armate terrestri e navali* *italiane nelle guerre del primo Settecento* (1701–1732), Ancona, Nuove Ricerche, 1996; MANNO, Antonio, (a cura di), *Relazione e documenti sull'assedio di Torino nel 1706*, estratto da "Miscellanea di Storia Italiana," Torino, Regia Deputazione di Storia Patria, Tomo XVII, 2° della serie, F.lli Bocca, 1878, pagg. 539–548; MUGNAI, Bruno, *La guerra di Comacchio: 1708*, in "Studi Storico-militari 1999," Roma, USSME, 2000; NICOLINI, Fausto, *L'Europa durante la guerra di successione di Spagna*, 3 Vols, Regia Deputazione Napoletana di Storia Patria, Napoli, 1937–1939; PAOLETTI, Ciro, *Errori d'impostazione storiografica e nuova valutazione dell'assedio di Tolone e della campagna sabauda in Provenza del 1707*, in *Studi storico-militari 2001*, Roma, USSME, 2004; PAOLETTI, Ciro, *Logistica e assedi delle guerre del settecento*, su "Panoplia," n. 27—28, anno VII, August - December 1996; Regia Deputazione per gli Studi di Storia Patria per le antiche provincie e la Lombardia, *Le campagne di guerra in Piemonte (1703–1708) e l'assedio di Torino (1706) – studi, documenti, illustrazioni,* Torino, F.lli Bocca librai di S.M., 1912; VICO, Giambattista, *La congiura dei principi napoletani del 1701*, Napoli, IEM, 1971.

About the 1718 War in Sicily, see CASTAGNOLI, Pietro, *Il cardinale Giulio Alberoni*, 3 voll., Roma, Ferrari, 1929; DI VITTORIO, Antonio, *Gli Austriaci e il Regno di Napoli, 1707—1734*, Napoli, Giannini, 1969; PAOLETTI, Ciro, *La guerra ispano-austrosabauda in Sicilia del 1718*, su "Rivista Italiana Difesa," anno XXI, n° 6, June 2003; ROSSI, Giovanni Felice, *Cento studi sul Cardinale Alberoni*, 4 Vols, Piacenza, Collegio Alberoni, 1978. **About the Polish and Austrian Successions**, the best available coeval source is the Anonymous made yearly history, printed in Venice and covering the period from 1730 till the end of the Napoleonic Era. The first volume concerning this period is ANOYNMOUS, *La storia dell'anno 1732–33*, Amsterdam, (Venice), Pitteri, 1735; following volumes are about the history of the years 1734–1749, one each year; then one can use ILARI, Virgilio – BOERI, Gian Carlo—PAOLETTI, Ciro, *La corona di Lombardia: guerre ed eserciti nell'Italia del medio Settecento (1733—1763)*, Ancona, Nuove Ricerche, 1997; BONAMICI, Castruccio, *De Bello Italico*, Augusta Vindelicorum (Augusburg), 1764; BONAMICI, Castruccio, *De rebus ad Velitras gestis*, Augusta Vindelicorum, 1764; BROGLIE, Jacques Victor Albert duc de, *La paix d'Aix-la-Chapelle*, Calmann-Lévy, Paris, 1895; *La battaglia dell'Assietta*, dattiloscritto originale in AUSSME, L 3, 11, Lavori svolti, Piemonte; LOGEROT, Ferdinando, *Memorie storiche del Regno delle Due Sicilie*, Soc. Napoletana di Storia Patria, Ms. XXVI-C-6; MINUTOLI, Daniele, *Rélation des Campagnes faites par S.M. et par ses Généraux avec des Corps Séparés dans les années 1742 et 1748*, 5 manuscript Vols. and 2 topographical atlas, Torino, Biblioteca Reale, M.S. Mil. 111; PAOLETTI, Ciro, *La battaglia di Casteldelfino*, su "Rivista Storica," Anno VIII, n. 7, 1995; PAOLETTI, Ciro, *La battaglia di Velletri del 1744*, a paper presented to the conference for the 250th of the battle of Velletri, Velletri, Novembre 17th 1994. About the **Corsican revolt**, the best available coeval source is the aforesaid Anonymous yearly history, printed in Venice and covering the period since 1730 till 1769. The last published work about this issue in miltary history is PAOLETTI, Ciro, *La Repub-*

blica di Genova e l'insurrezione corsa (1730–1769), on "Bollettino d'archivio dell'Ufficio Storico della Marina Militare," year XVII, December 2003.

Napoleonic Era

The minimum needed is: CUOCO, Vincenzo, *Saggio Storico sulla Rivoluzione di Napoli del 1799*, Napoli, Procaccini, 1995; FERRERO, Guglielmo, *Avventura: Bonaparte in Italia (1796–1797,"* Milano, Corbaccio, 1996; ILARI, Virgilio – CROCIANI, Piero – PAOLETTI, Ciro, *La Guerra delle Alpi (1792–1796)*, Roma, USSME, 2000; ILARI, Virgilio – CROCIANI, Piero – PAOLETTI, Ciro, *Storia militare dell'Italia giacobina, (1796–1802)*, Roma, USSME, 2001. CROCIANI, Piero – ILARI, Virgilio – PAOLETTI, Ciro, *Storia militare del Regno Italico (1802–1814)*, Vol 1° tomi I e II, Vol 2°, Roma, USSME, 2004; CAPPELLO, Girolamo, *Gli Italiani in Russia nel 1812*, Città di Castello, Comando del Corpo di Stato Maggiore del Regio Esercito—Ufficio Storico, Memorie Storiche Militari, Vol. VII, Fascicolo IV del 1912, 1912; COLLETTA, Pietro, *Storia del reame di Napoli*, Milano, Casini, 1989; CONTI, Giuseppe, *Firenze dopo i Medici*, Firenze, Marzocco, 1984; COOPER, Duff, *Talleyrand,* Verona, Mondadori, 1974; FERRARI, G. – GIACCHI, N., *Gli Italiani in Germania nel 1813*, Città di Castello, C.do del Corpo di Stato Maggiore del Regio Esercito—Ufficio Storico, 1914; GATES, David, *The napoleonic wars 1803–1815*, New York, Oxford University Press, 1997; SCHNEID, Frederick C., *Soldiers of Napoleon Kingdom of Italy*, Boulder. Westview Press, 1995; SCHNEID, Frederick, *Napoleon's Italian campaign 1805–1815*, Westport, Praeger, 2002; SCHNEID, Frederick C., *Napoleon's conquest of Europe: the War of the Third Coalition*, Westport, Praeger, 2005.

Risorgimento: 1814–1870

CAVOUR, Camillo BENSO conte di, *Epistolario*, 14 Voll., Firenze, Olschki, 1990–1994; CAVOUR Camillo BENSO conte di, *Diari (1833—1856)*, 2 Vols., Roma, IPZS, 1991; GARIBALDI, Giuseppe, *Memorie*, Torino, Einaudi, 1975; PAOLETTI, Ciro, *Latin America Warfare and Garibaldi's tactics*, in Acta of the XXIV Annual Conference of the International Commission for Militry History, Lisbon, 1998; SACERDOTE, Gustavo, *La vita di Giuseppe Garibaldi*, Milano, Rizzoli, 1933; ALBERINI, Paolo (edited by), *Adriatico 1848: ricerca e significato della contrapposizione marittima*, Acta of the conference held in Venice on September 25th 1998, Roma, CISM, 1999; GIACCHI Nicolò, *La campagna del 1849 nell'Alta Italia*, Roma, USSMRE, 1928; JAEGER, Pier Giusto, *Le mura di Sebastopoli*, Milano, Mondadori, 1991; MANFREDI, Cristoforo, *La spedizione sarda in Crimea nel 1855–56*, Roma, USSME, 1956; ADEMOLLO, Amedeo, *L'allagamento del Vercellese nell'aprile 1859*, in *Studi storico-militari 2002*, Roma, USSME, 2004; CEVA, Lucio, *Ministro e Capo di Stato Maggiore*, on "Nuova Antologia," year 121, fasc. 2160, October – December 1986; CEVA, Lucio, *Monarchia e militari dal Risorgimento alla Grande Guerra (1848–1915)*, su "Nuova Antologia," year 131, fasc. 2197, January – March 1996; COGNASSO, Francesco, *Vittorio Emanuele II*, Torino, UTET, 1942; GALLINO, Crescenzio, *La marina sarda durante la guerra d'indipendenza italiana del 1859*, su "Rivista marittima," n. 4, aprile 1877; MAS-

SARI, Giuseppe, *Vittorio Emanuele II,* Milano, Ediz. A. Barion, 1935; PINTO, Paolo, *Vittorio Emanuele II*, Milano, Mondadori, 1997; VISCONTI-VENOSTA, Emilio, *Ricordi di gioventù*, Milano, BUR, 1959; ABBA, Giuseppe Cesare, *Da Quarto al Volturno*, Firenze, Casini, 1966; BUTTà, Giuseppe, *Viaggio da Boccadi- falco a Gaeta*, Milano, Bompiani, 1985; JAEGER, Pier Giusto, *Francesco II di Borbone ultimo re di Napoli*, Milano, Mondadori, 1982; CEVA, Lucio, *Ministro e Capo di Stato Maggiore*, su "Nuova Antologia," year 121, fasc. 2160, October – December 1986;

The Kingdom of Italy

On Foreign interventions and Colonial policy 1869–1914 and 1919–39, except the Great War, see, apart from the general accounts like my *Gli Italiani in armi* and Lucio CEVA's *Le Forze Armate*, BANDINI, Franco, *Gli Italiani in Africa*, Milano, Longanesi, 1971; BOURELLY, Giuseppe, *La battaglia di Abba Garima*, Milano, Cogliati, 1901; GABRIELE, Mariano – FRIZ, Giuliano, *La politica navale italiana dal 1885 al 1915*, Roma, USSMM,1982; MAGNANI, Enrico, Il *manteni- mento della pace dal XIX al XXI secolo*, Roma, Rivista Marittima, 1998; MAZZETTI, Massimo, *L'Esercito Italiano nella Triplice Alleanza – aspetti della politica estera 1870–1914*, Napoli, ESI, 1980; DE COURTEN, Ludovica—SARGERI, Gio- vanni, *Le Regie Truppe in Estremo Oriente 1900–1901*, Roma, USSME, 2005; PAOLETTI, Ciro, *La Marina italiana in Estremo Oriente 1866–2000*, Roma, Uf- ficio Storico della Marina, 2000; Paoletti, Ciro, *La Marina italiana nelle operazioni di pace 1823–2004*, Roma, Ufficio Storico della Marina, 2005 (basically useful also for the interwar period interventions and for peacekeeping operations after Wordl War II); MALTESE, Paolo, *La terra promessa*, Cles, Mondadori, 1976; RA- MOINO, Pierpaolo, *Le forze armate italiane alla vigilia della guerra di Libia,* su "Analisi Difesa," anno IV, n. 35.0, June 2003; LEVA, Fausto, *Storia delle campagne oceaniche della Regia Marina*, 4 vols., Roma, USSMM, 1992; MOLA, Aldo Alessan- dro, *Giolitti: lo statista della nuova Italia*, Cles, Mondadori, 2003; PASQUALINI, Maria Gabriella, *Missioni dei Carabinieri all'estero 1936–2001*, Roma, Ente Editori- ale per l'Arma dei Carabinieri, 2002. On the **Great War and first afterwar period**, it is basic MINISTERO DELLA DIFESA – STATO MAGGIORE DELL'ESER- CITO, *L'esercito italiano nella Grande Guerra (1915–1918),*Roma, USSME, 1983, which is the Italian official relation about the Great War. Then, apart the general accounts like my *Gli Italiani in armi* and CEVA's *Le Forze Armate*, see: ALBERTI, Adriano, *L'importanza dell'azione militare italiana – le cause militari di Caporetto*. Roma, USSME, 2004; BANDINI, Franco, *Il Piave mormorava*, Milano, Longanesi, 1968; CACCIA DOMINIONI, Paolo, *1915–1919*, Treviso, Longanesi, 1979; FALDELLA, Emilio, *La grande guerra*, 2 vols., Milano, Longanesi, 1978; MON- TANARI, Mario, *Le truppe italiane in Albania 1914–20, 1939*, Roma, USSME, 1978; GERRA, Ferdinando, *L'impresa di Fiume*, Milano, Longanesi, 1978. On the **1919–1939** period, a part the general accounts like my *Gli Italiani in armi*, CEVA's *Le Forze Armate* and BANDINI's *Gli Italiani in Africa*, one can see about **Libya:** GRAZIANI, Rodolfo, *Cirenaica pacificata*, Mondadori, Milano, 1934 and *Verso il Fezzan*, Tripoli, Cacopardo, 1930; about **Ethiopia 1935–39:** BOTTAI, Giuseppe,

Diario 1935–1944, Milano, Rizzoli, 1982; LONGO, Luigi Emilio, *La Campagna Italo-Etiopica (1935–1936)*, 2 tomes, Roma, USSME, 2005; PIGNATELLI, Luigi, *La guerra dei sette mesi*, Milano, Longanesi, 1972; PEDRIALI, Ferdinando, *L'Aeronautica italiana nelle guerre coloniali – Africa Orientale Italiana 1936–40: dalla proclamazione dell'impero alla Seconda Guerra Mondiale*, Roma, USSMA, 2000; about the **Spanish Civil War:** ATTANASIO, Sandro, *Gli Italiani e la guerra di Spagna*, Milano, Mursia, 1974; CEVA, Lucio, *Le Forze Armate*, Torino, UTET, 1981; BARGONI, Franco, *L'impegno navale italiano durante la Guerra civile Spagnola (1936–1939)*, Roma, Ufficio Storico della Marina, 1998; about **Albania** there is only the aforesaid book by MONTANARI, *Le truppe italiane in Albania etc* and PAOLETTI, Ciro, *L'operazione "Oltremare Tirana"*, on "Storia Militare," n.23, agosto 1995, the only recently (!) printed work on this topic.

About **World War II 1939–45:** apart the general accounts like my *Gli Italiani in armi* and CEVA's *Le Forze Armate*, see for: **France,** AZEAU, Henri, *La guerra dimenticata – storia dei quattordici giorni di battaglia tra italiani e francesi nel giugno 1940,* Verona, Mondadori, 1969; DE LORENZIS, Ugo, *Dal primo all'ultimo giorno*, Milano, Longanesi, 1971 (also relevant for Yugoslavia, Russia, Corsica and Italy); GALLINARI, Vincenzo, *Le operazioni del giugno 1940 sulle Alpi Occidentali*, Roma, USSME 1981; **Northern Africa,** BARNETT, Correlli, *I generali del deserto*, Milano, Longanesi, 1964; CACCIA DOMINIONI, Paolo, *El Alamein 1933–1962*, Milano, Longanesi,1964; DI GIAMBARTOLOMEI, Aldo, *Il Servizio Informazioni Militare italiano dalla sua costituzione alla Seconda Guerra Mondiale*, Roma, SMD-SIFAR, 1957; MONTANARI, Mario, *Le operazioni in Africa Settentrionale*, 4 vols, Roma, USSME, 1993–2000; **Eastern Africa:** LEONE, U., *La guerra in Africa Orientale*, Roma, USSME, 1971; LOFFREDO, Renato, *Cheren (31 gennaio-27 marzo 1941)*, Milano, Longanesi, 1973; **Yugoslavia,** LOI, Salvatore, *Le operazioni delle unità italiane in Jugoslavia*, Roma, USSME, 1978; **Greece,** CECOVINI, Manlio, *Ponte Perati: la Julia in Grecia*, Milano, Longanesi, 1973; CERVI, Mario, *Storia della Guerra di Grecia*, Verona, Mondadori, 1969; MONTANARI, Mario, *L'Esercito Italiano nella Campagna di Grecia*, 3 vols, Roma, USSME, 1980; Museo Storico dei Granatieri, *I Granatieri del 3° Reggimento nella guerra contro la Grecia*, Roma, s.i.,1943; **Russia,** CARLONI, Mario, *La campagna di Russia*, Milano, Longanesi, 1970; CORRADI, Egisto, *La ritirata di Russia*, Milano, Longanesi, 1968; **Italy,** BROOKE, Alan Francis, *War Diaries 1939–1945*, London, Phoenix Press, 2002; BARTOLI, Domenico, *La fine della Monarchia*, Milano, Mondadori, 1966; CAPPELLANO, Filippo – ORLANDO, Salvatore, *L'Esercito Italiano dall'armistizio alla Guerra di Liberazione: 8 settembre 1943 – 25 aprile 1945*, Roma, USSME, 2005; Commissione Italiana di Storia Militare, *La partecipazione delle Forze Armate alla Guerra di Liberazione e di Resistenza: 8 settembre 1943 – 8 maggio 1945*, Roma, CISM, 2003; LUALDI, Aldo, *Nudi alla meta*, Milano, Longanesi, 1970; MECCARIELLO, Pierpaolo, In Nome dello Stato—le forze militari di polizia in Italia 1943–1945, Roma, USSME, *L'azione dello Stato Maggiore Generale per lo sviluppo del movimento di Liberazione*, Roma, USSME, 1975; **Social Republic,** PANSA, Giampaolo, *Il gladio e l'alloro*, Milano, Mondadori, 1991; SAXON, Timothy D., *Hidden treasure: the Italian war economy's contribution to the German War effort (1943–1945)*, in Acta of the XXX Conference of the International Commission of Military History, Rabat, Commission Marocaine d'Histoire Militaire, 2005.

The Italian Republic, 1946–2006

Apart the general accounts like my *Gli Italiani in armi* (useful up to 2000) and CEVA's *Le Forze Armate*, (useful till 1980) one can see only: Commissione Italiana di Storia Militare, *L'Italia nel dopoguerra – L'Italia nel nuovo quadro internazionale: la ripresa (1947–1956)*, Roma, CISM, 2000; DI CAPUA, Giovanni, *Come l'Italia aderì al Patto atlantico*, Roma, EBE, 1971. In fact, a part the aforesaid books, there are practically no good histories, or no histories at all, of the Italian armed forces from 1946 to 2006, and one must seek to collect a great number of articles of interviews of top ranks and essays. Most important seem to be: **about Policy**, PASTORELLI, Pietro, *L'ammissione dell'Italia all'ONU* in, Commissione Italiana di Storia Militare, *L'Italia nel dopoguerra – L'Italia nel nuovo quadro internazionale: la ripresa (1947–1956)*, Roma, CISM, 2000; SALIMBENI, Fulvio, *Il confine orientale*, in Mola, Aldo Alessandro (a cura di), *Il marchesato di Saluzzo – da Stato di confine a confine di Stato a Europa*, atti del convegno per il IV centenario della pace di Lione, Saluzzo, 30 novembre -1° dicembre 2001, Foggia, Bastogi, 2003; FRESCOBALDI, Dino, *Quando l'Italia è stata determinante*, su "Nuova Antologia," year 134, fasc. 2209, October – December 1986; LAGORIO Lelio, *Euromissili e dissuasione: le motivazioni tecnico-operative della scelta di Comiso*, su "Quadrante," n. 14/15, sept. 1981; **about Armed Forces, their structure and personnel,** *Cambia il vertice di SME*, su "Rivista Italiana Difesa," anno XXI, n. 9, sett. 2003; *Decreto legislativo 31 gennaio 2000, n. 24 – Norme in materia di reclutamento, stato giuridico avanzamento del personale militare femminile; Decreto Ministeriale 4 aprile 2000, n. 114 – Regolamento recante norme in materia di accertamento dell'idoneità al servizio militare; Decreto del Presidente della Repubblica 15 giugno 1965, n. 1431 – Documenti caratteristici degli ufficiali, dei sottufficiali e dei militari di truppa dell'Esercito, della Marina e dell'Aeronautica; Decreto del Presidente della Repubblica 29 dicembre 1973, n. 1092 – Approvazione del testo unico delle norme sul trattamento di quiescenza dei dipendenti civili e militari dello Stato; Decreto legislativo 30 dicembre 1997, n. 498 – Modifiche alla normativa concernente la posizione di ausiliaria del personale militare, a norma dell'articolo 1, commi 97, lettera g), e 99, della legge 23 dicembre 1996, n. 662; Legge 10 aprile 1954, n. 113 – Stato degli Ufficiali dell'Esercito, della Marina e dell'Aeronautica; Legge 12 novembre 1955, n. 1137– Avanzamento degli Ufficiali dell'Esercito, della Marina e dell'Aeronautica; Legge 27 dicembre 1990, n. 404 – Nuove norme in materia di avanzamento degli ufficiali e sottufficiali delle Forze Armate e del Corpo della Guardia di Finanza; Legge 31 luglio 1954, n. 599 – Stato dei sottufficiali dell'Esercito, della Marina e dell'Aeronautica; Legge 5 novembre 1962, n. 1695 – Documenti caratteristici degli ufficiali, dei sottufficiali e dei militari di truppa dell'Esercito, della Marina, dell'Aeronautica e della Guardia di Finanza; L'Esercito*, in AA VV, *Elementi di diritto amministrativo militare*, Quaderni della Rassegna dell'Arma dei Carabinieri, Roma, Rassegna dell'Arma dei Carabinieri, 2001, pag. 65.

VAGNONI, Salvatore, *L'unificazione e il riordinamento dei ruoli normali, speciali e di complemento degli ufficiali dell'esercito, della marina e dell'aeronautica*, su "Quadrante," n. 17/18 e 19/20, ott. e nov. 1980. VAGNONI, Salvatore, *Unificazione e riordinamento dei ruoli normali, speciali e di complemento degli ufficiali dell'esercito, della marina e dell'aeronautica*, su "Quadrante," n. 21/22, dic. 1982; ILARI, Virgilio, *Storia del servizio militare in Italia*, Roma, Ce.Mi.S.S. – Rivista Militare, 1991; CERVONI, Francesco, *L'esercito Italiano alle soglie del XXI secolo*, su "Rivista militare," n° 5, sett/ott. 1999; CAMPAGNA, Luigi, *La logistica dei sistemi informativi e di Comando e Controllo*, su "Rivista Militare," anno CXLVI, n. 1, gennaio-febbraio 2002; CANINO Goffredo, *Esercito Italiano ed eserciti europei: i nuovi modelli di difesa a confronto*, su "UNUCI," n. 10, ott.1993; CORCIONE, Domenico, *Il nuovo modello di difesa 1993*, su "UNUCI," n. 9, sett.1993; VOZZA, Nicola, *Nuovi lineamenti dell'Organizzazione Logistica dell'Esercito*, su "Rivista Militare," n.3, 1993; ZUCARO, Domenico, *La nuova dottrina dell'Esercito*, su "Rivista Militare," n° 5 sett/ott. 1999; about **Budget and planning,** *Esercito—consuntivo 1985; programmazione 1986*, quaderno 1986 della "Rivista Militare"; *Esercito—consuntivo 1986; programmazione 1987*, quaderno 1987 della "Rivista Militare"; *Esercito—consuntivo 1987; programmazione 1988, quaderno 1988* della "Rivista Militare"; *Esercito duemila*, su "UNUCI," n. 11/12 nov. dic. 1997; *La Difesa: libro bianco 2002 – sintesi*, su "UNUCI," n. 5/6, maggio/giugno 2002; SCAGLIUSI, Pietro, *Il libro bianco della Difesa*, su "Rivista Marittima," agosto-settembre, 2002, pag. 117; *La Difesa: libro bianco 2002 – sintesi*, su "UNUCI," n. 5/6, maggio/giugno 2002; NATIVI, Andrea, *Bilancio Difesa '98: tra tagli e speranze*, su "Rivista Italiana Difesa," n. 12, 1997; *Obiettivi dell'Esercito per il 1988*, Roma, Stato Maggiore dell'Esercito, 1987; **Strategy, geopolitics, and tasks,** LURAGHI, Raimondo, *The Mediterranean, Italy and NATO*, in *Military conflicts and 20th century geopolitics* Acta of the XXV annual conference of the International Commission for Military History, Bruxelles, 2000; RAMOINO, Pier Paolo, *Une vision géopolitique italienne: La Méditerranée elargie*, in *Military conflicts and 20th century geopolitics* – Acta of the XXVII annual conference of the International Commission for Military History – Athens August 19th-25th 2001, Athens, Greek Commission for Military History, 2002; RAMOINO, Pierpaolo, *L'OTAN et la Marine Italienne dans la Méditerranée des années Cinquante*, in Acta of the XXV annual conference of the International Commission for Military History, Bruxelles, 2000; ARPINO, Mario, *Concetto Strategico del Capo di Stato Maggiore della Difesa*, su "Informazioni della Difesa," anno XX, n. 1–2001; CERVONI, Francesco, *La trasformazione dell'Esercito nel nuovo quadro geostrategico*, su "UNUCI," n° 9/10, sett./ott. 2000.CORCIONE, Domenico, *La nuova situazione geostrategica: il modello di difesa italiano*, su "Informazioni della Difesa," n.2, 1992; OTTOGALLI, Gianfranco, *Il ruolo delle forze terrestri nei moderni scenari*, su "Rivista Militare," anno CXLVII, n. 4, luglio-agosto, 2003; VIESTI, Antonio, *Compiti, dottrina e strutture dell'Esercito*, su "Rivista Militare," n.5, 1987.

Italian involvement in Peacekeeping

There are four main printed sources containing all the needed general information about all the peacekeeping operations that included Italian personnel. They are Enrico MAGNANI's *Oltremare – Le missioni dell'Esercito Italiano all'estero*,

Roma, SME, 1992 and *Il mantenimento della pace dal XIX al XXI secolo*, Roma, Rivista Marittima, 1998; and my *Gli Italiani in armi – cinque secoli di storia militare nazionale 1494–2000*, Roma, USSME, 2001 and, about only the Navy-involving operations, my *La Marina italiana nelle operazioni di pace 1823 – 2004*, Roma, USSMM, 2005. They include all the basic information about Italian involvement in Afghanistan 1989–1990 and 2001–05 (Isaf—Enduring Freedom –Active Endeavour), Albania (all the operations), Bosnia and Kosovo (former Yugoslavia, IFOR-SFOR and JOINT FORGE – JOINT GUARDIAN, Eufor-Althea, KFOR); Cambodia; Cashmir; Congo 1960; Congo Kinshasa Eupol; Corea; East Timor; El Salvador; Erithrea; Ethiopia; Hebron – Palestine (UNTSO); India-Pakistan (UNMOGIP); lraq; Ivory Coast; Kenia (Mountain NUBA); Kurdistan (Airone I and II and Provide Comfort); Kuwait; Lebanon (UNIFIL—Italair, Libano e Libano 2, Leonte); Macedonia; Malta (military cooperation agreement); Mozambico (Albatros); Namibia (UNTAG); Persian Gulf; Red Sea minesweeping; Romania; Rwanda; Somalia (AFIS, UNOSOM, Ibis, Ibis 2 and United Shield); South Chinese Sea – Boat People rescue; Southwestern Sahara (MINURSO); Sudan (Operation Nilo and AMIS II); Tiran Gulf – Sinai – Sharm el Sheik; Zambia.

Military Unit Index

Name Index

Personal and organization names, including operations, civil and military services, and military units greater than an army or less than a battalion

Place Index

(Names in parentheses are the Italian orthography)

About the Author

Ciro Paoletti, librarian, author of many official histories, has written many articles and essays and 15 books, this is the 16th and the first in English.